Praise for **A VAST CONSPIRACY**

"Toobin has risen to the challenge of rendering the chaos of the impeachment, what led up to it and its denouement, in a sharp prose style and in a manner that makes sense of a disastrous phase of American political history."

—MICHAEL COFFEY, *Publishers Weekly*

"A richly detailed narrative . . . [and] a fascinating read."

—WAYNE WOODLIEF, *Boston Herald*

"Compulsively readable. . . . *A Vast Conspiracy* delivers new information, provides arresting perspective and is a helluva read for all that."

—SHERRYL CONNELLY, New York *Daily News*

"A rich and readable reprise of the Clinton scandals by the *New Yorker* writer who shows brilliantly how the American legal system spun out of control."

—*Chicago Sun-Times*

"A new kind of war historian has emerged in the United States, one whose expertise lies in analyzing and describing the politely savage battlefields of high-stakes criminal and civil litigation. Jeffrey Toobin is the best of the breed. . . . *A Vast Conspiracy* is a seasoned prosecutor's sweeping indictment of the tactical mistakes made by the office of independent counsel Kenneth Starr, as well as the zealotry and clouded judgment of Starr's aides."

—JOEL CONNELLY, *Seattle Post-Intelligencer*

"Toobin offers the best account yet of the Clinton investigation."

—DAVID KUSNET, Baltimore *Sun*

"*A Vast Conspiracy* . . . takes the disparate characters, facts, and disjointed timelines and reassembles them smartly. . . . The book Windexes the filmy glaze caked on by daily spinning and leaking. . . . Toobin's writing is accurate and fearless . . . hugely entertaining."

—JAMES N. THURMAN, *The Christian Science Monitor*

"The most definitive book on the Clinton administration."

—MARK BONOKOSKI, *Calgary Sun*

"Other books doubtless will be written about the Clinton presidency. [*A Vast Conspiracy*] already may be the last word. . . . A must for political junkies, this even-handed, cold-eyed book also is required reading for those interested in the political and legal process. . . . An exhilaratingly readable book."

—CARLO WOLFF, Cleveland *Plain Dealer*

Opening Arguments: A Young Lawyer's First Case—
United States v. Oliver North

The Run of His Life: The People v. O. J. Simpson

A Vast Conspiracy: The Real Story of the Sex Scandal
That Nearly Brought Down a President

Too Close to Call: The Thirty-Six-Day Battle
to Decide the 2000 Election

The Nine: Inside the Secret World of the Supreme Court

The Oath: The Obama White House and the Supreme Court

American Heiress: The Wild Saga of the Kidnapping,
Crimes and Trial of Patty Hearst

A VAST CONSPIRACY

JEFFREY TOOBIN

A VAST CONSPIRACY

The Real Story of the Sex Scandal That
Nearly Brought Down a President

RANDOM HOUSE

NEW YORK

To McIntosh

Contents

Cast of Characters

David Brock, journalist, *The American Spectator*
Randall Terry, founder of Operation Rescue
Patrick Mahoney, clergyman, director of the Christian Defense Coalition
Cindy Hays, fund-raiser
Susan Carpenter-McMillan, antiabortion activist
Rick and Beverly Lambert, private investigators

FRIENDS AND ACQUAINTANCES OF PAULA JONES
Stephen Jones, husband
Debra Ballentine, friend
Pamela Blackard, friend and coworker
Dennis Kirkland, alleged former boyfriend

ARKANSAS STATE TROOPERS
Larry Patterson
Roger Perry
Ronnie Anderson
Danny Ferguson
L. D. Brown

ATTTORNEYS FOR MONICA LEWINSKY (IN ORDER OF APPEARANCE)
Francis Carter
William Ginsburg
Nathaniel H. Speights III
Plato Cacheris
Jacob Stein
Sydney Hoffmann

FAMILY OF MONICA LEWINSKY
Bernard Lewinsky, father
Marcia Lewis, mother
R. Peter Straus, fiancé of Marcia Lewis

ATTORNEYS FOR PRESIDENT CLINTON
Office of the White House Counsel
Bernard Nussbaum, counsel to the president
Charles F. C. Ruff, counsel to the president
Bruce Lindsey, deputy counsel to the president
Cheryl Mills, deputy counsel to the president
Jane Sherburne, special counsel to the president
Lanny Davis, special counsel to the president

Lanny Breuer, special counsel to the president
Gregory Craig, special counsel to the president

Personal Attorneys
Robert S. Bennett, Mitchell Ettinger, and Amy Sabrin of Skadden, Arps, Slate, Meagher & Flom
David Kendall and Nicole Seligman of Williams & Connolly

FRIENDS AND ACQUAINTANCES OF BILL AND HILLARY CLINTON
Jim and Susan McDougal, Whitewater investors
David Hale, former judge and businessman
Linda Bloodworth-Thomason, writer and producer
Harry Thomason, director and producer
Dick Morris, political adviser
James Carville, political adviser
Mickey Kantor, former trade representative and commerce secretary
Mark Penn, pollster, Penn, Schoen & Berland
Kathleen Willey, White House volunteer and accuser of sexual misconduct
Julie Hiatt Steele, onetime friend of Willey's

White House Staff
Betty Currie, personal secretary to the president
Nancy Hernreich, director of Oval Office operations
George Stephanopoulos, senior adviser to the president for policy and strategy
Rahm Emanuel, senior adviser to the president for policy and strategy
Sidney Blumenthal, assistant to the president
Paul Begala, counselor to the president
Bayani Nelvis, Navy steward
Glen Maes, Navy steward
Lewis Fox, uniformed Secret Service officer
John Muskett, uniformed Secret Service officer

OFFICE OF INDEPENDENT COUNSEL (OIC)
Kenneth Starr, independent counsel

Selected Other Attorneys (in approximate order of appearance in Starr's office)
Mark Tuohey III

Roger Adelman
John Bates
W. Hickman Ewing, Jr.
Jackie Bennett
Robert Bittman
LeRoy Jahn
Ray Jahn
Bradley Lerman
Brett Kavanaugh
Samuel Dash
Amy St. Eve
Solomon Wisenberg
Paul Rosenzweig
Bruce Udolf
Mary Anne Wirth
Michael Emmick
Karin Immergut

OTHER ATTORNEYS

Kirby Behre, attorney for Linda Tripp
James Moody, attorney for Linda Tripp
William Bristow, attorney for Danny Ferguson
Billy Martin, attorney for Marcia Lewis

JUDGES

Susan Webber Wright, U.S. district judge presiding over *Jones v. Clinton*
Norma Holloway Johnson, chief judge, U.S. District Court for the District of Columbia
William H. Rehnquist, chief justice of the United States

HOUSE OF REPRESENTATIVES COMMITTEE ON THE JUDICIARY (SELECTED MEMBERS)

Republicans (in order of seniority)
Henry J. Hyde, chairman
Bill McCollum
George W. Gekas
Bob Inglis
Ed Bryant
Bob Barr
James E. Rogan
Lindsey O. Graham

Democrats
John Conyers, Jr., ranking member
Barney Frank
Charles E. Schumer
Howard L. Berman
Rick Boucher
Jerrold Nadler
Maxine Waters

Republican Staff
Thomas E. Mooney, Sr., general counsel and chief of staff
David P. Schippers, chief investigative counsel

Democratic Staff
Julian Epstein, minority chief counsel and staff director
Abbe D. Lowell, minority chief investigative counsel
Jim Jordan, spokesman for minority staff

UNITED STATES SENATE
Trent Lott, majority leader
Tom Daschle, minority leader

Chronology

JUNE 30, 1994   President Clinton signs a reauthorization of the expired independent counsel statute.

AUGUST 5, 1994   The Special Division of U.S. Court of Appeals replaces Fiske with Kenneth Starr as independent counsel investigating Whitewater.

JULY 1995   Monica Lewinsky begins to work as an intern at the White House.

NOVEMBER 15, 1995   Monica Lewinsky and President Clinton have their first sexual encounter in his White House study.

JANUARY 4, 1996   White House aide Carolyn Huber finds copies of Hillary Rodham Clinton's billing records from the Rose Law Firm, which had been subpoenaed more than a year earlier.

JANUARY 18, 1996   Hillary Clinton subpoenaed to Kenneth Starr's grand jury.

JANUARY 26, 1996   Hillary Clinton testifies before grand jury.

APRIL 5, 1996   Monica Lewinsky is informed that she will be transferred from her job at the White House to one at the Pentagon. There she becomes friends with Linda Tripp.

MAY 28, 1996   Jim and Susan McDougal and Governor Jim Guy Tucker are convicted in the Whitewater case.

JUNE 24, 1996   Supreme Court accepts a writ of certiorari in *Jones v. Clinton* and agrees to decide whether President Clinton can be sued while in office.

AUGUST 1, 1996   An Arkansas jury fails to convict two bankers charged by Starr with felonies in connection with Bill Clinton's 1990 gubernatorial campaign.

NOVEMBER 5, 1996   Bill Clinton is elected to a second term as president.

FEBRUARY 17, 1997   Kenneth Starr announces plans to resign as independent counsel and accept a deanship at Pepperdine University. Later the same week, Starr agrees to continue his work as prosecutor.

FEBRUARY 28, 1997   During an assignation with President Clinton, Monica Lewinsky's dress is stained with his semen.

MARCH 24, 1997   Michael Isikoff meets Linda Tripp.

MARCH 29, 1997   Monica Lewinsky and President Clinton have their final assignation.

MAY 24, 1997   President Clinton tells Monica Lewinsky that they can no longer continue their relationship. Lewinsky refers to this event as "D-Day" or "Dump Day."

MAY 27, 1997   Supreme Court rejects President Clinton's bid for immunity from civil suits while in office. *Jones v. Clinton* is ordered to proceed.

AUGUST 3, 1997   In *Newsweek,* Isikoff publishes a story revealing Kathleen Willey's allegations.

NOVEMBER 3, 1997   Monica Lewinsky receives a job offer from the office of the United States ambassador to the United Nations.

NOVEMBER 5, 1997   Monica Lewinsky meets with Vernon Jordan for the first time.

DECEMBER 5, 1997   Jones's lawyers fax the witness list in the Jones case to President Clinton's lawyers. Monica Lewinsky's name is included.

DECEMBER 6, 1997   In a meeting with his lawyers, President Clinton denies having a sexual relationship with Monica Lewinsky.

DECEMBER 11, 1997   Monica Lewinsky and Vernon Jordan discuss her job hunt over lunch. Later in the day, Judge Wright rules that Jones's lawyers can ask President Clinton about his consensual sexual partners.

DECEMBER 17, 1997   President Clinton telephones Monica Lewinsky to inform her that her name is on the witness list for the Jones case. They discuss a sanitized account of their relationship.

DECEMBER 19, 1997   Monica Lewinsky receives a subpoena from lawyers for Paula Jones.

DECEMBER 22, 1997   Monica Lewinsky meets with attorney Francis Carter.

DECEMBER 28, 1997   Betty Currie drives to Monica Lewinsky's apartment to retrieve gifts given to Lewinsky by President Clinton. Currie takes them home and hides them under her bed.

JANUARY 5, 1998   Monica Lewinsky rejects the UN job offer.

JANUARY 7, 1998   Monica Lewinsky signs an affidavit, prepared by Francis Carter, denying a sexual relationship with President Clinton.

JANUARY 9, 1998   Monica Lewinsky receives an informal job offer, which she accepts, from Revlon. The offer is formalized four days later.

JANUARY 12, 1998   Linda Tripp contacts the Office of Independent Counsel and reveals her information about Monica Lewinsky's relationship with President Clinton. Also, in a secret hearing in Arkansas, Judge Susan Webber Wright urges both sides to settle the Jones case.

JANUARY 13, 1998   Linda Tripp wears a recording device and produces a "sting tape" of her lunch with Monica Lewinsky at the Ritz-Carlton.

JANUARY 14, 1998   Monica Lewinsky gives Linda Tripp written suggestions ("talking points") for how to prepare an affidavit in the Paula Jones case.

JANUARY 16, 1998   The Special Division grants Kenneth Starr authority to investigate whether Monica Lewinsky or others suborned perjury or obstructed justice. Linda Tripp arranges to meet Lewinsky at the Ritz-Carlton. There Lewinsky is taken to a hotel room and interviewed by prosecutors from the Office of Independent Counsel.

JANUARY 17, 1998   In a videotaped deposition in the Jones case, President Clinton denies a sexual relationship with Monica Lewinsky.

JANUARY 18, 1998   The *Drudge Report* publishes item alleging a sexual relationship between the president and an "intern." President Clinton meets with Betty Currie to discuss his contacts with Lewinsky. Over the next day, Currie makes repeated attempts to contact Lewinsky.

JANUARY 21, 1998   In the early morning, *The Washington Post* and ABC News disclose Starr's investigation of the alleged affair, including a denial from the White House. In midafternoon President Clinton denies allegations about Lewinsky in interviews with Jim Lehrer and others.

JANUARY 26, 1998   While speaking at the White House, President Clinton denies having "sexual relations with that woman, Miss Lewinsky."

JANUARY 27, 1998   On NBC's *Today* show, Hillary Clinton denounces a "vast right-wing conspiracy." Later, President Clinton delivers his State of the Union address.

FEBRUARY 4, 1998   Kenneth Starr rejects a proposed agreement granting Monica Lewinsky immunity from prosecution in exchange for her cooperation.

APRIL 1, 1998   U.S. District Court judge Susan Webber Wright grants President Clinton's motion for summary judgment in *Jones v. Clinton,* dismissing the case. Jones's lawyers announce plans to appeal.

JULY 17, 1998   Independent counsel Kenneth Starr sends a subpoena to President Clinton to testify before the grand jury.

JULY 27, 1998   In exchange for a promise of immunity from prosecution, Monica Lewinsky meets with prosecutors in New York and discusses her relationship with President Clinton.

JULY 28, 1998   Monica Lewinsky gives the Office of Independent Counsel her semen-stained dress.

AUGUST 6, 1998   Monica Lewinsky testifies before the grand jury. President Clinton wears a blue-and-gold Zegna tie.

AUGUST 17, 1998   In testimony before the grand jury, President Clinton acknowledges intimate contact with Monica Lewinsky. Later, he admits the affair in a televised address.

SEPTEMBER 9, 1998   Kenneth Starr submits his report to Congress.

SEPTEMBER 11, 1998   The House votes, 363–63, to release the Starr report.

SEPTEMBER 21, 1998   The videotape of President Clinton's grand jury testimony is released.

OCTOBER 8, 1998   The House votes, 258–176, for an impeachment investigation.

NOVEMBER 3, 1998   The Republicans lose five seats in the House in midterm congressional elections.

NOVEMBER 13, 1998   President Clinton agrees to pay $850,000 to settle *Jones v. Clinton.*

NOVEMBER 19, 1998   Kenneth Starr testifies before the House Judiciary Committee.

DECEMBER 11, 1998   The House Judiciary Committee approves four articles of impeachment against President Clinton.

DECEMBER 16, 1998   President Clinton orders air strikes on Iraq for its violation of weapons agreements.

DECEMBER 19, 1998   The House votes to impeach President Clinton, adopting two of the proposed four articles of impeachment. House speaker-designate Robert Livingston announces his resignation.

JANUARY 7, 1999   The Senate impeachment trial is formally opened by Chief Justice William H. Rehnquist.

JANUARY 14–16, 1999   The House managers present the case against President Clinton.

JANUARY 22, 1999   Senator Robert Byrd announces a plan to move to dismiss charges against President Clinton. Five days later his motion is rejected, 56–44.

FEBRUARY 12, 1999   The Senate votes to acquit President Clinton of both articles of impeachment.

Introduction

The story looks different now.

All stories, even all lives, take on a new cast with the passage of time. And while the facts haven't changed—sexual misbehavior, a media frenzy, and the disgrace of an American president—the saga of President Clinton's journey to impeachment seems especially evocative of its era and distinct from our own. More than two decades have passed since that last impeachment trial, and we can look back to the bizarre, often messy story told in *A Vast Conspiracy* and consider, with new eyes, some of the core elements of the scandal.

There are many routes back into the sprawling story told in *A Vast Conspiracy,* and I'll address a few of them here, but the question that seems especially urgent is the one that asks us to reconsider the relationship between Bill Clinton and Monica Lewinsky. Do the lessons of the #MeToo movement change our understanding of what happened between them and how we, as a society, responded to their affair?

In a word, yes. Monica Lewinsky started work at the White House in the summer of 1995, when she was twenty-two years old, a couple of months after she graduated from college. At the time, Bill Clinton was forty-nine and nearing the end of his first term as president of the United States. Their sexual relationship began six months later, during a temporary government shutdown. Because most White House employees were not permitted to work at the time, unpaid interns like Lewinsky were enlisted to keep the operation going. One night, Lewinsky's delivery of a slice of pizza to Clinton's small, private office in the West Wing led to a sexual encounter. There were several more between them over the next two years.

Phrases like "power imbalance" had barely entered the public lexicon when the story of the relationship unfolded—including when I wrote *A Vast Conspiracy,* in the immediate aftermath of Clinton's impeachment. Many people, myself included, had a rather wooden understanding of consent in sexual matters, one that didn't necessarily flinch at the immense power imbalance between the president of the United States and a young intern who worked for him. From that time forward, Lewinsky herself was candid about her belief that her relationship with Clinton was consensual, and that, for many, concluded the inquiry about the legal propriety of their encounters. By this reckoning, the only person with a legitimate grievance about their relationship was the betrayed wife, Hillary Clinton. But the Clintons' marital issues were a private matter between husband and wife, not a reflection of any broader societal or political problem.

That line—between the formal investigation of the relationship between the president and Lewinsky, and the private matter of the Clintons' marriage—is one that I basically endorsed in *A Vast Conspiracy.* Neither one, I asserted, was the public's business. Kenneth Starr, the independent counsel, should never have investigated a consensual relationship between Clinton and Lewinsky. And the problems in Bill and Hillary's marriage were no one's business but their own. Now I'm less sure about these conclusions. It is particularly difficult to imagine a greater power imbalance between two people than the one between Clinton and Lewinsky. Such a relationship appears today by its nature improper, almost certainly a firing offense for the senior party if it had taken place in a private company. In this particular story, it does seem clear that Lewinsky "consented" to the relationship, and even initiated it. But does that really tell us everything about the relationship's propriety? One of the things the #MeToo movement has taught us is that the notion of consent is more complex than a simple on/off switch. Power imbalances impose different obligations on people depending on their status. The more powerful party—here, the president, no less—is obliged to think beyond the question of formal, immediate consent.

Even before #MeToo, we saw clearly from the Clinton-Lewinsky scandal what happens when relationships with dramatic power imbalances end—and who suffers the most from the fallout. It's invariably the less powerful person who endures the most, both in social stigma and professional status. That was especially true in this story. During the scandal and in the years that followed, Monica Lewinsky has had a much tougher road than Bill Clinton, and that was predictable from the beginning. I have decided not to change the text of *A Vast Conspiracy*—it, too, is a document of the era—but if I did, I would certainly portray Lewinsky less harshly. In her early twenties, she made a mistake by getting involved with a much older, married man. But she paid a disproportionately heavy price. During the final two years of Clinton's presidency, she lived in a tornado of denunciation. The right decried her as an immoral vixen, and the left disowned her as the vehicle of their president's political destruction. Columnists and comedians mocked her relentlessly and cruelly, and the experience with the president haunted her postscandal life. Clinton himself, on the other hand, survived impeachment and left office at the end of his second term with his popularity intact. Only with the rise of the #MeToo movement, as women came forward to reveal the cultures of abuse and sexual misbehavior that pervaded institutions of power, have Clinton's actions drawn more critical attention. He deserved an earlier reckoning with his behavior, and she deserved a gentler one. (As for Starr and his investigation, I have no revisionist sympathy. Their fanatical determination to get Clinton for something—anything—looks no better now than it did when I wrote the book.)

One major irony of the Monica-and-Bill affair, and an especially unfair one, is how Bill Clinton's misdeeds haunted his wife's political career and may have even cost her the presidency. Consider just one example from Hillary Clinton's presidential run in 2016. Donald Trump invited four women who alleged improper sexual behavior by Bill Clinton to sit in the audience for his second debate with Hillary Clinton. To be sure, Paula Jones, Kathy Shelton, Juanita Broaddrick, and Kathleen Willey were in a separate category than Lewinsky; they alleged conduct that ranged from improper advances to rape. (None were ever proved.) Lewinsky claimed no such behavior. But all of these women had accused Clinton of sexual misconduct, and Trump sought to place responsibility for Bill's actions on Hillary. Trump's apparent success with this issue shows the persistence of widespread misogyny.

And so, of course, does the election of Trump himself. It's tempting to assert (as I have) that the reevaluation of Bill Clinton's conduct in light of the #MeToo movement reflects an important evolutionary milestone in our culture, in which we've awakened to the pervasiveness and danger of sexual harassment. But if that's true—if we have achieved a more enlightened state—how did Trump win the presidency, with a record that was worse on every personal and political level than Bill Clinton's? I don't pretend to have a full answer to that question, but one partial explanation seems to be in the deepening polarization of our politics over the past two decades. We are increasingly two societies, each with our own moral systems. Blue America (to use a simplified term) has self-consciously changed since #MeToo, and has become less tolerant of all forms of sexual oppression. Red America (exemplified by Trump) continues to see #MeToo as part of an epidemic of "political correctness," in which self-appointed elites police the behavior of ordinary Americans. In this respect, then, the story told in *A Vast Conspiracy* does look different today, but different Americas have drawn different lessons from it. The legacy of the story, like the country itself, is more divided than ever.

/ / /

Our beliefs about Clinton and Lewinsky's relationship may have changed over two decades, but what has certainly transformed in that time is the way we learn about such stories. Journalism is very different now. The Lewinsky story first came into public view in the early morning hours of January 18, 1998, when Matt Drudge hit send on a post on his eponymous website. Drudge was something new in the world: a hybrid figure who was both provocateur and journalist, aggregator and creator, who operated entirely in the online world. Drudge's story bore the headline NEWSWEEK KILLS STORY ON WHITE HOUSE INTERN, and though Drudge's report contained several errors, the gist was true: *Newsweek* had the story of a relationship between Clinton and an intern, and the magazine chose not to publish it. By launching the story into the public discourse via the Internet, Drudge's post announced a fundamental reordering of our media hierarchies, a process that has only accelerated in subsequent years. (The man who would cause the next, far more cataclysmic upheaval to this hierarchy, Mark Zuckerberg, was thirteen years old at the time.)

Clinton's impeachment was a media story as well as a political one, and it both announced and hastened the fragmentation of the media landscape that followed in subsequent years. Drudge's post itself was a good illustration of what was about to happen. He was an independent operator with a largely conservative audience. Because of the decentralized structure of the Internet, he was able to find and serve that audience without the intervention of any of the traditional powers—like *Newsweek*. The weekly news magazine did not have a particular ideological tilt, and it strove to serve a broad audience, both politically and geographically. The story told in *A Vast Conspiracy* basically killed that model and, soon enough, *Newsweek* itself. (The magazine technically still exists, though in a much-diminished form.)

It was not only the Drudge Report, which still thrives today, but Fox News that rode the Clinton-Lewinsky story to prominence from its infant status in 1998. Rupert Murdoch, the notoriously powerful media mogul who created and owned Fox News, came first from Australia and then from England, where newspapers had clear ideological profiles. They did not adhere to the kind of neutrality that was the norm in the twentieth-century U.S. newspaper market. Murdoch brought the ideological model to the United States. He recognized that the niche audiences of cable news represented a tremendous potential market for the ideologically slanted journalism that thrived overseas. Bill O'Reilly and Sean Hannity (then paired with the hapless Alan Colmes) brought nightly denunciations of Clinton to a largely conservative audience desperate to hear that message on television. Fox News never strayed from this position, and its massive audience has rewarded the network with remarkable devotion and consistent ratings.

What Murdoch missed, but Zuckerberg didn't, was that the Internet was even better than cable as a news service for telling people what they want to hear. The atomization of our media both reflected and created the political divisions present in the Clinton-Lewinsky story. With the rise of Fox News in the late 1990s, conservatives had a news network that would broadcast their views. The full flowering of the Internet came somewhat later, in the post–Bill Clinton era, when Facebook gave individual citizens a News Feed full of stories that reflected their own prejudices. There was a time when news only became "news" when it was announced by Walter Cronkite or *The New York Times*. The Clinton-Lewinsky story heralded a moment when media gatekeepers relinquished their monopoly over the news, in some cases even ceasing to exist. Broadcast network news, major newspapers, newsweeklies like *Newsweek* all surrendered their authority to the scrum of Internet competitors. Drudge's post announced the transition moment with precision.

This shift in the media landscape also influenced the actions taken by the two lead prosecutors of their eras— Kenneth Starr and Robert Mueller. Starr, the independent counsel who pursued Clinton for four years, made expansive use of the news media in his long quest to bring down the president. He held regular (if peculiar) news conferences at the foot of his driveway in suburban Virginia when he was taking out the trash. His staff also leaked to journalists with some regularity. In a very intentional way, Mueller, the special counsel investigating Trump, went the opposite direction. He gave no interviews, and his office produced no leaks. This was certainly a high-road approach by Mueller, but it's far from clear that it benefited his work. As Trump battered him with such intensity and regularity, Mueller decided to be intentionally disengaged—and, one can argue, suffered accordingly.

/ / /

I write this reappraisal of the Clinton scandal in the midst of the next impeachment fight. It is a measure of the toxicity of modern American politics that the effort to remove Donald Trump is the third impeachment process in the last forty-five years, when there was only one impeachment in the previous two hundred. While there are some similarities, the impeachment investigation of Trump is markedly different from the one faced by Bill Clinton. At this moment, though, this one seems destined to end the same way Clinton's did, with impeachment of the president in the House of Representatives and acquittal in the Senate.

At a substantive level, the two impeachments seem to be mirror images of one another. Clinton was impeached for acts that were violations of criminal law (that is, lying under oath, or perjury) but not abuses of his powers as president. Clinton clearly lied in his deposition testimony in the Paula Jones sexual harassment case, and probably lied in his grand jury testimony in Kenneth Starr's investigation. (His supporters' arguments that he conducted sufficient linguistic gymnastics to avoid outright falsehoods never seemed persuasive to me.) What was clear then, and remains clear today, is that the subject matter of Clinton's false statements related entirely to his extramarital affair with Lewinsky. Even if Clinton did lie, there was no allegation that he used his powers as president to excuse or facilitate those lies. All he did was lie under oath—a crime that could be committed by any individual, not just a president.

Trump's behavior, in contrast, may not have been a violation of criminal laws. In simplest terms, he demanded damaging information about his political opponents in return for releasing congressionally appropriated funds for Ukraine (as well as a White House meeting with the president of Ukraine). There is a plausible argument that Trump committed the crimes of bribery or extortion by doing so, but that theory seems like a stretch to me. What's far clearer is that Trump abused his power as president. This is true, too, in the other major accusations against him, which are obstruction of justice (by interfering with the FBI and special counsel investigations) and obstruction of Congress (by refusing to provide evidence demanded in the course of congressional investigations). These actions, especially the threat to withhold aid to Ukraine, could only be made by the president of the United States. To put it another way, anyone could have lied under oath about an extramarital affair, but only a president can control the power and purse strings of the federal government.

The contrast between the misdeeds of Clinton and Trump raises the question: Which is worse? Is it worse to commit a crime or to abuse presidential power? Which one comes closer to the definition of impeachable offenses provided in Article II of the

Constitution: "Treason, Bribery, or other high Crimes and Misdemeanors"? The framers had a clear answer to this question. In *Federalist no. 65,* Alexander Hamilton gave the most expansive treatment of the impeachment provision. He wrote that impeachable offenses were "of a nature which may with peculiar propriety be denominated POLITICAL, as they relate chiefly to injuries done immediately to the society itself. The prosecution of them, for this reason, will seldom fail to agitate the passions of the whole community, and to divide it into parties more or less friendly or inimical to the accused." Hamilton is saying that abuse of power is worse because it's an injury to society as a whole, which only a president, with his or her vast authority, can do.

This seems almost obvious—that impeachment should be reserved for abuses of power, for offenses against society—but Hamilton was also right in another way. Impeachment raises partisan passions like few other issues. This was true in 1998, and it is true now. One would hope that a subject as profound as impeachment would bring out the best in politicians and others in public life. But history has shown us otherwise. As recent events have demonstrated, the existential nature of the struggle over the survival of a president prompts atavistic surges of partisanship. The impeachment of Bill Clinton was almost entirely engineered and supported by Republicans; the impeachment of Donald Trump is so far a production led by the Democratic Party. (Democrats also led the fight to force Richard Nixon from office, and it was Republican defections, first in the House Judiciary Committee and then among Senate leaders, that led Nixon to resign.) For better or worse, the continued ferocity of our politics is easier to predict than any particular outcome.

To look back at a story like the one told in *A Vast Conspiracy* is necessarily to examine the arcs of history. But my primary interest in the matter has always been less in broad societal forces and more in the specific facts—and that is what has allowed the saga to live on, vividly, in the public imagination. That is, I preferred the messy specificity of the people involved and the sheer unlikelihood of the tale as it unfolded. It's a story that includes Alexander Hamilton and the *Federalist Papers,* but also Danny Traylor's law practice in Little Rock. And what vaunted figure of history compares to Linda Tripp, as she toggles between Lucianne Goldberg, her scheming literary agent, and Monica Lewinsky, her lovesick friend? It's the ultimate high and low story—with great issues about the nature of presidential power and low gossip about human folly. As a journalist, and a reader, that gets me every time.

January 2020

A VAST
CONSPIRACY

PROLOGUE

"This Is Danny"

This is Danny."

Every caller to the law office of Daniel M. Traylor received this greeting from the proprietor and sole employee of the business. There was no secretary, no receptionist, no other lawyer, and, technically speaking, no law office at all. Traylor operated out of a converted two-bedroom suite in a bedraggled apartment building on an unlovely corner of downtown Little Rock, Arkansas. Plywood panels had replaced the glass in many of the window frames at the Courtyard Apartments, and a few pieces of lawn furniture rusted on the wilted grass by the door. Across the street, "Poor Man Used Cars" had been out of business for years, but the sign—and a few battered hulks—remained.

"Thizz Danny."

That was how Traylor answered the phone on January 13, 1994, his thirty-eighth birthday, to hear the voice of an old friend and client. A few years earlier, Traylor and Debra Ballentine had worked together at a hazardous waste disposal company called ENSCO. She was a secretary and he was an in-house lawyer, and Traylor had handled Ballentine's divorce. He was the only lawyer she knew. She was calling on behalf of a friend.

"Did you see that article in *The American Spectator*?" Ballentine asked.

Until recently, few people in Arkansas had even heard of the magazine. At the time, its national circulation was about 200,000, but only a handful of copies of the conservative monthly ever made their way outside the nation's big cities. But in December 1993, the *Spectator* published an article entitled "His Cheatin' Heart," by David Brock, and at the time of Ballentine's call, the piece was still the talk of Little Rock. By coincidence, a few days before Ballentine's call, a friend in Buffalo had faxed a copy to Traylor.

The "heart" in question belonged to Bill Clinton, who at the time the article was published had been president of the United States for less than a year. Before that, he had served as governor of Arkansas for twelve years, and during his long tenure, his personal life had provided endless fodder for local gossips. There were rumors of affairs and girlfriends, but the news media in the state never followed up. For the most part, the local newspapers and television stations played by informal journalistic conventions that limited their coverage to Clinton's public life. But as the *Spectator* article illustrated, those rules were changing.

The bulk of the twelve-thousand-word article was devoted to interviews with two Arkansas state troopers, Larry Patterson and Roger Perry, who had served on Clinton's protective detail. "Over the years," Brock wrote, "the troopers have seen Bill Clinton in compromising situations with dozens of women." It was one story in particular that drew the attention of Debbie Ballentine—and her unnamed friend. Brock recounted, "One of the troopers told the story of how Clinton had eyed a woman at a reception in downtown Little Rock. According to the trooper . . . Clinton asked him to approach the woman, whom the trooper remembered only as Paula, tell her how attractive the governor thought she was, and take her to a room in the hotel where Clinton would be waiting. . . . On this particular evening, after her encounter with Clinton, which lasted no more than an hour as the trooper stood by in the hall, the trooper said Paula told him she was available to be Clinton's regular girlfriend if he so desired."

Traylor remembered the passage after Ballentine pointed it out to him. "That girl, that's my girlfriend, Paula Jones," Ballentine explained, "and she's just crying her eyes out because of what they wrote about her. Paula told me she was going to run down that

David Brock, leave him a message, and give him a piece of her mind. But I said she should go to a lawyer instead."

"Tha's right," Traylor told Ballentine, in his soft mid-South drawl.

"Would you mind talking to her?" she asked. Ballentine thought there might be a lawsuit in it. Danny Traylor had handled her divorce, Ballentine thought, so why couldn't he take care of the president of the United States?

"You just tell her to give me a call," Traylor replied, "and I'll see what I can do."

/ / /

That brief telephone conversation led—indirectly, improbably, but inexorably—to the first impeachment of an elected president in the history of the United States. Five years and one month after Ballentine's call, the events she set in motion concluded with a vote by the Senate that fell short of the two-thirds required to remove Bill Clinton from office. If Paula Jones had chosen any of a hundred different routes—if she had called Brock directly, or approached another lawyer, or sued the magazine rather than the president, or if she had done nothing at all—an extraordinary chapter in American history might have unfolded very differently or not at all. But instead, Paula called Debbie, who called Danny. In a simple sense, then, the root of this story is easy to trace.

But, of course, the real origins of this epochal crisis are more complex. The most famous explanation for the president's near downfall came from his wife. In an interview on NBC's *Today* show, on January 27, 1998—just a few days after news broke of her husband's relationship with a former White House intern named Monica Lewinsky—Hillary Rodham Clinton ascribed the president's difficulties to a "vast right-wing conspiracy" that had been pursuing both of them for years. Much evidence supports this view; the president's political enemies devoted enormous energy to bringing him down. At the same time, however, the first lady's explanation neglected the president's own very considerable culpability in the matter. Still, in retrospect, it does seem that there was a vast conspiracy behind the Jones and Lewinsky cases—just not the one that Mrs. Clinton had in mind.

In the years since the Second World War, there has been a conspiracy within the legal system to take over the political system of the United States. Describing his travels in America during the 1830s, Alexis de Tocqueville made the famous observation, "Scarcely any political question arises in the United States that is not resolved, sooner or later, into a judicial question." In fact, Tocqueville's observation would begin to come true only a century later. The process was set in motion shortly after the war, when Thurgood Marshall and a small group of lawyers at the NAACP Legal Defense and Education Fund entered upon the first sustained and successful attempt to use the courts to achieve political change. Their reasons were simple. Because it was difficult if not impossible for most African-Americans to register to vote, they lacked access to the political system; the judiciary was their only hope for ending legalized segregation.

Marshall's extraordinary success had unforeseen consequences. Court cases became a central part of any organized political activity—even for those groups who could have used the ballot instead of the subpoena. As activists quickly discovered, lawsuits had many advantages over traditional politics. They required just a few people, and they moved quickly, at least compared to biennial or quadrennial elections. Lawsuits allowed civil rights workers, feminists, environmentalists, and other activists of the political left a perfect shortcut. They didn't have to do the expensive and labor-intensive work of persuading the masses to support their views; instead, they enjoyed prestige and intellectual challenge in this new field, which they dubbed "public interest law."

This legal activism eventually extended even to criminal law. Marshall and his immediate political heirs used the courts to target and change laws; the next generation of activists used the courts to target and prosecute individuals. The liberal triumph over Richard Nixon in Watergate led the Democratic Party to seek to institutionalize its gains. To this end, Democrats created the independent counsel law, which gave the successors to Archibald Cox virtually unlimited power and tenure. And because of this obsession with ethics, not to mention their unpopular policy agenda, liberals fought their most successful political battles in the seventies and eighties in courtrooms rather than legislatures.

In Watergate and then Iran-Contra, the pursuit of Republican officials became a central obsession of the political left. When the independent counsel law came up for reauthorization early in President Clinton's first term, more Democrats than Republicans wanted him to sign it, and to his enduring regret, he did.

Then, of course, the inevitable occurred. The political right discovered that it, too, could use the courts to advance its agenda. Groups like the Federalist Society, the Landmark Legal Foundation, and the Rutherford Institute modeled their efforts on the work of their ideological adversaries at places like the NAACP and the American Civil Liberties Union. Conservatives used many of the same legal concepts that their adversaries had pioneered—freedom of speech, equal protection of the laws, and even, eventually, sexual harassment law—to achieve their aims. They copied the liberal rhetoric, too; the Republican prosecutors in Clinton's impeachment trial in the Senate took pains always to refer to the Paula Jones case as a "federal civil rights action." Toward the end of the century, it was extremists of the political right who tried to use the legal system to undo elections—in particular the two that put Bill Clinton in the White House.

In a similar way, Clinton's election prompted conservatives to put aside their misgivings about the criminalization of political disputes. With a Democrat in the White House, Republicans required only the barest of pretexts to demand that prosecutors be appointed. And once these prosecutors were installed, Republicans insisted that they pursue their Democratic targets with inventiveness and zeal. The Clinton years abounded in purported scandals that offered much in the way of colorful names—Whitewater, Filegate, Travelgate, to name only the best known—but little in the way of actual criminal offenses. The futility of the endless searches for criminals in the White House only spurred the zeal of the pursuers. Once again, the prosecutors were political heroes—this time for the other side.

/ / /

The legal system's takeover of the political system steered a great deal of partisan conflict from legislatures to courtrooms. But in terms of the substance of those disputes, the Clinton presidency took place at a paradoxical moment in American political history.

It was, at one level, a time of remarkable consensus between the major parties. The presidential election of 1996, between Clinton and Bob Dole, which took place at a critical point in the scandal, may have featured smaller differences on policy issues than had any other such contest of the postwar era.

But at the same time that Washington basked in an era of relative good feelings on the issues, the city experienced partisan rancor on a titanic scale. This had its roots in cultural, rather than political, ferment. Two of the great social movements of the late twentieth century, feminism and the Christian right, were ordinarily seen as ideological opposites. But in one critical respect, they pushed the country in precisely the same direction, toward the idea that the private lives of public people mattered as much as their stands on issues. The feminist insistence that "the personal is the political" meant that private conduct, particularly when it came to sex, served as a useful metaphor for a politician's public acts. Yet conservatives, too, under the motto "Character counts," began to weigh personal behavior as heavily as did their ideological rivals.

This fixation on the personal amounted to a tremendous gift to the news media, which were experiencing their own transformations during this period. In the early 1960s, when reporters heard tales of the voracious sexual appetite of President John F. Kennedy, they kept the information to themselves. Public disclosure of such matters was literally unthinkable; that is, it wasn't even considered. But feminists and evangelicals gave journalists the permission—the pretext—to go into areas that they wanted to examine anyway. The press could define tawdry voyeurism as the study of "character," but the labeling couldn't obscure the true nature of this new kind of reporting. In an ever more competitive market for journalists and journalism, a high-minded rationale for covering the sex lives of famous people was much appreciated. Some reporters took to the task with gusto. And this hunger for sleaze extended beyond the journalists who covered the stories for newspapers, magazines, and television. The book business—a critical part of this story—fed and exploited this trend as well.

And so the forces were arrayed. Politicians shunning policy for cultural warfare. The media using sex to sell. And all of it destined to wind up in court.

/ / /

Viewed in this way, the process that led to the impeachment of President Clinton can seem almost inevitable—the by-product of large forces in the sweep of history. But that, of course, is not the case. For while the Jones and Lewinsky stories did reflect their times, they also evolved out of a strange mixture of accident, coincidence, fate, and a bizarre cast of personalities. The peculiar population of this saga spanned a broad range in ideology and temperament, but its members did have some traits in common. Chief among them was the narrow pursuit of self-interest. No other major political controversy in American history produced as few heroes as this one. Instead of nobility, there was selfishness; instead of concern for the long-term good of all, there was the assiduous pursuit of immediate gratification—political, financial, sexual.

Chief among the antiheroes was the president of the United States. He believed, in an undoubtedly sincere way, that his private life was his own business, and that it had no impact on how he performed his public duties. In this, ironically, he may have been right. For all the piety of the authoritarians of the left and right about the importance of sexual fidelity of public persons, there remains no proof that monogamous presidents do better jobs than adulterous ones. (The evidence is actually somewhat to the contrary.) But Bill Clinton knew the implicit promises he had made about his own behavior. He thought he could get away with breaking them, and he couldn't. And when Clinton was caught in that most clichéd of dilemmas—a menopausal man having an affair with a young woman from the office—he reacted not with candor and grace, but rather with the dishonesty and self-pity that are among the touchstones of his character.

Yet the most astonishing fact in this story may be this one: in spite of his consistently reprehensible behavior, Clinton was, by comparison, the good guy in this struggle. The president's adversaries appeared literally consumed with hatred for him; the bigger the stakes, the smaller they acted. They were willing to trample all standards of fairness—not to mention the Constitution—in their effort to drive him from office. They ranged from one-case-only zealots in the cause of fighting sexual harassment to one-defendant-only federal prosecutors, and they shared only a willingness to misuse the law and the courts in their effort to destroy Bill Clinton.

But Clinton's enemies were not propelled only by political opportunism. There was greed, too. Several of his primary pursuers—each of whom played an essential role in the events leading to his impeachment—contemplated writing books about the president's sex life. Such incentives did not even exist a generation ago. But the transformed business of publishing inspired his former bodyguards in Arkansas, the journalist Michael Isikoff, Linda Tripp, and Paula and Stephen Jones. Only one of this group actually wound up writing such a book (so far), but some of the book projects—Linda Tripp's in particular—altered the course of events at several significant moments in this story. Indeed, at times in the Clinton scandals, commercial considerations even trumped political motives.

The Clinton scandals—using that term to define the events that led to his impeachment—consisted of three intertwined narratives. One of these stories, the Paula Jones case, occurred mostly in public; the second, Kenneth Starr's investigation, occurred mostly in private; and the third, the president's relationship with Monica Lewinsky, occurred almost entirely in secret. No single person knew the details of all three narratives as they were happening, and the stories unfolded at the same time as one another. When the president's relationship with Lewinsky became public in January 1998, the three strands merged into a single cataclysmic drama. But these crashing cymbals of constitutional portent could scarcely be imagined when Danny Traylor answered the telephone on his birthday.

1

What the Bubbas Wrought

The story that Paula Jones told Danny Traylor was a simple one—at first. She said the magazine article did refer to an actual incident. But, she explained, Brock had it all wrong.

During Clinton's last term as governor, Jones was twenty-four years old and working as a clerk at the Arkansas Industrial Development Commission. One day—she later determined it was May 8, 1991—Jones and a colleague named Pamela Blackard were working behind the registration desk at an AIDC conference at a Little Rock hotel called the Excelsior. After the governor and his security detail arrived, a trooper named Danny Ferguson stopped to chat with Blackard and Jones, whose last name was then Corbin. A little while later, Ferguson said that the governor, whom she had never met before, wanted to meet her in a room upstairs at the hotel. She agreed, and the trooper escorted her to the suite. The governor greeted her, made small talk for a few moments, and then began touching her. Jones rebuffed him and moved to sit down on the sofa. Clinton followed her there, then exposed himself and asked her to perform oral sex. She immediately jumped up, told him, "I'm not that kind of girl," and left the room. In the intervening almost three years, Jones said, she had told only a handful of people about the incident—her two sisters and her husband, as well as Blackard and Ballentine, both close friends.

Traylor and Jones spoke for only a few minutes in that initial conversation, and then she put her husband, Stephen Jones, on the telephone. For Traylor, the contrast between husband and wife was dramatic. Paula was hesitant, nervous, still embarrassed about the whole situation, and conspicuously uninformed about politics or the law. Steve, on the other hand, was enraged—at Clinton, at the troopers, and, it seemed to Traylor, at life in general.

Steve was thirty-three at the time, and he had just moved Paula and their son, Madison, to Long Beach, California, so he could pursue a career in show business. He had tried to make it as an actor in Little Rock, but there wasn't much of a market for his talents. He had basically had only a single small role—as the ghost of Elvis in Jim Jarmusch's quirky independent film *Mystery Train.* Like Elvis, Steve hailed from Memphis and had a soft Southern accent and sleepy good looks. For years, he had made a living as a ticket agent for Northwest Airlines, first at the Little Rock airport and now at Los Angeles International. Colleagues remembered him as quiet and a little sullen. When he did talk, it was often about sex. He'd probe coworkers—men and women—about the state of their sex lives, and he'd display photographs of his girlfriend Paula in skimpy costumes—garter belts, stockings, and the like.

Steve Jones also despised the governor. Even during his governorship, Clinton had an unusual ability to generate passionate hostility, feelings that often transcended mere political differences. Indeed, one cannot understand the long siege of his presidency without weighing the depth and breadth of these emotions. Clinton haters were sometimes so obsessed by their feelings that they acted against their own political or financial self-interest. During the 1992 presidential campaign, Steve had posted Bush/Quayle bumper stickers on his locker at the airport and had even worn a campaign button until his supervisors told him to remove it. But politics only began to explain the depth of Jones's feelings. There would come to be a personal dimension to Steve's feelings as well.

For his part, Traylor did a little legal research and made a revealing discovery. If he were to sue anyone on Jones's behalf, she would have a better chance of winning a case against the president of the United States than against a small magazine. The power of the news media had manifested itself in the legal world. Public figures like the president enjoyed no legal protections comparable to those erected, on First Amendment grounds, to benefit the press. For Paula Jones, it would be almost impossible to file a libel suit and win. (This was especially true because the *Spectator* identified Jones only by her first name; most readers could not have known that the story referred to her, so it could scarcely have damaged her reputation.) In most circumstances, that would be the end of the matter. A nasty story in a magazine generates either a libel suit or nothing. But at this early moment in the case, the fundamentally political nature of the dispute first revealed itself. Traylor was far from a sophisticated man, but he knew the only potential leverage he had in the situation was against Clinton. The *Spectator* would likely just ignore the threat of a lawsuit. But if Paula Jones pursued the matter against the president, it might embarrass him—and Clinton might pay something to avoid that fate. Besides, Steve Jones had never shown any inclination to take on the *Spectator;* Paula's husband, who was the driving force in the matter from the very beginning, wanted to go after Clinton.

In truth, Traylor never wanted to go to court at all. He made his modest living doing real estate closings and small commercial deals. The last thing he needed was to embark on a massive lawsuit. To assuage Steve, and to a lesser extent Paula, Traylor proposed that he try to "finesse" the situation. He thought he might be able to persuade Clinton to make a public statement about Paula—at best an apology but at least a statement clearing her of any improper conduct. Traylor might also win a small financial settlement. Traylor didn't know Clinton or anyone who worked for him; in a city and state full of people with connections to the president, this fact alone demonstrated just how obscure his law practice was. But Traylor made a few calls and figured he'd found the right man to use as an emissary to the White House.

A few days later, Traylor met George Cook after work around one of the battered linoleum tables at the Sports Page, a seedy bar downtown. By Arkansas standards, Cook, a real estate developer who had raised money for some of Clinton's campaigns, ranked as only a peripheral friend of the president's. But when Traylor called him to set up the meeting, Cook said that he could, if necessary, pass a message to the president's people in Washington.

As they sat down to their scotch and waters, Traylor described Paula's story.

"That's the most ridiculous thing I've ever heard," Cook told him, in a conversation both men remembered the same way. Cook identified some of the problems. It was old; it was unprovable; the *Spectator* story didn't even identify Paula by her last name. "Why would you take a case like that?" Cook asked.

"I know it's weak, but it could be embarrassing for the president," Traylor replied. "Now, I'm sure with my little brain and yours, we could work something out. These people are in dire straits, and they need money badly." Traylor never said anything about wanting an apology—only money and, later on, jobs. He mentioned that he thought $25,000 would be a good amount to settle on, but later in the conversation said $15,000 might close the deal.

Cook said it sounded like a shakedown to him. So Traylor tried another tack.

"What about a job? Her husband wants to work in Hollywood. How about if the Thomasons gave him a job? Wouldn't that work things out?" (The Clintons' friends Harry Thomason and his wife, Linda Bloodworth-Thomason, produced television comedies, including *Designing Women*.)

Cook said it would be illegal for the president to do that.

At the end of the evening, Cook did promise that he would call Bruce Lindsey, an Arkansas friend who now worked as a deputy White House counsel, and ask him if he thought the president might make a statement about Jones. A day later, Cook did speak to Lindsey, who told him to forget about the whole thing. "It's absurd," Lindsey said. "Just another crazy coming out of the ionosphere."

Cook called Traylor to report on his conversation with Lindsey. "But did you speak to the president?" Traylor asked.

"The president?" Cook replied incredulously. "If I tried to talk to the president about this, he'd have me committed."

Now Traylor was really stymied. He clearly wasn't going to get anything from the president without a fight. So he thought of another approach. Steve was not just angry at the president, he was fuming about the troopers' role in the *Spectator* story as well. "These no-good troopers were sitting around and talking about my wife," Steve told the lawyer. Trooper Danny Ferguson was not identified by name in the article, but Paula knew that he had been the source for the story about her. Traylor decided to call Ferguson's lawyer and see if he could make any headway with him. So Traylor rang Cliff Jackson.

/ / /

Jackson actually did not represent Ferguson, but Traylor made an understandable mistake. When the subject was Arkansas state troopers—or anti-Clinton activity—Jackson's name often came to mind.

The relationship between Bill Clinton and Cliff Jackson was the stuff of hack fiction. The parallels between their lives were so pat and obvious that it didn't seem possible they were real. But they were, and so were the implications of Jackson's sustaining obsession with his ancient rival. Before Traylor called Jackson, the Paula Jones case loomed as little more than a minor annoyance for the president. Jackson's determination and sophistication turned the matter into a major crisis.

Clinton and Jackson were both born in 1946, raised in neighboring small towns in Arkansas, and marked early for success in the future. Both were class presidents as undergraduates, Clinton at Georgetown and Jackson at Arkansas College. Clinton won a Rhodes Scholarship and Jackson a Fulbright, and they both arrived at Oxford in 1968. One was a Democrat and the other a Republican, and they both nurtured political ambitions in the same small state. They even vaguely resembled each other—tall, bulky men who played together on the same intramural basketball team in England. In temperament, though, Clinton was the extrovert, Jackson more the loner. Even with his hangdog shyness and sad blue eyes, Jackson's comparative reticence was never mistaken for diffidence about Clinton.

Through their time together at Oxford and then for the following few years, the two men shared a wary friendship, but in the letters that Jackson shared with reporters from that period, Jackson's hostility was always close to the surface. On August 27, 1968, Jackson wrote of Clinton to a friend: "His syrupy-sweet cultivation of friendships, and tendencies . . . to speak in superlatives about everyone and everything rather grates on my nerves." Still, despite their incipient rivalry, each saw the advantage in maintaining good relations with the other. Jackson even assisted Clinton in the first great crisis of his life, over the draft for the Vietnam War.

Jackson won a medical deferment from military service shortly after both men left Oxford. Clinton spent several years struggling with the issue, hoping, as he wrote in a famous letter to an Arkansas draft official, both to avoid a war he "opposed and despised with a depth of feeling I had reserved solely for racism in America" and at the same time "to maintain my political viability within the system." Jackson helped Clinton do that, and Jackson chronicled these efforts, as he was making them, in a series of letters to his then girlfriend in England. "I have had several of my friends in influential positions trying to pull strings on Bill's behalf," Jackson wrote in one such missive, "but we don't have any results yet. I have also arranged for Bill to be admitted to the U of A[rkansas] law school at Fayetteville, where there is a ROTC unit affiliated with the law school." Jackson may have exaggerated his efforts, but he did make some contacts on Clinton's behalf. As often happened in their relationship, however, Clinton managed to do Jackson one better. The future president succeeded in avoiding the draft, ROTC, and even Arkansas's lightly regarded law school. Jackson wrote his girlfriend, "Bill Clinton is still trying to wiggle his way out of the 'disreputable' Arkansas law school."

So Clinton went on to Yale. (Jackson went to the University of Michigan Law School.) In 1971, it was Jackson's turn to ask Clinton for help. Jackson was seeking references for his application for a White House fellowship (which he never won). Replying on Yale Law School stationery, Clinton wrote a long and revealing letter to Jackson, portraying himself as a man in some crisis about his own future, full of new doubts about his once-clear ambitions. "Glad to hear from you," the letter begins. "I will have to hold discussion of law practice for another time except to say I'm glad you have a job that pleases you. Can't say I look forward to it as much as you do, but I am trying at least to learn the stuff this year, and perhaps I'll figure out something to do with it that I can really care about."

The next paragraph contains a strange foreshadowing of a future scandal in Clinton's life. "About the White House Fellowships, the best story I know on them is that virtually the only non-conservative who ever got one was a quasi-radical woman who wound up in the White House sleeping with LBJ, who made her wear a peace symbol around her waist whenever they made love. You may go far, Cliff; I doubt you will ever go that far!"

As Clinton continued his letter, he offered some general observations about Jackson's chances. "You know as well as I do that past a certain point there is no such thing as a non-partisan, objective selection process," Clinton wrote. "Discretion and diplomacy aren't demanded so much by propriety as by the necessity not to get caught." Though the sentence is garbled, and the future president is only talking about Jackson's application for a fellowship, there is still something chilling about it. Indeed, it summons nothing so much as the advice the president gave Dick Morris on the night of the greatest crisis of Clinton's political life: "We'll just have to win." Continuing in the letter, Clinton wrote, "I don't mind writing to [Arkansas senator J. William] Fulbright for you, if you'll tell me what you want me to ask him to do, but you ought to know that he won't give your politics a second thought. It would look good for Arkansas if you got the thing."

Clinton closed with a meditation about their respective futures. "One final thing: it is a long way from Antioch to the White House, and it may not be a bad thing to make the leap. Just always remember it's far more important what you're doing now than how far you've come. The White House is a long way from Whittier and the Pedernales, too; and Krushchev couldn't read until he was 24, but those facts leave a lot unsaid. If you can still aspire go on; I am having a lot of trouble getting my hunger back up, and someday I may be spent and bitter that I let the world pass me by. So do what you have to do, but be careful." In a Christmas letter sent shortly afterward, Clinton again referred to his sense of malaise. "As to the 'disturbing undercurrents' in my letter," Clinton wrote, "they were not meant to sway you from your course, or to express disapproval at the kind of things you seem destined to do—only to say these things too must be considered. You cannot turn from what you must do—it would for you be a kind of suicide. But you must try not to kill a part of yourself doing them either."

In the next few years, however, Jackson and Clinton flipped positions. Clinton got his hunger back up, and Jackson left the fast lane, only partly out of his own choosing. In 1976, the same year that Clinton first sought public office, Jackson made his only run, as the independent party candidate to be the prosecutor for Pulaski County, which includes Little Rock. He lost, and as Clinton vaulted to national prominence, Jackson retreated to a successful but obscure law practice in Little Rock. His resentments simmered. By 1991, though he was only forty-five, Jackson had mostly retired from law practice and was living off his savings.

To fill his time, Jackson turned to anti-Clinton activism. The intensity of Jackson's animosity was exceeded only by the fervor of his denials that it existed. But Jackson was clearly obsessed by his former rival—and his resentments often involved the subject of sex. Indeed, as with Stephen Jones, the subject of sex was near the core of Cliff Jackson's hostility toward Bill Clinton. So Jackson formed a group called the Alliance for Rebirth of an Independent America and led a small delegation of allies to New Hampshire to campaign against Clinton. "I felt manipulated, exploited, and deceived," Jackson said. "Our slogan was, 'Please, Governor Clinton—don't do to America what you did to Arkansas.' And we talked about how he tripled the budget, but what we really went up there to do was talk about the character issue."

The journey to New Hampshire ended largely in embarrassment—the Arkansans were roundly ignored—but it taught Jackson an important lesson. He could inflict far more harm on Clinton by serving as a source for journalists than by campaigning himself. Journalists could sustain little interest in the success or failure of Clinton's policies as governor. But if Jackson could provide narratives—stories—for the national press, then he might hold their attention. Jackson's first foray into this realm involved the draft. Jackson was savvy enough to know that the story would hurt Clinton more if Jackson could portray himself as reluctant and conscience-stricken about whether to disclose his twenty-year-old letters to his girlfriend in England. (Several reporters repeated Jackson's descriptions of his "sleepless nights" as he weighed whether to go public.) In the end, Jackson put aside his purported misgivings and served as a chief source for the stories about Clinton and the draft, which were a major crisis for his campaign in early 1992.

Of course, the draft story failed to deprive Clinton of the presidency, but Jackson learned from the experience. He had erred by providing the information indiscriminately. By doing so, he had deprived any single journalist of an exclusive, which would have amplified the story's impact. Also, by circulating his complaints so broadly, Jackson had marked himself as a vocal critic of the president. That allowed Clinton's allies to dismiss any information that came from him. When he had another opportunity, Jackson would try not to repeat these mistakes.

In July 1993, Jackson received a call from Lynn Davis, a former director of the state police. (A Republican, Davis had run for Arkansas secretary of state in 1968, and Jackson had directed his campaign.) Davis said that he had spoken with four of Clinton's former bodyguards in the state police, and they wanted to go public with their accusations about Clinton's womanizing. There wasn't anything especially high-minded about the troopers' motives. As Jackson acknowledged, they felt outraged by Clinton's conduct, but at the moment they wanted to explore the possibility of writing a book or making speeches for pay. Nor did the troopers have any evidence of actual illegal behavior by Clinton. Over the years, they had facilitated Clinton's comings and goings for what they believed were assignations with women—and they knew they could sell that as a story about the president's "character." As one of the troopers, Ronnie Anderson, recalled in a sworn affidavit that was prepared but never made public in the Paula Jones litigation, Davis estimated that the quartet "could earn $2.5 million in royalties." The troopers wanted to keep their jobs at the same time they sold out their former boss, so they figured they needed a lawyer.

Jackson quickly agreed to help them. He met with the troopers—Anderson, Roger Perry, Larry Patterson, and Danny Ferguson—and proposed that he serve as their exclusive representative in their dealings with the press. Anderson, recalling the meeting in his affidavit, said that "it had become clear to me that Mr. Davis and . . . Troopers Perry and Patterson were only interested in bashing the Clintons and that any book we authored would be used to hurt Mr. Clinton politically. On numerous occasions, I specifically recall Cliff Jackson stating that he 'wanted to see President Clinton impeached' and that he would 'do anything to bring him down.'"

But at the end of the meeting, Troopers Anderson and Ferguson refused to participate in the project (at least for the time being), and Jackson could persuade only Perry and Patterson to sign the contract he had prepared. In the document, they promised that "Jackson will negotiate and arrange subject to the approval of bodyguards the initial timing, manner and terms in which their story is brought to the attention of the American people." Moreover, Jackson agreed that he would act "to secure compensation for all . . . damages suffered by them" and to find them "employment opportunities outside the state of Arkansas." This time Jackson would not repeat the errors he had made with the draft story. He would use his new friends in the news media to make the disclosures instead of trying to do it himself.

So Jackson called Bill Rempel, the reporter who had covered the draft story for the *Los Angeles Times*. Would he be interested in talking to the troopers? In the first week of August, Rempel flew to Little Rock to meet with the troopers. Jackson told the reporter to check in at a suite at a resort on Lake Hamilton, outside the town of Hot Springs, and the troopers would be delivered to him. The next morning, Jackson and Lynn Davis—accompanied by three grim-faced strangers—knocked on his door. The three men introduced themselves.

"I'm Bubba number one," the first one said.

"Bubba number two," said the second.

"Bubba three," said the last.

They explained that they feared for their lives if it became known that they were cooperating with the story, so they preferred not to tell Rempel their names for the time being. (The three were Patterson, Perry, and Anderson; Ferguson did not participate in this first meeting.)

Over the years, many of Clinton's enemies shared this melodramatic fear of physical reprisal, even though there never appeared to be any basis for it. Despite rumors to the contrary, all of Clinton's major critics over the years enjoy robust good health.

Jackson claimed that when Davis first approached him about representing the troopers, they were "under surveillance" at a McDonald's in Little Rock. In an interview with Laura Blumenfeld of *The Washington Post,* after the trooper story broke, Jackson refused to disclose the town or even the county where he lived. He said he had run a check on the license plates of a van that he thought was following him. "Not on file," he told Blumenfeld. "That means federal undercover enforcement." These persecution fantasies allowed Jackson and the others to justify virtually anything they did, because they weren't just bringing down Clinton, they were fighting for their lives.

Rempel listened to the troopers' tales with interest, but he told them from the start that there was no way he was going to write a story of this kind based on anonymous sources. He would consider writing it only if the troopers spoke on the record. When Jackson mentioned the possibility that Rempel might join the troopers in their book project, the reporter recoiled. There could be no business dealings between them. The meeting ended with considerable uncertainty that Rempel would pursue the story at all.

Dismayed by Rempel's hard line, Jackson decided to hedge his bets. He knew that the troopers' tale bore almost no relation to Clinton's duties as governor—or as president, for that matter. It was a story about Clinton's sex life. Even with the expanding definitions of "character" that were circulating in the press at the time, Jackson could not be sure that a major newspaper like the *Los Angeles Times* would ever publish the story. So Jackson needed a sure thing—a publication, and a reporter, that would be certain to publish the troopers' stories about Clinton and maybe help his clients write their book in the bargain.

Jackson's contacts were primarily in the mainstream news media, so he called a friend for advice about the conservative press. A year earlier, during the 1992 presidential campaign, Peter W. Smith, an investment banker from Chicago and a major contributor to Newt Gingrich's political action committee, had spent about $40,000 on public relations assistance in an attempt to persuade reporters to write stories about Clinton's personal life—especially the allegation that he had fathered a child with a black prostitute. At the time, Smith had tried to hire Jackson as the lawyer for the prostitute. That deal had gone nowhere, but the two men had kept in touch. In 1992, Smith had contacted David Brock, a conservative writer who wrote *The Real Anita Hill,* a bestseller that included many purported details about Hill's sex life. After a meeting in Washington in which Smith had the *Globe,* a supermarket tabloid, open in front of him, Brock declined to pursue the black prostitute story. But when Jackson called about the troopers in 1993, Smith thought Brock might be interested this time.

Brock was—though he needed a little persuasion. Smith paid Brock $5,000 for expenses, and the young author traveled to Little Rock to meet with the troopers, even though Jackson told him that he had promised the first exclusive on their stories to Bill Rempel. In August, Jackson persuaded the troopers to speak on the record to both Rempel and Brock, and the reporters took turns debriefing them in Arkansas hotel rooms. According to Brock, Jackson told the troopers they could each make a million dollars from a book on Clinton's sex life. Fresh from the success with his Anita Hill book, Brock was the perfect candidate to serve as ghostwriter. Anderson recalled in his affidavit, "Mr. Davis and Mr. Jackson introduced David Brock to us as a prospective author for our book." But Brock knew that if the troopers had been paid, that would discredit their story, so he limited himself to writing the article for *The American Spectator.* Rempel, too, worried about the troopers' profiting from their tale, so he received an assurance from Jackson that the bodyguards had come forward, as he ultimately wrote in his story, "without a promise of financial reward." (In fact, Smith eventually paid the troopers about $25,000 for their information—but *after* the stories about them were published. Smith also paid Jackson $5,000 in legal fees.)

Brock started his reporting by meeting Jackson and two of the troopers—Anderson and Perry—in a hotel near the Little Rock airport. As it turned out, this was a gathering of some historical importance—the first interviews for an article that would lead to the impeachment of a president. Fortunately, this first meeting was tape-recorded, and the audio record illustrated the nature of Brock's inquiry and the demeanor of his principal subjects.

"Okay, yeah," the tape began with Brock's voice. "We can go from your categories. Why don't we talk about the sleaze department first, the state of their marriage. What are we talking about—an open marriage?"

What followed was nearly three hours of the most vile gossip that can be imagined. The transcript of this noxious session stripped the "character issue" bare of its pretensions. The interview included the troopers' pointless rambling ("Chelsea is allergic to cats. I don't know why they got their cat in the first place") and their random conclusions ("She wouldn't divorce him if that sumbitch did it right in front of her. She wants the power"), but it consisted mostly of the troopers' recounting what they believed were Bill and Hillary's sexual antics. At first Anderson contributed a good deal to the conversation, including passing along rumors of an affair between Hillary and her law partner, Vince Foster. "It was just one of the known deals out there that every time Bill left, Vince would come over to the [governor's] mansion," he said. But by far the lead role went to Roger Perry, who, among other things, recounted how he heard Hillary scream at Bill one night, "I need to be fucked more than twice a year!" At another point, Perry said, "Bill Clinton was infatuated with the black women. He loved black women." Amid the giggling and cackling, Jackson limited himself to gentle admonitions to the troopers. "Stay on your topic of talking about sleaze," he said at one point. At another he asked, "Is this good stuff, David?" Later on, Jackson inquired, "Is this enough to give you a flavor?" Brock answered, "Give me a couple more"—and everyone laughed.

Through the fall of 1993, Jackson monitored the troopers' cooperation with Rempel and Brock. He pestered Rempel, who was later joined by his colleague Douglas Frantz, to move faster, but they encountered some resistance from their editors in Los Angeles, who were not yet persuaded that the stories amounted to relevant news about the president. Jackson also had a problem with the troopers. Jackson had promised the troopers that neither the *Los Angeles Times* nor the *Spectator* would publish their stories without a release from them. Anderson had never given one. Then, according to Anderson, one day in the late fall, Roger Perry called Anderson at home "asking me to attend a meeting at Mr. Jackson's office in Little Rock. He characterized the situation as one involving 'life and death.' I reluctantly agreed to attend."

Jackson assembled the same troopers as in the "three Bubbas" meeting—that is, all but Ferguson. This time, Jackson had another contract for the troopers to read, but not to sign. "In return for authorization to release the stories that had been provided regarding President Clinton," Anderson recalled, "the troopers were promised jobs for seven years at an annual salary of $100,000. The only limitation mentioned was that we would have to accept these jobs in a state other than Arkansas." Acting mysteriously, Jackson wouldn't say who would provide the jobs, only that they came from his Republican connections. The troopers were skeptical. How did Cliff know these offers were real?

If the troopers didn't believe him, Jackson replied, they could speak to "a high-ranking official in the Republican Party." Jackson had spoken to the guy himself.

Who's that? the troopers challenged.

"Bob Dole," he said.

None of the troopers followed up on Jackson's offer to contact Dole, but Perry and Patterson did sign the contract. Anderson declined. Jackson subsequently denied that he had offered the troopers a precise salary for seven years or that he brokered a meeting with Dole, but Anderson's version can be partly corroborated in an unusual way.

In that fall of 1993—as Brock and Rempel prepared their stories—Trooper Danny Ferguson grew nervous about the project, and he reached out to the president to discuss it. In a clear lapse of judgment, Clinton spoke twice to his former bodyguard, and the president took handwritten notes of the conversations with Ferguson. Clinton's scrawl shows that Ferguson and Anderson were saying much the same thing. "Troopers being talked to by lawyer—offered big $," Clinton wrote. "He says GOP in on— now talking about 100G/7 years—job and whatever get from book. . . . [H]e and R. Anderson know it's wrong, they don't know anything, all rumors not good for their families or mine."

/ / /

Reluctantly, the *Los Angeles Times* reporters found themselves in a race with David Brock to be first into print with the trooper stories. Rempel and Frantz grew frustrated as the editors in Los Angeles agonized about how, or if, to publish the story. Finally, though, Clinton himself sealed the *Times*'s decision to publish. The reporters learned that the president had called the troopers' former supervisor, Buddy Young, and asked him to talk to the former members of the security detail about their decision to cooperate with the reporters. Clinton even called one of the troopers, Danny Ferguson, directly. There was no evidence that Clinton made any threats against the troopers—though there did appear to be a suggestion that the president might provide federal jobs if the troopers kept quiet. Still, the president's direct involvement gave the *Times* the hook it needed.

Notwithstanding Jackson's promise to the *Times,* the *Spectator* story actually hit the newsstands first, on Friday, December 18, 1993, and the *Times* published on Tuesday, December 21. The timing turned out to be fortuitous for the White House. Because the *Spectator* published first, the troopers' tales became associated with Brock and his magazine's clear anti-Clinton agenda. Clinton's aides could thus lump the two stories together as part of a single right-wing hatchet job. And though the *Times* story was phrased more neutrally, both publications offered much the same rationale for publishing the troopers' accusations—the character issue.

The *Times*'s story sought to portray Rempel and Frantz's work as the modern model of political reportage. "Allegations about the personal lives of Presidents are not new," they noted, citing Thomas Jefferson and his slave Sally Hemings, Franklin Roosevelt and Lucy Mercer, and "the sexual conquests of John F. Kennedy. For most of this century, propriety generally required such matters be discussed only after the individual leaders were no longer alive. In recent years, however, those standards have been changing—propelling politicians, the public, and the news media onto uncertain ground.

"Today," Rempel and Frantz continued, "the question of what inference should be drawn from a particular example of private conduct remains a matter of intense debate, influenced in part by a widening belief that personal character may be as important to a leader's performance as political party or ideology."

From there, it was on to the allegations—the "new details about extramarital affairs." The troopers said they "were often called upon to act as intermediaries to arrange and conceal his extramarital encounters" and they "shielded his infidelities" from Hillary Rodham Clinton. As for Gennifer Flowers, the *Times* report suggested that by denying Flowers's accusations about their relationship in an interview on *60 Minutes,* Clinton had made the Flowers affair a legitimate story to pursue. This was, of course, the classic bootstrapping formulation that reporters often used. It may not be a legitimate subject to ask about, but once Clinton answered, the issue became his lying rather than the underlying conduct. Trooper Larry Patterson said he had never seen Clinton engaged in sexual activity with Flowers, but he had heard phone calls between them. In addition, Patterson said, following the governor's visits to her apartment building, "Bill would come back in a half-hour or so smelling like perfume."

In *The American Spectator,* Brock employed a different tone from that of the *Times*'s reporters, but his conclusion on the legitimacy of the subject was the same. Press coverage of the Flowers case, Brock wrote, "quickly devolved into a tortured colloquium on whether or not infidelity was a Legitimate Issue. . . . Though opinion polls showed that 14 percent of the electorate would not vote for an adulterer, the indifferent public response to the Flowers story may have convinced many in the media that the public desire for 'change' outweighed any concerns about Clinton's character." There was nothing "tortured" about Brock's interest in adultery and infidelity. In one passage that later drew a great deal of notice, Brock quoted Patterson as saying Clinton had said "he had researched the subject in the Bible and oral sex isn't considered adultery." (Perry actually mentioned this point in the original taped interview.)

In fact, Brock wasted little time on his rationale and devoted most of his energy simply to trying to humiliate the president and first lady, who, the author asserted, had "an inadequate sex life" with each other. "Listening to the audio monitor at the rear porch of the main house," Brock wrote, in a passage also drawn from the first interview, "Patterson said he sat in the guard house and heard Hillary tell Bill, 'I need to be f—ed more than twice a year.' "In another passage, "Clinton evidently couldn't resist bragging about his sexual exploits. On one occasion, Perry recalled, Clinton said that Gennifer Flowers 'could suck a tennis ball through a garden hose.'"

/ / /

It was, of course, the obscure section of the *Spectator* story about "Paula" that prompted Danny Traylor to call Cliff Jackson. But when Traylor called him, Jackson at first brushed him off. For one thing, Jackson didn't even represent Trooper Ferguson. For another, he had heard Ferguson tell the story to Brock, and he knew that the reporter had given an accurate account in the *Spectator* article. Traylor then recounted his client's version of the incident at the Excelsior Hotel. This interested Jackson a great deal. In a flash, Jackson could see that Paula Jones was not a putative adversary but rather a potential friend.

The appeal for Jackson was obvious. Instead of troopers passing along rumors and circumstantial evidence of sexual misconduct by Clinton, Paula Jones could provide firsthand testimony. Jackson asked to meet Jones, and Traylor—desperate for allies anywhere he could find them—agreed. Traylor had access to a shared suite of lawyers' offices in the First Commercial Building, one of the handful of office towers that dot the skyline of Little Rock. Lynn Davis, Debbie Ballentine, and Jackson joined Traylor and Jones around a desk and heard her repeat her story. As Jackson remembered it, there were tears in the young woman's eyes as she reached the end of her story. "I will never forget it as long as I live," she said. "His face was blood red, and his penis was bright red and curved."

At this point, though Traylor remained Jones's attorney in name, Jackson basically took over the representation. Jackson showed Traylor a copy of the original agreement he had signed with the troopers, and together they modified it into a six-page "Agreement for Legal Services" to cover Traylor's representation of Jones. It began with sixteen paragraphs summarizing the facts of the case to this point, each beginning with "WHEREAS." The provisions included:

> WHEREAS, the inaccurate published report [in *The American Spectator*] has caused Client great mental anguish, embarrassment, and distress in that it erroneously implies a

consummated and satisfying sexual encounter with Bill Clinton, as well as Client's willingness to continue a sexual relationship with him; and,

WHEREAS, Client, in order to clear her good name and to set the record straight, has decided to go public with the details of this encounter with Bill Clinton; and,

WHEREAS, Client, as a proponent of women's rights and workplace security believes that all persons, have a right to security in the workplace from unwelcome sexual harassment and intimidation, especially from employers . . .

The contract then went on to describe the obligations of Traylor and Jones. Jones "will not accept any 'hush money,' jobs or other inducement from Bill Clinton, his supporters or anyone else to cease and desist in their present effort to bring her unique information and perspective to the American people. . . . [Jones] will not be intimidated from the present course of action by threat or coercion of any kind." The agreement went on to empower Traylor to "negotiate and arrange . . . the timing, manner and terms in which her story is brought to the attention of the American people." It also allowed Traylor to arrange "any and all television, radio or movie contracts" and entitled the lawyer to one-third of all of Jones's earnings from such ventures. The contract was signed and dated on February 7, 1994. (Traylor left a copy of the agreement lying around the lawyers' suite he sometimes used, and the occupants of the suite passed it around, to much hilarity.)

The agreement left open precisely how Paula Jones was to bring her story to the attention of "the American people." Traylor and Steve Jones wanted to make a public demand for Clinton to apologize to Paula. "If you are hell bent on having a press conference," Jackson told them, "you have three choices. You can do it in Little Rock on your own and try to get the press to cover it. You can do it in Washington and try to get people to come. Or you can tag along with my troopers." Jackson and the troopers were planning a press conference the following week at the Conservative Political Action Conference (CPAC) in Washington. "There'll be a lot of press there," Jackson explained, "but you have to be aware that it's a conservative organization, and the White House will try to spin that." Frustrated by George Cook's brush-off and lacking any better ideas, Paula, Steve, and Danny agreed to go to Washington.

/ / /

"Has everybody had an opportunity to get a press packet? Raise your hand if you did not get a press packet."

Cliff Jackson stood at the podium on February 11, 1994, and surveyed the rows of seated journalists who were waiting, pens poised, before him. The hotel ballroom was nearly full. In addition to about fifty reporters and a half-dozen television crews, more than a hundred participants in the CPAC conference stood behind a velvet rope awaiting the beginning of his presentation. Jackson's press conference wasn't on the official calendar of events for the annual convention, but it was the most anticipated event of the year's festivities.

This was the fourteenth annual meeting of CPAC, and the event had grown each year—more people, more speakers, more passion. The event gathered the hard core of the right wing of the Republican Party, and they were, at this moment, united in passionate loathing of the new president. There were bumper stickers—WHO KILLED VINCE FOSTER?—and doctored photographs of a naked Hillary Clinton. Jackson and his troopers were greeted like heroes.

When the time came for the press conference, Jackson had arranged for a large sign to be placed just in front of him. TROOPER-GATE WHISTLE-BLOWER FUND, it said, with a post office box in Little Rock and an 800 number. Seated behind Jackson to his right were Patterson, Roger Perry, and Lynn Davis. To his left were the real stars of the day: Danny Traylor and Paula and Stephen Jones.

After making a pitch for funds for the troopers—who, as it turned out, were never fired from their jobs—Jackson turned to the next part of the program. "You'll hear the details," Jackson said. "I'm not going to steal her thunder." Then, instructing the reporters who were going to ask Paula questions, Jackson said, "Make it simple. And no follow-up questions."

"Ms. Jones," the first reporter began, "a lot of people want to hear this in your words. What was wrong in your view with what happened?"

The answer was the first time Paula Jones ever spoke in public. As her case stretched out over five years, Jones became a fairly accomplished public performer, but at this moment she was painfully awkward to behold. With her untamed Arkansas twang and her curls stacked so high that her hair bow was barely visible in the tangles, she projected a wounded innocence but painfully little sophistication. "What was wrong," Jones said, "is that a woman can't work in the workplace and be harassed by someone that high, and it's just humiliating what he did to me."

"Will you tell us in your own words something about what really happened in that room? Everybody has been vague," another reporter said.

"I will not speak on that," Jones replied.

The reporters, clearly perplexed, followed up. Jackson had read the relevant portion of the *American Spectator* article and denounced it as untrue, and Traylor had said vaguely that they were seeking an apology from the president. So, the journalists wondered, why weren't they suing the *Spectator*? Why wouldn't they say what Clinton had done? Why were they here?

"Understanding that you don't want to go into any great detailed description of what happened," one reporter ventured, "can you tell us just what happened in the room?"

"I'll just put it this way," Jones replied. "He presented hisself to me in a very unprofessional manner. I would call it sexual harassment, and that's all."

"Did he ask you to have sex with him?"

"A type of sex, yes."

After another reporter harangued Jones about the details of the encounter, Traylor jumped in. "I appreciate that concern, but you also have to appreciate our deference to the first family and you have to appreciate the sensitive nature of what we're discussing, but I am going to talk to Paula right now and ask her to give you kind of a blow-by-blow account . . ."

Snickers filled the room at Traylor's choice of words.

". . . of what transpired in the room."

Then, as the bewildered reporters waited, Traylor and Paula and Steve Jones conferred behind the podium.

When they finished, Paula expanded her story a bit. "When I went into the hotel room, then he proceeded to take my hand and pull me over, and then slide up my legs. I pushed him back. It was just humiliating for someone of that nature, you're supposed to trust somebody like that or I would never have went to that room. . . . Somehow it worked its way into, 'You have nice curves.' 'I love the way your hair goes down your body.' Garbage like that."

Finally, the reporters grew a little giddy with the sparring. "You have mentioned that he asked you to perform a sexual act," one person ventured. "Was this something that could have been performed without you taking your clothes off?"

The reporters groaned, and Traylor allowed, "The answer is yes."

Finally, as Jackson said they would take only one more question, one reporter asked, "Did the governor ask you to perform fellatio?"

"Excuse me?" said Paula.

"Fellatio?" he shouted back.

With that, Jackson closed the proceedings. Back in their room, Paula and Steve were distraught. So was Traylor. They knew the event had gone badly. (The press conference received little coverage, and the White House dismissed it. "It's just not true," said press secretary Dee Dee Myers.)

It had been two months since Paula's name surfaced in the *Spectator*, and the efforts on her behalf had ranged from ineffectual to catastrophic. The White House had dismissed her; the press had scorned her; her prospects for a lawsuit were dim and for a book or movie deal nil.

Amid the gloom of that February night in the capital, Cliff Jackson told the group he did have one idea. He had one final hope for keeping Paula's story alive. There was someone he wanted her to meet.

2

"Isn't That What Happened?"

In the summer of 1987, a new reporter joined the staff of *The Washington Post* and was assigned a desk next to that of Michael Isikoff. The rookie had never worked at a big paper before, and he had certainly never seen or heard anyone like Isikoff. Isikoff was rumpled, in the vanishing mode of old-time newspapermen—an imperfect shave, a mess of tousled hair, a collection of ill-fitting sport jackets, a habit of gnawing on Bic pens when he wasn't barking at someone on the telephone. But none of this was the real reason Isikoff stood out. What really amazed the newcomer was the subject matter of those high-decibel phone calls. *This* was what people reported on at *The Washington Post*?

Finally, the new arrival couldn't contain his curiosity any longer and asked Isikoff what he was working on.

I'm second-sourcing a blow job, Isikoff explained. (Isikoff doesn't remember this. He recalls it was the newcomer who made the joke.)

The story was the biggest of his career to date. In February 1987, a reporter named Charles Shepard of *The Charlotte Observer* broke the news that Jim Bakker, a celebrated televangelist who ran a religion and real estate empire known as the PTL Club, had deposited $265,000 into a trust fund for the benefit of a woman named Jessica Hahn. The purpose of this payment, it became clear, was to try to buy Hahn's silence about an adulterous encounter the former church secretary had had with Bakker in 1980. (Bakker's broadcast partner in the PTL Club was his wife, the famously makeup-slathered Tammy Faye.) Shepard's story set off one of the great journalistic chases of the era, as reporters began uncovering the corruption that permeated PTL and, as it turned out, several other ministries of the airwaves.

Isikoff—and the *Post* generally—had come to the story late, but he took after it with gusto. By late summer, Hahn had become a public figure herself, especially after she agreed to provide *Playboy* magazine with an interview and a photo shoot for a reported $1 million fee. Together with a similarly aggressive reporter named Art Harris, Isikoff decided to look into Hahn's background, and they reported on September 30, 1987, that "questions have been raised about the credibility of the ex–church secretary whose revelations toppled a multimillion dollar TV pulpit. . . . Some of the questions . . . focus on Hahn's alleged sexual experience."

The key source for the story was a thirty-five-year-old electrician from Massapequa, Long Island, Rocco Riccobono, who told the *Post* reporters that he had had a "brief affair" with Hahn. Isikoff and Harris wrote, "Contacted by *The Washington Post* over several weeks, Riccobono said his fling with Hahn was in 1978. Hahn, then 18, had recently been hired as a church secretary and was visiting the apartment of a friend. After his pregnant wife fell asleep in a bedroom, Riccobono said, he plopped down in front of a fire where Hahn 'seduced me on the couch.' Riccobono said, 'I didn't resist. I couldn't help it, my flesh is weak . . . I was with Jessica several times.'" (Asked to respond, Hahn said, "I had absolutely nothing to do with Rocco Riccobono.")

The reporters ran with the story for weeks—Harris found Riccobono and handled more of the sexual material, and Isikoff did more on the financial details—and when they exhausted the *Post*'s interest in the subject, they wrote two long freelance articles about PTL for another publication—*Penthouse.* The PTL story, they wrote, was "a saga of sex, sin and pseudosalvation"—and they emptied their notebooks of material that may have been too racy for their usual employer. In one of their tales about the Bakkers, there was even a foreshadowing of a bigger story in Isikoff's future. An anonymous former aide identified as Daniel recalled how Jim Bakker told him "about parking with Tammy Faye at Bible college, how they'd first had sex in his car. 'He was laughing,' recalls Daniel. 'He said Tammy had on a black velvet skirt, and he'd messed it up pretty badly by [ejaculating] all over it when they were petting.'"

/ / /

Isikoff had helped to invent an entire new field in American journalism—sexual investigative reporting. His work on the PTL story coincided with an even more famous moment in the history of this new territory. In May 1987, just as Isikoff and Harris were pursuing Bakker and Hahn, reporters from *The Miami Herald* were crouched in the bushes outside a town house in Washington where the presidential candidate Gary Hart was having a tryst with a woman named Donna Rice. The journalists who covered these stories never had any trouble coming up with rationales for their work. For Hart—for any politician—inquiries into sex life were said to reveal "character," or, in Hart's case, "recklessness." For Hahn, it was said that the public had a right to know that she was not as innocent as she claimed to be; it was true, as Isikoff and his partner wrote, that "questions have been raised" about her sex life—if only by the reporters themselves. At each of these landmarks of sexual investigative reporting, there were misgivings expressed inside and outside the journalistic world. But journalists moved in only one direction—toward more investigations and more disclosures about the sex lives of public people. These changes, of course, took place in an ever more competitive business environment for journalists, and sex, it need hardly be said, sold. Whether sexual investigative reporting was rooted in serious questions about character or merely in profitable voyeurism, there was more of it all the time.

Mike Isikoff was perfectly situated to take advantage of this new world. For one thing, he was good at his work. He did second-source blow jobs—and much else besides. Isikoff had journeyed to Washington in the great post-Watergate migration of investigative reporters. A native of Long Island, he had graduated from Northwestern's Medill School of Journalism in 1976, and he came to

Washington to work on a Ralph Nader project. Because many small newspapers could not afford to hire their own Washington correspondents, Nader believed that most members of Congress never received adequate scrutiny from the press. So he founded the Capitol Hill News Service, hired a bunch of energetic kids just out of school, and gave them each a state delegation to cover. Isikoff had Illinois.

A little more than a year later, at the age of twenty-six, Isikoff was being profiled on the front page of *The Washington Post,* his future employer, because of his first big scoop. Isikoff had been monitoring votes on the year's farm bill when, as the *Post* reporter wrote, "he noticed something funny about George Shipley," a congressman from east-central Illinois. Shipley was missing lots of votes that mattered a great deal to his rural district, so Isikoff tracked him down and asked him why. "My back hurts, Mike," the congressman said. "Sometimes it hurts so bad that I just have to stay in bed. But the folks back home don't know about it—and I don't want them to know." Isikoff wrote the story up for his subscribers, such as the Decatur *Herald,* and Shipley's missed votes as well as his comments about keeping his constituents in the dark generated a modest tempest back home.

Many reporters might have left the matter there, but doggedness was always Isikoff's trademark. In the course of following up his investigation of the congressman, Isikoff received a tip that at the same time Shipley was claiming he was too sick to vote, he was actually hosting a golfing fund-raiser for his campaign back in Illinois. The tip checked out, and Isikoff's story made news across the state. SHIPLEY ATTENDED FUND-RAISER WHILE TOO SICK TO VOTE, cried the headline in Decatur. Not long afterward, Shipley announced he would not seek reelection to Congress.

However, it was only when the *Post* profile was published several months later that the full story of Isikoff's scoop became clear. The tipster whose information ended George Shipley's political career was an Illinois businessman named Gene Stunkel. "Stunkel had decided, a few months before, to run against Shipley in 1978," the *Post*'s T. R. Reid reported. "He wanted to give Isikoff a tip that would embarrass the incumbent." There was a lesson in that, too.

/ / /

From the Capitol Hill News Service, Isikoff migrated to the *Washington Star* and, when that paper folded, to the *Post,* in 1981. He had done good work over a dozen years, covering a mix of subjects, mostly crime stories of one kind or another. He had never covered much national politics or dealt with the tangled motives of the sources in that unique setting. Cop stories—with clear good guys and bad—were his métier. And still, in more than a decade on the job, he had never made a splash like the one he had with the Bakkers. Isikoff's pugnacious insistence on doing things his way meant that editors never wanted him around for very long, and he tended to bounce from editor to editor, from beat to beat. He was a valuable reporter, his editors and colleagues invariably said about him, and he was also—the same phrase recurred—a pain in the ass.

Cliff Jackson had met Isikoff during the 1992 campaign, when the reporter had written some stories about Clinton's avoidance of military service during the Vietnam War. Jackson liked Isikoff, not least because they shared many of the same views about Clinton. Unlike Jackson, Isikoff was no conservative. But with friends, colleagues, and sources, the reporter never shied away from expressing his view that the new president was a pathological liar. Jackson and Isikoff also shared similar feelings about Clinton's sex life. Based on the reporting he had done, Isikoff referred to Clinton as a sex addict, and he believed that virtually all of his problems stemmed from this fatal flaw.

Invited by Jackson to the press conference at the Shoreham on February 11, 1994, Isikoff had attended and then filed a fourteen-inch story about Paula Jones's charges. But the paper didn't run it and referred to Jones only glancingly—and mockingly—in a story about the CPAC conference three days later.

Jackson knew immediately that the press conference had been a disaster, so while he was still with Paula and Steve Jones in their room at the Shoreham, he told them what he thought they should do next. "You are going to have to give a respected reporter an exclusive," Jackson said. "Mike is top-notch. He's honest. You should deal with Isikoff and Isikoff alone." Summoned to the hotel room, Isikoff met the Joneses and received their promise of full cooperation. Isikoff would have access to Paula, Steve, Debra Ballentine, Pam Blackard, even Paula's sisters. Paula and Mike hit it off right away. Isikoff had even seen Steve in *Mystery Train*.

So Isikoff received permission from his editors to go down to Arkansas and research Paula's claim. He spoke to the people that Jackson recommended, but it was difficult to find anyone else who might prove or disprove the story. (Ferguson wouldn't talk to Isikoff.) One of the perils of sexual investigative reporting was that the key evidence tended to be known by only two people. Through spokesmen, Clinton was denying Jones's accusations, so Isikoff's investigation seemed stalled at the impasse of he said/she said. So the reporter, stymied, took what he regarded as the logical next step. In an effort to prove whether Clinton had propositioned Jones, Isikoff would see if the president had made similar approaches to other women. Was there a pattern in Clinton's behavior?

The search for such "patterns" is a key element of sexual investigative reporting. At one level, it does make sense. Some men do display consistent aberrant habits in their dealings with women. But reporters who set off to identify such patterns essentially make a public figure's entire private life fair game. Isikoff set out to track down every rumor about Clinton's sex life that he could find in Little Rock, and there were a lot of them. Brock had been down this road before, and the two men talked. There were, in fact, a number of reporters from all over the country who had come to Arkansas in search of Clinton girlfriends, and Isikoff became their dean. As he began drafting his Paula Jones story, Isikoff included some of the tales of other women as corroboration of Jones's claim.

His editors weren't interested in the "pattern" evidence. They were skittish enough about getting into the Jones story at all; they didn't want to start in with other women who had not publicly complained about the president's behavior. On a day-to-day basis, Isikoff worked for three editors at the *Post*—Marilyn Thompson and Fred Barbash, from the national desk, and Karen de Young, the assistant managing editor. Concerned about Isikoff's lack of progress—and his zeal—his editors assigned two other reporters,

Sharon LaFraniere and Charles Shepard (who had come to the *Post* from *The Charlotte Observer*), to work with him on the Jones story.

The situation grew so tense that Isikoff began talking to editors in other sections of the paper—the Style section, which mostly did features, or the Sunday Outlook section, which did opinion pieces—about the story. On March 16, Thompson told Barbash (who happened to be standing in de Young's office) that Isikoff was shopping the Jones piece to other sections and generally driving her crazy. Barbash summoned Isikoff into de Young's office. In seconds, with Thompson seated on the couch beside them, Barbash and Isikoff were screaming at each other. Isikoff called Barbash a "fucking asshole" and stormed out. Barbash took umbrage and reported the epithet up the chain of command, and Isikoff was suspended without pay for two weeks. (In a preview of a tactic that would become standard in the Clinton scandals, supporters of the Jones story—that is, opponents of the president—leaked news of Isikoff's suspension to the conservative *Washington Times*. Other conservative publications picked up the reporter's saga, which these outlets spun as the *Post*'s buckling under political pressure from the White House—an interpretation that even Isikoff didn't believe to be true. But leaking the news of an anti-Clinton work-in-progress in effect dared the publication to run its story—and thus leveraged the investment of placing the story in the first place.)

Though Isikoff did return to work after the two weeks, he began seeking a job elsewhere. As for his "pattern" evidence against Clinton, Isikoff didn't want it to go to waste, so later, he met David Brock for a drink at the Four Seasons Hotel in Georgetown. Isikoff's further research on Clinton's sex life had begun (where else?) with tips from Cliff Jackson, and he had three names to pass along to Brock. He handed him a printout of some of his notes for his story.

Like Isikoff's editors, Brock found the material unpersuasive, and he never used it either.

/ / /

The only person who felt worse than Isikoff about his suspension was Steve Jones. It was Steve, far more than Paula, who was pushing her confrontation with the president. Now, it appeared, Isikoff's story might never appear. So Steve decided to take his own first steps toward the goals he had had all along—to make trouble for the president and money for himself.

In early April, Jones received a call from a television producer named Patrick Matrisciana, who specialized in conspiracy documentaries. His company, Jeremiah Films, produced films on the familiar obsessions of the extreme right, including creationism, alleged cover-ups about prisoners of war still in Vietnam, and the horrors of the gay rights and environmental movements. (One of his features, *The Crash: The Coming Financial Collapse of America,* came in a "Christian version" and a "Non-Religious version.") The filmmaker offered Jones $1,000 for an interview with him and Paula, and on April 9, Matrisciana set up a camera on a balcony of the Joneses' apartment building in Long Beach.

Eventually, a few clips from these interviews were included in an enormously successful documentary called *The Clinton Chronicles,* which was distributed by Jerry Falwell's organization. To a sound track of ominous music in the background, *The Clinton Chronicles* accused the president of drug-dealing, conspiracies to murder his enemies, and, almost incidentally, sexual harassment of Paula Jones. (About 150,000 copies of the tape were sold.) The brief snippets used in the documentary did not, however, do justice to the full interview Matrisciana conducted on that windy afternoon in April. The raw footage of the interview was never made public, but it was subpoenaed by Clinton's lawyers in the course of Jones's lawsuit.

"Have you got the tape rolling now?" Jones said as the camera was turned on. She had placed an enormous purple bow in her hair in a forlorn effort to tame the frizzy mane that ran down nearly to her waist and often blew into her face. She was nervous and giggly, and each time she fluffed a line, she looked to Steve, seated just out of camera range, for reassurance and advice.

"On May eighth, 1991," Paula said, "I was invited to sit at the reception desk at the Governor's Quality Management Ball." Conference, that is—she rolled her eyes at the mistake. In time, though, she picked up her rhythm and began to recite what was becoming a familiar story.

When she came to the moment when she and the governor

were together in the hotel room, she spoke with confidence about one subject. "Before I knew it, he asked me to 'kiss it'—that was the word he used. And I said, 'I'm not that type of girl.'" In time, Jones would give many versions of the encounter. The details often changed. Who said what, when. Where Clinton was sitting. How they moved around the room. But the one thing that never changed was Paula's response to Clinton's overture: "I'm not that kind of girl." (She repeated it three times in the Matrisciana interview.) There was a poignancy to that line, because she often looked at Steve when she said it. It was, in a real sense, what Steve wanted the message of the whole story to be. He told me as much when we spoke for the first time several years later. "See, I know Paula's telling the truth about what happened, because what he asked her to do, she won't do that," he told me. "I don't want you to feel sorry for me, but she just won't do that."

Continuing her narrative for the camera, Paula said, "I started to proceed down the hall to the door and I turned around—I was very, very angry—and I asked him, did Hillary ever give him any?" Paula may have found herself caught up in Matrisciana's and her husband's encouragement, because this line about Hillary never came up again in her accounts of her encounter with Clinton. "And I went down the elevator, went back to my registration desk, and I told Pam the whole story."

Paula then paused, a quizzical expression on her face, and turned to her husband. "Isn't that what happened?" she asked him. Needless to say, Matrisciana left that moment on the cutting-room floor. Still, why was Paula asking Steve what happened between her and Clinton?

A moment later, Paula was describing the impact of the incident on her marriage. "My husband is very outraged at what happened to me, very, very angry with the president over what happened." She looked at Steve. "What has it done, honey? It's pissed you off. I know that." Paula laughed, and then her face darkened and she stared at the floor. "Gosh, yes," she said quietly.

Paula finally made it all the way through her story, and Matrisciana asked Steve to walk over to her and kiss her. After six such takes, Steve then began speaking to the camera. He looked almost like a caricature of a Method actor—jutting out his chin, taking deep cleansing breaths, placing his hand on the bridge of his nose as he collected himself during long pauses. His performance would have bordered on the comical if not for the rage that poured from him.

"I'd like to take this a few steps further," Steve began. "I think Bill Clinton is perverted. I think he needs some deep psychological help, I really do. . . . It really irritates me that we've got this perverted doughboy in the White House. I really honestly feel sorry for his family. Every time I see Clinton, I see him with his pants down in front of my wife, and oh, God, it infuriates me."

On this day, however, Steve had another target for his outrage— the paper that was suppressing his wife's story. "I think the position of the editors of *The Washington Post* . . . is under the left foot of Bill Clinton. That's where they are, and every once in a while they creep their hand out from under the foot and give him a spit shine. That's how I feel about it."

Paula's husband didn't feel that way about everyone at *The Washington Post,* however. "When we were in Washington, Paula and I and Danny Traylor, Paula's lawyer, we sat down and we had about a three-hour conversation with Mike Isikoff," Steve recounted. "Paula gave the exclusive to *The Washington Post* and Mike Isikoff. . . . And Mike told Paula as far as he was concerned, he believed Paula and he thought the story should be told."

/ / /

On the morning of April 15, 1994, less than a week after Paula and Steve's interview with Matrisciana and one month after Isikoff was suspended, a large black bus pulled into a parking lot across the street from the offices of the Rose Law Firm in Little Rock. Three words were stenciled in red along the side of the customized motor coach: WAKE UP AMERICA! Right below, in bold white lettering, was a provocative question: SHOULD CLINTON BE IMPEACHED?

The bus had been rented by Randall Terry, the founder of the antiabortion group Operation Rescue, who had taken it to Little Rock to kick off what he called his Loyal Opposition Tour to seven cities. "Our motto is 'Loyal to God, loyal to the scriptures, and loyal to the Constitution,' in that order," Terry said at a press conference to kick off the tour. "There are a lot of people who are talking about alleged offenses the president has committed. But at this juncture, there are very few people willing to say what is on a lot of people's minds, and that is this: Should this man be driven from office?"

Even at this early stage in Clinton's presidency, Terry had no compunction about stating his goal—driving Clinton out of office. (Cliff Jackson had used the same kind of language with the troopers a few months earlier.) Of course, at the time, the notion seemed quixotic at best, but it revealed a frame of mind that was central to the story that followed. For the most part, Clinton's enemies forswore the usual forums of American politics—voting, legislating, and organizing—in favor of calls for his personal destruction. Politics had always been rough, and presidents like Lyndon Johnson and Richard Nixon had endured attacks as vicious as those launched against Clinton. But in the past the vituperation had generally been tethered to some matter of government policy, such as, say, the Vietnam War. With Clinton, the assaults were based almost entirely on his personal behavior, his "character." And few played rougher than Clinton's enemies. For example, just a few weeks before he arrived in Little Rock, the federal court of appeals in New York had upheld Terry's conviction on charges in connection with an incident during the 1992 Democratic National Convention, when a man had thrust a fetus at Clinton.

Terry was joined on his tour by the Reverend Patrick Mahoney, the executive director of a group called the Christian Defense Coalition, who announced at that first press conference, "We are going to be holding demonstrations at the Rose Law Firm and in front of Clinton's former church, asking them why they did not discipline this man, or excommunicate this man, or censure this man. This man is flagrantly promoting rebellion against God's word. We are going to grass-roots America and rip off the facade. This is the single most un-Christian administration in the history of this country."

So, on April 15, the tour did indeed kick off in the parking lot of Hillary's former law firm, and there Terry's motor coach was joined by a satellite uplink van belonging to Vic Eliason. A minister based in Milwaukee, Eliason used the van on behalf of the Voice of Christian Youth, an organization that syndicated radio programs to about two hundred religious stations around the country. Eliason, Terry, and Mahoney spent the day broadcasting from the parking lot, calling on a series of local guests, including a man who accused Clinton of participating in a conspiracy in the murder of his father. During the course of the call-in portion of the show, Mahoney heard the name Paula Jones for the first time. After a caller brought Jones's claims about Clinton to Mahoney's attention, he asked his assistant, Gary McCullough, to see if he could arrange to speak to her. McCullough tracked her down, and Mahoney, sitting in the satellite van, spoke to Paula for about forty-five minutes on the telephone.

It was a difficult time for Paula and Steve Jones—scant attention, little money, and no lawsuit. In addition to her paid session with Matrisciana, which had not yet been broadcast, she did two interviews for free. She and Steve spoke to a reporter from Pat Robertson's *700 Club,* which produced a taped spot. ("We want to warn our viewers that this interview contains graphic descriptions that are offensive to all of us, but especially for your children," the anchorwoman said in introducing the piece.) Paula and Traylor also appeared on a live local television program called *A.M. Philadelphia.* The lawyer was horrified to see that Paula wore what appeared to be a brown negligee for that interview.

Mahoney was the first person to show sustained personal interest in Jones and her story. Over the next few days, Mahoney called Paula and Steve several more times. They began praying together over the telephone. Gradually, Steve took over most of the communications with Mahoney, and they decided that they needed higher-powered legal help than Traylor could provide. There was one problem. Almost as soon as Mahoney heard Paula Jones's name for the first time, he heard a rumor that naked pictures of Paula existed somewhere. He knew this could be a problem if she embarked on a lawsuit against the president. In one of their first telephone calls, Mahoney asked Steve if these pictures existed. After checking with Paula, Steve told Mahoney the answer: there were no pictures.

Though he mostly operated on the fringe of American politics, Mahoney was a man of considerable sophistication, and he recognized that it would help Jones's cause—and hurt Clinton's—if she was represented by a feminist organization. After all, they were the ones who were supposed to be concerned about sexual harassment. So Mahoney persuaded Patricia Ireland, the head of the National Organization for Women, to participate in a conference call with Jones. But Jones was confused about the time, and she missed the call. Mahoney then fell back on his contacts in the religious right. That, he knew, was the most likely source of a lawyer who might want to sue Bill Clinton.

The anti-Clinton bus tour wound through the Midwest and finished its journey on Sunday morning, April 24, outside the Foundry United Methodist Church in Washington, where the president and first lady were attending services. Randall Terry led about twenty protesters in prayer.

"Father," he said, "this is not a Christian president."

A week later, Paula Jones had new lawyers.

/ / /

The search for new lawyers began, as did so much else, with Cliff Jackson. Traylor recognized from the start that he was in over his head, but he didn't even have the resources to know where to look for legal help. Jackson, on the other hand, did. Though he never spoke to Pat Mahoney, they independently came to the same conclusion about what kind of lawyer Jones would need. Jackson called it the "go-left" strategy, and he suggested that Traylor get in touch with the American Civil Liberties Union, the NAACP Legal Defense and Education Fund, Anita Hill, and Gerry Spence. Jackson even sought out a leftist lawyer he knew in Los Angeles. But these approaches came to nothing, and Jackson saw that the May deadline for the three-year statute of limitations was fast approaching. Go-left became go-right. So Jackson went back to Peter Smith, the Chicago financier who had underwritten Brock's article and then supported the troopers themselves.

Smith immediately went to work trying to find someone to represent Jones. He called a young lawyer in Chicago named Richard Porter, who had recently joined the firm of Kirkland & Ellis after serving on the staff of Vice President Dan Quayle. Porter did mostly corporate work, but he wanted to be helpful, so he called a lawyer in Philadelphia named Jerome Marcus. They had been classmates at the University of Chicago Law School, and they were politically in synch. Marcus was interested, so he and Porter arranged to have a conference call with Jackson to discuss the case. They liked what they heard, and so the two lawyers began speaking regularly with Traylor, offering to pitch in with some of the work that needed to be done if a lawsuit was going to be filed. As a litigator, Marcus had more to offer Traylor, and he even took a stab at a first draft of a sexual harassment complaint against the president. For Traylor, though, their help came with strings attached. The most important condition was absolute secrecy. Porter worked with a large corporate firm, and Marcus's firm, while smaller, had strong Democratic ties in Pennsylvania.

The involvement of Porter and Marcus marked the unofficial beginning of what became known much later, in Hillary Clinton's words, as the "vast right-wing conspiracy." This phrase lent their activities a more sinister cast than they deserved. There is nothing illegal or improper in one lawyer's assisting another in the way that Porter and Marcus (and later others) helped Traylor. The issue was not what they did but why they did it. In other words, what separated the actions of these lawyers from, say, those of the private attorneys who assisted Thurgood Marshall in his civil rights battles was the question of motive. Most public interest lawyers volunteer for a case because they believe in a cause—an area of law they want to change. Here, in contrast, Porter, Marcus, and their later recruits had no interest or expertise in sexual harassment law. To the extent they cared at all about the state of the law in this area, they were more sympathetic to defendants than plaintiffs. They joined the cause of this sexual harassment plaintiff because their agenda was to try—in secret—to damage Bill Clinton's presidency. Their involvement was a classic demonstration of the legal system's takeover of the political system. Indeed, Porter, Marcus, and their colleagues used this lawsuit like a kind of after-the-fact election, to use briefs, subpoenas, and interrogations to undo in secret what the voters had done in the most public of American proceedings. In time, this secret group of lawyers would call themselves, half-jokingly, "the elves."

As Danny Traylor saw it, though, the problem was that Porter and Marcus weren't doing enough. He valued their private assistance, but he needed a lawyer to stand up and take over the case for him. "When are you gonna stop chicken-shittin' around and get me a lawyer?" Traylor would ask the pair during their frequent phone calls in the spring of 1994.

Finally, though, Traylor did get a call from someone who wasn't just chicken-shittin' around. The lawyer searches led to Gil Davis and Joe Cammarata, who would remain anomalies during their three years of work for Paula Jones. Though virtually everyone else who participated in the case operated with a political agenda foremost among his or her priorities, the two of them behaved, in an old-fashioned sense, like lawyers. And though they resembled a mismatched comedy team—Davis the big and beefy Southerner, Cammarata the wiry and intense New Yorker—they acted with a degree of professionalism that was uncommon among the lawyers in the case. All they tried to do was help their client—and they were ultimately driven from the case because of it.

Their initiation to the case, however, revealed its political roots. To be sure, Davis was a Republican. He had served as a junior federal prosecutor during the Nixon years, and he was in the process of planning a run for the Republican nomination to be Virginia's attorney general. (He finished fourth in a primary in 1997.) But Davis was more iconoclast than ideologue, and the proudest achievement of his legal career was his twenty-year battle on behalf of a hillbilly farmer who won $39 million from Bethlehem Steel on a claim that the company had stolen the coal from underneath his land. (Davis made $6.5 million from the case, a fee that allowed him to dabble in politics and causes like Jones's.) It was the kind of David-and-Goliath struggle that appealed to Davis—which is how he saw Paula Jones's situation when he first heard about it in the last week in April.

Davis had sublet an office to Cammarata in his suite in Fairfax, a suburb of Washington. Though also a Republican, Cammarata had even fewer political ties than Davis. He had served as a lawyer in the tax unit of the Justice Department under George Bush, but his work involved the routine kind of litigation that carries over from one administration to the next. Cammarata wanted a little more excitement than he found in tax cases, so Davis agreed to share a few personal injury trials with him. On Monday, May 2, 1994, Davis told his younger colleague that he might have something more piquant than a slip-and-fall case to share.

The following day, Davis called Danny Traylor for a briefing. The most important thing he heard concerned the statute of limitations. The upcoming Sunday would mark three years since the alleged incident in the Excelsior Hotel, and that meant that Paula would have to file her case by Friday, May 6, or lose her right to do so. (Most sexual harassment cases are filed under Title VII of the 1964 Civil Rights Act, but that law's 180-day statute of limitations had long since expired. Most other possible claims had three-year statutes of limitations.) Almost as an aside, Traylor mentioned that he (actually the elf Marcus) had prepared a complaint for a lawsuit against Clinton. Traylor had already alerted the press that he was probably going to file it the next day. Davis asked him to fax it to his office so he could look it over.

Davis exuded laconic calm, while Cammarata nearly vibrated with nervous energy, and after they spent almost the entire Tuesday night reviewing Traylor's draft complaint, they had characteristic reactions to it. Davis thought it could use some work. Cammarata called Traylor on the phone and said, "Cancel the goddamn press conference. If you file that piece of shit, it's going to get thrown out." Then he turned to Davis and said, "I don't know what you think you're doing, but you're getting on a plane to Little Rock."

On Wednesday morning, May 4, they caught the first plane to Little Rock—but they received an important boost when they picked up the newspaper on the way to the airport. That day, the *Post* finally ran Isikoff's story, which bore Shepard's and LaFraniere's bylines as well. As the *Los Angeles Times* did with the trooper story, the *Post* used a pretext other than the underlying event as an excuse to publish the story. Clinton had just hired Robert S. Bennett, a well-known Washington litigator, to represent him in the case, and the *Post* made Bennett's hiring the focus of the piece. "Over the past three months," the front-page story read, "*The Washington Post* has interviewed Jones extensively about what she said happened in Little Rock's Excelsior Hotel. She said she was alone with Clinton in the room—making it impossible to independently resolve what, if anything, happened between them." Bennett was quoted as saying, "This event, plain and simple, didn't happen." Davis and Cammarata had been on the fence about whether to go through with filing the suit. The imprimatur of the *Post* on the story nudged them closer to proceeding.

The combination of Traylor's announced press conference, the appearance of the *Post*'s story, and the looming statute of limitations prompted a horde of journalists to descend on Little Rock.

After Davis and Cammarata (along with their paralegal, Bill Stanley) landed, they made it to Traylor's shared office suite around noon Wednesday, and they found Traylor as relaxed as ever. The Arkansas lawyer was fingering an inch-high stack of telephone messages, noting with amusement all the famous newspapers and networks that were calling him. (Bob Bennett had called several times, but the lawyers felt they'd gain a strategic advantage if they waited awhile before returning his call.) As it happened, the three men could see out the window to the front door of the federal courthouse, and they watched with astonishment as the crowd of journalists there swelled to more than a hundred.

Davis and Cammarata asked to meet their putative new client, and Paula and Steve Jones joined them later Wednesday afternoon. After Paula recited her story for the three lawyers, Cammarata asked to speak to her privately. He asked her something that Traylor had never thought to do in the four months he had represented her.

"Paula," Cammarata asked, "is there anything unusual about the way the president looks, you know, in his genital area?"

During the course of the day, Davis and Cammarata spoke to Debbie Ballentine and Pam Blackard—the woman who had heard from Jones on the day of the incident—as well as Jones's mother and sisters. This was the lawyers' due diligence check, to make sure they had a legal basis to proceed with the case. One thing they didn't do was revealing as well. Davis and Cammarata never spoke with anyone at AIDC, the agency where Jones worked. They never asked whether Jones was demoted or denied raises or promotions because of the incident. From the start, Jones's lawyers saw the case as about a crude pass, not employment discrimination.

On Thursday morning, May 5, Davis finally got around to returning Bennett's call. The two men knew each other vaguely from the time when they were both federal prosecutors in the early seventies, and so spent a few minutes on small talk. Finally, Davis said they would be filing Jones's case against Clinton by three o'clock that afternoon.

"I've talked to the president about this for hours and hours," Bennett said, "and this just didn't happen. You have no case."

The two men sparred inconclusively for a few minutes, and

then Bennett raised the stakes. "Did you know there are naked photos of your client?" (The president's lawyer had heard the same rumor Mahoney had.)

Davis said he didn't know about any naked photos, but he would be interested to see them if they existed. Bennett said he had not seen them yet. Then it was Davis's turn to spring a surprise.

"My client says your guy has a unique mark on his penis, and she can identify it."

What followed was a considerable silence.

By afternoon, Bennett had traveled the short distance between his office and the White House, and had camped out in the office of George Stephanopoulos, just down a small corridor from the Oval Office. Conferring moment by moment with the White House aide—and checking occasionally with the president himself—Bennett struggled for a way to avoid the filing of the lawsuit. What, he asked Davis, would it take to get Jones not to file her case? Davis said she wanted no money, no apology, just a statement clearing her name. So that afternoon, Bennett (with Stephanopoulos's assistance) and Davis spent much of the day trading drafts of a proposed statement to be made by Clinton. The last version read:

> I have no recollection of meeting Paula Jones on May 8, 1991, in a room at the Excelsior Hotel. However, I do not challenge the claim that we met there and I may very well have met her in the past. She did not engage in any improper or sexual conduct. I regret the untrue assertions which have been made about her conduct which may have adversely challenged her character and good name. I have no further comment on my previous statements about my own conduct. Neither I nor my staff will have any further comment on this matter.

The artful wording implied, but did not state, that Clinton had behaved properly, and it cleared Jones of her purported request to be Clinton's regular girlfriend. (Since that request was supposedly made to Danny Ferguson, Clinton could never have known whether it was made anyway.) As the negotiations continued that afternoon, Bennett said he would have to consult his client, and he went to the Oval Office. Bennett didn't tell Davis and Cammarata where he was going, but in their last conversation, Davis asked whether he had been able to reach his client.

"He's in the room," Bennett said.

Davis, Cammarata, and Paula and Steve Jones traded astonished looks. *He's in the room?*

Paula's lawyers had more or less agreed to the text of the statement, but they wanted to make sure that Clinton himself read it, not a White House spokesman. Was that okay with Clinton?

"I don't know," Bennett said. "Hold on."

Clinton told Bennett he would read the statement.

The two sides were very close. The one unresolved issue was a six-month "tolling" agreement in the statute of limitations. "We want to make sure that you don't take potshots at us in the press after we settle this thing," Davis told Bennett. "So we want to be able to reopen it if you do."

"No way," said Bennett. "No tolling agreement. It's a deal breaker." Davis wanted to close the deal or file the case before the court clerk closed at five o'clock. Finally, Bennett said, "Gil, we are talking about the president of the United States. You owe him every courtesy you could give him."

"You pushed the right button with me," Davis told him, and the two men decided to speak Friday morning.

Davis and Cammarata then sent their paralegal, Bill Stanley, to deliver a press statement to the throng of reporters who were gathered in the wilting heat in front of the Little Rock federal courthouse. Cammarata had written out a statement for Stanley to read: "For reasons I can't disclose, we shall file something tomorrow." But a moment before Stanley left, Cammarata crossed out the word "shall" and substituted "may." From their vantage point in the office tower, the lawyers watched the reporters envelop their paralegal as he waded into their midst with his script. Though he had only a single sentence to read, Stanley was jostled, questioned, and probed in so many ways—one reporter appeared to use Stanley's back as a writing surface—that it took him forty-five minutes to extricate himself from the scrum.

Overnight, however, the deal began to fall apart. The reason was Steve Jones. In a pattern that would recur throughout the case, Steve thought his wife's lawyers weren't fighting hard enough for her. Steve wanted an apology from the president—and he wanted money. The presidential statement that Bennett had agreed to amounted to a smidgen of the former and none of the latter. Steve wanted to sue the bastard. By Friday morning, Paula informed her lawyers that she did, too.

Davis did have a pretext for breaking off negotiations. In the course of the evening, CNN had broadcast claims by unnamed administration officials that Paula had backed off from filing her lawsuit because she knew she had no case and because her family opposed the lawsuit. Davis was sophisticated enough in the ways of Washington to know that in a White House with more than a thousand employees, it would be impossible to police what all of them said. Once more, Davis asked Paula, "Is there anything in your background you don't want to go into here? Because it's all going to come out."

Paula quietly said no.

So, in his way, did Clinton. He endorsed Bennett's decision to let Jones sue rather than agree to the tolling agreement. In light of all that followed from the filing of the Jones case, this decision has to rank as a monumental miscalculation. In six months, Davis and Cammarata might have lost interest and the case might have slipped quietly away. But six months would have put the decision at the beginning of Clinton's 1996 reelection campaign, when Clinton (and Stephanopoulos) thought it would generate even more attention. Clinton was also fatalistic about the inquiries into his past, with a substantial overlay of self-pity as well. No president, he said at the time, had been examined the way he had. If she wants to sue, the president said, let her sue.

On the morning of Friday, May 6, Davis sat down with a yellow pad and scratched out a letter to Bennett. "Bob," Davis wrote under the double-underlined "Confidential" at the top of the page, "I appreciate your efforts to resolve this dispute amicably." Though the letter nominally invited Bennett to resume negotiations, Davis knew that he had pushed Clinton's lawyer as far as he was going to go. "Further efforts to resolve these matters seem fruitless, as the tolling agreement is unfortunately a 'deal breaker,' as you have said," Davis concluded. "Therefore, the complaint will be filed today."

Cammarata had been polishing the complaint while Davis negotiated with Bennett. In the end, there were four counts. First, the lawyers claimed that Clinton denied Jones "equal protection of the laws" under the United States Constitution by "sexually harassing and assaulting her on May 8, 1991," and by creating "a hostile work environment" for her. Second, they said Clinton, Danny Ferguson, and others had "conspired" to deprive her of her constitutional rights. The third claim was "odious, perverse and outrageous" conduct—a seldom-used tort under Arkansas law. Finally, both Clinton and Ferguson, as well as the president's "agents and employees," had defamed Jones. The lawyers issued a statement that Jones had filed the lawsuit "with regret," adding that "any proceeds from this litigation, above the costs of the case, will be donated by my husband and me to a Little Rock charity."

It was late afternoon on Friday, May 6, when copies of the complaint were finally distributed to the journalists who had been waiting for three days in the stifling heat in front of the Little Rock courthouse. One reporter for a British tabloid even did a dramatic reading of selected portions to his exhausted colleagues.

"'. . . Clinton then approached the sofa and as he sat down he lowered his trousers and underwear exposing his erect penis and asked Jones to "kiss it."'

"And hey, mates," this refugee from Fleet Street bellowed into the Arkansas sun, "don't forget paragraph twenty-two. 'There were distinguishing characteristics in Clinton's genital area that were obvious to Jones.'

"Christ," he said. "I wonder what they were."

3

Party Girl

Before he was hired to defend President Clinton in the Paula Jones case, Bob Bennett never had a job interview with his prospective client. Rather, the lawyer was interrogated by his prospective client's wife.

That division of labor reflected the critical role played by Hillary Clinton in the long siege of her husband's presidency. The first lady had played a similar role in the hiring of David Kendall, the private lawyer who was originally hired to defend her and her husband in matters relating to Whitewater. But Kendall didn't believe in holding press conferences or attacking the Clintons' enemies in public, and Mrs. Clinton thought that was the kind of aggressive action that was needed by the spring of 1994.

In light of the portfolio the first lady wanted filled, it was no surprise that she turned to Bennett. He was fifty-four years old and the proprietor of one of the most glamorous and lucrative law practices in the country. Like many entrepreneurs, Bennett owed his success to a curious mixture of skill, timing, and luck. In the 1970s and 1980s, prosecutors began sending subpoenas to large corporations in investigations of defense-contractor fraud, corrupt campaign practices, and other complex offenses. Until this time, criminal defense work had been something of a backwater in the legal community, the province of the slick and often sleazy. But as Bennett and a handful of other lawyers recognized, the prosecutors' new targets could afford the fees that previously had been the exclusive province of Wall Street corporate lawyers. Because he was smart, resourceful, and happy to surround himself with the best younger talent—and because he had secured the Boeing Corporation as an early and loyal client—Bennett profited more than almost anyone else from the white-collar boom.

By the mid-nineties, Bennett was a senior partner in the Washington office of the colossal New York firm of Skadden, Arps, Slate, Meagher & Flom, where he charged about $475 an hour and took home well over $1 million a year. He had grown up in Brooklyn, big brother to William J. Bennett, the former secretary of education and drug czar, who was among Bill Clinton's most vociferous Republican critics. Bob was educated at the law schools of Georgetown and Harvard and served an apprenticeship at the United States Attorney's Office in Washington before he joined a law firm. In 1990, the Senate Ethics Committee hired Bennett to investigate five senators who were accused of intervening with federal regulators on behalf of the corrupt financier Charles H. Keating, Jr. He developed the consummate insider's law practice—a dollop of public service here, a touch of punditry there, and a host of big, unglamorous corporate clients to pay the bills. Perhaps Bennett's waistline did keep expanding so that he ever more closely resembled a Daumier villain, and he could never finish a meal without depositing a portion of it upon one of his expensive ties. He had a great life—and he knew it.

Still, the involvement of his client's wife in Bennett's defense of Clinton in the Paula Jones case created complications right from the start. She wanted to fight, not settle. When Bennett finally got around to seeing his client, the president also said he didn't want to settle, but not because he was eager for a fight. He didn't want to settle, Clinton told Bennett and others, because he couldn't do that to Hillary. A settlement would suggest that Clinton was admitting to Jones's charges, and the president said he could not put his wife through that kind of humiliation. This reluctance to settle had dramatic—and catastrophic—implications for the Clinton presidency, and it was rooted in the complex dynamics of the relationship between husband and wife.

So Bennett took his orders and fought. He began by stewing, obsessing, and seething . . . about Alan Dershowitz. In his many talk-show appearances, the Harvard Law School professor had expressed a theory about what Clinton should do: in Dershowitz's opinion, the president should have "defaulted" in Paula Jones's lawsuit against him. In other words, Clinton should have refused to defend himself and allowed the judge in the case to enter a verdict against him. The only issue then would have been damages. Because Jones could not prove that she was fired, denied promotions, or otherwise discriminated against, Clinton would have to pay only a modest sum, or perhaps nothing at all. Best of all, according to Dershowitz, a default judgment would spare the president the ordeal of testifying or even devoting much time to this distracting matter.

Dershowitz's theory did have an elegant simplicity. It was also completely insane. The press would have portrayed a presidential default as at best an act of contempt by the president toward the judicial process and at worst a full admission of Jones's claims. In the American system, generally only wanted fugitives and rogue governments default in court. More important, a default would *not* have excused the president from testifying. Jones's lawyers could have—and undoubtedly would have—forced Clinton to testify on the issue of damages. No serious lawyer or scholar joined Dershowitz in his quixotic notion. Yet Bob Bennett spent hours recruiting lawyer friends to rebut Dershowitz's position, asking White House officials to defend him in public, and generally agonizing about the harsh words that rained down on him from Cambridge.

Bennett's anguish made no sense at all—yet it arose from the precise reason the Clintons had hired him. Bennett had a superb team around him to prepare the legal work—younger partners like Mitchell Ettinger, who could research the facts, and Amy Sabrin, who could write the briefs. What separated Bennett from scores of other successful white-collar defense lawyers was his obsession with public, as well as legal, advocacy. Bennett inhabited the world of *Nightline* and *Rivera Live,* and this was where he believed the Paula Jones case would be won or lost. He worked the press ceaselessly, on the air and off, with bombastic press conferences and discreet off-the-record whispers. Shortly after Jones filed her lawsuit, Bennett even invited a reporter from *The New York Times Magazine,* Ruth Shalit, to his vacation home in Montana, took a business call there in private, then informed the journalist of the (unspecified) coup he had just engineered for a client. "That's called getting intelligence. That's knowing people. That's getting the inside track," Bennett told Shalit. "That's having inside your head a kind of wiring diagram of how Washington works."

In the president's calculus of self-interest, the Clintons made the right choice in selecting Bennett, who skillfully advanced his client's interests for more than four years. Bennett understood instinctively that the Paula Jones case was rooted more in politics than in law, and he defended it accordingly. The "vast right-wing conspiracy" had abused and manipulated the legal system to pursue Clinton. Less noticed—but no less real—was that Clinton's allies replied in kind. From the very start, Bennett used the language and techniques of politics to prevail in the Paula Jones case. That was what he was hired to do. But Bennett's spin, demagoguery, and exaggeration—no less than that of his adversaries—degraded the legal process as well. Bennett's behavior fed and even helped justify the public's cynicism about courts, lawyers, and law.

Of course, the client in this relationship—that is, the president of the United States—could have held Bennett back and insisted on the high road. In fact, the reverse occurred. It was the president's lawyer who had to restrain Clinton's headlong rush into the gutter.

/ / /

"Good afternoon," Bennett said to the nest of microphones arrayed before him. "First and foremost, the president adamantly denies these vicious and mean-spirited allegations. Quite simply, the incident did not occur."

When Bennett began his press briefing on the afternoon of May 6, the full text of Paula Jones's complaint had only moments earlier slithered out of the fax machine. But the president had built his career around the idea of a perpetual campaign, and a key tenet of that philosophy was never to leave an attack unanswered. The first news cycle to report the filing of the case would certainly include his lawyer's emphatic response.

"In a single term," Bennett said, "this complaint is tabloid trash with a legal caption on it. If it was a serious lawsuit, it would not read like a made-for-TV lawsuit. The language in the lawsuit just underscores the fact that this is not about the serious subject of sex harassment or civil rights. Indeed, it cheapens and it trivializes those important areas of the law. . . . This suit is about publicity, it's about talk shows, it's about money [and] book contract profits."

Bennett's opening statement lasted just five minutes, but he hit all of the talking points that would constitute the president's response to the case for the next four years: the "incident" did not take place; money and greed motivated Jones; the lawsuit was the work of the president's personal and political enemies. And yet Bennett was a lawyer, and so he spoke with precision as well as passion in behalf of his client. And in the details of what Bennett said on the first day of the Paula Jones lawsuit, there were the first flickers of caution in his denials on behalf of the president. Shortly after Jones's press conference in February, Mark Gearan, then the White House communications director, responded to Jones's claim by saying, "It is not true. He does not recall meeting her. He was never alone in a hotel with her."

At the May 6 press conference, one reporter asked Bennett, "Are you denying every particular in the lawsuit? Are you saying there was no approach by a state trooper, no meeting in a hotel room, no discussion between President Clinton and this woman?"

Bennett hedged—elegantly. Indeed, he used almost precisely the same words his client would employ four years later when he was asked about his relationship with another young woman, complete with the same disdainful reluctance to utter her name. "This president did not engage in any inappropriate or sexual conduct with this woman," the lawyer said. So, Gearan notwithstanding, perhaps Clinton did meet Jones in a hotel room.

And then there was a question of legal strategy. Bennett proclaimed emphatically that the "incident" did not take place, and he implied that he welcomed the opportunity to take on the accusation in court. But reporters asked whether a trial might involve a deposition by the president. Was that what Clinton wanted?

Indeed not, said Bennett. "Let's be practical and reasonable," he said, "Do the American people really want the president of the United States of America to be spending his time with lawyers rather than solving the problems of the times? I mean, that's just an absurd result in a democracy. And frankly, foreign countries laugh at us at the suggestion that somebody can spin a yarn and file a complaint, and be off to the races tying down the president of the United States."

Within these first answers were the seeds of Bennett's real strategy to win the case. In truth, the last thing Bennett—or Clinton—wanted was to challenge Paula Jones's story on the merits in a courtroom. In May 1994, only one date mattered to the president, and that was two and a half years away. He wanted all fact-finding—depositions, discovery, any inquiry into this case in particular or his sex life in general—put off until after the 1996 election. As if the point needed any clarification, Clinton's White House counsel at the time, an old Washington hand named Lloyd Cutler, took Bennett to brunch at the Four Seasons Hotel to deliver the message in person.

"The win is getting it beyond the election," Cutler told him. "Nothing else matters."

But because of the election, Clinton couldn't just win the case. He had to win the case the right way. Or, more precisely, he had to be seen as having won the case the right way. Clinton had always enjoyed the support of feminists, and women generally voted for him in greater numbers than men. Clinton had opposed the nomination of Clarence Thomas to the Supreme Court and spoken eloquently in support of laws prohibiting sexual harassment. So, not surprisingly, the question arose at Bennett's first briefing of whether he was going to defend the president in the same way that Thomas's supporters had defended him—by attacking his accuser.

"Are you going to go into the character of this woman . . . Bob, the folks at the White House are saying that you are going to go after this woman's character and reputation."

"I feel sorry for her at this point, and that's not really my style," Bennett said.

/ / /

On June 8, exactly thirty-three days later, under the golden arches of one of the two McDonald's restaurants in the sleepy Arkansas town of Cabot, Mitch Ettinger of Skadden Arps shared a meal with a fellow named Dennis Kirkland. Kirkland had a tale to share about Paula Corbin Jones.

Kirkland had graduated from Cabot High School in 1985, and in the summer of 1987 he had attended a graduation party for the school. At the time of the party, he was nineteen and Paula Corbin was twenty. Before that evening, they had never met.

Kirkland recalled that he was drunk at the party, and he guessed Paula was, too. He told Ettinger that he "talked trash" to Paula for about ten minutes, and then she grabbed his crotch. Within ten minutes of their meeting, he took Paula to a van parked nearby, and there she gave him a "blow job." They returned to the party, where he shared news of his good fortune with several of his friends. Still later at the party, Kirkland told the lawyer for the president, he observed Paula giving blow jobs to three of his friends, whom he named. Paula gave Kirkland her phone number at the party, and they kept in touch for a while. Over the next several weeks, they met several times, usually at Paula's mother's apartment. From there they would go to Camp Robinson, a National Guard facility in the area, and have sex. Kirkland stopped calling when he began seeing the woman who would become his wife (and whom, he told Ettinger, he was now divorcing and fighting for custody of their kids).

Bob Bennett hoarded the report of Kirkland's interview like a trophy of war. Of course, he couldn't make any public reference to what he called, in private, the story of the "blow-job boys." Bennett's public silence and private joy about the blow-job boys illustrated how the political imperatives of the case created twisted pretzels of irony. Because of Clinton's feminist base, Bennett couldn't even acknowledge that Jones's background or reputation was relevant to her case, much less that he was studying her life with care. Bennett also had to keep his work secret, because if it was disclosed, conservatives would claim to be outraged. But in ordinary circumstances, conservatives believed that a woman's background was fair game in a claim of sexual harassment, so their anger would be just as phony as Bennett's denials of interest in Jones's sex life. So Bennett dissembled to trump the Republicans' own duplicity. This graceless standoff served as a metaphor for a larger lesson of the case—that the merger of law and politics degraded both.

The question Bennett so greedily explored had a slight relevance to the case. Paula Jones had filed a defamation suit, claiming that she had been damaged in "her good name, character, and reputation." So Bennett had the right to examine her standing in the community. Similarly, in her complaint, Jones had asserted that after Clinton had approached her in the room at the Excelsior, she "became horrified, jumped from the couch [and] stated she was 'not that kind of girl.'" In the same way, then, Bennett had a right to ask what kind of girl Paula Jones was.

Still, fundamentally, even these justifications served as pretexts. Like their adversaries—like, indeed, the reporters who covered the case—all the president's lawyers really cared about was the sex. Despite denials that were as indignant as they were false, the subject of sex subsumed everything in this case.

/ / /

As the sun moves across the Arkansas sky, the shadows from the huge concrete towers of the Lonoke grain-drying cooperative stretch out along the town's main drag. On some days, a visitor might be forgiven for thinking the shadows move faster than anything else in Lonoke. The railroad tracks that once ran up the grassy median strip of Front Street are gone, and these days only a few cars stop at the handful of surviving businesses in town. Pedestrians are few. Now and then, someone walks into Blackard's Dry Cleaners, which is run by the family of the woman who was sitting next to Paula at the registration desk at the Excelsior. The big business in town is minnows. Since the sixties the locals have been replacing their rice farms with ponds, where they raise Lonoke's gift to America's bait shops. Around city hall, they even call Lonoke the minnow capital of the world.

Today, of course, Lonoke is best known as the hometown of Paula Jones. (It's not far from Cabot, which nurtured Dennis Kirkland.) In a case filled with authentic pornography, there may be at least a moral obscenity in applying microscopic biographical attention to Paula Corbin Jones. Until the moment she took on Bill Clinton, her life was mostly sad, mostly ordinary, and entirely alien to the world of government and law. She must be the only significant political figure of the century who could say, as she once did to me, "The Republicans? Are they the good 'uns or the bad 'uns?" After Paula became famous, friendship with her became a kind of industry, as acquaintances, boyfriends, and even relatives cashed in on her notoriety. To the extent possible, it is important to try to separate truth from financially induced exaggeration. The life of Paula Jones does contain some clues to what happened between her and the governor in 1991—and to why, years later, her case spiraled into history.

Paula Corbin was born on September 17, 1967, the last of Bobby and Delmer Corbin's three daughters. The lives of Paula and her sisters were dominated by the harsh tenets of the First Church of the Nazarene, where the family worshipped and her father sometimes preached. It was part-time, unpaid work, and Bobby Corbin supported the family as a pattern maker in a local mill where they made dresses for Sears. The three Corbin girls dressed in clothes that Delmer Corbin made from the scraps of fabric Bobby brought home from work. Nazarene prohibitions defined the girls' lives. They couldn't drink, dance, wear pants or makeup, roller-skate, watch television, or even visit friends' houses. Paula wore thick glasses, and her hair flowed down her back. Early family pictures from Paula's girlhood show all three girls with long hair, because haircuts were also prohibited by the family's rules. Their isolation was intense. Delmer even fetched the girls from school so they could eat lunch at home.

When Paula became a teenager, the family's life, never easy, turned even more troubled. While Bobby was on a disability leave, he was laid off from the mill, just short of the time needed to qualify for a pension. Two years later, in 1984, he died of heart failure while playing gospel music on the piano at a senior citizen's home. Paula's sisters dropped out of high school and married. Paula struggled on at Lonoke High and then transferred to neighboring Carlisle High because it required fewer credits for graduation.

As the girls hit their teenage years, their parents' control over them dwindled. By the time of Bobby's death, Paula was in full-scale revolt against the rules of her childhood. It is this period of her life—from about 1984 until she met Steve Jones in 1989, from age seventeen to twenty-two—that drew most of the attention after she filed her case against the president. For a while, she commuted the thirty-five miles to Little Rock, first to secretarial school (from which she dropped out), then to a series of retail sales jobs, from which she was invariably fired because of tardiness, absenteeism, or inattention to her work (she worked at a pest control company, sold Swatch watches at a department store, and did clerical work for Hertz and a trucking company—where she was reprimanded for her provocative dress). In 1988, the small family home on Front Street burned down—the family had no insurance—and Paula lacked a permanent place to live for a while. During this time, she dated a fellow named Mike Turner for a few months, and he arranged for them to be photographed together in nearly naked embraces. (Both wore skimpy bikini bottoms.) In other words, the rumor that both Pat Mahoney and Bob Bennett had heard about photographs was true.

After Paula became famous, Turner sold the photographs to *Penthouse.* Turner had kept not only the pictures of his long-ago girlfriend but a handful of notes that Paula had written to him. The tone of the letters differed considerably from what one might expect from the horrified ingenue who recoiled in horror from Bill Clinton's pass. In one note to Turner, for example, Paula wrote, "I miss every inch of you . . . but I miss some inches more than others," and, in another, "Your [sic] great in bed." Paula's brother-in-law Mark Brown said Paula told him that by the time she was seventeen, she had had sex with fifteen men. (Paula's arrival in the public spotlight brought to the surface splits in her family that had simmered for years. Charlotte and Mark Brown denounced Paula as a fabricator and fortune-hunter; her other sister, Lydia Cathey, stood by Paula.)

Certainly there was no shortage of men in Little Rock who claimed to have been involved with her during this period. Certainly, too, there was little doubt that Paula's life began to change when she met Steve Jones in 1989 at BJ's Star-Studded Honky Tonk in Little Rock. Unlike her previous boyfriends, Steve was conservative and controlling, and Paula tamed her free-spirited ways when they were together. Jobs came and went; she had never held a job for longer than four months. Then her old friend Pam Blackard suggested she apply for work with Pam's employer, the Arkansas Industrial Development Commission. It took two tries, but finally Paula obtained work as a documents examiner for $6.35 an hour. Her duties at the AIDC never amounted to much more than making delivery runs to other government offices and typing employment applications into a database. These limited duties were not entirely surprising, because she typed only twenty-four words a minute. (In an employment test for alphabetizing, she got only twenty-three out of thirty-four answers correct.)

Still, she made an impression on her coworkers, who nick-named her Minnie Mouse because of her tight dresses, hair bows, and peripatetic manner. In the early nineties, the Arkansas legislative session used to feature parties for legislators and lobbyists nearly every night of the week. Paula went to so many that the fellows in payroll never learned her name; they just called her "party girl." Her good-natured spaciness made her something of a legend around the office long before she became famous. Once, in an oft-repeated tale, a coworker asked her to cash a check for him. Hours later, he asked Paula about his money. She put her hands on her hips, shook her head, and said, "I don't know where that is!"

In the months leading up to the conference at the Excelsior, it was possible to see that two sides of her character—her wild past and staid present, her flirtatious history and hopeful future with Steve—remained close to the surface. She had worked at AIDC for only two months when her boss, Clydine Pennington, asked her if she wanted to work at the registration desk at the Governor's Quality Management Conference on May 8, 1991. It was far from an ordinary assignment for Paula. Pennington remembered her bubbling excitement as she reported for work that morning, before she headed over to the hotel. She had dressed for the occasion—short culottes, black hose, high heels, and a big bow in her hair. Just before she left for the short drive to the hotel, Paula asked Pennington, "Do you think this skirt is too short?"

Pennington didn't lie. "Actually, I do, Paula, but I guess there's nothing you can do about it now."

Paula smiled and said, "I'll just stay behind the table." Then she was gone.

/ / /

In the spring of 1994, the events that took place at the Excelsior prompted Paula Jones to file a lawsuit against the president of the United States. The case—a private action against a sitting president for actions taken before he was elected—was often described as unprecedented, but that wasn't exactly true. A few days before John F. Kennedy was elected president, several disgruntled delegates who had attended the Democratic National Convention in

Los Angeles filed a lawsuit against him. The delegates had been standing in front of a hotel trying to flag down a taxi to go to a party given by the famous Washington hostess Perle Mesta. Kennedy saw them waiting and offered them his car and driver, which they accepted. Kennedy was not a passenger. During the subsequent ride, the car collided with another, and that accident became the basis for the suit. In a foreshadowing of the Jones case, the plaintiffs in *Bailey v. Kennedy* used the discovery process to try to obtain embarrassing information about the Kennedy family finances in interrogatories sent to Attorney General Robert F. Kennedy. Rather than answer such questions, the Kennedys settled the case for $17,750, a considerable sum in 1963.

But though there had almost never been a case like *Jones v. Clinton,* presidential power has been one of the most controversial areas of constitutional law over the past several decades. In a series of cases, the Supreme Court was asked to weigh how and whether the laws that govern other citizens apply to the president. The most famous of these cases arose out of Watergate. In *United States v. Nixon,* the Court upheld Judge John Sirica's subpoena of the White House tapes in the criminal trial against those charged in the Watergate cover-up. Because the subpoena was narrowly drawn and the material sought was indispensable to a fair trial, the Court unanimously ruled that Nixon had to produce the tapes. To rule otherwise, the Court held, would place the president above the law.

It was a less-known case that created the real ideological divide over presidential power and immunity from court processes. In 1970, an Air Force management analyst named A. Ernest Fitzgerald had been fired after he gave testimony before Congress about cost overruns on Air Force projects. Fitzgerald sued President Nixon, and the case reached the Supreme Court in 1982. A bitterly divided Court ruled, five to four, that Fitzgerald had no right to bring his case.

According to Justice Lewis Powell's opinion for the Court, the president enjoyed absolute immunity from liability for acts within the "outer perimeter" of his official duties. "Because of the singular importance of the President's duties," he wrote, the "diversion of his energies by concern with private lawsuits would raise unique risks to the functioning of government. . . . The sheer prominence of the President's office" would make him "an easily identifiable target for suits for civil damages. Cognizance of this personal vulnerability frequently could distract a President from his official duties, to the detriment of not only the President and his office but also the Nation that the Presidency was designed to serve." In a dissenting opinion in which he was joined by the Court's liberal wing, Justice Byron White thundered that the court's decision "places the President above the law . . . [and] is a reversion to the notion that the King can do no wrong."

The Fitzgerald case—and cases like it—defined the terms of the debate over presidential power for a generation, with conservatives seeking the protection of the president from the distractions of litigation and liberals believing that the chief executive should be treated more like an ordinary citizen. As a legal matter, the Paula Jones case followed in this tradition—posing the question of whether a sitting president should be forced to defend a private lawsuit. Of course, the analogy between the Jones case and that of Fitzgerald was close but not exact; the Pentagon employee's civil suit against the president was based on Nixon's official, not private, actions. Still, in the Jones case, if liberals and conservatives had stuck to their principles, the liberals would have supported Jones's right to sue and the conservatives would have backed the president's claim of immunity.

Just the opposite occurred. In another example of how law and politics polluted each other in the course of this case, the Jones lawsuit found liberals feeling a president's pain and conservatives speaking out for a lowly citizen. This hypocrisy was on vivid display in the genteel forum of the *MacNeil/Lehrer NewsHour* for May 24, 1994. Lloyd Cutler, the White House counsel and a stalwart Democrat, envisioned a legal quagmire for the president if the Jones case was allowed to proceed. "Suppose there were twenty libel suits filed against the president," Cutler said. "Would he have to defend all those libel suits?"

The conservative who embraced Paula Jones's cause on the program could scarcely bring himself to pay lip service to Clinton's obligations as president. "I think the dignity of the presidency and the rightful conduct of that office is of paramount importance and justifies protecting the president against the kinds of lawsuits that history tells us presidents are subjected to." (*Rightful* conduct—an important qualification.) But this case—and this president—was something altogether different. "This is a novel situation, which suggests to me that we elect as president of the United States not perfect individuals but people who have conducted themselves in a way that at least thus far in our history has not given rise to private civil litigation against them." It was a difficult sentence to parse, but the implication seemed to be that other presidents may not have been "perfect" but the Paula Jones case potentially represented a new and unprecedented level of presidential misfeasance. It was a thought that the spokesman for Paula Jones's position on the program, a former Republican official named Kenneth W. Starr, would have ample opportunity to reflect upon in the months to come.

4

"I Love This Man"

It's not easy to make this kind of call, Cliff Jackson said.

Jackson was agonizing once again about whether to supply a reporter with another damaging tale about Bill Clinton. But just as he had with the draft stories, the trooper stories, the Paula Jones stories, and his journeys to New Hampshire to campaign against his former Oxford schoolmate, Cliff Jackson said he had suffered through more purported sleepless nights. Then he decided that, well, yes, he would continue his campaign to destroy the president.

"Bill," Jackson said, "there's someone on my dock who wants to talk about Whitewater."

That was how Jackson greeted the *Los Angeles Times*'s Rempel in a telephone call in the fall of 1993. At the time, the two men were in touch almost daily, because Rempel was working on Jackson's tip about the troopers and Clinton's sex life. Now Cliff had something else for Rempel. He had Whitewater.

The story—Whitewater—had existed on the periphery of the political world since March 8, 1992, just after the New Hampshire primary, when *The New York Times*'s Jeff Gerth published the first story about it. CLINTON JOINED S&L OPERATOR IN OZARK REAL ESTATE VENTURE, the headline read. The lead to Gerth's story matched the neutral tone of the headline: "Bill Clinton and his wife were business partners with the owner of a failing savings and loan association that was subject to state regulation early in his tenure as Governor of Arkansas, records show.

"The partnership, a real estate joint venture that was developing land in the Ozarks, involved the Clintons and James B. McDougal, a former Clinton aide turned developer. It started in 1978, and at times money from Mr. McDougal's savings and loan was used to subsidize it. The corporation continues to this day, but does not appear to be active." Gerth's story was as notable for what it didn't say as for what it did: there was no allegation of illegal conduct on the part of the then governor.

While Gerth was working on his article for the *Times,* the Clintons' side of the story was presented by an old friend of theirs named Susan Thomases, a New York lawyer who was quoted extensively in the piece. According to James B. Stewart's book on Whitewater, *Blood Sport,* when, at long last, Gerth's piece was published, "Thomases was thrilled. She thought it was incomprehensible."

Thomases had a lot of company in that view. The same phrases would reappear in the continuing coverage of the Whitewater story—"conflicts of interest," "failed savings and loan," "subject to state regulation"—yet no one could ever say with precision, much less with the specificity required for a criminal case, what Bill and Hillary Clinton had done wrong. Many of the stories invoked two familiar phrases of this accusatory era, words that had in common both their ubiquity and their meaninglessness: "appearance of impropriety" and "unanswered questions." Indeed, with an almost comic circularity of reasoning, the very existence of the inquiries about Whitewater was seen as proof that they were justified. The *New York Times* editorial page often spoke this way. "Much as President Clinton might wish," the editors wrote in a typical passage, "the curious saga of his and his wife's dealings with the owner of a failed Arkansas savings and loan association just won't go away. It keeps popping up in Congressional inquiries and newspaper accounts. . . ." Or on another occasion, the eve of one of the many congressional hearings on Whitewater, the paper intoned: "Mr. Clinton came to Washington promising to end the casual conflicts, favoritism and insider deals of the Reagan-Bush years. The very existence of these hearings attests that he has done little to honor that commitment."

One thing, however, was clear from the start. The Whitewater development itself, about two hundred acres located in a remote and inaccessible region of north Arkansas, had been a failure. Bill Clinton had not even been elected governor yet when, on an evening in early 1978, he and Hillary first discussed the purchase of the property with Jim and Susan McDougal, over dinner at a restaurant in Little Rock called the Black-eyed Pea. Later that year, the Clintons began investing in the project, and they eventually sank about $70,000 into the venture, although the precise amount was in dispute. At one point, in a rather pathetic attempt to generate interest in the area, Hillary Clinton paid for a small model house to be built on the property. The idea succeeded only in drawing a horde of photographers to the doorstep of the luckless souls who lived there at the time Clinton became president. Eventually, the homesteaders grew so fed up with serving as backdrops for the endless Whitewater stories that they hung a large banner that said, GO HOME, IDIOTS! (To this day, the Clintons have never visited the Whitewater property.)

Still, the story never exactly went away. It received a smattering of attention in the press, and investigators in various bureaucracies of the federal government kept an eye on Whitewater as well. After Clinton was elected, the Whitewater case (if it was a case) remained in the same sort of limbo, the subject of occasional attention in the press but little sustained interest by law enforcement. In the Clinton White House, the Whitewater investigation belonged in the bailiwick of a lawyer named Vincent W. Foster, Jr., a former partner of Hillary Clinton's in the Rose Law Firm. Foster actually spent most of his first months on the job as deputy White House counsel dealing with inquiries about another so-called scandal—the firing of several workers in the White House travel office in May 1993. Alerted to possible improprieties in the operation of that office, the White House had moved swiftly to replace the career officials who worked there. But the Clinton administration figures who handled the matter, including Foster, blundered. Based on the way the story was covered in the press, it looked as if the Clinton people had mistreated the long-serving incumbents, who had close ties to many White House reporters; worse, it seemed that the Clinton people were trying to replace the travel office with individuals with personal and financial ties to the first family. (Years of investigation of "Travelgate" produced no criminal charges against any Clinton appointees.)

This minor flap turned into a tragedy on July 20, 1993, six months into Clinton's presidency, when Vince Foster was found dead of a self-inflicted gunshot wound in a park outside Washington. In an apparent suicide note that was found torn in pieces at the bottom of Foster's briefcase in his White House office, the lawyer wrote, "I made mistakes from ignorance, inexperience and overwork. . . . No one in the White House, to my knowledge, violated any law or standard of conduct, including any action in the travel office. There was no intent to benefit any individual or specific group. . . . The public will never believe the innocence of the Clintons or their loyal staff. . . ." In the aftermath of the suicide, many reporters decided to take a fresh look at all the subjects that had been within Foster's jurisdiction, including Whitewater. Still, the problem remained: there wasn't a witness who could say that the Clintons had done anything illegal in connection with Whitewater.

Then, at last, there was a witness. His name was David Hale, and he was sitting on the dock outside Cliff Jackson's house.

/ / /

In the Ozark Mountains of north Arkansas, not far from the Booger Hollow Trading Post and the seven-story-tall statue of Jesus Christ in Eureka Springs, the biggest summertime crowds used to gather at Dogpatch U.S.A., the amusement park based on the Al Capp comic strip. Visitors sipping Kickapoo Joy Juice strolled past the statue of General Jubilation T. Cornpone among actors dressed as Li'l Abner and Daisy Mae. The hillbilly theme even extended to the food signs. "Onbelievublee delishus Fish Vittles Kooked fo' Sail," boasted one offering. The park opened in 1968 and at one point drew as many as a million visitors a year, but once Capp stopped drawing the cartoon in 1977, the appeal of Dogpatch waned. In 1993, it went out of business for good.

The closing represented more bad news for David Hale that year. He had helped to found the park, but it represented just one of his many business interests. In some respects, David Hale was the consummate small-state wheeler-dealer who dabbled in politics, law, and finance, the kind of enthusiastic booster who would wind up (as Hale did) as national president of the Jaycees. He was the chief judge on the small claims court of Little Rock and a friend to virtually all of the state's political establishment. (As the journalist Murray Waas has pointed out, Hale was also a devout Baptist who frequently noted that one of his businesses manufactured church pews.) Hale even ran a bank of sorts, a company called Capital Management Services, which was authorized by the federal Small Business Administration to make loans to disadvantaged and minority borrowers. Among his many obligations, Hale also found time to be a professional thief.

In 1986, Hale's friends Jim and Susan McDougal came to him with a business proposition. (As it happened, this conversation also took place at Little Rock's Black-eyed Pea.) As operators of Madison Guaranty Savings & Loan, they wanted Hale's company to lend $300,000 to Susan McDougal for the husband-and-wife team to use in their various business ventures. Hale did make the loan, and it was never repaid. What happened to the money has always been something of a mystery. Jim McDougal said that $110,000 of it went to the Whitewater investment that he shared with Bill and Hillary Clinton. (Madison went bankrupt in 1989, costing taxpayers more than $49 million, which made it a rather modest failure by the standards of the S&L era.)

It was the story of this $300,000 loan that was at the heart of what David Hale told the *Los Angeles Times*'s Bill Rempel after Cliff Jackson introduced them, and one part of Hale's tale was especially significant. Hale told the reporter that Bill Clinton had personally asked him to make the loan to Susan McDougal. In that conversation, according to Hale, the then governor said that his name could not appear on any of the loan documents. To the extent that there has ever been an accusation of criminal wrongdoing against Clinton on Whitewater, this was—and is—it. Hale suggested that Clinton urged him to make a loan under false pretenses; according to Hale (though this was never entirely clear), Clinton knew that the money for the McDougals was really going to their shared Whitewater investment, even though Susan was ostensibly borrowing it for her marketing business. It was something less than an earth-shaking crime, and even if Hale's story was true, Clinton's actions may not have been a crime at all. But virtually the entire long investigation of Whitewater flows from this single purported conversation between Hale and Clinton in February 1986. (From the beginning, Clinton denied that any such conversation ever took place.)

Though Jackson peddled the trooper story only to Rempel and David Brock, he shared David Hale more widely. In the fall of 1993, Hale talked to *The Washington Post* and *The New York Times* as well as to Rempel, and the stories in all the various outlets dribbled out throughout the fall. "Clinton told reporters last week that he and his wife had done nothing improper," Rempel and Frantz wrote in one such story. "But such allegations, raising questions of possible conflicts of interest and abuse of office by the then-Governor of Arkansas, continue to be nettlesome." All of the reports in all the papers contained some version of this disclaimer. There's no proof Clinton did anything wrong—but the existence of the inquiries remained a problem.

One thing that wasn't entirely clear in these stories was David Hale's motivation in coming forward. Hale had one goal—to see an independent counsel appointed in the case. Throughout the fall of 1993, Hale was being investigated by the United States attorney in Little Rock in connection with a variety of fraud charges, most particularly the theft of $3.4 million from the Small Business Administration—a case that had nothing to do with Clinton. Hale's lawyer was trying without success to negotiate a plea bargain with the United States attorney in Little Rock that would allow Hale to avoid jail time. (Hale had other problems as well, including investigations of his involvement with a burial insurance fraud and a kickback scheme with suppliers at his own courthouse.) Hale did not succeed in avoiding indictment. The grand jury in Little Rock charged him in the SBA case on September 23. But his hopes of lenient treatment still rested in getting a new, independent prosecutor placed in charge of the case. Hale had been caught stealing thousands of dollars; his tale about Bill Clinton was, he hoped, his ticket to leniency.

The interviews that Jackson arranged for Hale succeeded in keeping the story alive in Washington. As Jackson knew they would, *The Washington Post, The New York Times,* and the *Los Angeles Times* spent the rest of the fall battling one another for preeminence in the story—which at this point consisted mostly of determining which investigative body was investigating White-water (the U.S. attorney or the Resolution Trust Corporation) and how much, if anything, Clinton administration officials knew about these investigations. Had the RTC—the government agency charged with examining bankrupt savings and loans—made a "referral" suggesting a criminal investigation of Whitewater? Who knew of it—and when? To be sure, the Clinton officials botched their handling of the inquiries in the winter of 1993 by acting unduly defensive. White House aides—at the direction of Bill and Hillary Clinton—refused to make public all of the first family's documents on their investments. George Stephanopoulos protested the appointment of Jay Stephens, a prominent Republican, by the RTC to investigate Whitewater.

In light of these disclosures, the underlying events of the White-water transaction all but disappeared from the news coverage. By December, when news broke that White House lawyers had removed some documents about Whitewater from Vince Foster's office after his death, Whitewater had turned into a bona fide media frenzy. (The lawyers said they removed the documents because they believed they contained privileged communications between Foster and his clients, the Clintons.) Congressional hearings on the subject were planned for the spring. Through it all, the evidence against the Clintons bordered on the nonexistent. (This was true even after the Whitewater documents finally were released—and after Stephens made his report, which exonerated the Clintons.)

Throughout December, members of Congress began calling on Attorney General Janet Reno to appoint a special prosecutor in the case. The law governing independent counsels had expired in 1992, when Republicans who were upset with Lawrence E. Walsh's conduct of the Iran-Contra prosecution blocked its renewal. Reno wanted to wait to make any appointment of a prosecutor until the law was renewed, which was expected to be in mid-1994. But during the second week in January, when Clinton set off on a major tour of Central Europe and the former Soviet Union, virtually all the questions that followed him involved Whitewater and the appointment of a special prosecutor. On January 11, in the Ukraine, Clinton sat for a brief interview with Jim Miklaszewski of NBC News, who asked him only about Whitewater. Clinton waxed indignant, saying, "I'm sorry you're not interested in this trip. My thinking is this is a situation without precedent in American history. I mean, all these people say, 'We don't believe this man's done anything wrong. There's no evidence that he's done anything wrong. There's never been a credible charge that he's done anything wrong.'"

Still, that night, the president and his advisers bowed to political reality. In a conference call between the president's party in Europe and his legal team gathered around the Oval Office in Washington, only one adviser spoke out against asking Reno to make the appointment. According to James Stewart, White House counsel Bernard Nussbaum warned that asking for a special prosecutor when there was no evidence of wrongdoing on the part of the president would amount to a historic blunder. "The frustration of finding nothing in Whitewater will make them investigate every one of your friends," Nussbaum said. "They will broaden the investigation to areas we haven't even contemplated."

"But this is about Whitewater," someone said to Nussbaum.

"No," he replied forlornly. "This will be a roving searchlight. . . . They will chase you, your family and friends, through the presidency and beyond."

Clinton's political advisers overrode Nussbaum and persuaded Clinton to request the appointment of a special prosecutor. This was a tremendous victory for both David Hale and Cliff Jackson. Hale would achieve his goal of cutting a plea-bargain deal that would lead to lenient treatment for his crimes. Jackson accomplished even more. By the end of February 1994, Jackson had set in motion both the Paula Jones case and the Whitewater independent counsel—which would, in time, converge and then nearly consume Bill Clinton's presidency.

On January 12, with the president still overseas, Stephanopoulos made the official announcement that the president would ask Reno to appoint a special prosecutor. He hoped that the appointment of a special prosecutor would bring the matter to "a speedy and credible resolution."

/ / /

In 1875, just five years after the Department of Justice was created, President Ulysses S. Grant appointed the first outside independent prosecutor (who was also the secretary of the treasury) to investigate the St. Louis Whiskey Ring, a scandal within his administration. Grant ultimately forced the prosecutor to resign because of his aggressive tactics. In 1952, President Harry Truman's attorney general appointed a Republican special prosecutor to examine possible wrongdoing within the Department of Justice. Two months later, that prosecutor, too, was fired. In 1973, Attorney General Elliot Richardson appointed Archibald Cox, a Democrat, to investigate Watergate. On October 20 of that year, President Nixon fired Cox in what became known as the Saturday Night Massacre.

The need for and the problems with special prosecutors have long been a part of American history. The dilemma at the heart of the issue can be simply stated. In cases of possible wrongdoing by senior members of a president's administration, or by a president himself, his subordinates may have a conflict of interest in conducting the investigations. But if "independent" prosecutors are appointed, who is to supervise them? Can any check be imposed on their power without creating the same kinds of conflict of interest that necessitated their appointments in the first place?

Congress tried to answer these questions with the Ethics in Government Act of 1978, which created the modern independent counsel system. Passage of the law served in many ways as the unofficial beginning of the era when the legal system took over the political system. The idea behind the law was to use judges to depoliticize high-profile investigations; the role of the judges, the theory went, would protect everyone involved from charges of conflicts of interest. The experience of Watergate was still fresh in the legislators' minds when they wrote the law, and the Saturday Night Massacre was the danger they most wanted to avoid. They worried more about abuses of the prosecutor than by the prosecutor.

In this one respect—avoiding more Saturday Night Massacres—the law was successful. In virtually all others, however, the law failed, and it expired, unmourned, in 1999—a monument both to the law of unintended consequences and to the cost of good intentions. The structure of the law changed little over two decades. When the attorney general found "reasonable grounds to believe that further investigation is warranted" of the president and certain other high-ranking officials, she was required to apply for the appointment of a prosecutor to a panel of three senior federal judges, who were, in turn, preselected by the chief justice of the United States. The three judges, known as the Special Division, then selected the prosecutor and defined his or her jurisdiction. To guarantee their independence and to prevent their targets from waiting them out, the prosecutors themselves would determine how long their investigations should take. (A midcourse change in the nomenclature offered a hint of the more substantive problems with the law. In 1978, the law used the title "special prosecutors," the designation that had been used for Cox. But in 1982, worried that "prosecutor" sounded too accusatory, Congress changed the name of the office to "independent counsel.")

In one of many ironies surrounding the law, it actually hastened the politicization of the legal process it was designed to combat. In part this was an inevitable by-product of a more skeptical age. It became more difficult to present any decision by anyone, including a judge, as neutral or apolitical. Still, the law itself seemed designed almost willfully to make these problems worse. All of its attempts to depoliticize decision-making seemed only to inject more politics into the process. The press, of course, with its zeal for confrontation and investigation, served as an important constituency in favor of the law. The prospect of politicians in jail always made a better story than the usual work of the federal government, so the news media could always be counted on to provide a forum for those who wanted investigations begun and prosecutors appointed.

Still, even on its own terms, the law never worked. For example, notwithstanding the hopes of the authors of the law, there was nothing self-evident about how to determine when an independent counsel should be appointed. The Whitewater controversy in late 1993 was only the first of many times during the Clinton administration when Republicans charged that the attorney general was ducking the appointment of an independent counsel to protect her boss, the president. Instead fomenting arguments about the propriety of the underlying behavior, the law encouraged this kind of proxy politics—endless, enervating debates about whether prosecutors should be appointed. Again contrary to the naïve hopes of the bill's framers, the method for appointing independent counsels also politicized the process, for judicial participants in the independent counsel process could scarcely be seen as Olympian neutrals. Chief Justice William H. Rehnquist served as a Republican political operative before he came on the bench, and there he opposed Clinton's agenda in almost every way he could. Therefore it was not surprising that he named, as head of the Special Division, a judge named David B. Sentelle, an even more avid anti-Clinton partisan from North Carolina. Decisions made by Sentelle had no greater claim to political neutrality than those made by Clinton's attorney general. And the biggest fallacy of all behind the law was that independent counsels themselves would perform better—and earn more public respect—than the prosecutors they replaced.

None of these flaws in the independent counsel law were secrets in 1993 when the Clinton administration began to weigh whether to apply the law to itself. At that moment, Lawrence E. Walsh, who had been appointed by the Special Division to investigate the Iran-Contra affair, was finally winding down his seven-year investigation. By the time it concluded, Walsh's probe offered a primer on the ills of the law—undue length, unwise prosecutions, excessive zeal on the part of the prosecutors. (I served as an associate counsel on Walsh's staff for the first three years of his investigation.) In the politicized environment of independent counsel investigations, few Democrats protested Walsh's excesses. Similar excesses by a Republican prosecutor would lift the scales from Democratic eyes. At that point, however, their protests drew little sympathy from the other side of the aisle.

/ / /

So, on January 12, 1994, the president announced that he wanted a special counsel appointed in the Whitewater affair. It was up to Attorney General Janet Reno to name the prosecutor.

The situation was analogous to that which faced Attorney General Elliot Richardson in 1973. Because the independent counsel law had expired—it would be reauthorized six months later—Reno had complete freedom to select a Whitewater prosecutor. Richardson chose Cox. Whom would Reno select?

She convened her top advisers, and the list was narrowed to a familiar list of big-shot lawyers and ex-prosecutors. Reno asked her deputy, Phillip Heymann, to sound out the leading candidates. He spoke to former senator Warren Rudman, former FBI and CIA director William Webster, former deputy attorney general Donald Ayer—and Kenneth Starr and Robert Fiske.

There was never any real contest for first choice. Fiske was the class of the field. Under President Ford, he had been named the United States attorney for the Southern District of New York, and he was kept in that sensitive position by President Carter. In recent years, he had worked as a white-collar criminal defense attorney at the New York law firm of Davis Polk & Wardwell. Fiske was a throwback to another era, when lawyers dipped in and out of public service and maintained some independence from the political process. He was sixty-three years old, prosperous, and content. He was not gunning for another job in the future. In a press conference to announce his selection on January 20, Reno called him "the epitome of what a prosecutor should be." Reno had made the perfect selection—and she had done so without the cumbersome superstructure of the independent counsel law.

Fiske, in turn, also started out the right way. He announced he was taking a leave from his firm and moving to Little Rock. He hired a team of seasoned prosecutors, and when he gathered the group together for the first time, he had two words of advice for them: "Lawrence Walsh." By that he meant that he was not going to repeat Walsh's mistakes. He was not going to bring marginal cases, he was not going to see his investigation politicized, and most of all he was not going to take seven years. They were going to work fourteen hours a day seven days a week, determine if there were any crimes to prosecute, bring their cases, and then go home.

At the press conference with Reno announcing his appointment, Fiske had said he was going to investigate the death of Vince Foster as well as the Whitewater land deal. Foster's death had become a mainstay of the right-wing-conspiracy industry—Pat Matrisciana did an entire documentary on the subject—but Fiske didn't waste any time reaching a conclusion. In a report released on June 30, 1994, six months into his tenure, Fiske said that Foster had indeed committed suicide. By coincidence, that same day, President Clinton signed the reauthorization of the independent counsel statute. Almost as a formality, Reno sent a request to the three-judge Special Division to ratify her appointment of Fiske as special prosecutor in the Whitewater case. Fiske had an impeccable reputation, his investigation seemed off to a promising start, and there was no reason to think the court would want a new prosecutor to start from scratch.

/ / /

The independent counsel law contained essentially no provision for how the prosecutors were to be selected. The law simply left the decision up to the Special Division. Yet these judges were almost intentionally ill-suited to the task. For one thing, the law called for appeals court judges to serve on the Special Division. Prosecutors and defense lawyers practice mostly before trial court judges, so the Special Division was unlikely to have any firsthand knowledge of the skills of the people they appointed. The Special Division judges were also supposed to be old—by law. The statute called for the appeals court judges to be "senior," that is, semiretired. But older judges were even less familiar with the talent pool than their younger colleagues. The law had no provision for standards, for applications, for judicial review of the hiring decision, or for public disclosure of how or why any appointment of an independent counsel was made.

So there was no warning from the Special Division of the action it would take on August 5, 1994. On that day, the Special Division rejected Reno's request to appoint Fiske as independent counsel. Instead, the three judges fired him and replaced him with Kenneth W. Starr as the new prosecutor in the Whitewater case. In its brief statement accompanying the change, the three-judge court stated, "It is not our intent to impugn the integrity of the Attorney General's appointee, but rather to reflect the intent of the [Independent Counsel] Act, that the actor be protected against perceptions of conflict." Thus, in Washington's endless loop of perceived and actual conflicts of interest, Fiske was both hired and fired to avoid conflicts of interest.

Because the appointment process of independent counsels was kept from public view, only one fact became publicly known about how the Special Division came to replace Bob Fiske with Kenneth Starr. An anonymous eyewitness told *The Washington Post* that on July 14, Judge David Sentelle had lunched at the Capitol with both of the senators from his home state of North Carolina—Jesse

Helms and Lauch Faircloth. Both Helms and Faircloth were ferocious critics of the president, especially on Whitewater, and Faircloth in particular had argued that Fiske had gone too easy on the Clintons. The timing of the lunch suggested that the senators were lobbying Sentelle to dump Fiske—which the judge promptly did. All three participants issued denials that they had discussed the Whitewater case at all during the lunch. According to Helms, they had talked of "Western wear, old friends, and prostate problems."

In fact, behind the scenes, the three-judge panel was engaged in a decorous struggle over the Whitewater independent counsel—one that, again, revealed the political roots of this fight. Sentelle and Judge Joseph Sneed, who were both Republicans, wanted Fiske replaced with Starr. They thought the appointment by Reno had fatally compromised Fiske, giving his continued supervision of the case the "appearance of impropriety," but they saw no such problems with appointing an outspoken Republican opponent of Clinton's like Starr. John Butzner, the one Democrat on the panel, believed there was no need to replace Fiske, a man of impeccable credentials and impartiality. If someone new had to be brought in, Butzner favored naming a former federal appeals court judge named John Gibbons, who agreed, as did Starr, to be interviewed for the job. But when Gibbons came to Washington to meet with the judges, he said that he felt he had a conflict of interest because he was involved in an unrelated case in which the firm of White House counsel Lloyd Cutler had also appeared. It was a remote conflict, far less dramatic than the many instances where Starr's political and personal agenda had clashed with Clinton's. But with Gibbons out, Butzner had little choice but to go along with the offer to Starr—who accepted with alacrity.

/ / /

Within a few days of his appointment, Ken Starr gathered Fiske's prosecutors around a conference table in their offices in suburban Little Rock. Fiske had staffed the case leanly, hiring fewer than a dozen lawyers, mostly people he had known from the U.S. Attorney's Office or Davis Polk. Starr, who had never met any of them before, began by noting the awkwardness of this first meeting. He said he understood their loyalty to, and affection for, Fiske.

"I love this man," Starr said of his predecessor.

The remark only increased the fury that several of the Fiske lawyers already felt toward Starr. The Whitewater prosecutors believed that Fiske would conduct a fair and thorough investigation. They regarded the Special Division's act as an abomination, an unjustified slap at a decent and honorable man. By accepting the job, Starr had made himself party to the hijacking of their work. They wanted no part of anyone who would have done such a thing.

But there was another reason the prosecutors were angry. In the days before he was fired, Fiske had told his staff that he was considering hiring an outside lawyer to handle some appeals on behalf of the office. Under his charter from Reno, Fiske had the right to file civil suits against the president, and the prosecutor knew that Clinton was claiming, in the Paula Jones case, that he was immune from being sued. Fiske told his staff that he was talking with the lawyer who had been so outspoken against Clinton on the issue of presidential immunity in the Jones case—a fellow named Ken Starr. In other words, at the same time that Starr was negotiating with Fiske about handling appeals, Starr was also talking with the Special Division about taking Fiske's job. Starr had never disclosed to Fiske that he had been approached by the Special Division, and Fiske's staff regarded this omission as a particular betrayal. "I love this man," indeed.

But Fiske had promised that he and his staff would assist Starr, so they began briefing the new independent counsel on the progress of their investigation. They had progress to report on two fronts. Earlier in 1994, Webb Hubbell, the associate attorney general, had resigned amid charges that he had overbilled his clients and defrauded his partners at the Rose Law Firm, where he and the first lady had worked before Clinton's election. Fiske's lawyers said that Hubbell was ready to plead guilty and cooperate with the Whitewater investigation. Second, the lawyers said they were making good progress on the case at the root of most of the Whitewater stories in the press—the one based on David Hale's fraudulent $300,000 loan to Susan McDougal, who with her husband, Jim, were the Clintons' partners in the original Whitewater project. (Fiske had already worked out a plea-bargain deal with Hale himself, meaning that the former judge and church pew entrepreneur had gotten what he wanted out of the appointment of a special prosecutor.) The idea behind all of Fiske's actions was the same simple notion underlying most investigations of white-collar crime. The prosecutors would convict these lesser figures and then offer them leniency if they would testify against higher-ups, specifically the president and first lady.

"We won't write our 5K letters until we see whether these people cooperate," one of the lawyers said to Starr.

"What's a 5K letter?" the new independent counsel replied.

There was really no reason Starr should have known about 5K letters, but the prosecutors were stunned nonetheless. Since the federal sentencing guidelines went into effect in 1987, judges have had much less leeway to set the length of prison terms in cases before them. The guidelines determine the sentences, unless prosecutors make a motion to reduce the prison terms under guideline section 5K1.1. These motions—known as 5K letters—are the way prosecutors reward cooperators. By 1994, they were as familiar to criminal lawyers in the federal courts as speed limits were to highway drivers. But until he was hired by the Special Division to investigate the president of the United States, Starr had never prosecuted or defended a criminal case. So the prosecutors explained 5K letters to him. As Starr was the first to acknowledge, he would need a lot of help from his staff.

/ / /

Much later, Kenneth Starr became one of the most reviled men in America when his opponents in the Clinton White House succeeded in defining an indelible public image of the man. He was Babbitt with a badge—a minister's son from San Antonio who shined shoes for fun as a kid, jogged to the cadence of hymns as an adult, and then called down legal hellfire and brimstone as a prosecutor. In one of the impromptu press conferences that Starr liked to give in the driveway of his home, in McLean, Virginia, he compared himself to Joe Friday, but his awkward public manner could scarcely have differed more from the just-the-facts-ma'am *Dragnet* detective's. Unable to talk about the evidence in his job as independent counsel, Starr instead offered pious lectures. "There's no room for white lies. There's no room for shading," he said, standing in his driveway. "You cannot defile the temple of justice."

In fact, Starr did fit an archetype, but it is neither Joe Friday nor Inspector Javert. Starr was a consummate Washington careerist who navigated the capital more by self-interest than by ideology. His defining attribute—more important even than his piety (which was real), his intelligence (which was considerable), or his energy (which was phenomenal)—was his ability to attract powerful mentors. In 1975, he clerked for Chief Justice Warren Burger. Then he spent four years in the law firm of President Reagan's first attorney general, William French Smith. In 1983, when Starr was just thirty-seven years old, Burger and Smith engineered his appointment to the United States Court of Appeals for the District of Columbia, the second-most-important court in the nation.

On the court, Starr had a chameleon-like ability to mix with every faction and clique. Once, after an oral argument in the courtroom, Starr found himself in the middle of a real argument between liberal and conservative colleagues, who looked like they might come to blows. "When we went into the robing room after the argument, Judge [Laurence] Silberman and I got into a famous contretemps. We really got into it, and he threatened me with bodily harm," Abner Mikva, who went on to become White House counsel, recalled. "The whole time, Ken kept looking at the ceiling. You could see it was like he was saying to himself, 'I'm not here. I'm not seeing this.' He was a gentle person who looked to avoid controversies." In 1989, President Bush persuaded Starr to step down from his lifetime judicial appointment and become solicitor general—the government's chief advocate before the Supreme Court. Nicknamed the Solicitous General for his deferential style in front of the justices, Starr argued for a series of conservative positions, particularly on abortion and affirmative action. Yet Starr, like Bush himself, never convinced the hard-core right that he was one of them. In 1991, he lost out on an appointment to the Supreme Court because conservatives in the Justice Department branded him a "squish"—an unreliable conservative. (The seat went to Clarence Thomas instead.)

After Clinton was elected in 1992, Starr became a partner in the Washington office of the law firm Kirkland & Ellis, where he earned more than $1 million a year. In the fall of 1993, just as the Whitewater stories were starting to break, Starr was summoned from his profitable exile for a different, sensitive assignment. The Senate Ethics Committee was investigating Robert Packwood for sexual and other misconduct, and the presiding Democrats asked

Starr to review Packwood's diaries for material relevant to the case. In announcing Starr's assignment, *The Washington Post* observed, "Even those who regularly crossed swords with him credited him with being fair. He was not seen as ideologically driven." In the days before Monica Lewinsky, the Packwood case passed for pretty salacious stuff, yet there was never a leak from Starr or a complaint about him in the course of his work.

Far from limiting himself to his law practice and the short stint with the Ethics Committee, Starr showed an almost compulsive desire to join organizations, give speeches, and stay in the mix. He lived, it seemed, to fulfill the old saying that if you want to get anything done, ask the busiest man in town. Starr served as an active member of a breathtaking number of professional associations, including the American Bar Association, the American Law Institute, the American Bar Foundation, and the American Judicature Society. In light of his experience as a former judge, he agreed to serve as president of the Institute for Judicial Administration. He taught a class on constitutional law one day a week at New York University School of Law. He even found time to direct an obscure organization called the Council for Court Excellence. In light of this record of compulsivity, it was no surprise that Starr would simultaneously negotiate for a position with Fiske—and for Fiske's job.

Yet all of Starr's frantic volunteerism could not obscure a fundamental fact about him. He was a committed political conservative who stood outspokenly opposed to Clinton on virtually every controversial issue of the day. Before 1994, he had served in prominent jobs, but never in any that included close scrutiny by the press. Because of this, his personal style may have caused almost everyone to misjudge him. By nature, he deferred to others. Lips pursed, almost leaning backward during most conversations, Starr was polite to the point of obsequiousness. In a city full of (literally) snarling partisans, Starr's manner set him apart. There was a time in Washington when lawyers could move up in the profession—to judgeships, high administration positions, and the like—in a largely nonpartisan way. But Starr came of age at the time when the legal and political systems were merging and one had to take a stand with one side or the other to chart a route for personal advancement. Politely but unmistakably, Starr had done just that, and by the time he was named independent counsel, he had long ago signed on with many of the people who wanted Bill Clinton destroyed.

Indeed, while Starr was no ideologue himself, he had always surrounded himself with them. He may have been a member of the middle-of-the-road ABA, but his real friends belonged, as did Starr, to the Federalist Society, the partisan fellowship that provided the intellectual energy behind the Reagan revolution in the courts. He had been hired by the right-wing Bradley Foundation—which financed, among other things, *The American Spectator*—to defend a school-choice program in court. Starr served on the legal-policy advisory board of the Washington Legal Foundation, another conservative think tank. In his work at Kirkland & Ellis, he represented Brown & Williamson and Philip Morris, two tobacco companies whose interests clashed with the Clinton administration's at every step. He had, of course, already spoken out against the president's legal position in the Paula Jones case, and he was on the verge of submitting a brief in her case on behalf of still another conservative organization, the Independent Women's Forum. Starr had even offered advice to Gil Davis, Jones's lawyer, about how to handle the issue of presidential immunity from civil suits. None of this activity was improper or even surprising. It simply reflected the legal world in which Ken Starr lived before he answered the Special Division's summons in August 1994.

The nature of that world was, in fact, what Phil Heymann learned about Starr when he first examined his record at Janet Reno's request. No one doubted Starr's intelligence or his integrity. But Heymann also heard a warning: Look at the people around him. Starr was a man who had never prosecuted a case in his life. Someone would have to teach him the rules. As Heymann and anyone else with experience in the criminal justice system knew, many of these rules—about fairness, judgment, and proportionality—weren't written down, and some prosecutors followed them more closely than others. Starr would be more dependent than most potential prosecutors on the people he hired. More than almost any independent counsel in history, Starr's destiny would be in the hands of his staff.

Where, Heymann worried, would Starr get his advice?

5

A Really Big Crush

Today is October fifth, exactly eight weeks since I became IC," Starr would begin a typical meeting of his staff in Little Rock during 1994, "and this is what I have not accomplished. We're not going to be Lawrence Walsh. I'm not going to be here forever."

Almost without exception, the Fiske prosecutors fled their jobs as soon as decency permitted. But Starr surprised the stragglers—and the new arrivals as well. His staff nearly matched Fiske's in their experience and professionalism. In his Washington office, the top people included Mark Tuohey III, the former president of the District of Columbia Bar Association; Roger Adelman, a former high-level prosecutor in Washington; and John Bates, who had just left a senior position in the United States Attorney's Office in Washington. In Little Rock, Starr recruited the husband-and-wife team of Ray and LeRoy Jahn, who were experienced federal prosecutors from San Antonio, and Bradley Lerman and Amy St. Eve, both veterans of the U.S. Attorney's Office in Chicago. Several of these lawyers had the perspective of having worked as defense attorneys as well as prosecutors. Starr even adopted Fiske's obsession with Walsh. Like his predecessor, Starr vowed a quick and fair resolution of the matters before him. He asked his staffers for commitments of just one year, because he believed—and here his inexperience showed—that was all it would take to finish the investigation. (Unlike Fiske, Starr did not take a leave from his firm, so he continued making his seven-figure salary during his first four years as independent counsel.)

On the whole, Starr successfully capitalized on the cases Fiske's staff had begun. On December 6, 1994—just four months into Starr's tenure—Webster Hubbell pleaded guilty to defrauding the Rose Law Firm and its clients of more than $400,000. On June 7, 1995, Starr indicted Jim Guy Tucker, Clinton's successor as governor of Arkansas, and two others in a bankruptcy-fraud case. (After a protracted series of appeals on legal issues, all of the defendants eventually pleaded guilty in the case, which concededly had nothing to do with the Clintons.)

Then, on August 17, 1995, just after the first anniversary of his hiring, Starr unveiled the results of his Whitewater investigation. Starr's grand jury in Little Rock charged Tucker and James and Susan McDougal in a conspiracy case involving Madison Guaranty Savings & Loan. Starr's staff called it "the 825 case," because the complex chain of events began with a loan of $825,000. The theory was that Tucker and Jim McDougal conspired to have Madison Guaranty Savings & Loan lend this amount to a third party, who, in turn, shared the proceeds with David Hale. Hale's company—which was supposed to make loans to minorities—then used this money to obtain a fraudulent loan of $1.5 million from the Small Business Administration. The only link to Clinton concerned his famous (and disputed) conversation with Hale in February 1986. There, Hale claimed that Clinton asked him to lend some of the $1.5 million to the McDougals, whose business ventures included the shared investment in Whitewater. Of course, Clinton claimed that this by then nine-year-old conversation never took place, and in any event the alleged conversation scarcely related to Starr's conspiracy case. But that purported David Hale conversation was as close as Starr could get to the president.

All in all, the 825 case was a typical, if rather small, federal white-collar-crime prosecution—complex, unsexy, and based on the testimony of a cooperating witness (Hale) who was probably more culpable than anyone who went to trial. And as the months devoted to pretrial preparation passed, the prospect of tying the president into this conspiracy faded even more. Hale's uncorroborated word would never suffice to bring down a president. Jim McDougal—an eccentric, mercurial man whose financial reverses had driven him from a life of white suits and Jaguars to a new home in a trailer—was publicly defending Clinton and denying Hale's charges. His ex-wife, Susan, was not speaking out in public, but her lawyer was saying she also rejected Hale's accusations. Even if the two McDougals would eventually flip on Clinton (and Jim did), their words would likely mean little. The experienced prosecutors in Starr's office began to realize that their Whitewater case would begin—and end—with the trial of Tucker and the Mc-Dougals. Starr's prosecutors had gone to where the evidence had taken them—and it wasn't very far.

In a peculiar way, these early days of the Starr investigation almost helped the Clinton presidency. Because of Starr's probe, all the important evidence was protected by the shield of grand jury secrecy, and there were never any leaks of consequence (perhaps because there was so little incriminating evidence to leak). Starr was considering using most of the Whitewater witnesses in the grand jury or at trials, so he deprived the multiple congressional investigations of Whitewater of these potential stars. The hearings on Whitewater—which included those chaired by Alphonse D'Amato, of New York, and Jim Leach, of Iowa—attracted little interest outside of Washington.

Strangely enough, 1995 proved to be a year of renewal for the Clinton presidency. The previous year had been consumed by disasters—the appointments of Fiske and then Starr, the failure of the Clinton health-care plan, and, worst of all, the midterm congressional elections. In November 1994, Republicans regained their majority in the Senate and, astonishingly, won a majority in the House of Representatives for the first time in almost four decades. In the days after the rout, the president was reduced to protesting wanly that he was still "relevant" in a city that seemed to belong to the new speaker of the House, Newt Gingrich. But guided by his resurrected Svengali, Dick Morris, Clinton co-opted some elements of Gingrich's "Contract with America," rejected the more extreme parts of the program, and positioned himself at the moderate center of American politics.

The defining moment of Clinton's comeback came in the fight over the federal budget in November 1995. At the time, Clinton chose to pick a fight with Gingrich and company over Medicare rather than "triangulate" between the congressional Republicans and Democrats. The more the president vowed to protect that prized entitlement, the higher he went in the polls. As the showdown loomed, more good news came Clinton's way. On November 8, Colin Powell announced that he would not run for president in 1996, leaving only the elderly and uncharismatic Bob Dole as Clinton's likely opponent. On November 14, Clinton denounced Gingrich and Dole for their "deeply irresponsible" insistence on cutting Medicare "as a condition of keeping the government open." Clinton refused to sign their budget, and nonessential federal workers were sent home that day.

The following morning, the second day of the shutdown, the White House had a giddy, almost euphoric feel to it. The few staffers who were allowed to come to work scrambled to complete the marathon budget negotiations in what felt like, for some, a no-grown-ups slumber party. The morning of November 15 brought the president even better news. At a breakfast with reporters, Gingrich said that he had sent a tougher budget bill to the president because of the way he had been treated on Air Force One during the trip to Israel for the funeral of Prime Minister Yitzhak Rabin. "You land at Andrews Air Force Base and you've been on the plane for twenty-five hours and nobody has talked to you and they ask you to get off the plane by the back ramp. . . . It's petty," Gingrich said, "but I think it's human." Gingrich's remarks caused an immediate sensation, and by noon George Stephanopoulos arranged for an official White House photograph of Gingrich and Clinton on the flight to be released to the news media. Suddenly, the president—and everyone else—could see a clear path to one of the most extraordinary political rebirths in American history.

At exactly 1:30 P.M. on November 15, according to the computerized Workers and Visitors Entrance System (WAVES), an intern named Monica Lewinsky entered the White House. She didn't leave until eighteen minutes after midnight the following morning.

/ / /

For Bill Clinton, the political showdown with the Republicans in 1995 paralleled another moment four years earlier. Clinton had endured several rocky months in 1991 when he was trying to make up his mind about whether to run for president. In his last reelection campaign for governor of Arkansas, he had pledged not to seek higher office, and he was struggling to climb away from that promise. President Bush was still basking in the success of the Persian Gulf War. In the midst of these troubles, Clinton traveled to Cleveland to give the keynote address at the national meeting of the Democratic Leadership Council, the collection of moderate Democrats he then chaired. Speaking from only a handful of notes, Clinton gave what was widely regarded as the best political speech of the year. "We're here to save the United States of America," he said. "Our burden is to give the people a new choice rooted in old values. A new choice that is simple, that offers opportunity, demands responsibility, gives citizens more say, provides them with responsive government, all because we recognize that we are community." The national press corps gave the speech rapturous reviews. On this day, more than any other, Bill Clinton became a realistic possibility as a presidential candidate. It was a day, like the one in November 1995, of the most powerful kind of adrenaline rush an American politician can enjoy. It was May 6, 1991, two days before Bill Clinton appeared at the Governor's Quality Management Conference at the Excelsior Hotel.

Henry Kissinger's observation that power is the ultimate aphrodisiac has become a cliché because it made the obvious sound original. Politicians have led charged sexual lives through all of history. In some cases, no doubt, they have used their power to coerce unwilling partners, but just as surely many women have sought them out. In the twentieth century alone, the ranks of presidential adulterers include, among others, Warren Harding, Franklin D. Roosevelt, and John F. Kennedy—a terrible president, a great president, and one viewed ambivalently by history. In other words, their sex lives revealed little about their presidencies—or their "character." Clinton, too, strayed during his long marriage—a damning fact about him as a husband but one with no bearing on his record as a public man.

In part because of his status as a symbol of sybaritic baby boomers, Clinton developed the reputation of a kind of Lothario, somewhere between a suave seducer and a relentless conqueror. If his dealings with Monica Lewinsky were any indication, however, both descriptions seem wrong. To be sure, few relationships would shine under the kind of microscopic attention that was focused on the president and the intern, but Clinton appeared more miserable than joyous in his sexuality—guilt-ridden, selfish, compulsive. Bob Bennett once told Clinton as much. Having surveyed private investigators' reports and interviews with dozens of purported lovers, the lawyer told the president, "This stuff would kill your reputation." Clinton never hid his interest in sex. His handshakes with pretty women lingered, and he leered without apology. But there was a lot more talk than action.

Once the squalid details of the Lewinsky story broke, some of his old friends shared a rueful memory. During the early days of the 1992 presidential campaign, when Clinton's staff was small and the circumstances intimate, one young woman confided to another that she had had an erotic dream about one of their colleagues—George Stephanopoulos, whom she barely knew. Somehow this story reached the candidate, and it prompted him to initiate a series of late-night conversations with staffers about sexual fantasies. Clinton never laid a hand on anyone during these talks in airplanes and hotel rooms, but they occurred in an atmosphere thick with sexual tension. When it was Clinton's turn to talk, he often returned to the same scenario: that he was standing in a doorway as a woman kneeled before him and performed oral sex.

/ / /

When Monica Lewinsky gave a deposition during Clinton's impeachment trial in 1999, she was examined by Tennessee congressman Ed Bryant, one of the House impeachment managers. Bryant decided to break the ice with a few questions about Lewinsky's background. "Tell me about your work history, briefly," he said, "from the time you left college until, let's say, you started as an intern in the White House." Lewinsky looked at the congressman as if he were crazy (not for the last time in their interview, either).

"Uh, I wasn't working from the time . . ." she said.

"Okay," her nervous inquisitor replied and turned to another subject. Bryant had forgotten that Lewinsky had no real "work history" before she came to the White House. Lewinsky graduated from Lewis and Clark College in May 1995 and began her internship two months later, shortly before her twenty-second birthday. (Lewinsky was six and a half years older than Clinton's daughter, Chelsea.)

Lewinsky had been raised in Beverly Hills, the daughter of a moderately prosperous oncologist and a socially ambitious housewife. In a home, and a town, where learning mattered less than looks, Lewinsky had spent most of her brief life obsessed with her weight. She drifted from one high school to another, from a mediocre junior college to a modestly regarded university, and made little impact anywhere she went. By the standards of most Americans, her life was privileged—expensive schools, private lessons, powerful friends, and plenty of money for clothes and vacations. Yet once she became famous, Lewinsky did little but dwell on her supposed privations—that her parents divorced, that a mean boy had called her "Big Mac," that she lacked "self-esteem." Before she became obsessed with the president of the United States, her only other serious interest in life was dieting.

Indeed, even beyond the fact that Lewinsky and Paula Jones both entered Bill Clinton's life at politically exhilarating moments for him, the two women had a great deal in common. Owing to differences in social class, Lewinsky appeared more sophisticated and worldly than Jones. Still, their similarities were considerable, starting with their ages (Monica was twenty-two, Paula twenty-four) and their personalities—both bubbly, outgoing, and friendly. They also lacked talent, learning, wit, great beauty, interest in the outside world, or knowledge of politics. The most important thing they shared was an apparent sexual availability. Clinton told his trooper Danny Ferguson that Paula had "that come-hither look." Lewinsky just said to Clinton, Come hither.

Before November 15, 1995, Clinton and Lewinsky had never had an actual conversation, though she later asserted they had engaged in "intense flirting" through eye contact. During the shutdown, all but ninety of the 430 employees of the White House were furloughed, so unpaid interns took up the slack. Lewinsky was assigned to the office of Leon Panetta, the chief of staff, just down a corridor from the Oval Office. Clinton spent most of the day negotiating with congressional leaders, and he popped in and out of Panetta's office several times. To Lewinsky's credit, she never portrayed herself as any kind of victim of Clinton's advances. Indeed, her own account of that day demonstrated how hard she tried to seduce the president. Her efforts began with a now-famous gesture. Noting that Clinton was alone for a moment in Panetta's office, she lifted her jacket and gave the president a quick glance at the top of her thong underwear, which showed above the waist of her pants. Clinton, Lewinsky recalled, smiled enigmatically.

A little later, according to the methodical accounting of the Starr report, "En route to the rest room at about 8 P.M., she passed George Stephanopoulos' office." In fact, Starr's sleuths failed to note that this venture alone was a pretty bold gesture. To cross Clinton's path, Lewinsky had chosen the bathroom that was closest to the president's domain in the West Wing. As she had hoped, Lewinsky found the president alone in Stephanopoulos's office. (Stephanopoulos himself was lobbying on Capitol Hill.) Clinton noticed Lewinsky, beckoned her in, and made small talk, asking her where she had gone to school. Instead of answering, Lewinsky blurted out, "You know, I have a really big crush on you." Clinton invited her to his private study, a few steps away. There they kissed for the first time. Lewinsky recalled breathlessly that "his eyes were very soul-searching, very wanting, very needing and very loving." They soon parted, but before the end of the evening, Clinton found Lewinsky alone in Panetta's office and invited her to meet him in Stephanopoulos's office again. To prepare for this second meeting of the night, Lewinsky removed her underwear.

There was a kind of poignancy in where Clinton chose to take Lewinsky at that point. The couple went to the tiny hallway that ran from the closed door to Stephanopoulos's office to the closed door to the Oval Office. On one side of this hallway was a tiny bathroom, on the other a door to Clinton's private study. It was the only place in the White House where the president could pretty much guarantee that he would not be seen by anyone. For all that Clinton may have wanted to pursue women during his presidency, his encounters with Lewinsky illustrated the logistical challenges. It took not only a determined partner, but one who didn't mind awkward and degrading circumstances. Monica Lewinsky fit the bill.

In the protected hallway, Clinton and Lewinsky began to kiss again, but they were interrupted by the telephone ringing in his study. In the surreal deadpan of the FBI summary of Lewinsky's interview on the subject, the agent recounted: "The President began kissing her and she unbuttoned her jacket. The President pulled her bra up (he only unhooked her bra once in subsequent sexual contacts) and put his hand down into her pants. The President received a phone call from a Congressman or Senator. While talking on the telephone, the President kept his hand in LEWINSKY's pants to stimulate her, thereby causing her to have an orgasm or two."

As the Starr report described what followed, "While the President continued talking on the phone, she performed oral sex on him. He finished the call, and, a moment later, told Ms. Lewinsky to stop. In her recollection: 'I told him I wanted . . . to complete that. And he said . . . that he needed to wait until he trusted me more.'" (At that moment Clinton could not have known how right he was to worry about the consequences of what became known, delicately, as "completion.") The Starr authors concluded their description with one of the report's several gratuitous and cruel observations about the Clintons' marriage. "And then I think he made a joke," the report quoted Lewinsky as saying, "that he hadn't had that in a long time."

/ / /

Sixteen months later, on March 29, 1997, Clinton and Lewinsky had their final sexual encounter. But it would be a mistake to think of their affair as lasting nearly a year and a half. They never had more than sporadic contact, and they had "sex" with each other—using the term in a loose, colloquial sense—only about a dozen times. Moreover, nearly all of the physical intimacy between them took place within a few months of the government shutdown. Indeed, there was only one month when they had sustained contact. (Their relationship can be reconstructed with this kind of precision because Lewinsky possessed an extraordinary memory, and her friend Linda Tripp persuaded her to make a computerized matrix of all of her contacts with the president. In addition, the Starr prosecutors forced Lewinsky to supply minute-by-minute accounts of all of her dealings with Clinton.)

The month of glory for the Clinton-Lewinsky relationship was

January 1996. After their first encounter on November 15, they had another two days later, while the government shutdown was still in effect. Clinton orchestrated this second rendezvous by asking Lewinsky to bring him a slice of pizza. As on the first occasion, Clinton was lobbying congressmen on the telephone while Lewinsky performed her ministrations. Lewinsky, who moved to a junior position on the president's legislative staff after the shutdown, worried that with the return of the normal White House operations, the president would forget about her. Lewinsky recalled for her friend Linda Tripp, in one of their taped telephone conversations, "You know, I mean, when this first happened, I mean, I said to my mom, I said, 'Well, I think he just fooled around with me because his girlfriend was probably furloughed.'" But around lunchtime on New Year's Eve, Lewinsky engineered a visit to Bayani Nelvis, one of the president's Navy stewards, and she succeeded in running into Clinton. At that meeting, Lewinsky quizzed the president about her actual name—he had been calling her "kiddo"—and when he passed the tests, she performed oral sex on him. For the first time, he was not on the telephone.

The New Year's Eve encounter set off a month of regular contact between them—which is of interest chiefly because of what else was occurring in Clinton's family life. The most intense month of his relationship with Lewinsky was the worst month of Hillary Clinton's tenure as first lady. On January 4, 1996, Carolyn Huber, a White House aide and former office manager at the Rose Law Firm, discovered 115 pages of Hillary Clinton's billing records from her time at the firm. Huber reported that she had found the records the previous August in the Clintons' residence area at the White House, and had then taken them to her own office and forgotten about them. Starr's prosecutors had subpoenaed the documents more than a year earlier, and the Clintons' lawyers had been unable to produce them. As White House officials never tired of pointing out, the substance of the records generally backed what Hillary had said all along—that she had done "minimal" work at the Rose firm for Madison Guaranty. Still, no one could erase the suspicion that surrounded the documents' mysterious vanishing and reappearance.

The story of the billing records hit the newspapers on Saturday, January 6. The following day, Clinton telephoned Lewinsky for the first time. She later testified, "I asked him what he was doing and he said he was going to be going into the office soon. I said, oh, do you want some company? And he said, oh, that would be great." Later that afternoon, Clinton called Lewinsky at her desk to arrange their meeting. He said she should bring some papers by the Oval Office. He would leave his door open, catch a glimpse of her "accidentally," and then invite her in. The operation went perfectly, and they spoke for about ten minutes in the Oval Office and then went to his private bathroom. The Starr report recounted, "The President 'was talking about performing oral sex on me,' according to Ms. Lewinsky. But she stopped him because she was menstruating and he did not. Ms. Lewinsky did perform oral sex on him." In the course of this encounter, Lewinsky noticed that the president was looking at a cigar in "sort of a naughty way." She told him, "We can do that too, sometime."

The next day's newspaper brought a thunderous attack against Hillary Clinton. In a column headed "Blizzard of Lies," in *The New York Times* of January 8, William Safire began, "Americans of all political persuasions are coming to the sad realization that our First Lady—a woman of undoubted talents who was a role model for many in her generation—is a congenital liar." In his daily briefing on the day after the article was published, press secretary Michael McCurry said that Clinton had told him that if he were not president, he "would have delivered a more forceful response to that [column] on the bridge of Mr. Safire's nose." (The same day, a three-judge panel of the federal appeals court in St. Louis ruled that Paula Jones could proceed with her lawsuit against the president. This was only a temporary setback for Bob Bennett's strategy of delay, because he still could appeal the issue to the full appeals court and then on to the Supreme Court—all of which would likely take enough time to push the issue past the election in November. Still, the appeals court decision served as a reminder of the potential costs of Clinton's personal behavior—a warning, of course, he chose not to heed.)

All through the week after the Safire column, White House lawyers tried to convince the prosecutors in Starr's office that the first lady had made an innocent mistake in not providing the documents earlier. By this time, Starr was already almost six months past his self-imposed (and obviously unrealistic) deadline of one year to complete his investigation, and the Whitewater trial of Tucker and the McDougals wouldn't even begin until the spring. He had come up with nothing against the Clintons, and the frustrations of an already long and inconclusive investigation were starting to weigh on his staff. Moreover, the experienced lawyers on his staff were starting to drift back into private life. The high-handed and contemptuous style of David Kendall, the Clintons' private lawyer for Whitewater, irritated Starr's people as well.

The mysterious reappearance of the documents led to a dramatic confrontation behind the scenes. Starr's deputy John Bates told Jane Sherburne, of the White House counsel's office, that Starr was planning to obtain a search warrant for the living quarters of the White House, to look for another box of documents relating to the Rose Law Firm. After heated negotiations, Bates agreed to forgo the search warrant, but in return for this concession Sherburne herself would have to do the search. So Sherburne crawled through every room in the residence, searching everywhere from the bathrooms to the underwear drawers. As required by the agreement with Starr's office, Sherburne even combed through Chelsea Clinton's possessions. "After I finished," Sherburne recalled, "I felt like standing in the shower." The White House lawyer never found what Starr was seeking.

White House lawyers pleaded with Starr's people to take Mrs. Clinton's deposition in private and spare her the indignity of parading up the steps of the courthouse like any other witness. (In the midst of these negotiations, on January 16, Mrs. Clinton left on her tour to support sales of her new book, *It Takes a Village: And Other Lessons Children Teach Us.* The president took advantage of her departure that night to call Lewinsky for their first round of phone sex.) The Starr team thought the discovery of the documents made the prosecutors look ridiculous, so they were not inclined to cut the lawyers—or Hillary—a break. So on Thursday, January 18, Hillary Clinton became the only first lady in American history to be subpoenaed before a federal grand jury.

Clinton spent the next weekend preparing for his State of the Union address, which he would give on the following Tuesday. On Sunday afternoon, Clinton and Lewinsky had a genuinely accidental meeting near the Oval Office, and the president invited her in. Before he ushered her into the private office, Lewinsky asked him whether their relationship was "just about sex, or do you have some interest in trying to get to know me as a person?" Clinton assured her that he "cherishes the time that he had with me." Even Lewinsky thought this remark was a bit excessive considering how little time they had spent together, but it didn't deter her from another sexual encounter. After a moment commiserating about the first death of an American soldier in Bosnia, Clinton and Lewinsky returned to the private hallway, where she performed oral sex in the manner he preferred.

After most of their encounters, Lewinsky simply left through the Oval Office. But their January 21 session ended with a scene out of a pornographic bedroom farce. When the president, as was his custom, stopped Lewinsky before completion, the couple faced a dilemma, because there were visitors waiting just outside the Oval Office. (The guests were Jim and Diane Blair, family friends from Arkansas; Jim was the Tyson Foods executive who had set up Hillary's brief but successful foray in commodities trading.) In order to avoid being seen, Lewinsky tried to leave through the office of Betty Currie, who was Clinton's personal secretary, but the door was locked. When Lewinsky came back to tell the president that she would have to find another exit, she found him in the office of Nancy Hernreich, Currie's boss, masturbating. Lewinsky wound up leaving through the Rose Garden.

The high point of the State of the Union address two days later came when Clinton defended the person the newspapers were calling his "embattled" wife. Turning to Hillary in the gallery above the House chamber, his eyes moist with tears, the president said, "Before I go on, I would like to take just a moment to thank my own family, and to thank the person who has taught me more than anyone else over twenty-five years about the importance of families and children—a wonderful wife, magnificent mother, and a great first lady. Thank you, Hillary!" (Two years later, Betty Currie hid beneath her bed some of the gifts that Clinton gave Lewinsky. Among them was an official copy of the 1996 State of the Union address, which was inscribed, "To Monica Lewinsky, With best wishes, Bill Clinton.") Three days after Clinton's speech, on Friday, January 26, Hillary Clinton made her way past the cameras into the United States Courthouse, where she testified before the grand jury for more than four hours.

The next Sunday afternoon, February 4, Clinton again telephoned Lewinsky to arrange another "accidental" encounter, which ended back in the hallway in the customary way. For the first time, Clinton and Lewinsky had a post-"coital" conversation of some duration, about forty-five minutes. According to Lewinsky, they chatted about her combat boots ("like Chelsea's," said Clinton), how they had lost their virginity, and Monica's mistreatment by an earlier married boyfriend, Andy Bleiler. An actual conversation with Lewinsky may have been the thing that cured the president of his infatuation, because the next time he summoned Lewinsky, two weeks later, it was to break off their relationship. On Presidents' Day, Clinton invited Lewinsky to the Oval Office and announced that—for her good as well as his—their sexual relationship had to end.

Their January idyll was over—as was the public crisis for Hillary Clinton. For Starr's prosecutors, the grand jury appearance itself was really the only form of punishment they could inflict. They had no grounds to make a case against the first lady for obstruction of justice—they couldn't prove that she had intentionally hid the documents—so the matter of the billing records faded to an inconclusive muddle.

How, then, to explain the juxtaposition of Clinton's fling with Lewinsky and his defense of his wife? The most likely answer is that they were simply separate events. Both the president and the first lady shared a passionate desire to defeat the political enemies who had pursued them for years. Even in 1996, before Starr became a mortal enemy, the prosecutor was far from a friend, and the president did not have to muster false outrage in order to stand by Hillary against his (or Safire's) assault. How then to explain the affair? Pop psychological analyses of the president have often characterized him as a man of split personalities—a good Clinton and a bad Clinton, the policy wonk and the party animal. This explanation seems too facile. Not every adulterer suffers from multiple personality disorder. Clinton had affairs during his marriage, and he had never paid a calamitous personal or political price. Clinton pursued Lewinsky for the same reason he had pursued other women—because, presumably, he enjoyed the excitement and the sex, such as it was. These relationships were simply the way he lived. One part of his life never interfered with the other—as long as he didn't get caught.

/ / /

On May 28, 1996, Governor Jim Guy Tucker and Jim and Susan McDougal were convicted in "the 825 case"—the trial that grew out of the failure of Madison Guaranty. The jury had believed at least some of the testimony of David Hale, who was the star witness for the prosecution. (After making a plea bargain with Starr, Hale ultimately served less than two years in prison for his various crimes.) The president had testified by videotape from the White House, and he had denied ever discussing a loan with Hale in February 1986, but Clinton played a largely peripheral role in the case. Notwithstanding their convictions, the McDougals still stood by Clinton's version of the facts of the case, so Starr had no way to use his victory to advance his investigation. In any event, Starr soon lost the chance to capitalize on the McDougal convictions. In another case he brought, against a pair of Arkansas bankers for violations in connection with the financing of Clinton's 1990 gubernatorial campaign, the trial ended with the jury failing to convict on any count.

So, coming up on its second anniversary, the Starr investigation was running out of steam—and yet, in the curious manner of independent counsels, it wasn't slowing down either. A week after the convictions in the Whitewater case, Attorney General Janet Reno gave Starr jurisdiction over "Filegate"—the unauthorized receipt of about three hundred confidential FBI files by low-level officials in the Clinton White House in 1993 and 1994. Even among the most fevered anti-Clinton activists, there was never a suggestion that the president ordered these files to be obtained or that he saw them once they arrived. The only people ever implicated in the entire file fiasco were Craig Livingstone, a beefy former bar bouncer who became the director of the White House office of personnel security, and his aide, Anthony Marceca.

The idea that anyone committed any crime in Filegate was dubious at best. Career prosecutors at the Justice Department could have handled this modest investigation with no difficulty. Still, in the poisonous atmosphere of Washington in the nineties, and under the broad mandates of the independent counsel law, Reno turned the matter over to Starr. Any controversy that hit the newspapers—as Filegate did—was instantly transformed into a putative criminal case. In the inverted logic of *The New York Times*'s editorial page (and others), the very existence of the inquiries proved how serious they were. In this way the legal system continued its takeover of the political system. Once again, a new set of victims paid the price—the witnesses who had to hire lawyers, the targets who had to live in fear, the investigating agents who had to turn away from more important work, and the public, which was distracted from the real business of government and, of course, had to pay the bill.

There was one more victim—Starr himself. At a time when he was thinking about moving on with his life, Washington's conflict-of-interest culture dropped another unwelcome gift in his lap. Starr could have, and probably should have, turned the Filegate case back to the Justice Department, but only a prosecutor sure of his own judgments (a Bob Fiske, for example) would have had the self-confidence to take that kind of step. Burdened with Whitewater, Travelgate, the Foster suicide, and now Filegate, Starr made it clear that he would not take any public action in these investigations through the presidential election in November. Though the Whitewater case—the original reason for his appointment—had just about run its course, Starr was heading into year three of his investigation with no end in sight.

The Clintons, of course, had no sympathy for Starr's troubles. For them, the expansion of Starr's jurisdiction to include Filegate was followed by a piece of good news. On June 24, 1996, at the end of the Supreme Court's term, the justices announced that they would hear the case of *Jones v. Clinton* during its October term. This decision meant that Bob Bennett had succeeded in his most important goal in the case. The case could not be resolved before the election. Though it had been filed in May 1994, Bennett had delayed it for more than two years, and the Supreme Court's decision meant that no one would be able to take depositions in the case until 1997 at the earliest.

On November 5, 1996, Bill Clinton was reelected after a campaign in which Starr's investigation figured hardly at all. His margin of victory was held down by the emergence, shortly before the election, of what became known as the campaign finance scandal—even though, as with Filegate, scarcely anyone could even articulate any criminal offense the president might have committed. On this issue, Reno would spend much of the following several years in another controversy about whether she should appoint independent counsel. Ultimately, she declined to do so. (Meanwhile, of course, the campaign finance laws—which were clearly the root of the "scandal"—remained unchanged.)

The election also served as an opportunity for Ken Starr to take stock. By that time, he had won his cases against Hubbell, Tucker, and the two McDougals, but their cooperation hadn't brought the prosecutors any closer to the Clintons. With the investigation stalled, the prosecutor tried to declare defeat. On February 17, 1997, shortly after Clinton was inaugurated for a second term, Starr announced that he would be stepping down to become dean of the Schools of Law and Public Policy at Pepperdine University, in Malibu, California.

The White House reacted with quiet satisfaction to the news that Starr was, in effect, surrendering, and decamping to a school of modest reputation in a beach community known for starlets, bodybuilders, and surfers, to take a job partially financed by Richard Scaife, who had also subsidized *The American Spectator* and a variety of anti-Clinton causes. But the Republican right was outraged. In a typical example of conservative pique, William Safire declared that Starr had "brought shame on the legal profession by walking out on his client—the people of the United States." Four days later, Starr announced contritely that he had changed his mind about Pepperdine, and he promised to stay on until the end of the investigation. Still, as Bill Clinton began his second term in office, Kenneth Starr had effectively concluded his work as independent counsel.

6

"Joan Dean"

In the first two years of its existence, the Starr team had behaved in the tradition of honorable law enforcement. For the most part, they had investigated crimes rather than people and operated by the same general standards as other federal prosecutors. Notwithstanding his own political and personal distaste for the president, Starr himself appeared content to depart for Pepperdine without inflicting many wounds on his chief target. In sum, Starr had nothing to do with keeping the case against Clinton going at this low moment. The forces of culture and money took care of that.

Clinton's election as the first baby-boomer president had unleashed powerful resentments against him. It was Clinton's perceived moral lassitude and self-indulgence—far more than his political views—that outraged his critics. The president's conservative adversaries in what became known as the culture wars never represented a majority of Americans, but they were a market—especially for books. When Starr flagged, the forces of capitalism took temporary custody of the anti-Clinton campaign.

The first person to tap the anti-Clinton market with great success was a former FBI agent named Gary Aldrich. For Clinton's adversaries, Aldrich provided one of the few bright spots in the otherwise dismal year of 1996. In late June, Aldrich published a book titled *Unlimited Access,* an account of his brief tenure in the Clinton White House. Aldrich had a minor job coordinating the background investigations of new employees, but he parlayed his contacts among disaffected career staffers into a remarkably hostile narrative about the first family and the people around them. The book received a good deal of publicity when it first appeared, mostly because of its allegation that the president regularly ducked his Secret Service protection and made "frequent late-night visits to the Marriott Hotel" for assignations with a woman who "may be a celebrity." The former agent noted gravely that the story of the Marriott trysts had been provided to him by "a highly educated, well-trained, experienced investigator." Aldrich's scoop was marred somewhat by the fact that it turned out to be fictional; shortly after the book was published, Aldrich's "source" was revealed to be David Brock, the erstwhile chronicler of the troopers' tales, who had merely asked Aldrich about rumors of Clinton's late-night wanderings.

Despite his errors, however, Aldrich managed to express a coherent message about the president, and in time, the book emerged as a sort of urtext of Clinton-hating. He wrote at one point, "If you compared the staffers of the Bush administration with those of the Clinton administration, the difference was shocking. It was Norman Rockwell on the one hand, and Berkeley, California, with an Appalachian twist on the other." Aldrich charged that the White House social office hung pornographic ornaments on the White House Christmas tree, and that the men on Clinton's staff wore earrings and the women no underwear. Some of these charges were provably false, but that was almost beside the point. Aldrich tapped into a genuine cultural fault line in the country, and his book was an enormous success. *Unlimited Access* spent nineteen weeks on the *New York Times* bestseller list and sold even more copies than its unofficial videotape counterpart, Patrick Matrisciana's *Clinton Chronicles.* (Like so many of Clinton's adversaries, Aldrich included an obligatory passage about how "I might even be in danger, if the stories coming from Little Rock were true—about how so many enemies of the Clintons ended up having fatal 'accidents.'" Like all the others who expressed this fear, Aldrich survived to tell his tale.)

The core of Aldrich's complaints concerned sex. In one passage, as Aldrich sat musing about one of Newt Gingrich's appearances on *Meet the Press,* the author observed, "I nodded in agreement when Gingrich said that the Clintons and their staff were throwbacks to the 1960s counterculture." (At the time, Gingrich himself was engaged in an extramarital affair with a House staffer two decades his junior.) Aldrich's disgust at gay staffers, at the president's supposed affairs, and at the first lady's disrespect for her husband poured forth on nearly every page. In this respect, Aldrich had a kindred spirit on the White House staff. They spoke nearly every day, and they kept in touch after he retired. This former colleague watched the success of Aldrich's book with pride— and more than a little envy. And Linda Tripp decided to follow in Gary Aldrich's footsteps.

/ / /

One of the ironies of Linda Tripp's emergence as a conservative heroine was that, in truth, she represented one of the archetypes that the right wing most despised. She was the civil service lifer, whose mastery of the arcana of job rights, seniority, pay levels, and retirement bred in her a sense of entitlement that scarcely existed anymore in the private sector. She could figure out her pension benefits to the third decimal. By the time she injected herself into the story of the Clinton presidency, she, like so many people in this saga, had already had a difficult and unhappy life, and she had learned that she could rely on no one except herself.

Tripp liked to refer to herself as a "hick from Morris County," a largely rural part of New Jersey where she was born in 1949. Linda Carotenuto's father was a high school teacher who married a German woman he met during his service in World War II. Tripp's adolescence, like Lewinsky's, was marred by her parents' acrimonious divorce, which was precipitated by her father's adulterous relationship with a coworker. In 1971, she married Bruce M. Tripp, a career Army officer. They spent two decades together, raising two children near a string of Army bases. Tripp had a series of what she called "jobettes," mostly secretarial, as her husband worked his way up to colonel. In 1990, when their children were teenagers, they divorced.

The following year, Tripp found a job at the White House as a secretary for a group of people on the communications staff, and she quickly earned a reputation for diligence and competence. She was kept on after Clinton's victory, but her attitude toward her employers changed. As with Aldrich, her complaints ran more to the cultural than the political changes she saw at the White House. (In fairness, the arrogance of many members of the new Clinton team alienated even some potentially sympathetic members of the permanent White House staff.) Aldrich later told an interviewer, "Linda Tripp and I and about two thousand other permanent White House employees shared a scorn for what we were seeing."

Under Clinton, Tripp was assigned to the counsel's office, which proved to be a magnet for controversy in the early days of the administration. The turning point in her career came with Vince Foster's suicide. Tripp would sometimes boast that she was the last person to see him alive—"I served him his last hamburger," she said—and she was an eyewitness to the panic and chaos that followed his death. In a series of e-mails that were disclosed during the many investigations of Foster's death, Tripp was withering about her superiors. Tripp called her boss, Bernard Nussbaum, and two of his colleagues "the three stooges" and wrote in another message, "So it took until Monday to figure out if [the briefcase] should be looked at? Christ. And we're the support staff?"

Notwithstanding her distaste for many of the Clinton staffers, Tripp made it her business to learn as much as she could about their personal lives, especially if they intersected with the president's. According to Tripp's grand jury testimony, no fewer than three women at the White House confessed to her that they had had sexual contacts with Clinton. Two of them, Lewinsky and Kathleen Willey, became well known, but Tripp enthusiastically shared news of the third with the grand jury as well. Debbie Schiff had parlayed a job as a flight attendant on Clinton's 1992 campaign plane into the position of receptionist in the West Wing of the White House.

"One day," Tripp said, in a particularly breathless moment in her testimony, Schiff "came up to me and said, 'I won.' And I said, 'What did you win?' And she said, 'I have my twenty minutes every morning.' I said, 'With who?' She said, 'With the president.' And I said, 'For what?' And she said, 'You figure it out.' Subsequently, she said they had a sexual relationship. . . . She was so comfortable in his presence that she would, for instance, come in and wear his shoes and traipse around the Oval Office complex and out in the lobby wearing his shoes. And she's tiny, just a little tiny girl, and he is a big man, and it was obvious right away that she was wearing gunboats on her feet compared to her little feet. So—" At this point, the prosecutor from Starr's office finally cut in and ended the bizarre monologue. But Tripp's meticulous recounting of Schiff's purported activities showed how much attention she paid to the president's sex life. (For her part, Schiff denied to Starr's prosecutors that she had had a sexual relationship with Clinton.)

In time, though, Tripp felt the need to escape the White House, and she arranged an advantageous departure. In the spring of 1994, Bernard Nussbaum, the White House counsel who had been her direct supervisor, was forced to resign, and Tripp had to look for a new job. There was an opening for a political appointee in the press office at the Pentagon. The job involved scheduling interviews with the then secretary of defense, William Perry. Following the usual policy for political appointees, the supervisor of the position, a fellow named Willie Blacklow, sought a "priority list" of candidates from the White House. When he got the list, Blacklow was astonished to see it contained only one name—Linda Tripp. Blacklow had seen many such lists, but he had never before seen a job-seeker preemptively eliminate all competition. Blacklow wanted someone else for the job, and he protested about the one-name list to his own boss, Cliff Bernath. "The White House is trying to shove somebody down my throat, and I am not going to take it," Blacklow said. But Bernath pointed out that anyone who possessed the bureaucratic skills to put herself on a list of one was going to get hired.

Willie Blacklow could have been Linda Tripp's *Doppelgänger*. Before he was hired as a deputy assistant secretary of defense, the last time Blacklow had visited the Pentagon was when he and several thousand others had tried to levitate the building, in a famous anti–Vietnam War protest of 1967. He spent most of the intervening decades as a press secretary to various liberal congressmen. Not surprisingly, then, his first meetings with Tripp were inauspicious. Within a week of arriving, she told Blacklow that she wanted a private office, which no one at her level received at the Pentagon.

He told her no. She went over his head to Bernath, who told her the same thing. Officials in Secretary Perry's office began to complain about Tripp's peremptory manner. Tripp also had a great deal of trouble getting along with the woman with whom she shared a cubicle, Susan Wallace. The two women had screaming fights, and their desks soon had to be separated.

But worse was to come. Tripp accused Wallace of listening in on her conversations. Much later, when Tripp's name became synonymous with the surreptitious whir of a tape recorder, some Pentagon colleagues would shake their heads at the memory of one particular Tripp outburst. "She's eavesdropping on my phone calls!" Tripp screamed about Wallace. "I'm going to sue that woman!"

Blacklow recognized that he had to make a change. He shifted Tripp to another job, where she ran a program that each year allowed a group of prominent civilians to tour military installations. She succeeded in this difficult job, and she and Blacklow even developed a friendship of sorts, based largely on their shared need to sneak cigarettes in "pigeon alley," a small airspace between the D and E rings of the Pentagon. For the most part, Tripp kept her political opinions to herself, but Blacklow would sometimes bellyache about the difficulties of getting a decision out of the president's people. "It's crazy over there at the White House," Blacklow sighed.

"You don't know the half of it," Tripp replied.

/ / /

When Aldrich's book was published, in the summer of 1996, Tripp had already been gone from the White House for almost two years. But the former secretary couldn't resist investigating whether she, too, might cash in in the same way. She told her idea to Tony Snow, a journalist who had served with her in the Bush White House. Snow said Tripp needed a literary agent. "You ought to talk to Lucianne Goldberg," Snow said. "She's a piece of work."

Lucianne Goldberg seemed to emerge from a virtual space somewhere between the Republican National Convention and the bar scene in *Star Wars*. She had banked a lifetime of obsessions—about sex, gossip, secret tape recordings, tell-all books, and conservative politics—as if in preparation for her moment in this case. She acted throughout with a kind of joyous malice, pretending at every moment to be outraged by one thing or another (usually the behavior of Bill Clinton), but in truth she was thrilled to be, finally, at the center of the action. Like Norma Desmond descending the staircase at the end of *Sunset Boulevard*, with her heart full of murder and longing, Goldberg was ready for her close-up. But unlike Desmond, the silent-screen diva who was left behind in a changing world, Lucianne Goldberg reflected the new face of American politics—personal, petty, and mean.

Born in Boston in 1935, Lucianne Cummings dropped out of high school at sixteen and claims to have had fifteen jobs before she was twenty-one. Since then, she has had nearly that many careers. She was a clerk at *The Washington Post,* ran a one-woman public relations firm (the sign on the door boasted of nonexistent offices in London and Paris), and served as a Democratic campaign worker and low-level White House staffer under Lyndon Johnson. After an early marriage and divorce, she married Sid Goldberg, a Republican who worked for a newspaper syndicate. In 1972, a friend of Sid's, the right-wing columnist Victor Lasky, introduced Lucianne to Murray Chotiner, a veteran political operative for President Richard Nixon. Chotiner hired Goldberg at $1,000 per week to be a spy on George McGovern's campaign plane as the representative of the fictional Women's News Service. After Watergate, she wrote a couple of less successful novels on her own, and began work as a literary agent, mostly for conservative authors with incendiary tales to tell. (Goldberg claimed to have ghostwritten Maureen Dean's bestselling novel, *Washington Wives;* Dean denies this. Goldberg's most recent novel, *Madame Cleo's Girls,* published in 1992, featured a literary agent who "was known for her representation of sensational nonauthors and their ghostwritten stories.")

In 1985, Goldberg materialized at the second trial of Claus von Bulow for the attempted murder of his wife, Sunny. The literary agent was trying to sell a book by one David Marriott, who was, among other things, a male prostitute, a drug dealer, and an acquaintance of several people involved in the case. Marriott had hidden a recorder in his jockey shorts and made tapes of von Bulow and others. Marriott's tapes turned out to be less than dispositive, and he never wrote a book, but at the trial in Providence,

Rhode Island, Goldberg became friendly with the writer Dominick Dunne. For the next thirteen years, they spoke almost every morning; they hashed over the tabloids and Goldberg listened to Dunne's tales of life on the A-list dinner circuit.

Virtually all of Goldberg's projects appeared to involve, in one way or another, tell-alls and tapes. *Madame Cleo's Girls* concerned the efforts of a celebrated madam to recite (on tape) and then sell a sensational memoir about her famous clients. The story mixed soft-core sex ("It got better and better until he stopped counting the orgasms"), nose-against-the-glass voyeurism ("The black Super Puma helicopter hovered above the Mosby Media office tower"), and breezy contempt for the famous in general and politicians in particular ("The Connecticut lawyer who paid to watch Sandrine masturbate while he sat on the couch chewing the ear of a teddy bear was running for Congress and had gone back to his home district to campaign"). There wasn't much of a theme to the novel—"Everyone is for sale" was about as close as it came. Nor was there a clear pattern to Goldberg's life. As she often said, she hated being bored, and she loved "dish."

That, more or less, was the picture Goldberg presented of herself. A political thrill-seeker. A good-time girl. With her cigarette holder and her booze-and-nicotine-ravaged voice, Goldberg made herself into a caricature, a kind of joke—the "Auntie Mame of politics," as one former client described the image. Yet this picture served to free Goldberg from any real responsibility for her actions. This, too, was a pattern in her life. In fact, in addition to crazy stories and many laughs, Goldberg left a trail of wreckage behind her.

Goldberg's literary agency was more of a hobby than a business. She operated it out of her home and never made much of a living from it. One advantage of Goldberg's preference for one-shot sensational authors was that few people wanted to do business with her for a second time. Her best-known client, the celebrity biographer Kitty Kelley, sued Goldberg for breach of contract and fraud and won a judgment of $41,407. (Goldberg's lawyer in that case then sued her for not paying his bill; Goldberg never contested the suit, and the judge entered a default judgment against her, which she never paid.) Goldberg used to tell friends that she had two sons who were killed in an automobile accident—a made-up story.

Her marriage was often troubled; a friend was surprised to discover, after she lent Goldberg her apartment several times so she "would be closer to the theater," that she was using it for private afternoons with a prominent Washington writer.

Once Goldberg emerged as a national figure, many people who knew her well were astonished to hear the strict, moralistic tone she took toward the president's behavior. "He's such a weak man, such a bad man," she said any number of times. In one interview, she said, "We're all saying 'blow jobs' at dinner parties. I mean, I'm old enough to be shocked by that. . . . He is the president of the United States. He sets the moral tone for this country." Like many of Clinton's critics, Goldberg displayed contempt for the president's roots in Arkansas. "Borderline trailer trash," she called him—which recalls Aldrich's dismissal of the president and his friends as having Berkeley values "with an Appalachian twist."

Yet Goldberg's books abounded in blow jobs—and phone sex and bondage and more—and she often told a story about herself that resembled the one Monica Lewinsky would tell Linda Tripp. On any number of occasions, Goldberg told friends that when she worked in the White House—that is, when she was just a few years older than Lewinsky was in 1995—she had had an affair with President Johnson. There is, of course, no way to verify the claim now; and Goldberg, after she became famous, took to denying that she had ever said she had slept with Johnson. Still, the irony— her outrage at an affair that seemed to duplicate one she had claimed as her own—was extraordinary.

In any event, Goldberg was only too happy to chat with Linda Tripp about her book idea. From the moment they first spoke in 1996, Lucianne Goldberg took on the role of Linda Tripp's id, always pushing her to do what she, Tripp, really wanted to do anyway—that is, destroy the president and make some money in the bargain. After all, as Goldberg wrote of her fictional alter ego, this agent "prided herself on being a 'closer.'"

/ / /

"This is going to be bigger than Gary Aldrich," Goldberg confided on the telephone. "She was right in the center. They can't get anything on her. We need to do it fast. I just can't tell you her name yet. Let's call her 'Joan Dean.'"

Goldberg was talking to Maggie Gallagher, a conservative columnist for the *New York Post.* After a few conversations with Tripp, Goldberg was ready to move. Gallagher agreed to talk to Tripp on the telephone, hear her story, and then prepare a book proposal. All through July 1996, Gallagher and Tripp would speak almost every night—a total of fifteen or twenty hours of conversations. In their talks, Tripp told Gallagher that she was worried that the financial payoff for the book would not justify the risk it would present to her career. She was a political appointee at the Pentagon, so she no longer enjoyed civil service protections. Tripp told Gallagher she was earning about $80,000 a year, more than she had ever expected she would make in her life. Still, she plowed ahead, with Tripp rambling into the night and Gallagher scribbling notes. Tripp's paranoia prompted her to impose one condition for their conversations—a rather extraordinary one, in light of what was to come. Tripp refused to allow Gallagher to tape-record their conversations.

Gallagher shared Tripp's rather starchy and proper demeanor, and they convinced each other that their book was not really about Clinton's sex life. It was, they said, a more generalized exposé of the shoddy operations at the White House. Goldberg, in contrast, had no such illusions. She knew the appeal of the book lay in what Tripp could say about what she called "the graduates"— women employees at the White House who purportedly owed their careers to their sexual relationships with Bill Clinton. (At the time of Tripp's 1996 book proposal, her list of graduates did not include Monica Lewinsky, who had not yet confided in Tripp.) Goldberg knew the sex would sell the book, and she boasted to Alfred Regnery, the head of the right-wing publishing house that had scored with Aldrich's memoir, that she had another hot one in the pipeline for him.

The trio of women—Goldberg, Tripp, and Gallagher—decided to title the book *Behind Closed Doors: What I Saw at the Clinton White House,* and Gallagher's proposal eventually ran to fifty pages. The chapter on the "graduates" was entitled "The President's Women." On August 6, Gallagher traveled to a restaurant in New Jersey, near Tripp's mother's home, to meet Linda in person for the first time. Tripp had only minor changes to make on the proposal, and Goldberg prepared to begin circulating it. Then, just a few days later, Tripp called Goldberg and pulled out of the project. She felt that the financial risks did not justify the rewards, especially since Gallagher was going to receive a third of the proceeds. Gallagher was miffed. She had put in all the work on the proposal for no compensation, and now there was not going to be any payoff at the end. But Gallagher's anger paled next to Goldberg's. In part, her concern was simply financial; no book meant no money for the agent. But it was more than that, too. For Goldberg, Tripp's book represented a passport to the action, the deal flow, and a chance to embarrass a president she despised. On the telephone with Tripp, Goldberg scoffed at her misgivings. "Who do you think you are," Goldberg asked her putative client, "the queen of England?"

/ / /

With the Tripp book project on what turned out to be a temporary hold, another chronicler of Clinton's personal life was getting back into business. A few days after Jones filed her lawsuit against the president, Isikoff had quit *The Washington Post* and signed on at *Newsweek,* where he served as the in-house expert on Clinton's sex life. As Bob Bennett and Lloyd Cutler had figured when the suit was filed more than two years earlier, the press had lost interest when the case bogged down in appeals on legal issues. But shortly before the 1996 election, Stuart Taylor, Jr., had written a widely read piece on the case in *The American Lawyer,* suggesting that the case deserved to be taken seriously. The election, the Taylor article, the presence of an expert like Isikoff, and, of course, the inherent sex appeal of the story pushed *Newsweek* to revisit the Jones case as 1997 began.

As part of his reporting for the story, Isikoff called Joe Cammarata. In the long time since the case had been filed, Cammarata had had relatively little to do on behalf of his client. The briefs were mostly drafted by the "elves"—especially Jerome Marcus in Philadelphia and George Conway in New York. (Marcus and Porter had recruited Conway after they read an op-ed piece he wrote about the case.) Cammarata answered press queries and sorted out the curiosity seekers and other peculiar callers who gravitate toward people in the news. As it happened, Cammarata had gotten one of those strange phone calls right before Isikoff telephoned.

The woman had actually called several times but refused to leave a name or a number. Finally, Cammarata took the call. The story she told was extraordinarily detailed—and potentially very helpful to Paula Jones's case. The woman said that she and her husband had been fund-raisers for Clinton during the 1992 campaign. After the election, she had worked as a volunteer at the White House and then been hired as a clerk in the counsel's office. In November 1993, when she was still a volunteer at the White House, she had gone to see the president about getting a paid job. While they were in Clinton's private office, the president had touched her breasts and placed her hand on his penis. They were separated only because the president was interrupted by a phone call.

Though she refused to give her name, the woman gave Cammarata more details that would make her easy to identify. She said that her husband, who had been suffering business reverses, had killed himself on the very day she was groped by Clinton. His death had been mentioned in several right-wing-conspiracy publications that often referred to the "mysterious" deaths of people connected to Clinton. She even mentioned one of these outlets—something called the *Guarino Report*. After her husband's death, the woman said, she had been given a White House job and had even attended several overseas conferences with the American delegations, including one to Jakarta and another to Copenhagen.

The call presented Cammarata with several choices. In light of all the detail she had supplied, it wouldn't be difficult to track her down himself. But Cammarata didn't have a lot of resources for private investigators, and, more important, simply learning the woman's name wouldn't give him any leverage to win a settlement with the president. For that, the woman's name would have to become public. Her story would have to embarrass Clinton—and serve as a warning of the disclosures that were likely to come at trial. It would be better, then, for Cammarata if someone else tracked her down and then made her name public, especially someone at a credible national publication. That would help his case—and it would be free.

Such were Cammarata's thoughts when he received Isikoff's call. An intrepid reporter like Isikoff could easily find the woman, and then he'd have a nice scoop. So the lawyer told Isikoff about the call. Their recollections differed about the terms of the exchange. Cammarata said that Isikoff promised to supply him with the name before he published it. Isikoff recalled no such promise. But the gist of the agreement was the same. Even if Cammarata had to wait to read her name in the magazine, he would eventually get what he wanted—an advantage in his lawsuit against the president.

Cammarata's leak to Isikoff was analogous to the last important leak the reporter had received about Clinton's sex life. Cliff Jackson had learned from his disastrous press conference with Jones that he could not hope to gain political leverage simply by making the charges himself. He needed the sanction of a national publication. Cammarata faced the same dilemma. If he simply learned the woman's name and then disclosed the story himself, the news undoubtedly would have been greeted with skepticism. That's why Cammarata, like Jackson, needed Isikoff—to invest his damaging information about the president with the prestige of Isikoff's employer.

There was nothing extraordinary about this strategy. No one leaked more, or better, than the Clinton White House. But the business of leaking illustrates an important difference between covering crime (which Isikoff had done for most of his career) and covering politics (which he found himself doing in the treacherous waters of the Jones case). In crime, leaks generally come only from law enforcement, and a reporter must assess on his own whether the charges have merit. (After all, it's difficult to call, say, the Gambino crime family for its side of the story.) But in politics, leaking often represents a strategic choice for a candidate or a cause, and sophisticated reporters inform their readers not just of the facts, but of the context in which the story was developed—that is, which side is leaking and why. That was Isikoff's challenge as Jackson, Cammarata, and soon others tried to use him for their personal or political advantage.

Based on Cammarata's information—fund-raisers for Clinton, husband suicide, job in the White House—Isikoff quickly identified the woman as Kathleen Willey. (After hearing and seeing Willey much later, Cammarata was certain that Willey herself had called him. Willey denied calling the lawyer.) Willey met with Isikoff for an off-the-record interview in her lawyer's office and related what had happened between her and the president in what Isikoff later called "gripping and microscopic detail."

Willey and her husband had first met Bill Clinton during the 1992 campaign. After Clinton won the election, Kathleen had come to work as a volunteer at the White House. But in the first few months of the Clinton presidency, the Willeys' life began to disintegrate. Ed Willey's law business was failing because he had been caught embezzling funds from a client. Kathleen could no longer afford to work for free, so on November 29, 1993, Willey told Isikoff, she had obtained an audience with the president in order to ask for a job on the White House staff. After Willey told the president of her family troubles, Clinton told her how sorry he was—and then kissed her. This was no social kiss; according to Willey, he put his hands in her hair and up her skirt.

"What else?" Isikoff wanted to know. "Did he put your hands on his penis?"

"Yes, he did," Willey replied.

"Was it erect?" the reporter wanted to know. Indeed it was.

Continuing her story, Willey told Isikoff that she had emerged, shaken and upset, from the meeting with Clinton, and when she returned home to Richmond, she learned that her husband had killed himself earlier that day.

Isikoff immediately looked for a way to corroborate the story of Clinton's pass at the job-seeker. Had she told anyone right away? As a matter of fact, she said, she had told a friend of hers who was working at the time in the White House counsel's office. A woman named Linda Tripp.

Isikoff did two things after he heard Willey's tale. He was now convinced, he wrote later, that "Clinton was far more psychologically disturbed than the public ever imagined." So he started writing up a book proposal. He and his friend Glenn Simpson, a reporter for *The Wall Street Journal,* came up with an idea for a book that would explain all of the Clinton scandals. The theory was that Clinton was a sex addict, and that virtually everything that had gone wrong in his presidency—from Whitewater to Paula Jones to the health care debacle—could be explained by the crippling effects of Clinton's obsessive pursuit of sex. (Health care failed, the theory went, because the president had no ability to control the first lady because he feared that she wouldn't defend him in the sex scandals.)

The other thing Isikoff did was try to find Linda Tripp and see if she would back up Willey's claim about what had happened between her and the president. On the morning of March 24, 1997, Isikoff went to the Pentagon and located Tripp's office. The imperious bureaucrat initially shooed the reporter away from her desk, but agreed to meet him when she took a cigarette break a few minutes later.

Isikoff outlined Willey's charges and asked Tripp if it was true. Tripp wouldn't answer, not until she spoke to Willey herself.

Tripp had one more thing to say, as Isikoff was about to leave. "There's something here, but the story is not what you think it is," she said cryptically. "You're barking up the wrong tree." By this time, unknown to Isikoff, Linda Tripp had a new friend.

/ / /

The president's attempt, in February 1996, to cut off his relationship with Monica Lewinsky had been less than fully successful. The frequency of their contacts never approached the halcyon days of the previous month, but their encounters didn't stop altogether, either. On the Sunday afternoon of March 31, Clinton summoned Lewinsky to the study for the first time since their breakup a little more than a month earlier. (It was on this occasion that they made erotic use of one of the president's cigars. Lewinsky told her biographer, Andrew Morton, that after the experience with the cigar, "she realized she had fallen in love." One FBI interview with Lewinsky on this subject included a revealing disclosure about the real taboos of the Clinton era: "The president did not smoke the cigar because smoking is forbidden in the White House.")

On the following Friday, April 5, 1996, Lewinsky was fired from the White House staff. Her departure was the work of Evelyn Lieberman, a deputy chief of staff who made it her business to monitor White House staffers (especially women) for inappropriate behavior around the president. Lieberman regarded Lewinsky as a "clutch" who tried too hard to be around the president. But Lewinsky was also let go because she wasn't very good at her job.

Lewinsky and her boss, Jocelyn Jolley, were terminated on the same day. The two women were responsible for directing routine correspondence from Capitol Hill to the correct office in the White House. According to Lieberman and others, they did it slowly and inaccurately, and a change was needed regardless of Lewinsky's behavior around the president. As Timothy Keating, Clinton's director of legislative affairs, told the Starr investigators, Lewinsky "spent too much time out of the office and not enough time doing what she should have been doing." Neither woman was thrown off the government payroll, however. Jolley was given a temporary job in the General Services Administration, and Lewinsky was dispatched to the public affairs office of the Pentagon.

By almost any standard, Lewinsky's new job was better than her old one. It came with a raise, the opportunity to travel, and increased responsibility. Still, Lewinsky was shattered by the change. She devoted the next year and a half to finding a way to return to the White House and proximity to Clinton. Notably, in all of these efforts, Lewinsky displayed no interest in what she might actually *do* at the White House. This is not entirely surprising, since she admittedly had no interest in politics or the workings of government. (Indeed, it suggests that the decision to fire her was a pretty good one in the first place—and that she was lucky to get the job that she did.) Two days after her transfer, on Easter Sunday, April 7, Lewinsky made a teary appeal for a stay of execution in an audience with the president in his private study.

Lewinsky later described this meeting with Clinton in one of the conversations that Tripp surreptitiously taped. "He called me at six o'clock and he said, you know, 'Hi,' and I said, 'Hi.' And this was, like, the Ron Brown thing." (The secretary of commerce, who was a close friend of Clinton's, had just been killed in an airplane crash.) "I said, 'How are you doing?' He was like, 'Oh, I'm okay. It's so bad, da, da, da.' I said, 'I know.'" Following this moment of shared grieving, Lewinsky told the president, "Well, I have more bad news for you. . . . Guess whose last day is tomorrow. . . . Can I please come and see you?"

"So I went to see him," Lewinsky went on, "and he—you know—and I was so upset, and he said, 'Well, let me see what I can do,' you know. He said—he says, 'Why do they have to take you away from me? I trust you so much,' you know. And then—then he said, 'I promise you . . . if I win in November, I'll have you back like that. You can do anything you want. You can be anything you want. You can do anything you want.'

"And then," Lewinsky continued to her friend, "I made a joke, and I said, 'Well, can I be the assistant to the president for blow jobs?' He said, 'I'd like that.'"

Before this conversation with the president ended, Lewinsky again auditioned for that position (this time while the president was on the telephone with his adviser Dick Morris). Their interlude was interrupted when Clinton's aide Harold Ickes arrived in the Oval Office to see the president. Lewinsky scurried out a side door. They didn't see each other privately for the rest of 1996.

/ / /

Lewinsky's title at the Pentagon was confidential assistant to the assistant secretary of defense for public affairs, Kenneth Bacon. She was, in essence, the secretary to the press secretary. For most twenty-two-year-olds, it would have been a dream job—full of glamorous travel with high-level delegations to the best hotels in the great capitals of the world. But Lewinsky didn't see it that way. She was consumed by a single interest in life: waiting for the president to call her for phone sex, a visit, or best of all, a job (any job) back at the White House. She moped, ate a great deal, and did this job rather badly as well, especially under time pressure. (She was supposed to do transcriptions for Bacon, and she did not type well.) On her Day-Timer at work, Lewinsky kept track of the days since her last sexual encounter with the president and the days until the election, when, she hoped, she would return to the White House.

A small bright spot in Lewinsky's otherwise grim existence came shortly after she started at the Pentagon. She noticed that one of her colleagues in the public affairs office had decorated her work space with "jumbos" of President Clinton—the large-format photographs that are displayed throughout the White House. Lewinsky wondered if the owner of the photographs had also worked at the White House. As Tripp later testified in the grand jury, "I had the jumbos and she begged me for one of the jumbos." So on the basis of this aspect of their shared past, Monica Lewinsky and Linda Tripp struck up their friendship.

Despite the difference in their ages—Tripp was twenty-four years older than Lewinsky—the two women had more in common than just their prior place of employment. They both loved to gossip, and they shared an intense interest in clothes, hair, and dieting. Tripp recalled later that she always knew that Lewinsky was a big fan of the president's, but she never noticed anything unusual about her interest in him until August 1996, when the young woman traveled to New York to attend a gala fund-raiser on the occasion of his fiftieth birthday. At this event, Lewinsky contrived to place herself near the president, and then, in the words of one of her FBI debriefings, "LEWINSKY reached behind herself to fondle and squeeze the President's penis." Lewinsky didn't share that detail with Tripp at the time, but she began to hint that she had a big secret in her recent past.

At first Lewinsky would say only that she had had an affair with "someone" at the White House. She called him "Handsome" or "the Big Creep"—the latter because of the way he had ended the relationship—and finally she admitted her lover was the president. (Lewinsky had already shared the news with her mother, her Aunt Debra, a therapist, and a handful of friends—in all, eleven people.) Tripp, who had just dropped her book project with Gallagher and Goldberg, was as interested in listening as Lewinsky was in talking.

As the presidential election approached, Lewinsky was racked by nervous tension over whether she would finally be allowed to return to a job at the White House. (She also had an abortion in this period, the result of a brief relationship with a Pentagon colleague.) After Clinton's victory over Bob Dole, the president never delivered on the promise of a job, but he did agree to see Lewinsky again. After her departure from the White House, she had begun cultivating the president's personal secretary, Betty Currie, who came to serve as Lewinsky's conduit for messages to, and occasionally from, Clinton.

On February 28, 1997, Currie invited Lewinsky to watch the taping of the president's weekly radio address. When the couple retreated to his private office after the speech, Clinton gave the former intern a pair of belated Christmas gifts—a blue glass hat pin and an edition of Walt Whitman's *Leaves of Grass*. For the first time in nearly eleven months, Monica began performing oral sex on the president, but this time their encounter would end differently from all the others. As Lewinsky later testified to Starr's prosecutors, "I finished"—and she was wearing a blue dress from the Gap. (There was only one more sexual contact between them. On March 29, with the president still on crutches from his knee injury at the golfer Greg Norman's house in Florida, Lewinsky once again performed oral sex "to completion" while, as she put it to Starr's prosecutors, Clinton "manually stimulated me" to four orgasms. Still consumed with her White House job hunt, Lewinsky left the president with a copy of her résumé on this day.)

By this time, Lewinsky was keeping Tripp apprised moment to moment on the progress of her relationship. The two women gave somewhat contradictory accounts of Tripp's behavior in response. Tripp asserted that she gave no advice on how Lewinsky should sustain the relationship, but Lewinsky said Tripp goaded her to keep it going. Lewinsky's account is far more persuasive. If Tripp had really disapproved, she could have simply cut off contact with Lewinsky; indeed, if that had been Tripp's attitude, Lewinsky probably would have wanted nothing to do with her. Instead, the pace of their contacts only accelerated. It was, for example, in the spring of 1997 that Tripp suggested that Lewinsky use the Excel spreadsheet software on her computer at the Pentagon to make a grid of all her contacts with Clinton. That way, the older woman said, Monica could identify the "patterns" of the relationship. This, however, was a plainly bogus pretext for Tripp to secure documentary evidence of the subject that had long obsessed her—the president's extramarital sex life.

And, by coincidence, it was at this time that Tripp met a man who shared her obsession with that subject. On March 24, 1997, Mike Isikoff came calling at the Pentagon to ask about Kathleen Willey. This was, as Tripp told him, "barking up the wrong tree."

/ / /

But still, Isikoff wanted to know about Kathleen Willey. The reporter began shuttling between the two women, trying to sort out what (if anything) had happened between Willey and the president. He later wrote that "the relationship between Tripp and Willey turned out to be a lot more complicated than I suspected." Though Tripp had befriended Willey at the White House and tried to help her find a paying job there, Tripp came to think that Willey was trying to steal Tripp's own job in the counsel's office. Tripp's departure to the Pentagon had ended the budding competition between them, but some bitterness lingered. More important, even though Willey promised Isikoff that Tripp would back up her story about the president's crude pass, Tripp did no such thing. According to Tripp, it was Willey who had schemed to ensnare the president.

Isikoff's inquiries illustrated the difficulties of sexual investigative reporting. According to Tripp's later testimony, while they both worked in the White House in 1993, Kathleen had complained about her marriage to Ed Willey and tried to have an affair with the president. "They both had—appeared to have—not very good marriages, and it just seemed to be as consenting adults," she said. Tripp had indeed seen Willey after her November 29 meeting with the president, but she had been anything but distraught by the encounter. "I can just tell you that she was very excited, very flustered, she smiled from ear to ear the entire time," Tripp told the grand jury. "She seemed almost shocked, but happy shocked." (Clinton would provide still a third version of what happened between him and Willey. He acknowledged meeting with her in his private office, but said that he had only comforted her about her husband's travails. Starr's prosecutor Jackie Bennett challenged Clinton about this incident in the president's grand jury deposition: "You placed her hand on your genitals, did you not?" Clinton bristled, saying, "Mr. Bennett, I didn't do any of that, and the questions you're asking, I think, betray the bias of this operation that has troubled me for a long time.")

But before Isikoff had a chance to put his reporting in the magazine, he was, in a way, beaten to the punch. In late June 1997, Matt Drudge visited Washington at a time when his celebrity was still rather modest. Two years earlier, Drudge had started posting various news items and gossip—mostly early reports of weekend movie grosses along with occasional news of show business contract disputes—on the fledgling World Wide Web. His popularity grew with that of the Internet, and Drudge soon developed a following in the tens of thousands, especially among journalists. Drudge wrote with a cranky anti-Clinton slant, but his juicy tidbits and old-time tabloid style made his intermittently reliable

Drudge Report a must-read in political and media circles. By the time he toured *Newsweek's* offices, in the summer of 1997, he could promenade through them like a visiting dignitary. (On the same trip to Washington, Drudge was guest of honor at a dinner thrown by the ubiquitous David Brock.) In a conversation with Drudge at *Newsweek,* Isikoff accidentally confirmed that he was working on an article about a possible act of sexual harassment by the president in the White House.

Drudge ran a vague item on his web site about Isikoff's research on July 4, and then tried hard to follow up. It wasn't too difficult, because by this time, Cammarata had already located and subpoenaed Willey. The elves—the conservative lawyers who were helping the Jones team—began leaking to Drudge. Laura Ingraham, later a network journalist, introduced Conway to Drudge, and Conway told Drudge about Willey. Drudge's items put pressure on Isikoff and *Newsweek* to give the story their imprimatur. It was the same strategy employed with the leaks to *The Washington Times* after Isikoff's suspension in 1994—to goad a national publication into running a story that would damage the president.

Isikoff went back to Willey to try to persuade her to put her story about Clinton on the record. She wouldn't talk, but among Cammarata, Tripp, and Willey's friend Julie Hiatt Steele—who told Isikoff that Willey had earlier asked her to lie about the incident with the president—the reporter had enough to cobble together a story for the magazine. Entitled "A Twist in Jones v. Clinton," Isikoff's story hit on August 3, 1997. "The phone call was provocative, to say the least," it began, describing the mysterious caller who had tantalized Cammarata in January. "She refused to give her name," the article went on, "but offered enough details to allow Cammarata to track down the woman he believes made the call: Kathleen E. Willey." This was artful phrasing on Isikoff's part. The caller did offer enough details "to allow Cammarata" to track her down, but that wasn't exactly what happened. As Isikoff implied later in the article, Cammarata had used Isikoff to track her down and make her story public—which was what the lawyer had wanted all along. Of course, the story included Bob Bennett denying, on Clinton's behalf, that he had made a sexual advance toward Willey.

Isikoff's story also included one more significant, if garbled, passage. Isikoff quoted the then obscure Linda Tripp as saying she remembered seeing Willey after her alleged encounter with the president, and she looked "disheveled. Her face was red and her lipstick was off. She was flustered, happy and joyful." Tripp wanted "to make it clear that this was not a case of sexual harassment." In this instance, Tripp's comments both help and hurt the president—suggesting that Willey was lying but also that some consensual sexual activity might have occurred. But Isikoff quoted Bennett as saying only that Tripp "is not to be believed." Tripp later cited this comment as turning her from a loyal soldier in the administration to a determined enemy. It was a debatable claim—for example, Tripp had already planned an anti-Clinton book—but the Bennett comment gave her the pretext she needed to turn against Clinton completely.

In any event, Isikoff had his scoop, albeit with an annoying postscript. In his last report on the Willey story, Matt Drudge had added a characteristically provocative kicker. ISIKOFF BOOK BLOWUP, Drudge's headline screamed. "Was investigative reporter Michael Isikoff holding back his wild Kathleen Willey White House sex tale for a book? Talk around the NEWSWEEK offices has Isikoff compiling stories on various Clinton scandals for a collection—Willey was to be one of the 'newsworthy' sell points of the project." It was not true that he was holding back, but just the same, Isikoff and Glenn Simpson decided to put their book idea aside. As it happened, however, two other book projects in the case were just then coming to life.

7

Their Tabloid Hearts

Bob Bennett could not put off the Paula Jones case forever. He had accomplished his primary goal of postponing depositions and other fact-finding until after the 1996 election, but even the most skillful stalling tactics could only delay, not prevent, the inevitable showdown in the Supreme Court. When that day came, Bennett would have to be ready for one of the great constitutional confrontations of the era.

Bennett had never before argued a case in the Supreme Court, and he wondered if he was the right man for the job. Bennett knew that to the extent the justices regarded this case as about the presidency—not about the current occupant of the job—he had a better chance of winning. Perhaps he should let a law professor argue the case for Clinton, to emphasize the broader stakes of the issue. Bennett made this point to Walter Dellinger, the acting solicitor general, who would be representing the Justice Department in arguing that the Jones case should be put off to the end of Clinton's term in office.

Dellinger, himself a professor on leave from Duke Law School and a savvy politician in his own right, told Bennett he had it wrong. Bennett was what the case needed, a savvy trial lawyer who could explain to the Court just how vicious and time-consuming a modern lawsuit could be for a defendant. I'll handle the Constitution, Dellinger told Bennett. You tell them about the real world.

The Jones forces prepared with similar care. The brief had been written principally by the chief "elves," George Conway in New York and Jerome Marcus in Philadelphia. Conway arranged for Gil Davis, the easygoing Virginian who would argue the case, to be subjected to a moot court by two of the most distinguished conservative lawyers in Washington. In a prep session downtown, Robert Bork, the former appeals court judge and defeated Supreme Court nominee, and Theodore Olson, a top Justice Department official in the Reagan administration, grilled Davis in the manner that he could expect from the justices. It's common in Washington for politically plugged-in lawyers to prep their allies for battle in the Court. In one way, though, it was unusual to see Bork and Olson arguing against presidential prerogatives, since in other circumstances they invariably sided with the executive branch. But this case was different, because Bill Clinton was the defendant.

A tingle of anticipation ran through the Supreme Court chamber when the case was finally called for argument on January 13, 1997. The justices themselves, primed for the historic moment, scarcely let a lawyer on either side complete a sentence without jumping in with questions. Dellinger at least had a chance to make his core argument, that "the public's interest in the president's unimpaired performance of his duties must take precedence over a private litigant's interest in redress." But he took a drubbing from the Court. Justice Scalia: "We see presidents riding horseback, chopping firewood, fishing for stick fish, playing golf . . . really, the notion that he doesn't have a minute to spare is, is just not credible." Dellinger parried that attack gracefully, quoting President Reagan (who appointed Scalia) to the effect that "presidents don't have vacations; they have a change of scenery." Dellinger warned that litigation can be "all-consuming and all-absorbing," but Chief Justice Rehnquist scoffed, "Surely that may be true of an individual with an ordinary job, but with all the pressing concerns that the president has, one would think it would be less true of him."

On May 27, 1997, the Supreme Court ruled unanimously that Clinton had no right to delay the lawsuit. Paula Jones was imme-

diately entitled to return to the district court for the case to proceed. There is, in retrospect, something almost endearing about
the obtuseness of Justice John Paul Stevens's opinion. Despite the
political differences among them, the nine justices shared a hard-
won disengagement from the ways of the real world, and their
opinion in the Jones case sang out their collective ignorance. It
had been decades since any of them had tried a case as a lawyer.
Despite Bennett's and even Dellinger's warnings, they knew nothing of the hurly-burly of modern trial practice, much less in a politically charged environment.

The thesis of Stevens's opinion was that since the Jones lawsuit
related entirely to Clinton's unofficial conduct, the case had no
bearing on his presidency and accordingly he should enjoy no
special right to delay it. Besides, Stevens went on, the trial of this
matter would be no big deal. "As for the case at hand," the justice
wrote, "it appears to us highly unlikely to occupy any substantial
amount of [Clinton's] time." This was all, of course, precisely
backward. It is *because* the case related to Clinton's personal life—
and a sexual matter, no less—that it would receive much *more* attention than if it concerned the mere operations of government.

With a naïveté that in other circumstances might be seen as
admirable, they decided simply that Clinton was not above the law
and that this plaintiff deserved her day in court. The case was the
perfect vessel for both the prurience of the media (which led,
among other things, to the proliferation of book plans) and the
efforts of the president's political adversaries (which led everyone
from Robert Bork to Lucianne Goldberg to latch on to the Jones
cause). Davis and Cammarata had filed the case in part because
they knew how distracting it would be for Clinton—and because
they hoped to leverage the president's discomfort into an advantageous settlement. In a political culture where the "character issue"
was ascendant, the Court failed to recognize that nothing could
be more distracting to a president than a sexual harassment lawsuit.

/ / /

At the time of their victory in the Supreme Court, Gil Davis and
Joe Cammarata had represented Paula Jones for more than three
years. And now, they decided, it was time to parlay their legal vic-

tory into an advantageous settlement for themselves and their client. As they knew better than anyone, their prospects for victory at trial were small. Jones had waited three years to file her case, she had no proof of any damages, and it was far from clear that an Arkansas jury would believe her, as opposed to the president of the United States, about what happened at the Excelsior Hotel. It was time for the Jones team to cash in.

With the case back before a trial court, the plaintiffs now had the right to issue subpoenas for witness depositions. In a classic demonstration of the triumph of the legal system over the political system, the two Jones lawyers began using subpoenas to illustrate the political costs of a trial to the president. Davis and Cammarata subpoenaed David Maraniss, Clinton's biographer, for all information he had about several women rumored to be romantically linked to Clinton. They subpoenaed Betsy Wright, Clinton's top aide during his governorship, for "the list of the names of women William Jefferson Clinton had allegedly had affairs with and the places where they were said to have occurred." And, of course, thanks to the mystery phone call to Cammarata in January, both the lawyer and Mike Isikoff had tracked down Kathleen Willey, who was also subpoenaed. In truth, several of these subpoenas were poorly drafted, and Judge Susan Webber Wright might have quashed them at some point later in the case. But these early efforts sent a clear signal to Bob Bennett. Settle—or else.

Bennett got the message. He and his partner, Mitch Ettinger, an earnest and clean-cut former Air Force lawyer, played bad cop/good cop with their adversaries, but they sent out clear signals that they were willing to deal. On August 5, 1997, the two lawyers invited Davis and Cammarata to a secret late-night negotiating session to see if they could settle the case before any more damage was inflicted on either side.

In the conference room eleven floors above the deserted streets of downtown Washington, Bennett played the heavy. "This case is bullshit," Bennett announced near the start. "We're wasting our time even talking to you." In fact, though Bennett called himself a trial lawyer and often spoke of how much he looked forward to cross-examining Paula Jones, he hadn't conducted a single jury trial since he joined Skadden Arps in 1990. Lawyers in large firms almost never go to trial; it costs too much to pay them, and besides, the risks of gambling with a jury usually run too high. Notwithstanding his bluster, Bennett wanted to settle.

Ettinger had responsibility for making that point. "Maybe there's some way we can work this out," he said.

Davis and Cammarata hoped so. At the time of the meeting, they had done hundreds of hours of work for which they had not yet been paid. The fund-raising efforts for the Paula Jones legal fund had generated more attention than money. The first efforts in this area had been started by the Reverend Patrick Mahoney, the antiabortion activist, shortly after he first spoke to Jones in Little Rock, just after her ill-fated press conference with Danny Traylor and Cliff Jackson. Davis preferred to have someone he knew run the fund, so he asked Mahoney to yield control of the effort to a veteran Washington fund-raiser named Cindy Hays, who directed the fund for the next three years. Hays raised a little more than $200,000, but most of that money had been spent on expenses—printing, transportation, travel, and the like. The meeting in Bennett's conference room came at a propitious time for the Jones lawyers for another reason. Just two days earlier, Isikoff's story on Kathleen Willey had broken in *Newsweek*, giving the Clinton lawyers a taste of what was in store if they allowed the case to go to trial.

In a first round of halfhearted settlement negotiations in 1996, Jones's lawyers had asked for $1.4 million. Still hopeful that the Supreme Court would put the case over until the end of Clinton's term, Bennett had rejected the request out of hand, and Davis and Cammarata had come back with $1.2 million. Bennett again said no. But things quickly got serious on this August night in 1997. When Davis and Cammarata indicated a willingness to accept a six-figure settlement, Bennett started to pay attention. Bennett had tested out various settlement possibilities on some of his contacts in the news media. The consensus seemed to be that the lawyer could portray any payment of less than $1 million as a legitimate effort to dispose of a distraction to the president.

In the days leading up to the meeting, Bennett had brought the results of his informal survey back to his client with a simple message: Settle for under $1 million and put the case behind you. The president—as well as his wife—were reluctant. They had been battered by these sorts of allegations for years, and they found that the only way to respond to them was to fight them. If you settled, according to Clinton's reckoning, you just encouraged more of these people to come forward.

The recklessness of Clinton's approach, especially at this moment, is breathtaking. In May he had finally ended his sexual relationship with Lewinsky (though their phone sex would continue into November), but she kept pressuring him for a job back at the White House. On July 3, she had written him a starchy letter—"Dear Sir," it began—complaining about the lack of progress in her job hunt, and warning that she would "need to explain to my parents exactly why that wasn't happening." A day later, Clinton met with her and scolded, "It's illegal to threaten the president of the United States." Their meeting ended on a happier note, but Lewinsky's job situation, not to mention her equilibrium, remained unsettled. Thanks to the Supreme Court, the Jones lawyers could send out subpoenas to anyone they chose. Clinton also knew that Lewinsky worked with Linda Tripp, who was talking to Isikoff about Kathleen Willey. In the summer of 1997, in short, Lewinsky's name could have surfaced at any moment. Still, Clinton wanted to fight the lawsuit, if only, he said, to avoid embarrassing his wife. Bennett, however, talked him into a more conciliatory position. For less than $1 million—but with no apology!—Clinton would settle the case.

In the formal complaint, Jones had demanded $700,000. In the conversation with Davis and Cammarata, Bennett said there was a possibility that the president could agree to that figure. Both in public and in private, Bennett had said that he would never agree to a settlement that the president would have to pay out of his own pocket. But Bill Clinton owned a pair of general-liability insurance policies—one with a subsidiary of Chubb and the other with State Farm—and Chubb had implied that it would pay as much as $350,000, as half of any settlement, to resolve the case. State Farm was balking at paying anything, but Bennett thought he might find a way to fund the other half. (Bennett had explored the possibility of raising money for a settlement with a close friend of the president's—Vernon Jordan.)

But there was one more thing. In her complaint, Jones had asserted that she had seen "distinguishing characteristics in Clinton's genital area" when he purportedly exposed himself to her.

Jones had signed a secret affidavit describing the characteristics. As the meeting wound down, Bennett told his adversaries, "I gotta have the affidavit. I think it's horseshit, and I want it." Bennett felt that if he could discredit the accusation about Clinton's anatomy—a subject that had drawn a great deal of amused public attention—he could cast doubt on Jones's entire case. He believed that if he could prove that there were no "characteristics" he could deny that his client had admitted anything by settling.

Bennett subsequently tried an enticement for his adversaries to produce the affidavit. "We'll show you our best evidence," he promised. Bennett was talking about the blow-job boys. He figured if Jones knew that he had unearthed Dennis Kirkland and his friends, that would spur her to settle. Bennett thought of the sex evidence as a kind of nuclear deterrent. The potential effect of its disclosure on both sides would lead both of them to the bargaining table. In a narrow sense, Bennett's strategy was sound, and it appeared to work. But in the history of the American presidency, the moment when Bill Clinton's lawyer threatened this young woman with the public airing of her alleged serial fellatio with strangers will surely rank among the less admirable chapters.

Davis said it sounded as if they were making progress. Cammarata—wiry, intense, the younger and more detail-oriented of the lawyers for Jones—said there were other conditions that had to be satisfied. Jones, he said, still wanted an apology from the president for his behavior in 1991. Never, Bennett said: "If you want ten dollars and an apology, you're not going to get it." Jones's lawyers said that they would have to check with their client but thought they might have the outline of a deal: a $700,000 payment, and a statement in which Clinton acknowledged no improper conduct by Jones, giving her a chance to accomplish her stated goal of "clearing her name."

Cammarata and Ettinger went downstairs to Ettinger's office, where they sat at his word processor and typed up the mutually acceptable language for the statement. In the key passage, the settlement said that "the parties agree that Paula Corbin Jones did not engage in any improper or sexual conduct on May 8, 1991, and that the allegations and the inferences about her published in . . . the American Spectator are false and their adverse effects on her character and reputation regrettable." The statement said Jones had done nothing wrong; thus, by omission, the lawyers fudged the issue of what Clinton had done on that day. At Ettinger's insistence, the statement also noted pointedly that "the insurers for President Clinton" would be paying the money. Close to midnight, the four men reconvened and agreed that progress had been made. Cammarata and Davis said they would call Jones for her approval in the morning.

The Jones lawyers left Bennett's office thinking the case was as good as over. They had not figured on Paula Jones's new best friend.

/ / /

As their case made its way through the courts, Paula and Stephen Jones lived a secluded and lonely existence on the other side of the country from their lawyers. On most mornings, Steve took the one family car from their home in Long Beach to his job behind the Northwest Airlines ticket counter at Los Angeles International Airport. Paula spent most days alone in their one-bedroom apartment with their two young sons. Now and then she would take the boys to a local playground. She was lonely for home in Arkansas.

Not long after the case was filed, Cindy Hays tried to get a California-based antiabortion activist named Jane Chastain to attend an event with Paula. Chastain couldn't make it, so she invited a friend of hers to take her place: Susan Carpenter-McMillan.

McMillan had a grand helmet of immobile blond hair, a bombastic manner, and a life story that seemed like a petri dish of California eccentricity. She had been born approximately fifty years before she met Paula, into the family of a Los Angeles land developer. Both her mother and her grandmother were ordained ministers in the church of Aimee Semple McPherson, the charismatic revivalist (and huckster) of prewar Southern California. McMillan had become a public figure largely though the route of confessions about her own traumas. A longtime antiabortion crusader, McMillan also disclosed in a tearful interview with the *Los Angeles Times* that she had had an abortion when she was twenty-one and was a student at the University of Southern California. She also had another abortion many years later.

Starting in about 1980, McMillan helped to create a new form of political activism. According to her business card, she was the

"Media Spokes Woman" of "The Women's Coalition," which consisted entirely of herself. Her labors were underwritten by her husband, Bill McMillan, a personal-injury attorney, and she used their palatial home, in the Republican stronghold of San Marino, as her base of operations. In earlier days, political leaders came to prominence because of their leadership of or affiliations with organizations—political parties, say, or churches or labor unions. McMillan, in contrast, took a postmodern approach to political influence and her own celebrity. Solely because she was energetic and effective on television, and because her name appeared on the Rolodexes of talk-show bookers, McMillan became a prominent public voice on such issues as abortion, chemical castration for child molesters, and conservative causes generally. Her métier was speaking, not doing. She simply had opinions on things, and she was skilled at expressing them. McMillan kept a yellow Post-it note near the glass door to her office so that she could tell visitors when she was not to be disturbed. "I am on the air," the note said. Thanks to the Jones case, she was on the air a lot.

Each room of the McMillan manse was decorated in a different color scheme: peach living room, white dining room, green den, and a hand-carved mahogany study for Bill. Statues of cherubs abounded. To be sure, it was a long way from Paula and Steve's one-bedroom in Long Beach, and after their victory in the Supreme Court, McMillan more or less adopted the couple and their two boys. McMillan wrested control of the legal fund from Cindy Hays, and she used it to start paying personal expenses for Paula and Steve—airplane tickets, boarding for their dog. McMillan got the legal fund to pay for a cellular phone for Paula, and the two women spoke up to a dozen times a day. I spent time with McMillan during this period in 1997, and I overheard her side of many of her conversations with Paula. McMillan often spoke to Jones in baby talk. "Hi, my Paula-poo," she would begin in a singsong voice, and she would conclude the chats with the recitation "I dub-boo, I dub-boo, I dub-boo." She called Paula "the little sister I never had."

McMillan reveled in her role as Jones's "Media Spokes Woman," and she realized that the key to her survival in that role was keeping Steve as well as Paula happy. (Davis and Cammarata, who did their best with the uphill task of portraying their case as nonpolitical, regarded McMillan as a menace. But they were thousands of miles away, and McMillan ignored them.) For McMillan, Paula was never a problem. The phone calls and occasional shopping trips met all of her needs. But Steve had a different agenda. He wanted money. In the summer of 1997, McMillan had an answer for him—a book deal.

Through a friendly Hollywood producer, McMillan made contact with Adrian Zackheim, an editor at HarperCollins in New York. Without telling Davis or Cammarata, McMillan invited Zackheim to meet with Paula and Steve in the restaurant of the Peninsula Hotel in Beverly Hills. On the appointed day, Zackheim arrived at the hotel, and McMillan introduced them to the couple. Paula, however, simply said hello, indicated that McMillan was authorized to speak on her behalf, and excused herself to the other room of the restaurant for the duration of Zackheim's meeting with McMillan and Steve Jones. (This peculiar arrangement was McMillan's attempt to allow Paula to answer in a deposition that she had never talked to a publisher about a book deal.) Zackheim then had the experience of listening to McMillan and Steve rage about Clinton for about three hours—without hearing a word from the putative author of the book. Not surprisingly, Zackheim and HarperCollins passed on the project.

McMillan realized that she had to put together a more polished presentation if she was going to deliver for Paula and especially Steve Jones. So she spoke to Gary Thomas, a well-known ghostwriter in the Christian book market who also ran the Center for Evangelical Spirituality, in Washington State. Thomas and McMillan knew each other from their work in the prolife movement. (He had just completed Norma McCorvey's book, a chronicle of the born-again experience of "Jane Roe" of *Roe v. Wade.*) After speaking with McMillan, Thomas produced a full-fledged proposal for a book to be entitled *Still Standing: The Inside Story of Paula Jones.*

"Paula Corbin Jones," the proposal began. "Polls show that over 90% of the public recognize her name, but this book will provide the first true and detailed account of how a young, unknown woman from Arkansas was humiliated and abused. . . . It will be an inspiring message which leaves the reader with admiration for the grit, tenacity and perseverance of a modern-day Joan of Arc."

Over the nine double-spaced pages in the proposal, Thomas did his best to mine a book's worth of material out of a ten-minute encounter in a hotel six years earlier. ("Chapter Two will take the reader, second by second, through Paula's meeting with then-Governor Clinton. With candid yet respectful language, Paula will explain the governor's conduct.") McMillan loved the proposal and called Thomas's literary agent in New York to talk strategy.

The whole book project underlined just how much Paula was a spectator to the tumult that her case produced. Steve wanted the book more than she did. McMillan wanted the case to go on more than she did. Behind Paula's back, McMillan could be withering about her. She told Thomas's literary agent, "This is not a smart cookie. There is not much going on upstairs." But smart cookie or not, McMillan told the agent that Paula had real news to disclose in the book: "We know what it looks like," McMillan said.

What what looks like? the agent replied.

The president's penis! At first McMillan wouldn't tell the agent precisely about the famous distinguishing characteristic, but at last she explained, "Well, you know, his penis isn't necessarily straight." With this kind of material, McMillan and the agent agreed that they should shoot for a $1 million advance. (Notably, many of Clinton's enemies were obsessed with the appearance of his penis. Right around this time, the elf George Conway, who had tipped Matt Drudge to the Willey story, sent an e-mail message to Drudge saying that "the distinguishing physical characteristic that Paula Jones says she believes she saw is that Clinton's penis is curved when it is erect." Drudge didn't use the item.)

/ / /

Cammarata and Davis knew nothing of the negotiations for a book by their client, and they were astonished when Paula rejected the settlement offer they had extracted from Bennett and Ettinger. Actually, Steve did most of the talking to the lawyers—and McMillan orchestrated his response. The money was acceptable, Steve said, but the language in the proposed settlement agreement was not. Steve and McMillan had two objections to the "stipulation of settlement" that Cammarata and Ettinger had written out on August 5. First, it did not include an "explicit" admission by

Clinton that he was in the room with Paula at the Excelsior. Second, the settlement did not include an "explicit" admission that he did what Paula said he did—that is, drop his pants and ask her to "kiss it."

Cammarata and Davis were apoplectic. In a series of phone calls over the next week, they made the same points over and over to Paula and Steve. The settlement was a victory for her. She would receive the full amount for which she had sued. Her demands were unreasonable. Clinton would never apologize—and there was a good chance that if the case went to trial, she would lose. Paula, Steve, and especially Susan Carpenter-McMillan wouldn't budge.

Finally, in desperation, on August 19, the two lawyers wrote an extraordinary twelve-page, single-spaced letter begging their client to accept the settlement. "We firmly believe it is the best we can ever obtain," Davis and Cammarata wrote, "and delay in acceptance will be very harmful to your interests. . . . **It is a complete victory for the interests you seek which are the redemption of your character and reputation.**" The lawyers spoke with extraordinary candor about the weaknesses of her case—"Bear in mind defendant Clinton has persuaded millions of voters he is credible"—and about the real motivations behind the case.

"You will lose all prospect of selling your sealed affidavit once that affidavit is disclosed, as it must be, to our opponents," the letter stated. (Davis and Cammarata knew that Paula and Steve wanted to sell their story—and especially Paula's assessment of the president's penis—but they didn't know the negotiations were ongoing.) "You will recall they seek its production from you now," the letter went on, "and we believe they will be successful in getting it. Once disclosed to our opponents, it is more likely to become a matter of public knowledge." In touting the secret about the president's penis to the literary agent, McMillan had demonstrated her lack of understanding of the legal process. The Jones team would have to disclose it if the case went to trial. But McMillan was right about the book's prospects if the case was settled. The market for a book from Paula would disappear—as would demand for McMillan herself on the talk-show circuit. As Davis and Cammarata were candid enough to admit, their fees already amounted to $759,870.40—more than the amount Clinton was prepared to pay. The lawyers would certainly discount their final bill, but still, the $700,000 was going to look a lot smaller after the lawyers took their cut. Not so a book deal—and that would vanish altogether if the case were to settle.

Davis and Cammarata made a canny observation toward the end of their letter. Over three years, Paula had never before asked for an apology from Clinton. "Your focus has changed from proving that you are a good person, to proving Clinton is a bad person. That was never your objective in filing suit." That was true. But destroying Clinton (and promoting herself) was Susan Carpenter-McMillan's objective from the start. In a way, the two lawyers had isolated the difference between cases based on law and those based on politics. An apology wouldn't help clear Paula's name—it would only damage Clinton's. But that was now the objective for the case.

In the midst of these tense negotiations between the lawyers and their client, on August 22, both sides had to appear in front of Judge Wright in Little Rock. (Ironically, even though the lawsuit was ultimately pending for more than four years, this brief conference would be the only public court session before her in the entire matter.) Signs of tension between Jones and her lawyers were evident in the courtroom. Moments before Judge Wright took the bench, Jones was still seated in the second row of spectators, wedged between her husband and McMillan. The parties in civil cases rarely attend pretrial proceedings, especially routine conferences like this one, but the Joneses and McMillan had flown across the country from their homes for the forty-minute court session. McMillan said later that she had brought Paula and Steve to Little Rock as a signal that they, not the lawyers, were running the plaintiff's case. McMillan also wanted the lawyers to know that she remained Paula's closest adviser. When Davis and Cammarata took their seats at the counsel table, McMillan had to nudge Paula to go sit with them.

Wright ran the conference with relaxed confidence as she ticked off the matters that needed to be resolved before trial. In a written ruling issued that day, in response to a motion by the defense to throw the case out, Wright had dismissed only one of Jones's counts. The judge ruled that the trial would go forward on Jones's claim of conspiracy to deprive her of civil rights and on her claim of intentional infliction of emotional distress, but she dismissed Jones's claim that Clinton had defamed her. Wright also let stand Jones's defamation case against Danny Ferguson. Now, the judge asked, what about a schedule for trial?

Bennett asked for an early trial date—in January 1998—as if to prove that Clinton had nothing to fear. The judge consulted her calendar and found that she wouldn't have time for the trial until May. Looking morose and saying little, Cammarata consented. The defense asked for a jury of twelve, not six. A unanimous jury was required in cases such as this, and Bennett assumed that it would be difficult to put together a jury of a dozen Arkansans willing to rule against their most celebrated native son. When the hearing ended, Jones ignored her lawyers and rushed back to join her husband and McMillan.

Even before the courtroom cleared, Cammarata approached Mitch Ettinger with an urgent question: "Is the insurance gone? Is it gone?" Clinton's lawyers said that it probably was. Cammarata knew that under the terms of Clinton's Chubb and State Farm policies the companies were technically obligated to pay for Clinton's defense only on certain counts against him, and now the judge had dismissed the pertinent part of the case. As Cammarata expected—and as Bennett confirmed with the insurance companies shortly after the hearing—both companies now refused to contribute to a settlement, or even to pay Bennett's future fees. Bennett would later persuade the insurance companies to remain in the case, but Wright's order only dimmed whatever lingering chance of a settlement had remained.

After the hearing, Davis and Cammarata made several more fruitless phone calls to Paula and Steve, asking them to reconsider their opposition to the settlement. On August 29, the two lawyers sent another long and detailed letter to Jones. It began by noting that "serious differences have arisen between us" and announced that "we believe these differences are so basic as to make it necessary for us to withdraw as your counsel as a consequence of your refusal to agree to a settlement." They warned that "our opponents may portray your refusal as a money-grubbing attempt to further develop this story for profitable book rights, and portray you as inspired and under the influence of right-wing Clinton-haters."

This, indeed, summed up Davis and Cammarata's own view of their client at this point. "A perception of greed and hatred on your part will lose the public relations battle for your good name which your lawyers have worked long and hard to build up."

In September 1997—three years after the case was filed and nine months before it was scheduled to go to trial—Paula Jones had to find herself new lawyers. Susan Carpenter-McMillan took charge of the search.

/ / /

"Hello?"

Linda Tripp answered the phone at 10:23 P.M. on September 18, 1997.

"Linda?" asked Lucianne Goldberg.

"Hi."

"Hi, dear, how are you?"

"Thanks for calling," said Tripp.

"That's all right," Goldberg answered.

"I, uh, number one, didn't expect you to, necessarily, and I wouldn't have blamed you if you hadn't."

"Oh, why not?" the agent asked.

"Oh, I know that it was an awkward situation," Tripp replied, "and then I, in retrospect, feel very badly about it."

It had been more than a year since Tripp pulled out of her book project with Goldberg. Tripp had already started taking notes of her conversations with Lewinsky, and she knew what a sensational story she had. Sheepishly, she had approached Tony Snow once again and asked him if Goldberg remained too mad at her to resume their plans for a book. Snow's call to Goldberg prompted this call to Tripp—which Goldberg taped.

Goldberg and Tripp spoke three times in September 1997—the agent taped two of the calls—and the transcripts rank among the most extraordinary documents in the entire saga of the Clinton scandals. In many ways, these conversations built a template that the rest of the scandal followed.

First, though, Tripp had to explain why she had gotten back in touch. "I wanted to chat with you about something that is—is completely ridiculous," Tripp began. "Um, last September, a young lady who shall remain nameless for the time being took me in as her confidante, and, as it turns out, she had been a, quote, 'girl-friend of the Big Creep.'"

"Mmm," Goldberg purred.

"For—and still is," Tripp went on.

"Mm-hmm."

"Uh, she was twenty-one and an intern when it started."

Tripp then gave a brief summary of the Clinton-Lewinsky relationship, noting, "I've just written down dates, times, phone calls. He's heavy into phone sex." She explained that the pair generally met on Sundays in the White House, after the unnamed woman was cleared in by Clinton's secretary. (Goldberg was fascinated by the details, saying at one point, "Do you think there's a taping system in the Oval Office? . . . The slurping sounds would be deafening.")

Regarding the former intern, Tripp said, "This is so explosive, it makes the other thing [her previous book idea] pale."

Goldberg understood the stakes, but she seems to have had a brief pang of conscience, if only for the benefit of her tape recorder. (Much later, Goldberg jauntily dismissed criticism about the ethics of her tape-recording a friend, writing in an article in *Slate*, "Note to anyone who calls me after closing time: Expect to be taped. It's legal and it saves me pawing around my night table for paper and a pen." All true—except that it was Goldberg who called Tripp.) "The publicity might destroy her and you," Goldberg told Tripp. "I mean, I love the idea. I would run with it in a second. But do you want to be the instrument of this kid, really, um—"

The answer was vintage Tripp. "Well, let's—let me give you some history. She is from Beverly Hills. She, uh, had a very privileged upbringing. She's not a naïve. I mean, she's definitely sophisticated. Um, she was not a victim. Um, she's had affairs with married men before." In other words, who cared if Lewinsky was destroyed if it would help Tripp's book project?

For a moment, it seemed, Goldberg forgot that she was a book agent as well as a political provocateur, and she proposed, "Is there any way to have, uh, this Ms. X . . . shall we say reached by the Paula Jones people?" Even though Tripp hadn't said anything about sexual harassment, Goldberg knew that "Ms. X" could prove to be an asset to the Jones lawyers. No, Tripp said, Lewinsky wouldn't agree to help the Jones team, and anyway, Tripp reminded Goldberg to keep her eye on their book project—which was, after all, the reason she had resumed contact in the first place.

"I had just scrubbed my whole Maggie [Gallagher] product and started from scratch and come up with a whole different spin"— this one centered around Lewinsky, Tripp explained. But Goldberg was worried that Tripp would look like a "nut case" if she went public before the unnamed woman did. So she suggested leaking the story to Mike Isikoff and then writing the book.

This was where the stories, in all their gothic complexity, began to merge. Responding to the suggestion that she leak to Isikoff, Tripp said, "Oh, I could do that in a minute." His story about Willey had just run a few weeks earlier. But there was a problem with this strategy. "But then he'd write the book," Tripp explained. "He'd write the whole thing."

Goldberg, thinking of *Newsweek,* interjected, "No, he only has a certain amount of space."

"Oh, no," Tripp replied. "He's working on a book deal. He's doing an all-the-president's-women kind of thing." According to Isikoff, Tripp was wrong: Isikoff and Simpson had agreed to drop their book idea more than a month earlier, and all his reporting on Tripp and Willey in 1997 was for *Newsweek.* Isikoff did write a book on Clinton, but he said the project didn't get under way until a few months later. But Tripp factored into her plans that Isikoff was a potential competitor in the Clinton sex book market. (Of course, this scheming about book projects was taking place at the same time as Susan Carpenter-McMillan was courting publishers with promises that Paula Jones would deliver the precise dimensions of the president's penis.)

What to do amid this tangle of motives? For the moment, Tripp and Goldberg resolved to give Isikoff enough of the story to cloak it with the respectability of *Newsweek,* but they would omit enough so that Tripp could write her own book. Goldberg could scarcely contain her excitement, saying, "I'm very interested in this, needless to say . . ."

"Well, I'm glad," Tripp answered

". . . my tabloid heart beats loud," Goldberg concluded.

/ / /

A few days later, in a conversation that (ironically) Goldberg did not record, she first suggested that Tripp tape her own telephone conversations with the still unnamed young paramour of the president's. Tripp's notes were fine, Goldberg said, but the only way anyone would believe that the relationship actually took place would be if the woman said so in her own words. In a third conversation, on September 29, which Goldberg did tape, the agent raised the issue once again. "I checked that out. One-party taping is fine . . . it's fine. There's no problem with that," Goldberg said. The agent had received bad legal advice—she said later it came from a journalist friend. Unlike in New York, one-party taping was not legal in Maryland, where Tripp lived. But Tripp, who had a lawyer at the time, did not think to ask anyone except her literary agent, and after this talk, she went out and bought a voice-activated tape recorder at Radio Shack. (Later, when Tripp became a reviled public figure because of her taping of Lewinsky, she justified her behavior by asserting that she was just "protecting herself" in the face of Lewinsky's demands that she lie under oath. The tapes of Tripp's conversations with Goldberg demonstrate just how preposterous Tripp's explanation was. In the fall of 1997, Tripp had not been subpoenaed for anything, so Lewinsky couldn't have asked her to lie under oath. The Goldberg tapes showed that Tripp taped Lewinsky for simple reasons—to gather material for a book and to help destroy a president she despised.)

As Goldberg and Tripp weighed their next steps in this third conversation of September, the possibility of a competing Isikoff book remained. Tripp told Goldberg that she had hedged when Isikoff asked whether she was writing a book. According to Tripp, Isikoff suggested that they could cooperate in pursuing their respective studies of the president's sex life. Quoting Isikoff, Tripp said, "And he said, 'Well, in the present climate, I doubt you'd find a publisher. . . . But if I were to, uh, work with you and, you know, allow some of this to get out into the mainstream media, then that would set you up for a'—which is precisely what you and I had talked about."

"Right," Goldberg agreed. They had indeed discussed just this plan in their first conversation of the month.

If events unfolded as Tripp said they did, this would be dubious ethical territory for the reporter. In the book that he did write on the case, which was entitled *Uncovering Clinton,* Isikoff claimed that Tripp "invented" this conversation with him and said it was "ridiculous" to think he would have settled for just part of the story. Tripp was obviously not lying about her own interest in writing a book. Tripp told me that she did not invent the conversation.

And Goldberg, for her part, continued to behave as if Tripp and Isikoff were in cahoots. She also wanted a few more details about the sex between Clinton and the former intern. (G: "It's just blow jobs?" T: "It's not just. It's also been, to the extent that both of them are exposed totally . . . he'll like press it to almost penetration." G: "This poor woman. She must be going out of her mind.") Finally, Goldberg asked Tripp to set a meeting so both of them could dribble out a few details to Isikoff and launch Lewinsky's name into the mainstream news media. Tripp agreed. "It does twist me in knots," Tripp explained. "And every day that I have to listen to her, I keep thinking, 'The bastard should be exposed.'"

/ / /

Tripp set up the meeting between herself, Goldberg, and Isikoff in cloak-and-dagger fashion. She gave Isikoff the code name "Harvey" and Goldberg the moniker "New York." At six o'clock on the evening of October 6, the trio assembled at the Washington apartment of Lucianne's son Jonah. In his book, Isikoff—who at this point had spent a half decade investigating Bill Clinton's sex life and who was about to learn the name of the former White House intern who was the president's lover—asserted that he regarded this meeting as no big deal. "The issue that was much more on my mind at that moment," Isikoff wrote, "was the latest on the campaign finance scandal."

The October 6 meeting marked the third important moment in the case when Clinton's enemies used Isikoff to launch attacks about the president's purported sexual behavior. First, Cliff Jackson had given him the exclusive with Paula Jones; second, Joe Cammarata had set the reporter on the trail of Kathleen Willey; now, finally, Tripp and Goldberg were giving him the biggest story of all. In each of these cases, Clinton's accusers could have made the charges themselves; but as the ill-fated Jones press conference of February 1994 showed, the news media tended to discount direct accusations. Better, instead, to feed the charges to an interested reporter. This did carry a risk. Some journalists might have discounted the allegations, or, more likely, they might have focused more on the motives of the accusers than on the accusations themselves. But Jackson, Cammarata, Goldberg, and Tripp had invested their time and efforts in Michael Isikoff wisely. While he did note their roles and motivations in his articles, he reported their allegations in great detail, giving them full exposure in the national media, as they wanted.

For the meeting in Jonah's apartment, Tripp had brought two samples of her tapes along with her. She volunteered to play them for Isikoff, who was somewhat rushed because he had to appear on CNBC's talk show *Hardball*. But the reporter had a fair question: "What good is it going to do to hear a voice if I don't know whose it is?" This was the question that Isikoff had been asking Tripp since April, when she first told him about the former intern. "Tripp hesitated," Isikoff recounted. "She looked at Goldberg, who seemed to nod."

"Okay," Tripp said. "Her name is Monica Lewinsky."

Isikoff started taking notes as Tripp began giving him the outline of Lewinsky's relationship with the president. The idea that the president had promised Lewinsky a job back at the White House interested Isikoff. Could he call some sources there to check it out? Tripp said no. She feared that Isikoff's snooping would get back to Lewinsky, who would then realize that Tripp had betrayed her confidences. Isikoff could not follow up at all on the leads that Tripp and Goldberg were giving him.

So what about the tapes? Tripp said there was no "smoking gun" in these conversations, but did Isikoff want to hear them? All of those present agree that Isikoff did not listen to the tapes, although they remembered his reasons differently. Goldberg asserts that Isikoff had to make a television appearance and simply ran out of time. Isikoff himself says the fact that Tripp taped Lewinsky without her consent troubled him, and that he feared becoming "part of the process" of her ongoing taping of her young friend. An internal FBI memo of Tripp's version of the facts says, "Isikoff refused to listen to the tapes for 'ethical' reasons, but suggested that Tripp make additional tapes"—a charge that Isikoff denies. Asked in the grand jury whether Isikoff actually discussed making more tapes, Tripp said, "I don't know that Mike Isikoff did. I mean, he encouraged me to continue my taping. He didn't say create more tapes as did Lucy, but it was understood that clearly I needed to document what I was trying to document." Moreover, Goldberg promised Isikoff that he could see courier receipts of Lewinsky's gifts to the president—because the agent had arranged for Tripp to propose that Lewinsky use a company that was run by one of Goldberg's relatives. In any event, the meeting ended with everyone agreeing to stay in touch.

But something important had occurred as well. Up to this point, the three important narratives of the story—the Starr investigation, the Jones case, and the Clinton-Lewinsky relationship—had existed separately from one another. But now two of them were about to be joined. As the fall of 1997 wound down, Tripp would continue taping, Isikoff would keep monitoring her progress, and Lucianne Goldberg would make sure that the lawyers for Paula Jones knew all about Monica Lewinsky.

8

"Good Strong Christian Men"

On the morning of September 9, John Whitehead opened *The Washington Post* on his Virginia estate and discovered that Paula Jones needed new lawyers. A darkly handsome man of Bill Clinton's age, Whitehead never read newspapers out of idle curiosity. When he saw the right kind of story, Whitehead jumped.

Whitehead represented a fusion of the diverse forces that had shaped his unlikely life. A working-class kid from Peoria, he drifted through the sixties with a joint in one hand and a beer in the other. He wrote for alternative papers, shrugged his way through the University of Arkansas Law School (where he met a young professor named Clinton), and graduated from pot to cocaine and LSD. He played *Sgt. Pepper* every day. Then, in 1974, he accepted Jesus Christ as his personal savior and turned his life around—mostly.

From the day he was born again, Whitehead devoted his professional life to the burgeoning Christian-right political movement, but he never entirely abandoned his antiestablishment roots, either. In 1982, he founded the Rutherford Institute, a conservative public interest law firm based in Charlottesville, Virginia, named to honor an obscure seventeenth-century Scottish cleric who had argued for the primacy of God's law over man's. By the mid-nineties, Rutherford had a staff of fifty, a budget of more than $4 million a year, and a network of cooperating attorneys around the country. (The model was Thurgood Marshall's NAACP Legal Defense Fund.) The institute never made its name on one big case, but Whitehead attached himself to scores of smaller fights for his favorite causes—against evolution in schools, for prayer in schools, and for home schooling. (For his part, Whitehead didn't belong to any church and instead conducted religious observances for his family at home.)

The Rutherford Institute had once done legal work for Jerry Falwell's Liberty University but, more recently, had feuded with Pat Robertson. Whitehead's agenda seemed more personal than political. Except for the cases it actually litigated, the Rutherford Institute appeared to exist mostly to promote its founder, who was paid nearly $200,000 a year. Rutherford paid to broadcast Whitehead's radio commentaries (*Freedom Under Fire*) and to promote his speeches, and the institute even distributed copies of the United States Constitution with Whitehead's picture on the cover. Whitehead never lost his taste for rock and roll, and the institute published a slick glossy magazine called *Gadfly,* edited by his son, which included decidedly nonsectarian articles on people like Frank Zappa and Patti Smith. Whitehead wasn't above recalling a little counterculture poetry to make his points. For example, Whitehead shared many Clinton critics' abiding interest in the distinguishing-characteristic issue, and the lawyer took to announcing that the president would have to submit to a physical examination to settle the issue. "Someone is not telling the truth in this case," he said. "And, you know, it's like the Bob Dylan song when he says, 'Even the president of the United States sometimes must have to stand naked.'" In truth, Whitehead was as much publicity hound as partisan. (He did, however, come to share the obligatory fear of being murdered that came with being a Clinton adversary; after taking the Jones case, Whitehead bought a remote-control starter for his car, to detonate bombs before he got too close.)

Whitehead knew of Susan Carpenter-McMillan from the pro-life movement. After he saw the story in the *Post,* he decided to give her a call and tell her he had a lawyer in mind for her case. Like almost every lawyer who represented Paula Jones over her long legal battle, Whitehead had other priorities besides his client—himself, the movement, his press clippings.

/ / /

When Whitehead called McMillan, he told her the Rutherford Institute would agree to underwrite litigation costs for the lawsuit—lawyer travel, copying, the preparation of deposition transcripts—but would not pay the legal fees themselves. This wouldn't necessarily pose a problem, because he had some lawyers in mind for Jones who would agree to handle the case on a contingency-fee basis. Like Davis and Cammarata, the new lawyers would not ask for anything up front—and unlike their departed predecessors, they were anxious to wage war on the president no matter what the cost. The new team would be led by a Texas lawyer named Donovan Campbell, Jr. McMillan invited Campbell and a few of his colleagues to come to Los Angeles and meet with Paula and Steve to see if they made a good fit. (The conservative activist and frequent talk-show guest Ann Coulter had volunteered earlier, but she lacked the resources to take on Bob Bennett and his troops at Skadden Arps.) In a press conference in front of Susan Carpenter-McMillan's home on October 1, it was announced that Paula was now represented by the firm of Rader, Campbell, Fisher and Pyke, of Dallas, Texas.

Don Campbell served on the board of directors of the Rutherford Institute, but he could scarcely have differed more from John Whitehead in temperament or disposition. Whereas Whitehead had a laid-back, almost libertarian approach to politics, Campbell practiced a punitive, judgmental brand of law. He was renowned in Dallas for leading a long and successful effort to reinstate the Texas sodomy law after it was found unconstitutional, and for picketing performances of *Torch Song Trilogy* at a local theater. He abhorred homosexuality and adultery—and Bill Clinton.

With discovery deadlines looming, Campbell and his colleagues entered the case just in time. Indeed, for a few harrowing days at the end of September, Jones had had no lawyers at all. So Jones had had to act by herself at one critical moment in the case. "Where is it?" Mitch Ettinger had been demanding of his adversaries for weeks. "We need to see it," Bob Bennett insisted. In the confusion following Davis and Cammarata's departure, though, the Jones team had never supplied a piece of evidence that Clinton's lawyers had been seeking for more than three years.

Then, at 5:55 P.M. on September 29, 1997, Paula Jones herself had finally answered these demands with a two-page fax sent from her home. The cover page was written in her own flowery hand.

Mr. Robert S. Bennett
Skadden, Arps
fax #202-xxx-xxxx

Dear Mr. Bennett,
Here is the affidavit you requested. I just received a copy of this today from Mr. Cammarata. Before today, I did not have the original of this copy.

Paula C. Jones

The second page read as follows:

AFFIDAVIT

State of Virginia;
County of Fairfax, to wit:

I, Paula Corbin Jones, after being duly sworn, state as follows:

1. I am the plaintiff in the case of Paula Corbin Jones versus William Jefferson Clinton and Danny Ferguson, Civil Action No. LR-C-94-290, pending in the United States District Court for the Eastern District of Arkansas.

2. In the Complaint, paragraph 22, in Civil Action No. LR-C-94-290 I allege that there were distinguishing characteristics in William Clinton's genital area that were obvious to me.

3. I briefly observed the erect penis of William Jefferson Clinton in a hotel suite of the Excelsior Hotel on May 8, 1991. That is the only time I have seen his genital area, and I have never had it described to me by anyone, nor have I read anything on that subject.

4. Mr. Clinton's penis was circumcised and seemed to me to be rather short and thin. I would describe its appearance as seeming to be five to five and one-half inches, or less, in length, and having a circumference of the approximate size of a quarter, or perhaps very slightly larger.

5. The shaft of the penis was bent or "crooked" from Mr. Clinton's right to left, or from an observer's left to right if the observer is facing Mr. Clinton. In other words, the base of Mr. Clinton's penis, to an observer facing Mr. Clinton, would be further to the left of the observer than the head of the penis.

Paula Corbin Jones

Joe Cammarata had prepared the affidavit with Jones shortly after she filed her lawsuit. Robert C. Lockhart, Jr., a notary public in Cammarata's law office in northern Virginia, had recorded that the affidavit was signed on May 26, 1994. Perhaps noting the magnitude of the historical moment, the notary had written in the time as well: "10:15 A.M. (EDT)."

Clinton's lawyers read the document with amusement—how could one not?—but also with relief. Anticipating the release of the affidavit, Bennett had had the surreal experience of questioning the president of the United States about what his erect penis looked like. Counsel had been assured that there was nothing out of the ordinary, and this information had been corroborated by Clinton's urologist, Dr. Kevin O'Connell, of Bethesda Naval Hospital. But if Jones had made some truly exotic claim, like a distinctive birthmark, it might have led to a great deal of embarrassing litigation on this unseemly topic. The information in the affidavit did not suggest anything terribly out of the ordinary, and Bennett thought that the judge—and even Jones's new lawyers—would finally leave this doleful subject alone.

But Bob Bennett was wrong about his new adversaries. Don Campbell and company did not wish to let go of the subject of Bill Clinton's penis—and that foretold a great deal about the future course of the Paula Jones case.

On the very first day that Campbell's team took over as Jones's new lawyers, they submitted a new set of interrogatories to the president. These are questions that the defendant is required to answer in writing, under oath. Campbell asked: "Please state the name, address, and telephone number of each and every medical doctor who has performed any surgery or medical procedure on your genitalia at any time after May 8, 1991."

In other words, the Jones lawyers were suggesting that, as a litigation tactic in the Jones case, Clinton had undergone surgery to change the appearance of his penis.

Another question demanded, "Please state the name, address, and telephone number of each and every individual (other than Hillary Rodham Clinton) with whom you had sexual relations when you held any of the following positions: a. Attorney General of the State of Arkansas; b. Governor of the State of Arkansas; c. President of the United States."

Not surprisingly, Clinton refused to answer both questions, replying that the questions had "been propounded solely to harass, embarrass and humiliate the President and the Office he occupies." Privately, the Clinton team began referring to their new adversaries in Texas as the Branch Davidians.

These intrusive demands for information established the plaintiff's legal strategy for the remainder of the case. The Dallas lawyers would largely ignore the facts of Paula Jones's alleged encounter with the president at the Excelsior Hotel. They also ignored the client herself and her meddling husband. Jones's new lawyers instructed her to drop her book plans, which had been the subject of embarrassing leaks that fall, and simply to remain silent pending the trial. Instead, Campbell's team decided to focus almost exclusively on Bill Clinton's sexual history. There was a nominal justification for this strategy—Campbell said at the time, "His custom, pattern, and practice of harassment is clearly relevant to the legal issues in the case." In fact, the relevance of Clinton's prior sexual history was a debatable legal point, but at this stage the Jones lawyers had virtual carte blanche to question anyone about almost anything they wanted. It was an opportunity Clinton's enemies had been seeking for more than a decade—an open-ended fishing expedition, with subpoena power, into every rumor that had ever been told about Bill Clinton.

The Jones lawyers worked, in effect, as the legatees of Gary Aldrich, the former FBI agent whose memoir made the cultural critique of the Clinton presidency. The Jones lawsuit was based on the concept of "harassment," but in the fall of 1997 Campbell made no distinctions between women who were alleged to have had consensual encounters with Clinton and those who charged that he had made unwanted advances. To track down Clinton's sexual history, the Rader Campbell firm retained Rick and Beverly Lambert, a husband-and-wife team of private investigators. Some, like the singer Gennifer Flowers, whose accusations nearly ended Clinton's campaign in 1992 and who later wrote two books about her relationship with him, agreed to testify willingly. So did Dolly Kyle Browning, a Texas woman who wrote a self-published novel based on a purported romance with Clinton. Many more women fought the subpoenas, filing affidavits with Judge Wright saying that they had no information relevant to the case. Kathleen Willey went to court near her home in Virginia in an unsuccessful effort to avoid being ordered to give a deposition. (At the same time, in keeping with the spirit of the case, Willey made her own efforts to retain a literary agent and write a book about her encounter with Clinton. She ultimately demurred on her book project.)

But the Lamberts kept after their sexual investigation of the president, and they made their greatest effort to secure the testimony of a woman named Juanita Broaddrick. Her name had first surfaced in political circles during Clinton's last Arkansas gubernatorial campaign, in 1990, when there were rumors that she was going to accuse Clinton of raping her in the late 1970s. As of the fall of 1997, though her name had never made it into the respectable press, Broaddrick became a kind of holy grail. True, the alleged assault was so remote in time that Judge Wright would probably never allow the accusation to be aired in court, but if a deposition could be taken and then leaked, the plaintiff's team could accomplish their goal—damaging Bill Clinton, if not helping Paula Jones.

/ / /

"Are you Juanita Broaddrick?"
"Uh-huh."

"Ms. Broaddrick, my name is Beverly Lambert. I'm a private investigator. This is Rick. Could we talk to you for a few moments?"

"No, no, you can't. What's this about?"

"We're doing an investigation, working for the attorneys who are representing Paula Jones."

"That's what I thought. No, I don't want to talk to you."

Shortly after they were retained in the case, the Lamberts made their way to the small town of Van Buren, Arkansas, where Juanita Broaddrick lived. Their initial conversation with her was tape-recorded, and the transcript offers some revealing clues about their approach to their work and a woman who would eventually play a role of considerable importance in the Clinton saga.

Broaddrick said she had been pursued for years by reporters and "I just had to try and evade all of this." Her memories of Clinton were "not pleasant. . . . It's very private. We're talking about something twenty years ago."

Rick tried another tack. "Do you feel in your mind that Paula Jones . . . ?"

"Oh, she's telling the truth. . . . Anything she would say bad about him, she's telling the truth," Broaddrick replied.

Rick picked up the thought. "All of the attorneys we are working for are good strong Christian men, and they are taking it with the risk of knowing what could happen, and we are, too. We've already been warned about the dangers and what could happen." Even in private settings like this one, the myth of the Clinton hit teams surfaced.

"We're Christians," Beverly explained.

"You're a Christian?" Rick asked.

"Yeah," Broaddrick answered.

"The reason we took the case," Rick went on, "the reason those attorneys took the case, this is a law firm that is all Christians."

"There's just no way I can get on the witness stand and tell that," Broaddrick said with some finality. Then she referred the Lamberts to her attorney, who was also an Arkansas state senator.

"Is he a Democrat or a Republican senator?" Rick asked.

"Republican."

"Good," the investigator said.

Broaddrick stuck with her refusal to tell her story to the Jones team and filed a sworn affidavit stating, "I do not have any information to offer regarding a nonconsensual or unwelcome sexual advance by Mr. Clinton." She also gave a sworn deposition to the same effect. Broaddrick would later recant both of these statements and assert that Clinton had raped her.

Beverly Lambert certainly thought they were on the right track. Not long after their interview of Broaddrick, Beverly told me later, she saw a "black helicopter" circling over her family's farm, outside Tyler, Texas. Because the Lamberts regarded the helicopter as the prelude to a White House–sponsored assault to obtain their files from the Jones case, they promptly moved the records to a more secure location.

The pious murmurs of Campbell and the Lamberts had a different sound from the ribald prattle of Tripp and Goldberg, but they merely represented the sacred and profane sides of the same coin. As the end of 1997 drew near, the literary team on the East Coast and the legal team in Dallas had reached much the same conclusions—that the Jones case represented the best way to hasten Clinton's destruction. For the lawyers, their weapon was the subpoena; for the agent and putative author, their tool was the fragile psyche of one Monica Lewinsky.

/ / /

"You know what I just want to say to him?" Monica Lewinsky asked her friend Linda Tripp. "I just want to be like—you know what I think? I just have to say this. Okay?"

"What?" said Tripp.

"The most pathetic commentary on this entire relationship is that it will be two years next month, and I have no clue how he feels about me. . . ."

"I think you have a lot of information," Tripp answered. "You have to sort through what you feel resonates to you. I think—I think there is no one outside of you and him who can really determine what level of emotion was there. . . ."

And so the conversations went, for hour after droning hour. There were few better measures of Tripp's dedication to her book research and Clinton-hating than the simple fact that she tolerated Lewinsky's inane chatter for so long. Their talks occasionally drifted into areas like dieting and hair care, but mostly focused on a few themes: Monica's desire to leave the Pentagon for a new job at the White House; her uncertainty about Clinton's feelings for her; her resentment of the women who had succeeded in getting access to him; her frustration with Betty Currie for failing to engineer more frequent contact between her and the president. Yet despite the endless repetitions and slight variations on these leitmotifs, Tripp remained a rapt audience. "Now, listen to me," she said at one point. "If you get a call [from Clinton] tonight, I don't care what time it is, will you please call me?" On another day, Lewinsky made a rare inquiry about Tripp's life. "Oh, please tell me about your weekend," Monica offered. But Tripp would have none of it, answering, "Wait a minute. Come on, come on, come on. So what about Betty? What is Betty saying?"

Tripp posed in these conversations as a sort of wise aunt—commiserating, consoling, concentrating, as she often said, on "what's best for you." She expressed disdain for Clinton's behavior, but she also advised Monica on preserving her relationship with him. "You know," Tripp mused at one point, "I have to say this because I've thought about it a lot recently. If he for one minute considered someone doing this to his daughter—"

"Yeah, exactly," Lewinsky jumped in. "I thought the same thing, you know? I know. What would you tell your daughter to do?"

"Yeah, exactly," Tripp replied. "In fact, that's a question you might want to ask him. I mean, he would die rather than let this happen to Chelsea, but you're supposed to be a stoic soldier." ("Sigh," the Starr transcript advises.) "Some fifty-year-old man decides to have an intimate relationship with his [deleted] daughter, and then she—oh, it defies imagination. Well, who would want to with her?" (That last line, disparaging Chelsea's appearance, was an especially rich Tripp touch.)

For all the whining, though, Tripp and Goldberg, who were speaking to each other often during this period, made clever use of the conversations to close the vise on Clinton. For her part, Lewinsky still entertained dreams of resuming her relationship with the president. On September 30, 1997—the day before Donovan Campbell officially took over the Jones case—Lewinsky wrote Clinton a jokey memo in an effort to wangle an invitation to see him. Heading it "Memorandum for: Handsome; Subject: The New Deal," Lewinsky wrote that they had not visited or spoken in six weeks. She promised that she "will be on my best behavior and not stressed out when I come (to see you, that is)." She concluded by comparing herself to one of her presidential forebears. "Oh, and remember," Lewinsky wrote, "FDR would never have turned down a visit from Lucy Mercer!" Clinton did call Lewinsky late that evening, when, she testified later, they "possibly" had phone sex, but they also discussed the possibility that she might return to the White House. It was now ten months into the president's second term, and Lewinsky was no closer to returning to the White House than she had been when she was evicted a year and a half earlier. Monica was primed for disappointment, and on October 6, Linda Tripp dashed her hopes once and for all.

In a conversation taped on the afternoon that she and Goldberg would later meet with Isikoff, Tripp called Monica at the Pentagon and told her that she had no chance of ever returning to the White House. Tripp's friend "Kate" at the NSC had made it clear: Monica would remain persona non grata. Lewinsky later testified that this news from Tripp was "the straw that broke the camel's back." Tripp stoked her friend's anger and insisted that Clinton be made to pay for all the disruption he had caused in her life. On the telephone that evening, Tripp helped Lewinsky draft a letter to the president in which she demanded that he help her find a job, preferably in New York, where Monica's mother was moving. On the telephone, Lewinsky read a draft of her letter to the president: "'I'd like to ask you to secure a position for me.'"

"Right," Tripp said.

"Okay, fine . . . but you know, I don't know," Lewinsky jumped in, suddenly irritated. "Maybe I'm being an idiot. I don't want to have to work for this position."

"Say that again," Tripp replied.

"I want it to be given to me," said Lewinsky, displaying her sense of entitlement.

"Right," Tripp agreed. "You don't want to go through the whole interview process."

This conversation captured the first moment in what would become an important new chapter of the story—the president's role in Lewinsky's job hunt in New York. Indeed, in his impeachment trial, one of the main charges against Clinton was that he tried to buy Lewinsky's silence with a job in New York. Yet the record in the case shows that Tripp instigated this entire episode under false pretenses: Tripp had lied to Monica about her conversation with "Kate." In interviews with Starr's investigators, Kate Friedrich of the National Security Council denied ever telling Tripp that Lewinsky would never get a job at the White House; indeed, Friedrich had never even heard of Lewinsky until the story broke in 1998. Tripp had fabricated this "last straw" in Lewinsky's White House job hunt so that her young friend would start making new demands for the president to find her a different job. Had Tripp told Lewinsky the truth, the former intern might never have reached out to Vernon Jordan, Bill Richardson, and, of course, Bill Clinton in an effort to find a job in New York.

And as Tripp nudged Lewinsky to increase her demands on her former paramour, she made certain that the young woman continued to use the Goldberg family courier service. Apropos of nothing in particular one day, Tripp volunteered, "You're using a very reliable and reputable courier service." In the middle of October, Tripp called Isikoff with a message to call "New York." Isikoff did call Lucianne Goldberg, who, in turn, instructed him to call Jeff Harshman, the proprietor of Speed Service. At Goldberg's urging, Harshman showed Isikoff the receipts from the occasions when Betty Currie or her designee had signed for Monica Lewinsky's letters to the White House.

/ / /

As her dream of a White House job faded, Lewinsky's hold on reality seemed to go with it. She would call Betty Currie and Bayani Nelvis, one of Clinton's Navy stewards, as many as a dozen times a day to ask about the president's whereabouts. By this means, Lewinsky kept almost minute-by-minute tabs on Clinton's activities—all in the hope that there would be time for a phone call or visit between them. When she couldn't see him, Lewinsky would materialize in crowds at the White House and even plant herself along the routes of his motorcade, including his trips to church on Sunday mornings. Much later, during Clinton's impeachment trial, the question of whether Lewinsky was a stalker or a girlfriend became important. But that was a false choice. Lewinsky was both—a genuine, if occasional, sexual partner as well as an obsessed, unhinged fan.

In her dealings with the president, Lewinsky alternated between haughty presumption and abject whining. On October 16, she sent a package by courier to the president with a letter about her job prospects. "I am open to suggestions that you may have on work that . . . may intrigue me," the twenty-three-year-old wrote to the president. "The most important things to me are that I am engaged and interested in my work. I am not someone's administrative/executive assistant, and my salary can provide me a comfortable living in New York." She suggested a handful of advertising agencies, public relations firms, and media outlets ("anything at George magazine") that she regarded as acceptable. Earlier, when she had said she wanted to move to New York, Clinton had thought of finding her something with Bill Richardson, the ambassador to the United Nations. Betty Currie passed the idea to John Podesta, then the deputy chief of staff, who spoke to Richardson. After she had expressed some initial interest in the UN, Lewinsky changed her mind, writing in the same letter to Clinton that "I want a job where I feel challenged, engaged, and interested. I don't think the UN is the right place for me." Following up on the letter, Lewinsky also mentioned that she thought his friend Vernon Jordan might be able to come up with something for her in New York. Lewinsky later testified that Tripp had given her the idea of mentioning Jordan to Clinton.

Richardson, not knowing that Lewinsky had cooled on the idea of working for him, called her to set up an interview. To her surprise, the interview with Richardson, which took place at the Watergate Hotel, went well. (The night before the interview, Clinton called Lewinsky and, she later testified, "we talked about some of the different issues at the UN, and he gave me some suggestions of things I could say.") Thanks to a tip from Tripp, Isikoff arranged for the dining room of the hotel to be staked out by another *Newsweek* reporter, so he could see how the president was setting up his girlfriend with a job, but he missed Lewinsky as she walked to the elevators. For Monica, the good interview with Richardson was bad news. She took to wailing to Tripp about the injustice of Clinton's having forced her to apply for a job she did not want. In response, Tripp gave Lewinsky word-for-word instructions on how she should ask Clinton for help. "Well, when you do speak to him and he tries to snow you about the UN," Tripp said one day, "I think you just have to say, 'I really don't want to be seen as unappreciative. That's not the case. But I—I cannot work for the government anymore.... My experience with the government has been hellacious. It's been enough to last two lifetimes.'" Starr's transcripts of their conversations barely do them justice.

> LEWINSKY: I'm so frustrated and I'm so—I was trying to keep so many things in check. (*Crying.*)
> TRIPP: I know.
> L: And it's too hard. (*Crying.*)
> T: I know. But if it's any consolation . . .
> L: (*Crying.*) But, Linda, you have no idea how hurt I am that I'm not going back.
> T: I know.
> L: (*Crying.*) You have no idea.
> T: It's the worst. It's the worst. I know that . . . but your—your situation was grossly unfair. It was horrible, horrible. And then to think for a year that you're coming back, and then to find out, no, you're not. I mean, you've been a trouper through all this, Monica.
> L: (*Crying.*)

Lewinsky's tears could scarcely have had time to dry before Tripp picked up the telephone and relayed the contents of these calls to Isikoff and Goldberg. All of Tripp's plans—political, financial, literary—depended on being able to *prove* that the affair between Clinton and Lewinsky had taken place. Then, in the midst of Lewinsky's distress, Tripp was invited to her home at the Watergate, and she recognized a perfect opportunity to make her case.

Lewinsky had saved the blue dress from the Gap that she had worn during the sexual encounter in February, on the day when Clinton presented her with *Leaves of Grass*. According to Tripp, Lewinsky had proudly displayed what she thought were stains from Clinton's semen. The next morning, Tripp called Isikoff with news about the dress—and offered to steal it for him. After first noting the evidentiary problems with such an approach—where, the reporter wondered, would he get a copy of Clinton's DNA for comparison?—Isikoff wisely chose not to be party to any crime by Tripp.

Undeterred, Tripp then took news of the dress to Lucianne Goldberg. Her call prompted a strange moment of scandal convergence, because, as it happened, another one of Goldberg's clients happened to be visiting. The client was Mark Fuhrman, the disgraced former Los Angeles police detective who played a central role in the investigation of O. J. Simpson. Fuhrman, who had been introduced to Goldberg by Dominick Dunne, was writing a book about an unsolved murder in Connecticut. Remembering that DNA evidence had played an important part in the Simpson case, Goldberg put Tripp's question to Fuhrman, without mentioning the names of the people involved. Could months-old semen stains on a dress still be tested for forensic purposes? Fuhrman said (correctly) that they could, and Goldberg passed the information back to Tripp.

A few days later, Lewinsky, who regularly consulted Tripp about clothes, mentioned that she was thinking about wearing the dress over the upcoming holidays. "Then I'm gonna wear the navy dress I wore to the radio address that has the [deleted] on it for Thanksgiving," Lewinsky said.

Noticeably startled, Tripp stammered, "Well, how—you're—gonna get it cleaned?"

"Yeah."

"Oh, God."

"It's about time," Lewinsky explained. "Out with the old, you know?"

"Oh, that's too bad," Tripp said, and then, knowing her friend's obsessions, told Monica that her other clothes made her look thin.

The conversation meandered to other topics, but the two women picked up the subject of the Gap dress the next day. Tripp had obviously carefully thought through what she wanted to say and even offered a little introduction. "Okay, so one other thing I want to say to you that you can do what you want with . . . but I want you to think about this—and really think about it, instead of always just dissing what I say, okay?"

"I don't always dis what you say," Lewinsky said cheerfully.

"Well—"

"But sometimes you're such a—"

Tripp jumped back in with her prepared remarks. "You're very stubborn. You're very stubborn." ("Sigh.") "The navy-blue dress. Now, all I would say to you is: I know how you feel today, and I know why you feel the way you do today. But you have a very long life ahead of you, and I don't know what's going to happen to you. Neither do you. I don't know anything, and you don't know anything. I mean, the future is a blank slate. I don't know what will happen. I would rather you had that in your possession if you need it years from now. That's all I'm gonna say."

Lewinsky was amused. "You think that I can hold on to a dress for ten, fifteen years with [deleted] from—"

"Hey, listen," Tripp answered. "My cousin is a genetic whatchamacallit, and during O. J. Simpson, I questioned all the DNA, and do you know what he told me?" (This was a lie, of course.)

"I will never forget this," Tripp went on. "And he's like a Ph.D. and blah, blah, blah. And he said that on a rape victim now—they couldn't do this, you know, even five years ago. On a rape victim now, if she has preserved a pinprick-size of crusted semen, ten years from that time, if she takes a wet Q-Tip and blobs it there . . . they can match the DNA with absolutely—with certainty." (Fuhrman had specifically mentioned the Q-Tip test to Goldberg.)

"So why can't I scratch that crap off and put it in a plastic bag?"

"You can't scratch it off. You would have to use a Q-Tip." Exasperated, Tripp moved on to her larger point. "Believe me, I know how you feel now," Tripp resumed. "I just don't want to take away your options down the road, should you need them. And believe me, I know better than anybody probably, other than your mother, that you would never, ever use them if you didn't have to. I know this. Believe me. I—I just—I don't trust the people around him [Clinton], and I just want you to have that for you. Put it in a Baggie, put it in a Ziploc bag, and you pack it with your treasures, for what I care. I mean, whatever. Put it in one of your little antiques."

"What for, though? What do you think—"

"I don't know, Monica. It's just this nagging, awful feeling in the back of my head."

"What if I didn't have it?"

"Well, I know that. I'm just—I think it's a blessing you do," Tripp said, reaching toward a kind of peroration. "It would be your only insurance policy down the road. Or it could never be needed, and you can throw it away. But I—I never, ever want to read about you going off the deep end because someone comes out and calls you a stalker or something and . . . some, God forbid, awful like that. And in this day and age, there's nothing I don't—I don't trust anybody. Maybe I'm being paranoid. If I am, indulge me. I'm not saying you should do it if you don't want to. I'm just saying I think it would be a smart thing to do. And then put it somewhere where no one knows where it is but you. And you don't label it, obviously."

At that point, Lewinsky steered the conversation toward safer ground. But Tripp had made her point, and Lewinsky did ultimately remove the dress from her apartment at the Watergate and ship it to her mother's new home in New York for safekeeping.

Tripp behaved so odiously during this period that it is tempting to write off all of her conduct as that of an irredeemable conniver. For good reason, few Americans have been tempted to forgive Tripp's surreptitious taping of a vulnerable friend, especially given her coarse political and commercial motives. But Tripp must be given this: she was right about the dress. Many of Clinton's own friends regarded him as so untrustworthy on sexual matters that they believed the president would never have admitted his relationship with Lewinsky if she had not kept genetic proof. Without the dress, the subsequent investigation of the relationship might have come down to a he said/she said contest between Clinton and Lewinsky. In such a fight, Clinton's advocates would not have hesitated to attack Lewinsky's credibility, and her unstable behavior would have provided them plenty of ammunition. But the dress made Lewinsky bulletproof. Of course, preservation of the dress served Tripp's purposes; but it also served Lewinsky's, and for that, if little else, she has her erstwhile friend to thank.

So, as winter approached, Tripp, Goldberg, and Isikoff knew where all the evidence was—the dress, the tapes, the courier receipts, and the witnesses. All that was left now was to get it all in the hands of Paula Jones's new lawyers—and the reading public.

9

"Draw the Penis for Me"

Would you state your full name for the record, please?"

"Dennis Kirkland."

"And Mr. Kirkland, for the record, I am Bill Bristow, and I'm the lawyer representing Danny Ferguson, the Arkansas state trooper who has been sued by Paula Jones in this matter. I have issued a subpoena for you to appear here today for a discovery deposition."

In October 1997, almost three and a half years after Paula Jones filed her lawsuit, the lawyers on both sides began taking depositions from witnesses. In an ordinary civil case, lawyers conduct this form of questioning in order to gather evidence to use in motions for summary judgment—which is the trial judge's most important pretrial ruling on whether the case should proceed. So it was in the Jones case. But the inherently political nature of this lawsuit transformed the depositions as they did every other part of the case. The witnesses called, the questions asked, even the lawyers doing the questioning—all were chosen by both sides with an eye toward the public as much as toward Judge Susan Webber Wright.

Clinton's team had had its collective eye on Dennis Kirkland since he lunched at McDonald's with Mitch Ettinger, of Skadden

Arps, just weeks after the case began. He was the original "blow-job boy," in Bob Bennett's felicitous phrase, and he was a critical weapon in the defense effort to tar Jones's reputation and intimidate her from pushing ahead. This legal strategy, however, presented a political problem. Bennett's client had run for office as a champion of women's rights and, indeed, had spoken out in favor of Anita Hill, who had endured these kinds of attacks after she accused Clarence Thomas of making unwelcome advances toward her.

In public, Bennett had to avoid character assassination. This hadn't always been easy. Earlier in the year, in a brief appearance on the ABC News program *This Week,* Bennett had said, "If she insists on a trial, we'll have a trial. And, as my mother once said to me, be careful what you ask for, you may get it. I had a dog like that, who just wanted to catch cars. And he successfully caught one one day, and I have a new dog." Bennett's remarks were widely interpreted as a threat against Jones. The following day, the National Organization for Women issued a strongly worded statement saying, in part, "Women who file sexual harassment complaints should not face personal attacks designed to intimidate them into silence." (According to Susan Carpenter-McMillan, Jones wept when she heard Bennett's comments, thinking that Bennett had called her a dog.)

Bennett hastened to *Nightline* to offer a clarification. "I did intend to sound tough, because we will be tough," he told Ted Koppel. "But, Ted, I want to make it absolutely clear—absolutely clear—that in being tough we have absolutely no intention of dragging out Paula Jones's prior sex life or invading her privacy. And the reasons for that are several. One, I have a wife and three daughters who would kick me out of the house. Second, I represent a client who has done more for women than any president in the history of this country, and even if I were inclined to do that, which I'm not, he wouldn't permit me."

How, then, to square this approach with Bennett's zeal to make use of the blow-job boys? Bennett's answer was to use a surrogate. Danny Ferguson was the largely forgotten codefendant in this lawsuit, and Billy Bristow the forgotten attorney. Back in May 1994, just before the complaint was filed, Davis and Cammarata had thrown Ferguson's name in as a kind of afterthought. He was a defendant on only two peripheral counts in the case—that he conspired with Clinton to deprive Jones of her civil rights and that he defamed Paula by telling David Brock that she had asked to be Clinton's regular girlfriend. But this sloppy drafting of the complaint came back to haunt the Jones team. The tort of defamation addresses injuries to reputation, so a plaintiff in a defamation case puts the state of her reputation at issue. As the defendant in a defamation count, Ferguson had the legal right to examine Jones's reputation.

Clinton's defense team exploited this quirk in a most cynical way. By retaining Bristow, Ferguson had plugged into the Arkansas Democratic establishment. Indeed, Bristow was at that time engaged in a successful campaign for the Democratic gubernatorial nomination in 1998. (Bristow lost the general election to the incumbent Republican.) There was never any doubt who was running the case. Bennett not only represented the president but had the resources for private investigators and other expensive assistance. But Bennett made sure that all of the inquiries into Jones's sex life were made in the name of Clinton's codefendant, Danny Ferguson.

But as so often happened in this lawsuit, things did not work out precisely as planned—as was apparent early on in "Bristow's" deposition of Dennis Kirkland.

"Did you do anything to prepare for the deposition today?" he was asked.

"No," Kirkland said. Then he paused and corrected himself. "Ironed my shirt," he said. "I ironed my shirt."

/ / /

One question left unresolved by Dennis Kirkland's deposition was whether Paula Corbin had worse taste in men than Bob Bennett did in witnesses. In the course of questioning by Bristow, Kirkland did recount his purported night of passion with Jones a decade or so earlier. At "the back gate of Camp Robinson," in Cabot, Arkansas, Kirkland said, "[a]fter we got there, we kissed awhile. We had oral sex, and we had sex. . . ."

"How many hours had you known her at this point in time?"

"I'm going to say approximately three or four. . . ."

"Did she in any way appear to be offended by the idea of oral sex?" Bristow asked.

"No," replied Kirkland. "She unzipped my pants, you know, if you want to be just blunt."

"That's what I want," Bristow said.

But that was about as good as things went for the president on this day. As for the seriatim blow jobs that had so captivated Bennett, it turned out that Kirkland had only secondhand information about his friends' intimacies. "Never actually saw anything happen, but I had been told," he said. Moreover, Kirkland conceded that on the night in question, he had probably had "five, six, seven, eight even" beers. As for his life after this incident, Kirkland had lost his football scholarship at the University of Arkansas because of drug use, had been convicted of forgery, and made his living, such as it was, trying to "fix the fences and see after cows" at his grandfather's closed-down farm. One cannot imagine that a jury would have found much to admire in Kirkland, and Bennett and Bristow might have thought better of presenting his uncorroborated ten-year-old tale to the jury if the case had ever gone to trial.

In a way, though, Kirkland's deposition proved typical of several dozen that were taken by both sides in late 1997. Everyone—the witnesses, the lawyers, even the clients—was diminished by the degrading process of microscopic analysis. There were, for example, the Arkansas state troopers, whose supposed outrage at Clinton's behavior set the wheels of the case in motion. Buddy Young supervised Roger Perry and Larry Patterson, the aspiring authors who were Brock's primary sources for the *American Spectator* article. What, the Clinton lawyers wondered, did Young know of his subordinates' ambitions?

"You've got to know and understand Larry Patterson," Young replied. "Larry Patterson's mentality and objective in life was to sleep with as many women as he could. You could not have a conversation with Larry Patterson more than five minutes that sex didn't enter into it and whose britches he was trying to get in. . . . So any time that Bill Clinton had contact with an attractive lady, in Larry Patterson's mind, the objective was to get in her britches. . . . That's his view of life. That's what he did."

Did Patterson actually know of sexual misconduct by Clinton?

"I don't know," said Young, whom Clinton had appointed to a federal job, much to the resentment of other troopers. "I know that I doubt seriously that Larry Patterson can testify that he knows that Bill Clinton did anything along that line. He can speculate. He can equate what he saw with what he would have done if it was him, and that's what Larry did in most cases. If Bill Clinton had a meeting with a woman behind closed doors, Larry assumed it was for the purpose of sex, because that's what it would have been if he had been there. . . ."

And Roger Perry?

". . . Roger had to repay . . . two hundred and seventy dollars to the state to pay for long-distance telephone calls on our security telephone to his girlfriends. He fessed up, paid up, and that was the end of that deal."

Did he and Patterson hang out together?

"Yes, they did. They were both divorced, and they partied together regularly." (Closing the circle, Patterson went on to serve as the caretaker and a rent-free tenant on property that Cliff Jackson owned in Little Rock.) Based on Young's and the other depositions, it seemed just as likely that the troopers used Clinton to pick up women as that the governor employed them for that purpose.

/ / /

For all their shabbiness, however, the depositions do contain the best available clues for deciphering the events of May 8, 1991. The aftermath of the incident—Jones's lawsuit and Clinton's impeachment—so outweigh the underlying encounter that it's tempting simply to avoid the issue. Still, the question remains: What, if anything, happened in that room at the Excelsior Hotel? Only two people know for sure, but, based on the available evidence, it appears that Bill Clinton and Paula Jones both lied about the incident.

The speech at the Excelsior Hotel was a routine event for Governor Clinton, but it took place on a day that had a special intensity for him—and for Paula Corbin. His triumphant speech in Cleveland two days earlier had been politically intoxicating; he was finally going to be a realistic candidate for president. For her part, Paula Corbin had worked for the Arkansas Industrial Development Commission (AIDC) for only three months, and the day held portents for her, too. She was going to dress up, get out of the office, and have the chance to meet high-powered executives, including, perhaps, the governor. As her boss, Clydine Pennington, testified, "she was just excited."

That excitement carried over to the event itself—a conference of public- and private-sector executives on improving quality in goods and services. Paula had arrived early at the AIDC office, where Pennington had questioned her "inappropriate" attire. Paula then traveled the couple of miles to the Excelsior in a state car with a group of colleagues. She and Pam Blackard were posted at the registration table outside the ballroom (which is now known as the President Bill Clinton Ballroom), and they handed out badges to the 150 guests.

Clinton arrived at the hotel shortly after eight in the morning, and he was greeted at the door by his economic aide, Phil Price, who took Clinton to a room that had been reserved for him on the eighth floor. Clinton attended many events at the Excelsior, which is the biggest hotel in Little Rock, and the governor was often provided with a room to use while he was there. In the room, Price and Dave Harrington, the AIDC director, briefed Clinton on the plans for the day, and then they went downstairs to the ballroom. (Oddly, several AIDC staff members had distinct memories of this conference because the sound system faltered all day long, which was especially embarrassing for a conference devoted to "quality." Harrington later apologized to the attendees and offered refunds.)

Clinton left the ballroom after the first break, and he stopped to chat and snack on coffee and doughnuts. While Clinton was speaking in the ballroom, Paula and Pam Blackard had been having a flirty exchange with Ferguson, the bodyguard, asking to see his gun. Their attention was quickly drawn to the governor when he stood nearby. According to Ferguson, "I went over and started small-talking with her, and they were kind of giggling about the governor's pants being too short. And [Paula] said that she thought he was good-looking, had sexy hair, wanted me to tell him that."

Ferguson passed Paula's message along to Clinton. "He had come back that she had that 'come-hither' look," he testified. Clinton asked Ferguson to get the key to the room upstairs, saying that "he was expecting a call from the White House." (In his article,

David Brock scoffed at the notion that George Bush would have been calling Clinton at this point, but governors often talk to White House staffers. It is also possible that Ferguson heard a garbled message. Earlier that morning, Clinton had told Phil Price to return a phone call to "Senator Kerry." Price called John Kerry, of Massachusetts, but he learned that it was really Bob Kerrey, of Nebraska, who had telephoned. Clinton may have gone to the room to return a call to a senator, not the White House.)

As Ferguson was taking Clinton up to the room, the trooper testified, "he told me if Paula wanted to meet him, then she can come up." After Clinton was settled in the room, Ferguson returned to the ballroom and handed Paula a note with the room number on it, "thinking that if she wanted to go up, she'd go up." Paula and Blackard then discussed whether she should go upstairs. Blackard was "curious" about what Clinton wanted. Paula said she thought Clinton might offer her a job. "Go ahead and go up and see," Blackard urged.

Paula tracked Ferguson down and said she wanted to go see Clinton. "Do you want me to go with you?" Ferguson asked. Paula said yes, and they went up to the room together.

It is worth pausing to note what everyone's expectations might reasonably have been at this point. Paula's thoughts of a job offer seem dubious. By her own account, she and the governor had not yet exchanged a single sentence. On what basis might he have offered her a job? Moreover, she had sought out the introduction to Clinton, not vice versa. The governor understood that she wanted to meet him—knew that she thought he had "sexy hair"—and invited her to the hotel room. If she hadn't wanted to go, she could have remained downstairs. Clinton might have assumed that given her coquettish exchanges with Ferguson, Paula might be interested in a dalliance with him. That, of course, didn't give him the right to do anything she didn't want. But given both of their histories, a sexual encounter between the two of them might well have been on his mind—and hers.

In the years that followed, Clinton said many times, including under oath, that he had "no memory" of being inside the room with Jones. It seems virtually certain, however, that they were in the room together. She recalled its unusual arrangement—a couch with two chairs, but no bed. (Phil Price remembered it the same way.) It is hard to imagine how she could have invented that detail. Of course, her version of what happened inside the room became well known. *I-love-your-curves. I'm-not-that-kind-of-girl. Kiss-it. I-don't-want-to-make-you-do-anything-you-don't-want-to-do.*

Ferguson, Blackard, and Jones agree that she was in the room for somewhere around fifteen minutes. Ferguson had returned to the second floor, and when Paula saw him, she asked whether the governor was going to be at the conference for the rest of the day. He said they had to return to the mansion for lunch, but he didn't know the rest of their plans. "And then she asked me if the governor had any girlfriends," Ferguson testified. "She said that she would be his girlfriend." (Paula, of course, denied making any such remark, and this comment was the basis of her defamation suit against Ferguson.)

Paula later asserted that she was immediately distraught after the incident in the hotel room. She conveyed her anguish to Pam Blackard, at the registration table, and then immediately left the conference and drove to the office of her friend Debra Ballentine, in a building just outside downtown Little Rock. Ballentine testified that Paula arrived at her office at around 4 P.M. Ballentine's testimony raised an important question, however: At what time of day did Paula go up to Clinton's hotel room?

It was a critical part of Jones's case that the incident took place in the late afternoon. That would explain how she bolted the hotel for Ballentine's office. But the evidence strongly suggests that the incident took place before lunch. Oddly, there was an important event on the governor's calendar that day, but it wasn't the AIDC conference. Clinton hosted a lunch at the governor's mansion for, of all people, the crown prince of Luxembourg, who had recently invested in a factory in Arkansas.

Did Clinton return to the Excelsior after lunch? Clinton's lawyers tried hard to prove that he did not, but the matter could never be resolved with certainty. His schedule for the day was ambiguous. Ferguson insisted that he did not return to the hotel after the luncheon with the prince. (Neither did Price and Harrington, who would have accompanied Clinton.) Also, the hotel's electronic key system cut off Clinton's access to the eighth-floor room at 11:45 A.M. No one—not the guests or the speakers at the conference—could swear to have seen Clinton at the conference in the afternoon. In addition, Paula left her car at the AIDC, so it's hard to figure how she drove straight from the hotel to Ballentine's office. In short, it seems more than likely that Clinton's encounter with Jones took place in the late morning.

So what? What difference does the timing make? It means that Paula Corbin, far from being immediately horrified, waited all afternoon before she complained to her friends about the incident. She had hours to think about what effect the encounter might have on her then new relationship with the jealous Stephen Jones. It was only after she had a chance to worry about Steve that she decided to complain—to her friends, her sister, her mother.

But in the days immediately after the conference, Paula did not complain about Clinton—just the opposite, in fact. Several colleagues from the AIDC testified that she was very happy to have met the governor. According to Pennington, Paula "specifically told me that she was excited that she had met the governor, held her hand out to say that he had shaken hands with her, and that he liked what she had on, and he liked her hair, and she was . . . thrilled she met the governor." Paula told her boss she wanted to work for the governor and on his campaign for president. Cherry Duckett, the deputy director of AIDC, heard the same enthusiasm from Paula.

Even before the conference, Paula had hung around Clinton's office in the capitol building, routinely spending a half hour there twice a day when she made deliveries from the AIDC offices across the street. On the day after the conference, Paula told Carol Phillips, who was Clinton's lead receptionist at the capitol, that a trooper had arranged for her to meet the governor at the hotel. Paula said he had been "nice" and "gentle" and "sweet." Paula took to calling Phillips, asking about Clinton's schedule and when he might be in the office (behavior that roughly paralleled Lewinsky's calls to Betty Currie). Once Clinton did run into Paula in the hallway of the capitol, and he put his arm around her and said, "Don't we make a great couple—the beauty and the beast?" But other than this harmless banter, there was no further contact between them.

About a week after the conference, Danny Ferguson ran into Paula at the capitol. "She asked me if the governor had asked about her," Ferguson testified. "I said, 'No.' She asked me for a piece of paper. She wrote her phone number down and said, 'If he wants to talk to me, he can call me at this number. If my boyfriend answers, either hang up or tell him you've got the wrong number.'" Ferguson said he threw the paper away. Clinton never called. (Paula asserted that Ferguson asked her for her phone number, which she refused to give him.)

So where does all the evidence lead? All in all, the record suggests that Clinton and Paula Corbin had a consensual sexual encounter in the room at the Excelsior Hotel. Clinton, it seems, lied about it from the start. When Ferguson returned to the hotel room after Paula left, the trooper testified, the governor recounted, "Nothing happened. We just talked." As for the president's subsequent claims that he had no memory of the incident, that seems unlikely, no matter how eventful a life he has led. Clinton denied making the approach because he always denied these accusations—and because, with some justification, he thought that his sex life was his own business.

In this scenario, Paula's motives seem more complex. She may have had a fling that she quickly regretted, and then, as Clinton ignored her, her resentments simmered. When the *Spectator* article ran, almost three years later, she took it as an opportunity to settle an old score—as long as she could do so without enraging her jealous husband. The best clue to her motives may have come out in a chance encounter in the ever-small world of Arkansas. Just after the *Spectator* article was published, in December 1993, Paula came home from California to visit Arkansas with her baby son. Her friend Debra Ballentine had heard about the story in *The American Spectator* and asked her out to dinner to discuss it. They took their toddlers to the Golden Corral steak house in North Little Rock, and Paula spied a familiar face at a nearby table— Danny Ferguson. Ferguson's wife noticed that an unfamiliar woman was staring at him, so he turned to face her. After she passed by on a visit to the salad bar, Paula motioned Ferguson to come talk to her.

In testimony and interviews, Jones, Ballentine, and Ferguson remembered their conversation much the same way. Ferguson began by apologizing. He said he didn't know Brock was going to use her name—and he added that Clinton had told him nothing had happened between them. Then he explained a little about how the troopers' plans for a book had fallen apart. "I got screwed," Ferguson said.

Then—as so often happened in the many-tentacled Paula Jones case—the subject turned to money. There were differences in recollections about who brought the subject up first, but Jones wondered how much money the tabloids would pay for an account of her encounter with the president. Ferguson said that Roger Perry had told him the *Enquirer* would pay $500,000. Ferguson warned her about the consequences. "You better think about your family," he said, "because I've been through it, and they start to dig up dirt."

Paula was torn. She wasn't worried about dirt from her past, but she was concerned about Steve—how he would react to hearing "the whole truth." Toward the end of Ferguson's visit to Paula's table, she mused, "Five hundred thousand dollars would last me a long time." Here, it seems, was planted the idea that the *Spectator* article might mean money for Paula and Steve Jones.

A few days later, Ballentine decided to call the lawyer who had handled her divorce—Danny Traylor. "This is Danny," he answered. And so the Paula Jones case began.

/ / /

Through the fall of 1997, the depositions proceeded in an increasingly rancorous atmosphere. The ideologically motivated Dallas team remained obsessed with pursuing Clinton's alleged girlfriends, and the Clinton team, in turn, focused on Jones's commercial motives in filing the lawsuit. There was an antic session with Lydia Cathey, Paula's corroborating sister, when Bill Bristow sought to draw her out on the distinguishing-characteristic issue. (Q: "Did Paula tell you that there were distinguishing characteristics of the president's penis?" A: "Yes, . . . she worded it as, 'His dick was crooked. . . .'" Q: "Any more description than that? . . . Did it have a U-turn in it?" A: "No, . . . It was hard and crooked and gross. You know. That was the word she used. . . .")

On November 12, though, the case reached an important turning point. On that day, the lawyers all converged on Little Rock for a two-day deposition of the plaintiff herself. Bennett was well prepared. He began with a promising subject for the defense—Jones's employment record. This was, after all, an employment discrimination case, and one of the plaintiff's claims was that she had been denied promotions and raises because of Clinton's sexual harassment. Her prior record might offer some clue to her potential at AIDC.

When Paula Corbin was hired at AIDC, she had been out of high school for less than four years, but she had already held several different jobs (and dropped out of secretarial school as well). She sold shoes, which she quit to work at J. B. Hunt Transport, where she was fired for "talking too much," according to Paula. From there she went to Dillard's department store, where she was fired for lateness. Then on to Hertz, where she was fired for undetermined reasons—and so on to Crown Rental, Pestmasters, Holliday's Fashions, and finally AIDC. All in all, she had been fired from five of the seven jobs she had held before going to work for state government. It was an extraordinarily damning recitation of failure in the workplace.

From there, Bennett moved to a handful of other topics, starting with the incident itself. In this telling, Jones added a new, sinister detail—that, after she rejected his advances, Clinton "put his hand on the door to where I could not open it up any further, and he stopped me and he says, 'You're a smart girl. Let's keep this between ourselves.'" Had there been a trial, Jones would no doubt have been asked how she came to forget the detail of her false imprisonment in her earlier tellings of the incident. As her question to her husband on the outtake from the Matrisciana film illustrated—"Isn't that what happened?"—Paula's recollections were always a work in progress.

But the Clinton team felt it wasn't enough simply to show that Paula Jones's employment history was dismal and her story inconsistent—which were both perfectly appropriate subjects to explore in a deposition in a case of this kind. The next moments in the deposition show how grotesque this case became. Bennett's promises notwithstanding, the next portion of the deposition reads more like a verbal sexual assault than a legal proceeding. Clinton may indeed have "done more for women than any president," as Bennett once said, but these questions form part of his legacy as well.

At first the queries were simply embarrassing. Bennett called Jones's attention to her "distinguishing characteristic" affidavit.

"All right," Bennett said. "Now you say in paragraph five, 'The shaft of the penis was bent or crooked.' Is that right?"

"Yes."

"Could you sort of just show me what you mean on that piece of paper? Draw the penis for me. Show me what you mean by the shaft was bent or crooked."

"I have to draw it?" Jones asked.

"Yes," replied the president's lawyer.

"(Whereupon, witness complied)," the court reporter dryly noted.

But the true cruelty began when Bennett turned the questioning over to Bill Bristow. First question: "You made a statement at one forty-two this afternoon that you were not a bimbo. Would you tell me what your definition of the word 'bimbo' is?"

"Whoa, whoa," her lawyer Donovan Campbell sputtered, but there was little he could do. Judge Wright was going to rule on objections after the deposition, so Jones had to answer every question, no matter how outrageous. If the case came to trial, then Judge Wright would make her rulings on the admissibility of the disputed questions. Paula stammered a brief answer—"trailer park white trash," among other things.

"Now, Mrs. Jones, when you make a statement that the president's penis looks small to you," Bristow continued, "that implies a certain familiarity with the male anatomy—in other words, that you would be in a position to make comparative studies. Have you ever taken any anatomy courses . . . ?"

"No. . . ."

"So I would gather then that your ability to discern distinctive characteristics about a male penis would be based on experience that you have had in your life where you have had the opportunity to view other male penises, is that correct?"

"It—very few, if there were. Yeah, I made it probably on that assumption and plus he was a really big man and really overweight and it seemed like it was real little compared to his weight."

Bristow used these questions as an introduction to an extended tour of Paula Jones's sex life. He started with her husband, Stephen. "So you dated for three weeks and then began having sexual intercourse?"

"That's correct."

"And then, about a week later, according to your prior testimony, you moved in together, correct?"

"Correct. . . ."

"In fact, you had been pregnant for some period of time before you and Mr. Jones got married, is that not true?"

"That's true."

All of this was entirely irrelevant—as Jones's lawyers tried forlornly to point out. But Bristow was relentless. He asked about her high school boyfriend: "Is that who you lost your virginity to?" And her drinking habits: Was it ever "necessary for you to, quote, sleep off a drunk?" No, said Jones. He went on to ask about other boyfriends—Glenn Cope, Carl Fulkerson. The background check on Jones had been extensive. Next Bristow turned to Mike Turner, the noble soul who had sold his seminude photographs of Paula to *Penthouse* magazine.

Turner, it turned out, had saved several of the notes that Jones had written to him during their brief relationship—some had been quoted in the magazine article that went with the pictures— and Bristow now began confronting her with them. "Mike, gorgeous, thanks for letting me sleep with you and I love to snuggle up to your sexy soft body and wonderful butt. . . . Mike, thanks for a wonderful time I had last time. Your [*sic*] great in bed. . . . Mike, thanks for letting me sleep my drunk off over here. You're a real sweetheart. Let's do something soon, okay? . . . Love you, babe. Paula."

"Okay," Bristow resumed, "you do agree that you apparently had to sleep a drunk off?"

"Yeah," Jones conceded. "Probably so."

Ultimately, the responsibility for these questions belongs not with the lawyers who asked them but with the client who mattered, Bill Clinton. Bennett knew the political risks of this kind of strategy. So at each step in the case, he was especially careful to get approval for these personal assaults from the client himself—and from the first lady. Bennett always received the same message: Don't hold back.

For the few hours when Bennett and Bristow were haranguing their client in Little Rock, Donovan Campbell and his colleagues had little choice but to suffer in silence. At the very moment of Jones's deposition, however, Linda Tripp and Lucianne Goldberg were preparing to transform the case very much to the plaintiff's advantage.

/ / /

With her job search still unsettled, Monica Lewinsky had taken to writing Clinton ever more beseeching notes in an effort to see him. Her first meeting with Vernon Jordan, on November 5, had yet to produce results. "I am not a moron," Lewinsky asserted in a letter to Clinton sent by courier on November 11. "I know what is going on in the world takes precedence, but I don't think what I have asked you for is unreasonable.... I need you now not as president, but as a man. PLEASE be my friend." Clinton and Lewinsky talked the following evening, and he proposed she stop by briefly on November 13—the second day of Paula Jones's deposition—which would prove to be her most pathetic, and comical, visit to the White House.

That morning, Lewinsky began hounding Betty Currie. After several calls, Currie finally admitted that the president had gone golfing—news that prompted Lewinsky to go "ballistic," as she wrote in an e-mail to a friend. She announced that she was coming to the White House anyway, and Currie told her to wait in Currie's car in the West Wing parking lot. Lewinsky arrived to find the car locked—and then it started to rain. After getting a good soaking, Lewinsky persuaded Currie to let her in, and the two women hustled into the president's private study, where Monica awaited his return from the links. Noodling around in the president's desk, Lewinsky was delighted to see that he had kept several of her gifts to him, including *Vox*, Nicholson Baker's novel about phone sex, and *Oy Vey! The Things They Say: A Guide to Jewish Wit*. Clinton finally arrived from his golf game, with only a minute or two to talk. Lewinsky gave him an antique paperweight and showed him an e-mail describing the effects of chewing Altoid mints before performing oral sex. "Ms. Lewinsky was chewing Altoids at the time," the Starr report noted, "but the President replied that he did not have enough time for oral sex." He rushed off to a state dinner for President Zedillo, of Mexico.

Later that evening, Lewinsky reported all of these developments to Linda Tripp, who was by now thoroughly frustrated. She had no book contract. Isikoff had not yet written a story. The Paula

Jones case seemed to be going nowhere. And still this hysterical young woman was whining to her about the president in several long phone calls every day. She had to do something to break the logjam. So, just after she heard about Monica's latest misadventure at the White House, Tripp called Goldberg with an idea. Tripp said she wanted to be subpoenaed to give a deposition in the Jones case. That would finally get the information about Lewinsky's affair with the president to people who could do Clinton some real harm.

Goldberg took to the mission with gusto and embarked on a game of what might be called right-wing telephone tag. First, she called Alfred Regnery, the conservative publisher of Gary Aldrich's book—and that of Goldberg's client Mark Fuhrman. "This woman recently phoned me with some fascinating info, and she wants to be in touch with Paula Jones's lawyers," Goldberg told Regnery. "Call my friend Peter Smith," Regnery said. This was fitting. Smith was the Chicago financier who had bankrolled David Brock's original investigation of the trooper story, which had led to the publication of his article in *The American Spectator*. (Indeed, a year before the trooper story, Smith had tried to sell Brock on the Clinton-and-the-black-prostitute story.) Smith, in turn, directed Goldberg to Richard Porter, the former aide to Dan Quayle who had since made partner at Kirkland & Ellis, Kenneth Starr's law firm. Goldberg called Porter on November 18.

Porter was one of the original "elves," the group of conservative young lawyers who had been secretly advising the Jones lawyers throughout the case. Amazed by what he heard from Goldberg, Porter quickly e-mailed his fellow elf George Conway in New York. "There's a woman named Lewisky [*sic*]," he wrote. "She indulges a certain Lothario in the Casa Blanca for oral sex in the pantry." Porter's message went on to say that Betty Currie was "Lewisky's" contact at the White House and that Isikoff had been kept abreast of all the latest developments. Conway printed out the e-mail, made sure Goldberg's phone number was included, and faxed it to Don Campbell in Dallas. Just to make sure, he then called one of the lawyers in the Dallas firm to make sure that they followed up on the message.

There was an unmistakable sense of giddy delight as Clinton's enemies passed this juicy morsel to its intended recipient. Virtually all of these people—including Smith, Porter, Conway, Goldberg, and Tripp—had been hoping for years to catch Clinton in an adulterous affair. Of course, based on what they knew at that point, the president's conduct wasn't illegal, wasn't harassment, wasn't relevant in any way to his public duties; it was just a story about sex. But that was what they really wanted—and that went for everyone from the raunchy sophisticates like Goldberg to the "good strong Christian men" on the Jones team. In a small way, the smarmy tone of Porter's e-mail ("a certain Lothario") illustrated how the elves—and the right wing generally—were more obsessed with the details of Clinton's sex life than with the content of his character.

Conway need not have worried about a lack of interest on the part of Paula Jones's lawyers. On November 21, another one of Campbell's partners, David Pyke, called Linda Tripp at home. (Apparently unintentionally, Tripp taped the call—which, it appears, she put Goldberg on call-waiting to receive.)

"Ms. Tripp?"

"Oh, Mr. Pyke."

"How are you?"

"Well, thank you. Thank you for calling. . . . I don't know how familiar—familiar you are with my situation."

"Well," Pyke answered, "Lucy Goldberg filled me in to some degree."

Some of the details had been lost in the long telephone chain—Pyke thought Tripp worked at the Treasury Department, not the Pentagon—but the lawyer had the gist of the story. Tripp began by asking about the status of Kathleen Willey's deposition. Tripp's onetime friend had filed a motion, near her home in Virginia, to avoid testifying, but the judge in the case had just made a secret ruling that Willey would have to submit to a deposition. "Okay," Tripp said. "That would leave you open to deposing me?"

"Right," said Pyke.

But there was a hitch. Under normal circumstances, the subpoena for Tripp's deposition would go through her attorney, Kirby Behre. A young lawyer who had recently left the U.S. Attorney's Office in Washington, Behre had urged Tripp to stay out of the Jones case. Tripp told Pyke that Behre "has my best interests at heart, but he . . . feels strongly that I should not involve myself."

"Uh-huh," said Pyke.

"Um, I feel strongly that the behavior has to stop, um, or should at least be exposed."

Pyke then turned to the real reason for his call. "Ms. Goldberg told me about—that you've—you talked to a woman that's having a relationship with Clinton currently, is that correct?"

With her usual precision, Tripp said that "currently" wasn't exactly right. "It's in the process of ending, let's say. . . . It is very sad and the girl will deny it to her dying breath. Um, she is very, very angry with him because of the way he's handling this, but would rather martyr herself in a way rather than—than expose him."

Tripp then set out to construct a scheme, with Pyke, to deceive her own lawyer about her plans to testify. "I need to look hostile," said Tripp, so Pyke should pretend that she was not cooperating with their side. "My livelihood is at stake here," she explained. (This was a recurring theme of Tripp's—that because she was a political appointee, she would lose her job if her anti-Clinton activities were known. Yet even though her role became highly public—as did her illegal taping of Lewinsky—Tripp never lost her high-paying political appointment at the Pentagon.)

Tripp and Pyke agreed on a plan whereby "a subpoena would drop on your doorstep out of the blue," and only then would Tripp tell Behre about it. Tripp would pretend to be upset that she was being dragged into the case, but ultimately she would cooperate and tell her tale about Lewinsky under oath. "Hold on," Tripp said. "I'll get my calendar." In subsequent calls, Tripp and Goldberg told the Jones lawyers the correct spelling of the name in Richard Porter's e-mail—Lewinsky, not Lewisky.

/ / /

At 5:40 P.M. on Friday, December 5, the Dallas lawyers faxed their witness list to Robert Bennett, in Washington. Many of the names were unfamiliar to Bennett and his team, so they had an informal agreement with David Pyke to give a capsule summary of each potential witness's testimony. Bennett's partner Mitch Ettinger called Pyke for the rundown. As Ettinger read a name, Pyke would say, "He slept with that one," "He raped that one," "He harassed that one." It was a surreal litany.

The following afternoon, Clinton's lawyers met with the president in the Oval Office to discuss the witness list. It was an important meeting for Bennett and his team. They had the names of all the women that the plaintiffs had managed to track down during three months of depositions. The president now had his chance. If Clinton had even hinted that there might be a problem with one of them—if he had just raised an eyebrow—Bennett could still settle the case. Bennett prided himself on his ability to get clients to be straight with him, to confide their weaknesses and vulnerabilities. All these names would become public if the case proceeded to trial. This was the time for Clinton to cut his losses.

So in the course of the long meeting, the lawyers put the question to their client: "Monica Lewinsky?"

Clinton's confidant, the deputy White House counsel Bruce Lindsey, who was also there, didn't even recognize her name. Bennett explained that she was a young former White House aide. The plaintiff's lawyers were alleging Clinton had had an affair with her.

"Bob, do you think I'm fucking crazy?" the president said, according to two people present. "Hey, look, let's move on. I know the press is watching me every minute. The right has been dying for this kind of thing from day one. No, it didn't happen.

"I'm retired," he said. "I'm retired."

10

Consensual Sex

Clinton's lies to his lawyers on December 6 were even more extraordinary in light of what had happened at the White House earlier that day.

Lewinsky had wangled an invitation to a Christmas party at the White House the previous night, and she had seen the president only on the receiving line. This brief meeting sent Lewinsky into a new spiral of despair, and she made one of her periodic vows to be finished with the relationship once and for all. On Saturday morning, she decided to pack up all the Christmas presents she had been stockpiling for Clinton and leave them with Betty Currie at the White House. So at around ten o'clock, Lewinsky appeared at the southwest gate of the White House—bearing a sterling silver antique cigar holder, a mug from Starbucks, a tie, "a little box that's called hugs and kisses," and an antique book on Theodore Roosevelt that she had purchased at a New York flea market.

Lewinsky tried to summon Currie to pick up the packages but didn't get an answer from the secretary's phone number or her pager. Then, seeing Marsha Scott, a presidential aide whom she regarded as one of her White House enemies, Lewinsky detoured to the northwest gate. There one of the guards let slip that Currie was giving a White House tour to Eleanor Mondale, the television correspondent and daughter of the former vice president, who was visiting Clinton in the Oval Office. In the grand jury, Lewinsky was asked, "What was your reaction to that?"

"Not good. . . . Very upset. Hysterical."

Notwithstanding her resolution of that very morning to put Clinton behind her, Lewinsky dissolved into a jealous rage at the thought of Clinton with another "other" woman. Lewinsky stormed off to a nearby bar, telephoned Currie, and began screaming at her. Lewinsky thought Currie had deceived her by telling her that Clinton would be meeting with his attorneys in the Jones case on this day; here Monica had discovered that he was seeing a woman she regarded as a rival. (As it turned out, the lawyers were simply due at the White House later in the day.) At this point, Currie began to worry about finding herself in the middle of these intrigues, and she told Monica that she was concerned about being fired herself. Later that morning, Currie called Lewinsky at home and asked her to calm down. Monica demanded to talk to the president, who was then speaking with the attorney general. Moments later, Lewinsky called back again, and Currie at last put her through to Clinton.

At the start of what turned out to be a fifty-six-minute telephone call between the president and his former girlfriend, Clinton lashed out. "In my life no one has ever treated me as poorly as I have been treated by you," Lewinsky recalled him saying. "Outside of my family and my friends and my staff, I have spent more time with you than anyone else in the world. How dare you make such a scene? It's none of your business who I see." (For the record, he also denied any romance with Mondale. "In fact," Lewinsky recalls him protesting, "I set her up with her current boyfriend.")

Eventually both Clinton and Lewinsky recovered their equilibrium, and the president actually invited her back to visit him that afternoon. So, in her second trip to the White House of the day, Monica gave him his Christmas presents, and in return he promised that he would have some gifts for her later in the month. The president sat in his rocking chair, stroking Monica's hair as she sat on the floor at his feet. They chatted, as they often did, about their childhoods. Though she was now more or less committed to moving to New York, Monica left the meeting once more thinking that their relationship might resume. Their sexual encounters had begun twenty-five months earlier; they had broken up several times, but they'd last had phone sex only a few weeks earlier, and now here Clinton was still hinting that they might get back together. To be sure, Lewinsky should have realized much earlier that their relationship was doomed; but at the same time, Clinton kept tantalizing her with the possibility of reconciliation.

In sum, then, Clinton and Lewinsky probably spent close to two hours together, on the phone and in person, before five o'clock on December 6, 1997. About ninety minutes after Monica slipped out of the Oval Office, her place was taken by Bob Bennett and his colleagues, who arrived bearing the plaintiff's witness list in the Paula Jones case. When they reached the name Monica Lewinsky, the president dismissed—ridiculed!—the idea that he had had an affair with her.

/ / /

How could Clinton have been so brazen—and in the middle of the most publicized sexual harassment lawsuit in history? Of course, one can only speculate about the president's thought processes, but several conclusions seem apparent. First, like anyone having an extramarital affair, he was embarrassed to admit it. Second, he regarded the entire Jones case as a political vendetta against him, and he didn't feel obligated to be candid in a lawsuit brought by adversaries he so despised. Third, Clinton had often, perhaps always, lied about his sex life.

But there was another potential reason for his lies to his lawyers—indeed, a possible answer to the larger question of why he would have conducted the affair with Lewinsky when a sexual harassment case against him was pending. Clinton drew a clear distinction between sexual harassment and consensual sex. In his grand jury testimony, Clinton returned to this theme more than half a dozen times. Describing his relationship with Lewinsky, Clinton said, "There was no employment, no benefit in exchange, there was nothing having anything to do with sexual harassment." In Clinton's view, his consensual sexual activity had nothing to do with sexual harassment. (Lewinsky, likewise, never suggested that her relationship with Clinton involved any kind of harassment on his part.)

As it happened, Judge Susan Webber Wright was then wrestling with just this issue—the relevance of Clinton's consensual sexual relations to the issue of whether he sexually harassed Paula Jones. Over the many years the Jones case was pending, Wright became known to the public mostly through newspaper photographs, in which she appeared to be something of a schoolmarm—all pinched and nervous severity. She held her hair back with barrettes; her hooded eyes peered out from small, metal-rimmed spectacles. The details were the same in person, but the impression she left could not be more different. Susan Webber Wright was confident, funny, unbuttoned, even a little zany. This was a judge who, after a long and frustrating trial day, once announced to a jury, "I'm going to go home and abuse alcohol." Everyone knew it was a joke, but it was not one that most federal judges would make.

Susan Webber was the first of two daughters born to an up-and-coming young lawyer and his wife in Texarkana. Tom Webber, whose firm was known for producing civic leaders and judges, died when Susan was sixteen. His widow, forced to provide for Susan and her sister, Missy, went to work at a local bank. Fortunately, Susan excelled at school, and she won a scholarship to Randolph-Macon Woman's College, in Lynchburg, Virginia, and afterward she won another, to continue her studies for a master's in public administration at the University of Arkansas. She then enrolled in the university's law school and split the costs with her mother, paying her portion with earnings from summer jobs and part-time work. In her final year, Susan became the first woman to edit the *Law Review* and was in the running to be the class valedictorian.

It was at that moment that she played a role in an early legend about Bill Clinton. In 1973, following his graduation from Yale Law School, Clinton returned home to teach at the University of Arkansas School of Law. The next year, Susan Webber took Professor Clinton's course in admiralty law—a subject that was apparently of little interest in the landlocked state. Toward the end of the semester, Clinton turned his attention to what became his first political campaign, against the incumbent Republican congressman John Paul Hammerschmidt. Clinton was so distracted by his campaign that he lost some of the final exams, including that of Susan Webber.

The law school demanded that Clinton turn in grades for the course, so the young professor had a problem. He turned for help to his twenty-six-year-old girlfriend, Hillary Rodham, who came up with the idea of a deal for Susan Webber. Clinton would give her a B-plus in the class, and Webber wouldn't have to take the final again. But as a candidate for valedictorian, Webber needed a better grade. She rejected Hillary's deal and forced Professor Clinton to give her a new test—and got an A. Webber, who nevertheless missed out on the top position, immediately went to work as a volunteer on the reelection campaign of Representative Hammerschmidt, who beat the young professor handily. Clinton's first political success came two years later, in 1976, when he was elected the state's attorney general.

At that point, though, Susan Webber largely withdrew from most political activity. She became a professor at the law school of the University of Arkansas at Little Rock, married a senior colleague, and earned a solid, if unspectacular, reputation as a scholar in oil-and-gas law. In 1988, she dipped back into politics, heading a local organization of lawyers for George Bush, and two years later she was rewarded with a federal judgeship, largely through the sponsorship of the then ranking Republican official in the state—Representative Hammerschmidt. Still, Wright bore Clinton no apparent animus, and she presided over *Jones v. Clinton* with a steady, diligent hand.

In December, however, Judge Wright was confronted with a provocative dilemma. The president's deposition was scheduled for Saturday, January 17, 1998. The lawyers wanted Wright to rule on the scope of the questioning. Clearly, Clinton could be asked if he had ever engaged in sexual harassment. But could the president be asked about *consensual* sexual activities? The answers to such questions, of course, had the potential for great political embarrassment for the president. But more than that, the issue went to the heart of modern sexual harassment law. Is consensual sex evidence of, or even related to, sexual harassment?

As Susan Webber Wright sat down to study that question, she could not have known that her answer would turn out to be one of the more momentous legal decisions of the twentieth century.

The birthplace of American sexual harassment law can be identified with some precision: Ithaca, New York. The first use of the term seems to have been at a 1975 conference at Cornell when a group of feminists held a "Speak-Out on Sexual Harassment." A pioneering survey of working women that was published by *Redbook* magazine in 1976 raised the issue before a mass audience, and two years later an activist from Ithaca named Lin Farley wrote a book on the subject, entitled *Sexual Shakedown.* But the most important turning point may have been when a woman named Catharine MacKinnon came to town.

From her base in New Haven, MacKinnon became a feminist prodigy in the 1970s. During that time, she worked toward both a Ph.D. and a law degree at Yale, taught undergraduates, created the first women's-studies course at the college, worked with unions, and cofounded a progressive collective in which she practiced law with a handful of like-minded young attorneys. In addition, she traveled around the country as a guitar-playing folksinger. At a gig in Ithaca, MacKinnon heard a story about a Cornell secretary named Carmita Wood, who had been fired for rebuffing her boss's sexual advances. "My mind just went, This is it," MacKinnon said years later. "It was an epiphany experience. Everything I had heard about what sex inequality is, is not it. This is it."

MacKinnon's epiphany led to the recognition of a new legal form of employment discrimination—sexual harassment. To the extent that courts had dealt with the issue at all, judges had dismissed sexual overtures, like the one directed at the Cornell secretary, as "personal," and they found that they did not constitute a legally recognizable form of discrimination. When MacKinnon had nearly completed a paper on sexual harassment that she was preparing for an independent-study course at Yale, she heard about a lawsuit at the federal appeals court in Washington that raised precisely the issues she was addressing. In *Barnes v. Costle,* Paulette Barnes, a clerk at the Environmental Protection Agency, had sued her employer because, she said, her supervisor had retaliated against her for her refusal to sleep with him. The district court had dismissed her case on the familiar ground that the harassment was personal. MacKinnon gave a copy of her paper to a law clerk on the case in the federal appeals court, and, she asserted, "it became the basis of the decision." In 1977, the three-judge panel on the case reversed the district court and produced, as MacKinnon later wrote, "the most explicit treatment of the issues to date and a holding that sexual harassment is sex discrimination in employment." (The late George MacKinnon, Catharine's father—and a conservative Republican—was one of the judges on the panel.)

MacKinnon turned the paper into a book, *Sexual Harassment of Working Women,* which was published in 1979. Now in its twelfth paperback printing, it surely ranks as one of the most influential law books of the late twentieth century. Dense, closely argued, and relentlessly polemical, MacKinnon's book was dedicated to the proposition that "sexual harassment, the experience, is becoming 'sexual harassment,' the legal claim." MacKinnon's triumph reflected the liberal spirit of the era. Through the sheer force of their intellects—their brief-writing and legal skills— "public interest" lawyers like MacKinnon had transformed the politics of their times. The creation of sexual harassment law represented a paradigmatic example of the legal system's takeover of the political system—a dramatic change in social policy engineered by lawyers and judges rather than by voters and legislators. Like much work by public interest lawyers in this period, the new law of sexual harassment made enormous contributions to the cause of fairness in the workplace. And like other such developments, the law also bore the scars of the idiosyncratic circumstances of its birth.

MacKinnon later became better known for her crusades, with the writer Andrea Dworkin, against pornography than for her more important work on sexual harassment. The subjects were different, of course, but they shared certain common philosophical underpinnings. MacKinnon invariably portrayed men and women in a constant state of war—a war that the men were winning. This was especially true when it came to sex itself. MacKinnon long argued that in a patriarchal society, the notion of consent had no real meaning for women. The real question, as she put it in her book, was "whether women have a chance, structurally speaking and as a normal matter, even to consider whether they want to have sex or not." In the light of the argument of her book, MacKinnon's question was clearly rhetorical. When men have greater power and status than women—and that is virtually all the time— consent is a myth; in such circumstances, all sex is harassment.

This view came to be reflected in the law of sexual harassment. The law to a great extent drew little distinction between consensual sex and actual sexual harassment. Indeed, evidence that a defendant had engaged in consensual sex in the workplace came to be seen as evidence that he also engaged in sexual harassment. The distinction that Clinton emphasized so strongly in his grand jury testimony—that he had engaged in consensual sex, not sexual harassment—scarcely even existed under the law relevant to his case. The law virtually compelled Judge Wright to allow the Jones lawyers to ask the president about his history of consensual sexual affairs with women he met at work. It would be up to the women to say if they had "consented" to sex with the boss. And even if the women in these affairs "consented," they could be seen as evidence of a pattern of sexual harassment. Indeed, in the years leading up to *Jones v. Clinton,* the trend had been toward more, not less, disclosure of the sexual history of defendants. For that, in some measure, Bill Clinton could blame . . . Bill Clinton.

/ / /

In 1991, in the first of the major televised criminal trials of the decade, William Kennedy Smith was acquitted of raping an acquaintance in Palm Beach. During the trial, the rape-shield law offered the accuser only a limited defense from questions about her sexual history and behavior. But the judge in the case barred the prosecution from putting forth evidence that purported to show that Smith had assaulted three other women in social settings. The perceived imbalance—open season on the woman's past and cover-up of the man's—generated calls for change. The Clarence Thomas–Anita Hill hearings that same year played out some of the same themes and added to the momentum for reform.

As is so often the case, however, the legal cure may have been worse than the disease. In Congress, Susan Molinari, then a Republican representative from New York, introduced changes to the federal rules of evidence to allow juries in civil and criminal sexual misconduct cases to consider evidence that the accused had engaged in such misconduct in the past. But Molinari proposed such a broad definition of "sexual assault"—which included any attempted contact, "without consent, between any part of the defendant's body or an object and the genitals or anus of another person"—that it would apply to mere fanny-pinching as well as rape. But the criminal defense lobby was no match for the women's groups on this issue. When Clinton's crime bill stalled in the House, in 1994, the president called Molinari to see what he could do to win her vote. She agreed to vote for the bill if Clinton would accept her amendments on admitting the evidence of previous offenses in sex trials. "He told me that he was shocked that it wasn't part of the bill, and he supported it," Molinari recalled to Jeffrey Rosen of *The New Yorker*. "Clinton basically assisted me in passing that legislation."

The Molinari law referred to sexual relations "without consent," but as far as the questioning of defendants was concerned, many judges simply read those words out of the statute. It was up to women to decide whether they had consented or not; the men had to answer whether there was any sexual activity of any kind. Indeed, for better or worse, the law was so clear that Judge Wright's decision turned out to be more important than it was difficult. In a ruling that was released to the lawyers in the case at 5:33 P.M. on December 11—the time of day would later prove important— Wright held that "the plaintiff is entitled to information regarding any individuals with whom the President had sexual relations or proposed or sought to have sexual relations and who were during the relevant time frame state or federal employees." The judge drew no distinction between consensual sex and sexual harassment; the plaintiff was entitled to know about it all.

Altogether, then, as with the independent counsel statute, sexual harassment law became a monument to the cost of good intentions. Each half step in the law seemed rational at the time. Some employers did harass their subordinates, and men generally did have more power than women in the workplace. Defendants sometimes did succeed in withholding relevant evidence about their past conduct from juries. But the system that had been jerry-built in response to these problems created new ones. Evidence of consensual sexual activity was presumed to be relevant to what was, in fact, the totally unrelated question of sexual harassment. And in any event, because of the Molinari "reforms" to the rules of evidence, the line between consensual sex and harassment scarcely existed at all.

In practical terms, the ruling meant that President Clinton would have to answer questions, under oath, about his relationship with Monica Lewinsky.

/ / /

The same day as Judge Wright's order—December 11—Monica Lewinsky had a lunch date: turkey sandwiches and Diet Cokes in Vernon Jordan's law office in Washington.

Prodded by Linda Tripp, Lewinsky had asked the president to reach out for Jordan's help in her job search during the first week in November. Lewinsky first went to Jordan's office on November 5, described her interest in finding a job in New York, and received his assurance, "We're in business." But after that promise, nothing much had happened. Jordan was out of town for the last three weeks of November, and Monica, in the meantime, had received a job offer from Bill Richardson at the United Nations—a position she didn't want. Anxious to find something in the private sector in New York, Lewinsky nudged Betty Currie during the first week in December to remind Jordan to help her. Currie did, and on December 8, Jordan and Lewinsky set up their lunch for three days later.

Who did Vernon Jordan think Monica Lewinsky was? Why was he helping her—and, more important, why did he think the president wanted him to help her?

Jordan would later answer these questions with a careful vagueness. He said he enjoyed helping young people find their way; he was always happy to be of assistance to the president; he was not aware that Lewinsky was sexually involved with Clinton; he thought she was just a "bobby-soxer who was mesmerized by Frank Sinatra, who was quite taken with this man because of his position." There has never been any way to disprove Jordan's answers, but his professed ignorance about his new protégé strained credulity. Both Clinton and Currie had called him on Lewinsky's behalf, something they had never done for any former aide, much less a former intern.

Jordan's ignorance about the true nature of the Clinton-Lewinsky relationship was even more unlikely after his conversation with her over lunch on December 11. According to her grand jury testimony, Lewinsky told Jordan she "didn't really look at him as the president," and instead saw him "more as a man . . . and a regular person." She was upset "when he doesn't call me enough or see me enough." Jordan replied, "You're in love, that's what your problem is." When he said that, Lewinsky recalled, I "probably blushed or giggled, something like that." (In his own testimony, Jordan corroborated Lewinsky's general outline of their conversation.) In any event, after their lunch, Jordan went to work for the president's lovesick young friend, making introductions for her at American Express, Young & Rubicam, and MacAndrews & Forbes, the parent company of Revlon.

Vernon Jordan was not the only person who was monitoring the progress of Lewinsky's job hunt. Tripp, Goldberg, Isikoff, and the Dallas lawyers were speaking to one another almost every day in this period. Thanks to Tripp, of course, the Jones lawyers knew the details of the president's relationship with Lewinsky, and in mid-December, they began to tip their hand. On December 15, they subpoenaed Clinton for all "documents that related to communications between the President and Monica Lewisky." (The Jones team was still relying on the misspelling in Richard Porter's e-mail to George Conway.) This subpoena, in turn, appears to have prompted a late-night call from Clinton to Lewinsky the following night. In her obsessive way, Monica kept tabs on the first lady's schedule, knowing that the president called only on nights when Mrs. Clinton was traveling. Lewinsky knew that Hillary happened to be in town this week, so Monica was especially surprised, at around 2:30 A.M. on December 17, to receive a call from Clinton.

This phone call, which lasted forty-nine minutes, later served as a centerpiece of the obstruction of justice case against the president. According to Lewinsky, Clinton began their conversation by giving her a piece of sad news: Betty Currie's brother had been killed in a car accident. After they commiserated on that topic for a while, the president let Monica know of another unfortunate development: Lewinsky's name had appeared on the plaintiff's witness list in the Jones case. "It broke my heart when I saw your name on the list," Clinton said.

The question of what Lewinsky should do about it naturally

arose. First, Clinton said that her name on the list didn't necessarily mean that she would be subpoenaed; this was true. But if she was, the president went on, she could file an affidavit in an attempt to avoid testifying. This, too, was true; she could say that she had no evidence relating to sexual harassment—as indeed, in any real sense, she did not—and perhaps the judge would excuse her on that basis alone. In any event, Clinton said, if she did get a subpoena, she should let Betty Currie know about it.

At some point, the conversation turned to the "cover stories" that Clinton and Lewinsky had discussed in the past to explain her visits to the Oval Office. They discussed their old tales that Monica was visiting Currie, or delivering papers to Clinton. But— the critical legal question—did Clinton tell Lewinsky to put these cover stories in her affidavit? Lewinsky testified on several occasions that the president did no such thing. Moreover, the cover stories were not technically false; she had visited Currie and delivered papers. Of course, the cover stories were monumentally incomplete, but that is sometimes how attorneys use affidavits. Sworn statements that are misleading but literally true cannot be criminal. An affidavit can disclose what one side wants to disclose—and no more. Clinton and Lewinsky agreed that their relationship had nothing to do with harassment, the subject of the Jones case. So, in an understandable effort to spare both of them tremendous embarrassment, they struggled to come up with a way that they thought could excuse Monica from testifying. (In passing, Lewinsky mentioned that it would be a pretty good idea for Clinton to settle the Jones case—which was probably the best advice she ever gave him.)

Toward the end of their call, Clinton mentioned that he had some Christmas presents for Monica. Perhaps, he said, he should summon Betty Currie over the following weekend, and she could arrange for Monica to visit him. In other words, Clinton considered dragging his secretary away from mourning her brother to arrange another rendezvous with his twenty-something friend. Even Lewinsky had the compassion to say that they ought to leave Currie alone with her family. Lewinsky concluded with a promise to keep him posted—and then burst into tears as soon as she hung up.

Obstruction of justice by the president? Not even close. Lewinsky could have filed a truthful, if limited, affidavit that might have gotten her out of testifying in the Jones case. Suggesting that she do so was no crime. But sleazy, selfish behavior by Clinton? Absolutely. The costs of his affair with Lewinsky—in political, legal, and moral terms—were becoming clearer all the time. The president could have chosen candor, squarely facing the consequences of his personal misbehavior. Instead he hedged, equivocated, waffled, misled—and urged his former girlfriend to do the same. The president had the right to do what he did—which did not mean it was the right thing to do.

/ / /

Two days later, it became clear that the president had offered Monica false hope about avoiding a subpoena. On December 19, a process server called Lewinsky at her desk at the Pentagon and told her he had a subpoena for her. The subpoena called not just for her testimony, but also for her to produce "each and every gift" she had received from the president, including "jewelry and/or hat pins." The mention of the gifts should have tipped Lewinsky off that she had a mole in her life—and Tripp was the obvious suspect—but Monica didn't realize for some time that her friend was consorting with the enemy.

From the Metro station where she met the process server, Lewinsky staggered to a phone booth, in tears, to call Vernon Jordan. He invited her over, calmed her down, and said he was going to find her a lawyer. While she waited, Jordan made an appointment for Lewinsky to meet Francis Carter, a criminal defense lawyer, three days later. (Later that day, Jordan testified, he happened to attend a Christmas party at the White House and sought a private word with the president. Jordan told Clinton about Lewinsky's subpoena and asked him about the nature of his relationship with the young woman. Clinton denied any sexual relations with her.)

The subpoena to Lewinsky served as the trip wire for the explosion that nearly consumed the Clinton presidency. News of the subpoena ricocheted, ultimately, from Lewinsky to Tripp to Goldberg to the elves (and Isikoff) to Kenneth Starr. As always, in this case, political animus and greed were the salient motivators for virtually everyone involved—Linda Tripp, preeminently.

Tripp had orchestrated her own "surprise" subpoena from the Jones lawyers a few days before Lewinsky's, and, as planned, she took it to Kirby Behre, the young former prosecutor who had been advising her for some time. Tripp had confided to Behre that she had been tape-recording her conversations with Lewinsky. Unlike Goldberg, who was Tripp's original source on the legality of tape-recording, Behre actually knew the law—and he informed Tripp that she was committing a crime in Maryland. He not only urged Tripp to stop, but asked her to allow him to go to Bob Bennett and urge him to settle the Paula Jones case. If the case was settled, the tapes would never come to light, and Tripp would have no worries about being prosecuted for her illegal taping. Plainly, Behre gave Tripp the correct legal advice, but Tripp didn't want to hear it. It was a measure of Tripp's obsession with getting the president—and writing her book—that her reaction to Behre's advice was to tell Goldberg that she wanted a new lawyer.

For her part, Lewinsky had to decide what to do about the subpoena. On December 22, Jordan escorted Monica to Frank Carter's office. Jordan's role in December and January was suspicious in many ways—how much did he really know about Clinton and Lewinsky? Did he really want Monica to tell the truth?—but his decision to introduce Lewinsky to Carter suggests that Jordan wanted to play by the rules. Carter had spent many years as the director of Washington's public defender program and enjoyed a sterling ethical reputation. If Jordan had wanted Monica to testify falsely, he never would have taken her to Frank Carter. To Carter, the situation looked fairly simple. Lewinsky denied to him that there had been any kind of sexual relationship between her and the president. After their first meeting, he said that he would draft an affidavit for her to that effect—and that he thought, as a result, he could get her out of testifying.

That evening, December 22, Tripp taped her last telephone call with Lewinsky—even though Kirby Behre had just warned her that she would be breaking the law by doing so. More than ever, the transcripts read as if Tripp was speaking to the tape recorder as much as to Lewinsky. "Look, Monica," she said at one point, "we already know that you're going to lie under oath. We also know that I want out of this big-time. If I have to testify—if I am forced to answer questions and answer truthfully—it's going to be the opposite of what you say, so therefore it's a conflict right there." At another point, Lewinsky wondered about how the Jones lawyers could have developed such specific information about things like the hat pin. "Someone has told them something," Tripp said. "Now, do we think that's a little something or a lot something? Do they have specifics to ask us? We don't know this." "We" did know, of course—because Tripp herself was the Jones team's source.

The next day, Tripp called Isikoff and let drop that she and Goldberg would soon take her story of the whole case, along with her tapes, to a publisher for a book deal. Isikoff recalled that he was shocked that Tripp was planning to write a book. In retrospect, it's difficult to see why he was surprised. He had seen her 1996 book proposal; why else would Tripp be talking to the same literary agent about essentially the same subject—the president's sex life?

In any event, Isikoff immediately started to try to talk her out of it. The reporter appealed to her desire to see Clinton lose the Paula Jones case. A book proposal, he said, "would undermine her credibility and the credibility of her information." Isikoff was coaching Tripp on how to be a more effective witness against the president they both despised. And when he finished doing that, Isikoff called Goldberg and made the same pitch. If Linda sold a book, he warned, she would have to testify about it in her deposition. According to contemporaneous notes from Goldberg's side of the conversation, Isikoff said, "Don't see a publisher or they will ask about it in deposition." (As Isikoff later wrote his own book, this advice may have turned out to serve his own interest, as well as the anti-Clinton political cause.)

/ / /

But Goldberg had an even more immediate priority—finding Tripp a new lawyer. On the same day that Isikoff called her, December 23, Goldberg convened a conference call of two of the chief elves, Richard Porter, in Chicago, and Jerome Marcus, in Philadelphia. The agent passed along Tripp's fantasy that Kirby Behre was somehow in Bob Bennett's pocket; her evidence of Behre's perfidy, of course, was his advice that she stop committing the Maryland crime of illegal wiretapping. Porter and Marcus agreed to help out in the search for more ideologically simpatico counsel.

Goldberg had other exciting news for the lawyers: Vernon Jordan had told Monica to lie under oath in her deposition in the Jones case. This was a clear exaggeration of what Lewinsky had told Tripp in the taped phone call, but in the Lewinsky-to-Tripp-to-Goldberg-to-elves phone chain, it turned into an accusation that Jordan had committed a crime—something the elves were only too happy to hear. Porter and Marcus agreed to help out in the search for a new lawyer, with the added fillip that the entire matter might turn out to be criminal as well as civil. Goldberg never lost sight of Tripp's (and her own) financial goals either. According to the Goldberg notes, the lawyers "said it was a good idea to get her to a publisher."

The circle of people who knew about the Clinton-Lewinsky relationship was widening. There were Monica's eleven friends and relatives, and the core group of Tripp, Goldberg, and Isikoff, and now the elf team was putting the word out on the conservative legal circuit that an explosive witness needed a new lawyer. Marcus, who had helped Danny Traylor draft the original complaint on behalf of Paula Jones, was by this point in his fourth year of sporadic work on the case. A year later, he told Isikoff that the involvement of Clinton and Jordan in the machinations around Lewinsky in December 1997 suggested that this was a criminal—not just a civil—matter. But, the elf wondered, who would be the prosecutor?

/ / /

Just after Christmas, Lewinsky reminded Betty Currie that the president had promised her Christmas gifts. The secretary invited Monica to see the president at eight-thirty on the Sunday morning of December 28. The president greeted Lewinsky in the Oval Office, where he introduced her to his then new dog, Buddy, for whom Monica had brought a small gift. Then they went back into Clinton's private office, and he pulled a few knickknacks out of canvas bag from the Black Dog restaurant on Martha's Vineyard. He gave her a little marble sculpture of a bear, which he had received at the Vancouver economic summit; a blanket from Radio City Music Hall's Rockettes; a pin with the New York skyline; a stuffed animal wearing a Black Dog T-shirt; a box of chocolates; and a silly pair of sunglasses. The glasses, Lewinsky later testified, were "a long running joke with us," because she used to tease him about his sunglasses.

For about ten minutes, their conversation turned to her subpoena in the Jones case—another critical moment in the case against Clinton. (Lewinsky ultimately was compelled, in no fewer than ten separate interviews with law enforcement, to recount the details of this brief conversation.) Clinton speculated that it was Linda Tripp—or, as he called her, "that woman from the summer, with Kathleen Willey"—who was cooperating with the Jones lawyers. (Monica lied and said she had not told Tripp about the gifts.) Lewinsky then raised the question of what she should do with all the gifts, since they were called for in the subpoena. She suggested that she move them out of her apartment or perhaps give them to Betty Currie. Asked repeatedly about Clinton's responses, Lewinsky said that he either said nothing or "I don't know" or "Hmm." Of course, Clinton should have simply instructed Lewinsky to comply with the subpoena. But just as surely, his ambiguous response did not constitute obstruction of justice. Like so much of the president's conduct, his vague answer was shabby, but not illegal.

Their meeting in the study ended with what Lewinsky called a "physically intimate . . . passionate kiss." Lewinsky went home. They have never again seen each other in person.

A few hours later, Currie and Lewinsky spoke on the telephone and discussed how Currie was going to come over to Monica's apartment at the Watergate and pick up the president's gifts. Neither woman had a clear memory on the critical subject of who initiated the gift pickup. Lewinsky said it was Currie's idea; Currie said Lewinsky made the call. If Currie called, it would have been virtually certain that Clinton told her to retrieve the gifts that were under subpoena—an act that really might have been obstruction of justice. But if Lewinsky asked Currie to come over, that didn't implicate Clinton. On balance, the evidence suggests that the president did not participate in the plot to hide the gifts from the Jones lawyers. Not only did Currie deny that Clinton gave her any such instructions, his behavior was not that of a man who wanted gifts hidden. Why, after all, would Clinton give Lewinsky *more* gifts on December 28 if he was trying to get her to hide the ones she already had? Not even Clinton's most ardent accusers could ever explain why he would in one breath give Lewinsky gifts and in the next concoct a plan to get them back.

Before she parted with the president's gifts, Lewinsky scrawled in big letters on the box she gave to Betty Currie: "Please do not throw away!!!"

/ / /

All of these events—Lewinsky's panic over the subpoena, the gifts, Tripp's conversations with Goldberg and Isikoff, the elves' talent search for a new lawyer for Tripp—combined with the fast-approaching date of the president's deposition to make it feel as if the barometer were dropping in political Washington. So many people knew parts of the story that some leakage was inevitable. Rumors about women had swirled around Clinton for so long that his allies instinctively discounted them. But this was different. Something bad was happening for him—and to him. In light of all this, what was perhaps most extraordinary was that Clinton never suggested to Bennett that he find a way to settle the Jones case and make all these issues go away. The president sprinted heedless into the abyss. (The president and first lady spent a quiet New Year's vacation on a secluded estate in the U.S. Virgin Islands. It was in keeping with the spirit of the moment that after they were photographed doing a romantic dance on the beach, a robust debate ensued about whether their embrace was staged for the camera.)

As 1998 began, the president had one thing going for him. In the three great crises of this moment in his presidency—the Jones case, the Lewinsky relationship, and the Starr investigation—only two of them, Jones and Lewinsky, had so far merged. But then, at the end of the year, Lucianne Goldberg's talent hunt for the right new lawyer for Linda Tripp succeeded. George Conway, the New York elf, remembered an old friend in Washington who would be just right for the job. He's a little strange, Conway said, but all the elves agreed that Jim Moody's heart was in the right place.

11

Revenge of the "Peace Corps"

James Moody embodied the transformation of "public interest" law from a left-wing to a right-wing obsession. For this reason, it was fitting that he played a critical, if largely unsung, role in the transformation of the president's Lewinsky problem from a civil to a criminal concern—and from a potential embarrassment to a matter of political life and death.

Moody had been born forty-five years earlier, in Kansas City. He was a premature baby, and as was relatively common in those days, too much oxygen was pumped into his incubator. As a result, Moody became virtually blind. He could never drive and he read only large print, but he never let his disability interfere with his considerable academic gifts. At MIT, in the mid-seventies, he became a prototype of the mischievous nerd—he once schemed to blow up the Harvard football field—and after graduating, he came to Washington to work on arms control issues.

Disillusioned with the ability of government to accomplish much of anything, Moody became a committed libertarian and, after law school, devoted himself to making social change through the filing of lawsuits. He worked on his own, as a freelance activist and lawyer, dedicated mostly to pushing deregulation in the airline and agriculture industries. Big, lumbering, with a distracted personal style, Moody lived by himself and appeared to work all the time. He had a zealot's devotion, forswearing money and status in the name of fomenting political change. "This is the Peace Corps part of my life," he said, referring to this legal work. His social life, to the extent he had one, consisted of attending meetings of conservative legal organizations, like the Federalist Society, and Grateful Dead concerts.

In the first week in January, Tripp hadn't yet fired Kirby Behre, but that was just a matter of time. At the end of the week, Tripp went back to Behre's office and brought him a copy of her December 22 tape with Lewinsky. Behre was furious that his client had continued to break the law by taping the phone calls, and he again insisted on calling Bob Bennett to prompt a settlement in the Jones case. Instead, Tripp had a new idea. She now wanted to wear a body wire and tape-record more of Lewinsky's conversations. She had plans to meet Monica at the Ritz-Carlton Hotel in suburban Virginia on the following Tuesday. There, Tripp told Behre, she would record Lewinsky urging her to lie about her knowledge of the relationship with the president. Behre briefly considered this strange notion; in an even odder touch, Behre even had the man for the job. Behre's firm had worked with the private investigator for the defense in sportscaster Marv Albert's trial—which was, in a typically bizarre connection in this case, based on an assault that took place in the same Ritz-Carlton Hotel where Tripp and Lewinsky were planning to meet. Behre decided to think about Tripp's body-wire idea over the weekend of January 10 and 11.

That was not what Tripp wanted to hear. She wanted action. So, on that Friday, Goldberg gave Jim Moody's name to Tripp, and she called him at about five in the afternoon. Their conversation went on until practically eleven, interrupted only when Moody requested bathroom breaks. It was a measure of Moody's enthusiasm for the anti-Clinton cause that he scared even Linda Tripp. He was willing to work for free and willing to wire her up; as Tripp later testified, Moody "seemed to me to be someone with clearly a political agenda as opposed to just an attorney's advocacy role." Tripp called Goldberg and said, "This man sounds nutty to me over the phone."

On Monday, January 12, Tripp had a final meeting with Kirby

Behre, who said he would not wire her up for her conversation with Lewinsky the following day. That sealed it for Tripp. Moody would be her new lawyer, and he had an important first piece of advice. Jim Moody told his client to place a call to the office of independent counsel Kenneth Starr.

Even if Tripp wanted to contact law enforcement, it was by no means clear that Starr would be the right person to call. If one believed that Lewinsky, Jordan, and possibly Clinton were obstructing justice in Paula Jones's sexual harassment case, why was that any business of Kenneth Starr's? At that point, Starr had jurisdiction over the Whitewater case, as well as Filegate and Travelgate. The Jones case had nothing to do with those subjects. Later, Starr's lawyers would conjure up a connection between *Jones v. Clinton* and the rest of the prosecutor's jurisdiction. But that purported link never even occurred to Moody when he first suggested that Tripp reach out to Starr.

Moody went to Starr because he despised Democrats in general—and Clinton's Justice Department in particular. Most of his law practice consisted of "whistle-blower" and "false claims act" suits against the government. He later said, "I think they are a bunch of lazy crooks at the Justice Department." Moody told his new client to go to the independent counsel not because he thought he had jurisdiction over her case, but because Jim Moody regarded Ken Starr as an ideological kindred spirit and Bill Clinton as their shared enemy.

/ / /

During the crucial first two weeks in January, Moody wasn't the only conservative who had the notion of linking the Jones case to the Starr investigation. The story was converging on Starr's office from another direction as well. On the previous Thursday, January 8, Jerome Marcus, the Philadelphia elf, was scheduled to have dinner with an old friend from out of town, Paul Rosenzweig. Marcus and Rosenzweig had graduated from the University of Chicago together, in the same class as Richard Porter, the Chicago elf, who happened to be in Philadelphia that night as well. George Conway, the New York elf, decided to take a train down from New York to join the party. Of course, by this point, Marcus, Porter, and Conway had been working together for several years, providing surreptitious assistance on the Paula Jones case. Indeed, Porter had even tried to recruit the fourth member of their dinner party, Rosenzweig, to the Jones cause as well, but Rosenzweig had made other career plans: he joined the staff of independent counsel Kenneth Starr (who was, simultaneously, Porter's law partner at Kirkland & Ellis).

Over dinner at Deux Cheminées, a fancy French restaurant, Marcus told Rosenzweig about Monica Lewinsky—and about how, as he understood it, Vernon Jordan had asked her to lie about her relationship with the president in her upcoming deposition in the Paula Jones case. Marcus said there was a witness, Linda Tripp, who had tapes of Lewinsky making admissions. Shouldn't Starr be investigating this? Rosenzweig said he would pass the story back to his superiors.

On Friday, January 9, Rosenzweig told his boss in Starr's office, the prosecutor Jackie Bennett, about the approach from Marcus. Bennett was interested, but he would have to check with Starr, who was out of town until Monday. On Monday, January 12, Starr gave Bennett the go-ahead to receive any information that the witness might want to provide. Bennett told Rosenzweig to pass the news to Marcus. From Marcus the word went to Lucianne Goldberg and then on to Jim Moody and finally to the person who was the focus of all these fevered communications—Linda Tripp.

It was late on Monday night, January 12, when Goldberg finally reached Tripp at home. "You need to call Jackie Bennett at the Office of Independent Counsel and bring your entire story and evidence to him," she said. Bennett had stayed late to wait for Tripp's call.

/ / /

At that moment, Kenneth Starr had been the independent counsel for three years and five months. It had been nearly a year since Starr announced, and then recanted, his plans to step down and move to Pepperdine University. The office, as a whole, was stuck in a kind of netherworld—neither beginning nor ending investigations, neither expanding nor contracting, neither prosecuting nor exonerating, but instead living out the bureaucratic imperative that work expands to fill the time available. Because Starr, like all independent counsels, operated without restrictions on either the cost or the duration of his labors, the staff always took the long route.

Starr's office had been in operation for so long that there were distinct eras in its history, and though the machinations were largely invisible to the outside world, the cast had changed a great deal since 1994. Starr began with the same kind of staff that Robert Fiske had assembled—experienced, thoughtful lawyers who had worked as defense attorneys as well as prosecutors. But every one of Starr's first group of top deputies—Mark Tuohey, Roger Adelman, John Bates, Ray and LeRoy Jahn, Bradley Lerman, Amy St. Eve—had left the staff by 1998. This group had managed the investigation in the time-honored professional manner: begin by prosecuting the midlevel players, in the hope that they will turn against the top people. They had convicted Jim and Susan Mc-Dougal, won a guilty plea from Webster Hubbell, and pushed them to flip.

Jim McDougal did change his testimony and incriminate the president on the obscure matter of the single loan relating to the Whitewater development, but his ex-wife and Hubbell never changed their stories. In the face of powerful inducements, both Susan and Hubbell continued to insist that they knew of no illegal activities by the Clintons. Hubbell stuck to this story in the face of two subsequent reindictments on other charges. Susan McDougal, who was sentenced to two years in the Madison Guaranty case, chose to serve an additional eighteen months in jail for civil contempt rather than testify before Starr's grand jury. In time, the experienced prosecutors on Starr's staff did what veterans usually do in such circumstances. They gave up—or, to put it another way, they moved on. Because of their professional reputations and experience, the original Starr group had job opportunities in the private sector; they knew when it was time to quit. For better or worse, the case against the Clintons, they recognized, was over.

Those who stayed on with Starr generally fell into one (or both) of two categories—the unemployable and the obsessed. The investigation of Vincent Foster's suicide provided a tragicomic example of the perversity of the Starr office. Foster, a deputy White House counsel, died of an apparently self-inflicted gunshot wound on July 20, 1993, in Fort Marcy Park, in suburban Virginia. About a month later, the Justice Department, the FBI, and the Park Police jointly announced the results of their investigation into his death: he had committed suicide. But, in part because Foster had left a note containing references to the Clintons' financial troubles, Fiske, the first Whitewater prosecutor, decided to reexamine the case. On June 30, 1994, Fiske released a report in which he agreed that Foster had killed himself. But that wasn't enough for some in Congress, so the House Committee on Government Operations opened its own investigation, only to come to the same conclusion on August 12, 1994. The Senate Banking Committee did the same, filing its report on January 3, 1995.

What did Starr do, after these four separate investigations were concluded? He devoted nearly three more years to studying Foster's death, and on October 10, 1997, he, too, released a report stating that Vincent Foster had killed himself. Through such follies, year after year of the Starr investigation slipped away.

But the Starr veterans had produced something more than just accumulated frustrations. They couldn't make their case in court, but by 1998, Starr's core group of survivors had developed what amounted to a private narrative of the Clinton scandals—an overarching explanation for what had happened and why. Its principal author was a man named W. Hickman Ewing, Jr., and its principal subject was sex.

/ / /

Hick Ewing was one of the first prosecutors that Starr hired, in 1994. Ewing quickly impressed—and occasionally surprised—his new colleagues with his approach to law enforcement. One former Starr prosecutor recalled, "Most prosecutors at least say that they come to things with open minds, but Hick says that he presumes that a crime has been committed and his job is to proceed as if there is criminal conduct and then be convinced otherwise. Hick doesn't undertake an investigation with the supposition that the people are innocent. It struck me when he said it." Ewing's attitude might have been less surprising in a United States Attorney's Office, where prosecutors are often presented with known crimes to solve. But independent counsels were assigned, in the first instance, to determine whether a crime had occurred. Ewing once said, "After you've been doing this kind of work for ten, fifteen, twenty years, it doesn't take too long to determine whether somebody has committed a crime. You draw your preliminary conclusions, and then you shut this down or you proceed. We proceeded."

The Starr investigation was often portrayed as a personal contest between the independent counsel and the president, but Hickman Ewing may have been the one who really took it personally. He and Clinton resembled opposite generational archetypes in the culture war that defined so much of this story. If Clinton was the Ivy League–educated, draft-avoiding, philandering liberal who found success on the national stage, Ewing was the born-again Vietnam-vet conservative whose assignment in Little Rock represented his first legal job outside Memphis, Tennessee. Ewing's distinctive history, and worldview, shaped the independent counsel's investigation.

The prosecutor's father, William Hickman Ewing, Sr., was a legendary sports figure in Shelby County, the longtime football and baseball coach at South Side High School in Memphis. Ewing, who played football for his dad, attended Vanderbilt on a Navy ROTC scholarship and, after he graduated in 1964, served on active duty for five years, commanding a small patrol boat that ran along the coast of Vietnam. While young Hickman was in the Navy, his father's life turned sour. In late 1964, he was indicted for embezzlement, and he pleaded guilty the following year to stealing about $43,000 from the county government. He spent eighteen months in prison while his son was at war. His father's problems began after he got mixed up with politics; Hick's adversaries often suggested that Ewing's career represented a form of revenge against politicians.

In his boyhood and college days, Ewing shared the typical preoccupations of a Memphis youth—sports, beer, and Elvis. But Ewing had a spiritual awakening in 1977, a few years after he became a prosecutor, and he joined the First Evangelical Church, one of the largest and most conservative congregations in Memphis. Ewing left that church in the mid-eighties, and he and a small group of friends founded the Fellowship Evangelical Church, over which he usually presided as a lay minister. With his conversion, Ewing began to set aside time for prayer when he rose each morning, and he stopped drinking. He and his wife, Mary, had three children, and they sent all three to the Evangelical Christian School, in Memphis. Ewing's conversion came with a commitment to service as well as a habit of piety. Nearly every year, he traveled to rural Mexico to work with the Tlapaneco Indians. While Ewing rose through the ranks to become the United States attorney in Memphis, his wife volunteered as an antiabortion sidewalk counselor outside clinics in Tennessee.

When Ewing was replaced as United States attorney in 1991, his friends held a testimonial in his honor at a Memphis restaurant. Few politicians were present, but there were several representatives of Christian-right organizations, including the Reverend Donald Wildmon's American Family Association, Beverly La-Haye's Concerned Women for America, and FLARE (Family, Life, America, and Responsible Education Under God). "I feel like I've just been an instrument over these years, and God should get the glory," Ewing told the group. "I'm trusting the Lord for the next step. I don't know what the next step is."

Shortly after he left the government, Ewing told the Memphis *Commercial Appeal* that he had considered going to work at a place like the Rutherford Institute—the Christian-right organization that helped to underwrite Paula Jones's lawsuit against Clinton. He ultimately decided to open a one-man private law practice, with his wife as his secretary and sole employee until his daughter went to work for him, too. But less than three years after he left the government, Starr called him back to prosecuting. He made the three-hour drive from Little Rock to Memphis almost every weekend, to see his family and to go to church. In his car he had two cassette tapes: the Book of Deuteronomy and *The Comeback Kid Tour,* by Paul Shanklin, who performed anti-Clinton parodies on Rush Limbaugh's radio program.

/ / /

Ewing and other veterans of the Starr hard core made a conceptual breakthrough early in their investigation. At first, they had thought Bill and Hillary Clinton were motivated by greed, which was what usually drove corrupt politicians in their experience. But they decided that theory was wrong. Instead, they said, it was sex and politics that drove the president and first lady.

The subject first came up in connection with the suicide of Vince Foster. Like both Mrs. Clinton and Webb Hubbell, Foster was a partner in the Rose Law Firm who had come to Washington to work in the new administration. Foster's suicide, on July 20, 1993, unsettled the White House; investigators began attempting to learn more about documents, including the Clintons' personal legal papers, that had been taken from Foster's office soon after his death. There was much speculation in the news media that loyal White House aides had removed documents relating to Whitewater, but the Starr staff developed another theory. It was no secret that Mrs. Clinton regarded Foster as a trusted friend, and some prosecutors came to believe the extraordinary—and entirely unproven—theory that Mrs. Clinton had had an affair with Foster, and that her chief concern was keeping it secret. According to this scenario, the Clinton aides were worried that Foster had left behind something about his relationship with Hillary, such as a suicide note saying something like "We can't sleep together anymore." This sort of fanciful speculation had surfaced previously, but mostly in the more extreme elements of the Clinton-hating press.

That was only the beginning of the sex-driven theory underlying the Starr investigation. Some asserted that Clinton became involved in the fraudulent loan to Susan McDougal in the Madison Guaranty case because he was having an affair with her—something both she and the president denied. Ewing was convinced that the Clintons' friend deputy White House counsel Bruce Lindsey was the designated keeper of the secrets about the president's personal life, and the prosecutor undertook an elaborate effort to persuade Lindsey to flip. In 1996, Ewing led the prosecution of two Arkansas bankers—Herby Branscum, Jr., and Robert M. Hill—on charges that they misapplied bank funds and concealed cash transactions related to the Clinton gubernatorial campaign in 1990. In that case, Starr named Lindsey as an unindicted co-conspirator. The hope was that Branscum and Hill would be convicted, and then inform on Lindsey, who would, in turn, testify against the president. But Ewing's plan fell apart when the jury failed to convict the two bankers.

This failure, of course, exemplified the central problem with the Ewing thesis: he could never make it stick. As with the financial issues at the heart of the Whitewater case, neither Ewing nor anyone in Starr's office could tie the president or first lady to any criminal activity related to sex or anything else. It certainly wasn't for lack of trying. As late as 1997, FBI agents working for Starr's Little Rock office—which Ewing ran—started questioning Clinton's friends and associates about the then governor's relationships with women in Arkansas. They were the same sorts of questions Mike Isikoff had been asking three years earlier. In a demonstration of the endless circularity of the pursuit of Clinton, the FBI paid particular attention to his former bodyguards with the Arkansas state police—the same people, of course, who were David Brock's sources on the story that began the Paula Jones case. The Trooper Project, as it was known in Starr's office, also came to naught.

So when Linda Tripp called Jackie Bennett on the night of January 12, 1998, she found an audience primed to hear her tale of sexual misconduct and cover-up by the president. Bennett himself represented the hardest of the hard core. Though he had tried without success for some time to find a job with a private firm in Washington, Bennett was as committed as anyone to bringing Clinton down. Before joining Starr, he had spent much of the previous decade as a prosecutor in the public integrity section of the Justice Department, on a rough-and-tumble crusade against Democratic politicians in south Texas. There Bennett had mixed results. He won a conviction of former representative Albert Bustamante (as well as the Justice Department's John Marshall Award for the top prosecutors in the nation), but he also lost a case against Doug Jaffe, a businessman in San Antonio who was a big Democratic contributor. After Bennett lost one case, the trial judge delivered an unusual rebuke, saying, "I really wish you'd take a message back to [the Justice Department] that we're not interested in wasting our time on rinky-dink cases." Because of episodes like this, Bennett was known to some colleagues as "the thug."

To many people, then, including some veterans of the Starr office itself, the story of Monica Lewinsky seemed awfully far afield from the Whitewater-based jurisdiction of the independent counsel. But to the true believers who remained on Starr's staff, it was as if they had spent three years and five months waiting for Tripp's call.

As Jackie Bennett recalled the conversation for Michael Isikoff, Tripp initially pretended that she had "a friend" who was being asked to lie under oath in her deposition in the Paula Jones case. But she soon dropped the fiction, identified herself, and asked a question that had been haunting her since her conversations with Kirby Behre. Could Starr's prosecutors give her immunity if she had made illegal tapes? Bennett told her yes. He was intrigued to hear that Tripp had been interviewed by the Starr office in connection with the Foster suicide. Quickly, he had heard enough to want to meet Linda Tripp. He found Steve Irons, an FBI agent assigned to Starr, and two other prosecutors, Sol Wisenberg and Steve Binhak, and they piled into a car for the forty-minute drive to Tripp's home in Columbia, Maryland.

They didn't settle down in Tripp's living room until about 11:45 P.M. on January 12. As recorded in the six-and-a-half-page single-spaced FBI report of the meeting, Tripp gave her interlocutors an astonishingly distorted survey of the twists and turns of the case. The theme was Tripp as victim—of Bob Bennett, Monica Lewinsky, Kirby Behre, Vernon Jordan, Bill Clinton. Tripp dropped tantalizing details about Monica's soiled dress and talked at length about her tapes, but she lied about the real purpose of her recordings. "TRIPP believed that BENNETT and the White House would try to destroy her based on what she had seen them do to other people who got in their way," the report stated. "That belief ultimately motivated TRIPP to begin tape recording telephone conversations TRIPP had with MONICA LEWINSKY." Thus, Tripp conveniently said nothing about her plans to write a book—and never even mentioned the name Lucianne Goldberg. Moreover, Tripp did not say that, through Goldberg, she had herself told the Jones lawyers about Lewinsky, and that she had herself conspired with David Pyke, of the Jones team, for the "surprise" subpoena that was now causing her such anguish.

As the hours stretched on toward daybreak, Bennett had a decision to make. Tripp was scheduled to have lunch with Lewinsky on that very Tuesday, January 13. Should the OIC tape the meeting?

Tripp believed the situation was urgent—Lewinsky had to be recorded. But was there really an emergency? Tripp and Lewinsky were in regular contact; Tripp's deposition was not even scheduled; there would undoubtedly be more contact between the two women in the near future. At this point, Bennett had to make his decision exclusively on the basis of Tripp's word—and Rosenzweig's briefing from the elves in Philadelphia the previous week. But who was Linda Tripp? Who were those lawyers in Philadelphia and what was their role in all of this? Bennett could have waited a day or two to check out Tripp's bona fides and motives and weigh whether Starr's office ought to be investigating this subject at all.

But Jackie Bennett was not one for agonizing. That night he called the FBI technical services division and ordered up a body wire for the next day. Linda Tripp was going to be an undercover operative on behalf of the Office of Independent Counsel.

/ / /

On Tuesday morning, Lewinsky began her day with a visit to Vernon Jordan's office, to drop off some gifts for him. ("I spend a lot of time and am very particular about the presents I give to people," Lewinsky testified later.) The previous week, Monica had accepted a job in the Revlon public relations department at $40,000 a year, which was less than she was making at the Pentagon but still acceptable to her. Also the previous week, Lewinsky had signed the affidavit that Frank Carter had drafted for her. In the critical part, paragraph 8, the affidavit stated: "I have never had a sexual relationship with the President, he did not propose that we have a sexual relationship[.] The occasions that I saw the President after I left my employment at the White House in April 1996 were official receptions, formal functions or events related to the U.S. Department of Defense, where I was working at the time. There were other people present on those occasions." (Jordan had let the president know both when the job offer had come through and when Lewinsky signed her affidavit.) For setting her up with Revlon and Carter, Monica wanted to say thank you to Jordan.

Then, following her visit with Jordan, Lewinsky made her way to the Ritz-Carlton and her late lunch with Linda Tripp. (Tripp had arrived first to meet with her FBI handlers, who fitted her with a body microphone.) Downstairs, Tripp found a secluded table in the restaurant's smoking section. Monica arrived at 2:45 P.M.

"Listen," Tripp began, "I've been thinking about you nonstop."

The conversation lasted an excruciating three hours—always rambling, at times incoherent, but with a few identifiable themes. Lewinsky spoke with a maddening inconsistency. On the one hand, she professed continued loyalty to the president: "No matter how he has wronged me, how many girlfriends he had . . . it was my choice." On the other hand, Monica portrayed herself as holding out for a job from Jordan in return for her testimony denying the affair. As she told Tripp at one point, "I said, 'I'm supposed to sign, and I'm not signing it until I have a job.'" This latter statement by Lewinsky was false on two counts. In truth, Monica had already signed her affidavit, and she had already gotten a job through Jordan. At still another time, Monica seemed afraid that Clinton was going to have her killed: "For fear of my life, I would not cross these people."

The confusion illustrated the risk of basing a criminal case on meandering girl talk. Based on this conversation, it was clear that Monica was going to deny a sexual relationship with Clinton and she wanted her friend to do the same. Yet it wasn't apparent that Lewinsky actually felt she had to lie, or that anyone had asked her to withhold information about her relationship. Describing the draft affidavit, she said that she denied having a "sexual relationship" with the president. "I never had intercourse," Lewinsky explained, in a theme that they had discussed in earlier, taped conversations. "I did not have a sexual relationship." So, in this respect, Lewinsky apparently felt she could file a truthful, if misleading, affidavit. The only sure thing about what became known as the "sting tape" was that Lewinsky was a confused and troubled woman. Her attitude toward Tripp was muddled. She said at one point, "I look at you as a mom." Tripp replied, "I know that." Yet when Tripp went to the "bathroom"—in fact, to get her wiring adjusted—Monica checked Tripp's bag for a tape recorder, perhaps because Tripp had been instructing her, "Stop whispering. I can't hear." In the 262-page single-spaced transcript of the sting tape, it was possible to find support for virtually any theory of the case—Clinton was lying (or being lied to); Jordan was calling the shots (or responding to them); Lewinsky was filled with fear (or bravado); Tripp was the instigator (or the victim) of a conspiracy.

Near the end Tripp sighed, "I feel like we're in the middle of a John Grisham book."

/ / /

After the "lunch"—it was by then early evening—on January 13, Tripp's handlers retrieved the tape and took her back to the Starr office, on Pennsylvania Avenue, a few blocks from the White House. There the prosecutors gathered to listen to the tape and begin their debriefings of their newest witness. Both the review of the tape and the interview with Tripp took a long time, and it was well into the evening when a pair of prosecutors volunteered to drive Tripp back home to Columbia—the same forty-minute ride that Jackie Bennett and his colleagues had made one night earlier.

Tripp's escorts were Bruce Udolf and Mary Anne Wirth. These two prosecutors, along with a third, Michael Emmick, had joined Starr's office only in the past year, and in certain important respects they did not resemble their longer-tenured colleagues. Udolf and Emmick had led two of the largest and most important public corruption sections in any United States Attorney's Office in the nation, Udolf in Miami and Emmick in Los Angeles. Udolf and Emmick were both forty-five years old, with literally decades of high-level law enforcement experience with corrupt politicians between them. (Wirth had served as a federal prosecutor in New York.) Because Emmick and Udolf had essentially just joined the office, they shared few of the accumulated frustrations that had festered among the true believers. To a greater extent than their colleagues, they could treat the Clinton case as just another federal investigation, not a holy war. (Udolf, Wirth, and Emmick were also Democrats.)

At least at first, Udolf in particular had no problem with being a loner in Starr's office. After graduating from college, he had tried to make a living playing bass in a blues band, but then drifted into law school, at Emory University in Atlanta. After graduating, he took a job as a prosecutor in a small county north of the city where the district attorney had served for thirty-three years. Within a couple of years, however, the old-timer announced he was quitting and wanted Udolf to serve as his successor. When Udolf won the office, in 1982, he wasn't yet thirty years old, and he was voted out of office after just a single four-year term. But he caught the prosecuting bug and went on to a legendary career in Miami, where he convicted a passel of crooked mayors, judges, and cops. At the time he joined Starr's office, in mid-1997, Udolf was just getting over a bout with liver disease, and he and his wife had a new baby daughter as well. He saw the job with Starr as a sort of culmination of his prosecutorial career, the chance, in a relatively brief period of time, to put his skills to work in the most important forum in the country.

But for the night of January 13, Bruce Udolf was Linda Tripp's chauffeur. Tripp treated him to an extended monologue on her own heroism and what she would expect from the prosecutors in return. Udolf and Wirth (whom Tripp would come to dub "the witch") were horrified at the arrogance and sense of entitlement of their office's newest and closest ally.

The first thing Wednesday morning, Udolf sought out Jackie Bennett. Swarthy and excitable, Udolf never hid his feelings from friends or adversaries. "That woman," he told Bennett of his passenger of the previous night, "is a fucking cunt. If you want to get in bed with that bitch, you're going to pay for it eventually."

Bennett, taken aback, replied, "But she's credible."

"Any jury would hate that woman," Udolf answered.

/ / /

For her part, Monica Lewinsky spent the morning of Wednesday, January 14, at the word processor in her apartment at the Watergate. There she composed a document that would briefly become one of the most discussed writings in the country—the "talking points." In a way, the talking points were a logical outgrowth of her conversation with Tripp of the previous day. Among other things, Lewinsky had suggested that Tripp could file an affidavit with the Jones lawyers to avoid testifying. (Lewinsky's affidavit, drafted by Frank Carter, was intended for that purpose.) At the end of the work day on Wednesday, Monica, who had quit her job in preparation for the move to New York, picked up Tripp at the Pentagon and handed her the three-page draft of the affidavit.

The first words on the document were "points to make in affidavit." It then continued, "Your first few paragraphs should be about yourself—what you do now, what you did at the White

House and for how many years you were there as a career person and as a political appointee." The next section—the bulk of the document—consisted of a recounting of Tripp's experience with Kathleen Willey. At this point, Lewinsky believed that Willey was the only subject about which the Jones lawyers wanted to interrogate Tripp. In the talking points, Lewinsky accurately summarized Tripp's view of the Willey incident—that Willey had sought out the meeting with the president and that she was pleased, not distressed, by Clinton's interest in her. "I have never observed the President behave inappropriately with anybody," Lewinsky wrote in Tripp's voice.

Later, when the Lewinsky story broke and copies of the talking points were leaked to the press, the document became the subject of frenzied speculation. According to the working hypothesis of many observers of the investigation, the talking points were drafted by some high-level Clinton administration official—Vernon Jordan or Bruce Lindsey, maybe even the president himself. That person gave the talking points to Lewinsky for her to turn them over to Tripp as a script for how she should lie in the Jones case. In this way, the talking points were evidence of a conspiracy within the Clinton administration to obstruct justice in the Jones case. All this hypothesis illustrated, however, was the hysteria that afflicted Clinton's critics. For starters, every word in the talking points was *true;* thus, regardless of its authorship, there was no way the document could be evidence of a plot to obstruct justice. Lewinsky was simply assisting in Tripp's stated goal of avoiding testifying. (It was *Tripp* who was lying—by saying she didn't want to testify when, in fact, she had engineered her subpoena from David Pyke.)

Tripp immediately turned over the talking points to the FBI, and the agents prepared her for a monitored phone call with Lewinsky that evening.

Also on the afternoon of January 14, Jim Moody showed up unannounced at the office of Kirby Behre, to say that he was taking over the representation of Linda Tripp. He was there to pick up the case files and the tapes. Mortified, horrified, but mostly stunned, Behre called Tripp to confirm what Moody was saying. She did—but Behre said he needed a day to get the tapes organized. Moody, goaded by Tripp, was starting to panic about Behre.

What if he took the day to copy the tapes and give them to Bob Bennett? Moody wanted the tapes—now. He insisted on seeing the senior partner on the case, then the top partner in the firm. Behre stood firm.

Finally, Moody agreed to return the following day, when Behre, as promised, turned over Tripp's tapes. By this point, Moody was beginning to share his new client's paranoia, so he didn't take the tapes straight to his office. Rather, he engaged in a series of evasive maneuvers to avoid what he imagined might be White House surveillance. (Because Moody couldn't really see, he had a difficult time determining whether he was being followed.) He took a cab to the Capitol and walked through one entrance to the Russell Senate Office Building and out the other. He stopped at another Senate office. Then he took a cab to Georgetown, talked on a pay phone for a while, and finally took another taxi to his office.

That night, Moody shared the tapes with two of the elves. Lacking a good home sound system, Moody took the recordings to the home of Ann Coulter, the conservative activist, where he listened to them with her and George Conway, the New York elf, who happened to be in Washington on other business. One of the lawyers for Jones had faxed Lewinsky's affidavit to Moody, and Tripp's lawyer that evening sent it over to Starr's investigators.

/ / /

As Tripp drew the Starr investigators deeper into the intrigue surrounding her own and Lewinsky's affidavits and depositions, the question remained: Why was the Whitewater independent counsel investigating the Paula Jones case? What business was this of Ken Starr's?

Under the law, independent counsels were allowed to investigate matters that had been specifically referred to them by the Special Division and also "related" matters—a usefully vague term. The questions troubled some of Starr's prosecutors from the moment they heard of Linda Tripp's first phone call.

The issue didn't trouble Jackie Bennett. A beefy former offensive tackle in college, Bennett was Hick Ewing's counterpart in Washington. In practical terms, Bennett served as Starr's chief deputy in the Washington office in the same way that Ewing was Starr's deputy in Little Rock; but in a more profound sense, Bennett and Ewing were kindred political spirits as well. Bennett believed that Starr needed no additional authorization from the court to pursue Tripp's leads, but he was prevailed upon at least to inform the Justice Department of the developments on Wednesday night. At 10:18 P.M., on January 14, Bennett caught Deputy Attorney General Eric Holder by cell phone just as he was leaving a Washington Wizards basketball game.

"We are sort of into a sensitive matter," Bennett's notes of the conversation begin. "Breaking. Paying close attention to jurisdictional limits—confident sufficient jurisdictional nexus. Involves people at and associated with White House." At this stage, there was little Holder could say or do. They agreed to meet the following day, and on Thursday, January 15, Bennett led a delegation to Holder's office that included Mike Emmick, Bruce Udolf, and a younger lawyer, Stephen Bates, who took detailed notes. Bennett began by reciting Tripp's allegations. In Bennett's recitation, he replaced the murky tangle of the facts with perfect clarity. The evidence was "explicit. Lewinsky feared retaliation from the powers that be. She acknowledged she had lied or would continue lying. She told Tripp that she planned to sign a false declaration." In fact, the sting tape itself contained evidence to contradict all of these assertions, which Holder and his deputy could not have known. "The effort" at providing a false story in the Jones case "seems to go back to the President and a close associate of his, Vernon Jordan."

"We've had no contacts with the plaintiff's attorneys," Bennett explained. This was close to an outright lie—and an important one. For one thing, Starr himself had consulted extensively with Gil Davis shortly after the Jones suit was filed and had spoken out publicly in favor of her right to sue the president. That might have been worth mentioning when, in essence, Starr's office was about to start investigating whether Bill Clinton had committed a crime against Davis and his successors in the Jones lawsuit. But more important, Bennett had been tipped off about Lewinsky's existence less than a week earlier by his colleague Paul Rosenzweig—who had heard about her from Marcus, Conway, and Porter. Had the deputy attorney general known about the cozy alliance between the Jones elves and the Starr team, he might have asked a lot more questions about the origin of the investigation. But because

Holder was misled, he didn't pursue the issue. Bennett later asserted that the elves were really not "the plaintiff's attorneys," but only assistants to her attorneys or friends of Tripp's. The Starr office would later call for Bill Clinton's impeachment for playing similar word games.

The only other person to speak at the meeting with Holder was Bruce Udolf, who took a considerably narrower view of the evidence. "The allegations against the president are not as clear as those against Jordan," he said. When Udolf suggested that if the case only involved Jordan, perhaps the Department of Justice should take it over, Bennett jumped in: "We think it's real, and it involves the White House."

Bennett and Bates followed up the meeting with a letter to Attorney General Janet Reno, formally asking her to petition the court to expand Starr's mandate to include the Lewinsky matter. Mostly, the letter illustrated just how desperately the Starr team wanted to hold on to the nascent investigation. "For two reasons, we believe that Mr. Jordan's and Ms. Lewinsky's alleged efforts to suborn perjury fall within our jurisdiction," Starr wrote.

"First, Ms. Tripp is an important witness in our investigation," the letter stated. She was now apparently being urged to perjure herself in *Jones v. Clinton*. "Should she in fact perjure herself, obviously her usefulness as a potential witness in any trial would be greatly reduced, which is a matter of deep concern." This was a transparently bogus rationale. Tripp's role in Travelgate and the Foster investigation did not make her an important witness in Starr's ongoing work; Bennett didn't even recognize her name. Indeed, this rationale was so tortured that Starr didn't even mention it in his celebrated report to Congress later that year.

Second, Starr wrote that he was already investigating whether witnesses in his criminal case were promised jobs for their silence. "Ms. Lewinsky's statements suggest that the very same individuals are using the very same tactics in the civil case. In particular, we are already investigating Vernon Jordan for having helped arrange employment for Webster Hubbell." Starr had a better claim here; there was at least a surface similarity between the two cases—although, ultimately, he couldn't make the jobs-for-testimony case in either one. But the Vernon Jordan connection did serve as the narrow bridge to allow Starr to march his divisions from the failed land deal in Arkansas to the presidential boudoir.

Politically, there was little Reno and Holder could do except agree to Starr's request. Based on the sketchy, incomplete picture that Jackie Bennett had presented, the Justice Department could scarcely have refused to go to the three-judge court and ask to broaden the prosecutor's jurisdiction. By late in the day on Thursday, January 15, Starr was officially sanctioned to investigate obstruction of justice in *Jones v. Clinton.*

/ / /

There was never much debate in the Starr office about what to do next. They had to flip Lewinsky.

And, it turned out, they had to do it fast. On Thursday, Isikoff, responding to pressure from his editors to deliver something for *Newsweek,* had called both Betty Currie and Jackie Bennett to ask about Monica Lewinsky. (On the advice of Jordan and Bruce Lindsey, Currie said nothing.) Currie also alerted Lewinsky that Isikoff was asking about her. For his part, Isikoff was ferrying information between Goldberg, Tripp, and the prosecutors, in the process walking up to and perhaps over the line that separates observers and participants. The Goldberg notes recount, "Isikoff told me PJ lawyers told him about the feds coming in."

The prosecutors were clinging to the hope that they might maintain the element of surprise. Bennett invited Isikoff to the OIC offices and implored him to wait until the following week to publish. Isikoff was noncommittal—this was a decision for his editors to make—so Bennett had to assume the story would run. *Newsweek* would release its story on Sunday, January 18, so the Starr forces had two days at most—Friday and Saturday (the day of the president's deposition)—to use Lewinsky to make their case against Clinton.

Thursday night, Tripp and Lewinsky had their final telephone conversation, in which they rehashed the same material one more time. They detoured briefly onto the subject of Tripp's sex life (L: "We gotta get you laid." T: ". . . After seven years, do you really think there's a possibility I'd remember how?"), but came back to the subject of how they should testify in the Jones case. As always, the conversation ended inconclusively, and they agreed to speak in the morning. On Friday morning, on instructions from the OIC, Tripp set up a meeting with Lewinsky, at 11:30 A.M., in the food court of the Pentagon City Mall, near where the two women had had lunch on Tuesday.

Bennett, Emmick, and Udolf scrambled to choreograph the meeting between Tripp and Lewinsky. Steve Irons and Patrick Fallon, Jr., who were FBI agents assigned to Starr, would descend on Lewinsky as soon as Tripp identified her. They would then bring her up to a room in the Ritz-Carlton where she could be debriefed. Early that morning, Udolf had told the two agents to bring a female colleague with them. "You don't bring a woman to a hotel room without a woman agent," Udolf had said. But the agents, who enjoyed being labeled tough guys, ignored the prosecutor's advice and arrived by themselves.

At 12:45 P.M., as Tripp went down the escalator, she signaled Irons and Fallon, who were waiting. They descended on Lewinsky and told her that she was wanted for questioning in connection with an investigation of the president of the United States for obstruction of justice. The two agents quickly escorted Lewinsky to Room 1012 of the adjoining Ritz-Carlton Hotel. Tripp trailed behind and joined them in the small room.

Not long after the general outlines of the case became known, the interrogation of Lewinsky in Room 1012 became a symbol of the purported excesses of the OIC investigation. Starr's critics asserted that Lewinsky's rights were violated in any number of ways—that she was held against her will, prevented from calling a lawyer, threatened with abuse and other unspecified outrages. From the beginning, Starr was on the defensive about the hotel room encounter.

The independent counsel made trouble for himself by the way he defended the conduct of his investigators on this day. On at least two occasions in the subsequent year—in a letter to *Brill's Content* magazine and in his testimony before the House Judiciary Committee—Starr denied that anyone in Room 1012 had tried to persuade Lewinsky to make secret tape recordings of Jordan, Clinton, or others. Starr wrote to the magazine, "This Office never asked Ms. Lewinsky to agree to wire herself for a conversation with Mr. Jordan or the President." Starr's claim was so obviously false that it served mainly to illustrate a larger truth about his stewardship of the OIC. Starr's lack of experience as a prosecutor was such that he exercised almost no critical judgment on the key decisions made by his office. But controlled phone calls are the standard investigative technique for white-collar crime. Not surprisingly, the *entire purpose* of the approach to Lewinsky was to get her to flip on Jordan, Currie, and perhaps Clinton as well. With Isikoff's story looming, such calls were the only way to collect useful evidence in the brief time available.

But Starr's muddled defense should not obscure the fact that Lewinsky's treatment in the hotel room was entirely appropriate for an important witness in an unfolding criminal investigation. From the moment she arrived at 1:05 P.M., Emmick and later Jackie Bennett did encourage her to cooperate—and make the controlled calls. They told her she might be prosecuted and face a long prison sentence, which was a real, if remote, possibility. Regarding the dicey business of contacting her lawyer, the prosecutors didn't want her to reach out to Frank Carter, but they didn't stop her either. (The situation was complicated by the fact that the prosecutors regarded Carter as a suspect at that point; they believed he had prepared Lewinsky's false affidavit, but they didn't know whether Carter knew it was false.) If a narcotics suspect had been treated as Lewinsky was at the Ritz-Carlton, there might well have been public outrage about how she had been coddled. The discomfort with Lewinsky's treatment seemed mostly to have been a form of displaced anger. It wasn't the interrogation that offended people as much as the subject matter of Starr's investigation—one rooted in consensual sexual encounters.

/ / /

In truth, the showdown in Room 1012 traced a slow but sure trajectory from tragedy to farce. The prosecutors had agreed that Emmick would handle the questioning. An Angeleno, like Lewinsky, Emmick was also a handsome, easygoing type who had a reputation as a ladies' man. Compared to the overbearing Bennett and intense Udolf, Emmick was the obvious choice.

At first, though, Lewinsky was in no position to be questioned. She had launched into an angry tirade against the stone-faced Tripp, who was sitting silently on a sofa. "Make her stay and watch," Monica recalled saying to the agents. "I want that treacherous bitch to see what she has done to me." Soon enough, however, Udolf stepped in from the adjoining room and suggested that they let Tripp go on her way. "If we're going to flip this girl," Udolf said quietly to his colleagues, "we're not going to do it with that bitch in the room." Tripp was excused, but the agents told her to remain in the mall. Lewinsky was finally alone with her inquisitors.

Emmick tried to play the good cop, explaining that Starr's office wanted Lewinsky to cooperate in their investigation. Lewinsky listened in silence for a time, and then, almost without warning, she broke down in hysterical, unhinged sobbing. Emmick tried to calm her, but he couldn't break through. As Emmick fretted to his colleagues in the adjoining room, Lewinsky went on and on, for a full ninety minutes. Finally, at around three o'clock, she began to recover her equilibrium. Lewinsky asked to call her mother, and Emmick reluctantly allowed Monica to leave the room and make the call from a pay phone. Since she wasn't under arrest, Emmick couldn't stop her. "Well, that's it," Emmick told the agents. "She's never coming back."

But Lewinsky did return, and her mother, Marcia Lewis, called the room from New York. On the spot, Emmick decided to offer immunity to both Monica and her mother. Obviously stalling, Lewinsky asked if her mother could join the negotiations in person. Emmick didn't like the idea of the delay, but he had little choice but to agree. After weighing whether Monica should be escorted to New York or to the middle ground of Philadelphia, Lewis said she would leave immediately for D.C. As Lewinsky weighed the offer, Jackie Bennett arrived to play the bad cop. "You're twenty-four years old, you're smart, you're old enough, you don't need to call your mommy," he said. But Lewinsky wanted to wait for her mother—who feared air travel and was arriving by train.

As the minutes, and then the hours, began to pass, Emmick and his colleagues began to notice a transformation come over Lewinsky. She began to try to ingratiate herself with the investigators—and then display her own sense of entitlement. She said she had wanted to become an FBI agent herself. She told them a dirty joke. She said she wanted to go for a walk, so Emmick and the agents took her on a long amble through every level of the mall—into Crate & Barrel, a men's clothing place, and a few other stores. At one point, Lewinsky said she had to go to the bathroom and was gone for about fifteen minutes. Again, Emmick figured she had skipped. (In fact, she had tried unsuccessfully to tip Betty Currie about the investigation.)

When Lewinsky returned, and the whole group went to dinner at Mozzarella's American Grill. They returned to the room and watched the beginning of *There's No Business Like Show Business.* At around eight o'clock, Lewis called to say her train was delayed. At one point, Lewinsky said her contact lenses were drying out. An agent searched the mall for a drugstore, but the best he could do was persuade the Ritz-Carlton sundries store to reopen. When the agent returned with the solution, Lewinsky said, "That's cleaner. I wanted saline"—and the agent returned to prowl the mall again.

Marcia Lewis finally arrived at 10:16 P.M., and spoke to her daughter alone. At this point, everyone in the room was woozy from the combination of boredom and tension. Mother and daughter called Monica's father, Bernie Lewinsky, in Los Angeles. A lawyer friend of Bernie's, a fellow named William Ginsburg, called to speak to Monica and then to the prosecutors. Clearly, Lewinsky would not be cooperating. At 12:45 A.M., the agents escorted Lewinsky and her mother to Monica's car in the mall parking lot.

As she wandered the mall with her law enforcement escort on Friday, Lewinsky never noticed one of her more famous fellow shoppers. As it happened, Susan Carpenter-McMillan had chosen that very mall to shop for a new suit for her friend Paula Jones. Susan thought Paula deserved something special to wear to the deposition of President Bill Clinton the following day.

12

The Definition of Sex—and L-E-W-I-N-S-K-Y

All right," said Judge Susan Webber Wright. "The purpose of this hearing is really rather unusual. It's to enable the court to make some kind of decision concerning the scope of the deposition of President Clinton. This deposition will be an extraordinary event."

They were all in an unfamiliar courtroom. In an effort to avoid the scrutiny of the press, Judge Wright had called a hearing in the small federal courthouse in Pine Bluff, about forty miles south of her usual home base in Little Rock. The judge had even ordered the windows in the courthouse covered, so that no one could see that she was meeting with the lawyers in *Jones v. Clinton*. News of the meeting did not leak, and the secrecy prompted unusual candor, especially from the judge. It was the morning of Monday, January 12, five days before Bill Clinton would become the first sitting president in American history to be examined as a party in a lawsuit.

In her decision on December 11, Wright had already established the general ground rules for the examination of the president, but she wanted one last chance to clarify matters with the lawyers. Everyone recognized that the stakes for Saturday's deposition were at least as high as for the lawsuit itself. The opportunity to examine Clinton under oath had been a principal reason the Dallas lawyers agreed to represent Paula Jones. Like all the depositions in the case, the president's would take place in secret, but Bob Bennett understood the ways of politics well enough to know that some—or, more likely, all—of the president's words would eventually be made public.

Clinton had long ago stated that he remembered nothing about any meeting with Paula Jones in a hotel room, so his testimony on the incident itself was sure to be uneventful. The real controversy would involve what the plaintiff's lawyers called the "pattern and practice" issues—that is, Clinton's testimony about his relationships with other women. As Bennett told Judge Wright, "All they can really ask him is—is sex." In a practical sense, then, the president's deposition marked the culmination of the campaign by journalists (led by Brock and Isikoff) and activists (initiated by Cliff Jackson and his fellow Clinton-haters) to explore the secrets of Bill Clinton's sex life. At last they all had what they really wanted: Clinton under oath on the subject of adultery.

Wright spoke with a deep sense of unease about what was to come—the indignity, the seaminess, of it all. Like so few people in this story, Susan Wright had no agenda of her own, only a desire to provide justice in as fair and dignified a manner as possible. She had summoned the lawyers to make a last pitch to prevent her court, and the country, from heading into the abyss.

"The idea, of course, is to be above politics, to be removed from it. That is my goal," the plain-spoken judge began, but in light of how the case had proceeded, "I feel helpless. And for that reason, I would like for you all to settle this case. I want you to get the thing settled. This case needs—it just screams for settlement."

Bennett urged the judge not to hold out much hope that the case would end before the president's deposition. "Your Honor," he said, "with all due respect, I think we should use our time to focus on the deposition next Saturday and the trial. This case is not going to settle, as much as Your Honor wants it to settle. We are not going to even consider the amounts of money that they demand. Their latest demand, Your Honor, is $1.5 million, plus I have to take care of this $800,000 lien [filed by Jones's prior lawyers, Davis and Cammarata]. We are not going to pay it. We're not going to pay anything close to that. . . . I made every effort with Mr. Davis and Cammarata, we got reasonably close. . . . But I've had it."

In retrospect, Bennett's tough line might appear foolhardy, but he was only reflecting the views of his client and a realistic assessment of his adversaries. For all his bluster, Bennett would have been delighted to settle the case. As a lawyer who had not tried a case in a decade, Bennett was not one to take heedless gambles on the whims of jurors. The president and first lady thought that a settlement would simply prompt more claims against them, and they wanted to maintain a hard line with the Jones lawyers. That was fine with the team from Dallas. They had entered the case, it seemed, as much to humiliate the president as to compensate their client, and an amicable settlement would have done nothing to advance their political agenda. Paula Jones's legal situation had deteriorated, yet her lawyers had increased their settlement demand by 300 percent.

Judge Wright wanted to step up the pressure on the Jones lawyers in the only way she could—by signaling her feelings about the merits of their client's case. "I'll say quite candidly that with respect to Paula Jones's case, I think that it is unlikely"—here the judge hesitated, choosing her words carefully—"I think it's unlikely that a jury will find for her if this matter goes to trial.... And I regret, personally, that she was not willing to accept what was being talked about last summer. And I was prepared to tell her that I thought she should accept it.... I would have almost forced her to take it."

The judge was suggesting that she might throw the case out on summary judgment—the motion that the defendants would file as soon as depositions were completed. "As you know, the record with respect to sexual harassment aspect is weak at best.... I mean, Ms. Jones is just going to have a difficult time proving her case.... I'm going to look very carefully at the defendants' motion for summary judgment. The way it looks now, more likely than not, she will fail."

And in the event the judge let the case go to trial, Wright said that Jones could expect a tougher time. "I have been a lifelong resident of Arkansas," she said. "I'm aware of Bill Clinton's reputation for womanizing.... But he doesn't have the reputation of being a harasser. He doesn't. And you're not going to be able to find a jury with twelve people who have never heard that Bill Clinton is a womanizer. But I don't believe before this case was brought he ever had a reputation for doing anything other than just chasing skirts. You know, just having a good time. . . ." But the lawyers on both sides were in no mood to listen to this voice of reason.

So Susan Wright turned to the doleful task of listening to the plaintiff's lawyers summarize their case. She quickly recognized that they planned an extended tour of Bill Clinton's sex life. She didn't want to see the trial sidetracked in that way, but she knew, too, that the law left her little choice. "I'm also aware that in sexual assault cases, the Rules of Evidence promulgated by the Violence Against Women Act has certainly opened it up. So I can't say that you can't call any of the witnesses" regarding extramarital affairs, she said. Wright was referring to the change in the law that Susan Molinari had sponsored, and that President Clinton had championed. The judge knew, as perhaps the president did not, that the line between consensual and nonconsensual sex had blurred to the point that she would have to admit some evidence of both.

Jim Fisher, the lawyer from Campbell's firm who would question Clinton on Saturday, said the plaintiff's case would be divided into three parts. First, there would be evidence about the events at the Excelsior Hotel. Second, they would call "witnesses that relate to the pattern and practice issue, the habit evidence . . . focused on his harassment of other women." And finally, "the cover-up, the suppression of evidence, the intimidation of witnesses in a concerted, systematic effort to prevent our client and others like her from developing cases that they might bring." Fisher rushed through the first category—it was, of course, never of great interest to the Dallas team—and then moved on to the subject of other women.

"With regard to the pattern and practice evidence," Fisher said, "the evidence involving other victims, there are three troopers . . . Roger Perry, Larry Patterson, and L. D. Brown." They were, of course, part of the same group who had supplied Brock and Isikoff in the early days of the story. "With regard to the women themselves," Fisher went on, "they would include Kathleen Willey— Your Honor, do I need to refer to these individuals by a Jane Doe designation?"

For purposes of public documents, Wright had ordered several of the women to be referred to as Jane Does, in order to protect their privacy. But because they were meeting in secret session, the judge ordered the lawyer to use the real names. "Let's just give me the names, because it's confusing," said the judge. "Go ahead. Kathleen Willey."

Fisher resumed: "Beth Coulson," an Arkansas woman whom Clinton had appointed to a state judgeship (and who denied any improper relationship with him), "Monica Lewinsky. I believe that is spelled L-E-W-I-N-S-K-Y."

"Can you tell me who she is?" Wright asked.

"Yes, Your Honor."

"I never heard of her," the judge said.

"She's the young woman who worked in the White House for a period of time and was later transferred to a job at the Pentagon."

"All right," said the judge. "Thanks."

Fisher then resumed the litany. Shelia Lawrence, the wife of a major Democratic fund-raiser; Juanita Broaddrick; Gennifer Flowers; Dolly Kyle Browning, a purported high school girlfriend who claimed to have had an extended affair with Clinton; Marilyn Jo Jenkins, an Arkansas friend; Cyd Dunlap, an Isikoff discovery who claimed that Clinton had propositioned her in 1986. For all Fisher's talk about "harassment" and "victims," only three of these eight women—Willey (an alleged groping), Broaddrick (a claimed sexual assault), and Dunlap (an asserted proposition by telephone)—had had even arguably nonconsensual contact with Clinton.

And there was one more thing. "Depending on how the president's deposition goes," said Fisher, "we may designate an expert on sexual addiction."

Wright had been holding herself back during most of Fisher's presentation, but this was more than she could take. "Well, hold it now," she said. "I think, really, Gennifer Flowers and the troopers and Paula Jones is bad enough. And—because I'm not going to let you use my courtroom to—you know, just to—to spend a long time throwing dirt at the president." But Fisher was serious. He wanted the judge's permission to give a copy of the president's deposition to a psychiatrist who "will render an opinion whether an examination is warranted or not"—on the question of whether Bill Clinton was a sex addict. In other words, the Dallas team had come up with the same theory of their case as the one behind Isikoff's projected book.

The whole idea was absurd as a legal matter, more so because

Wright had never heard the phrase "sexual addiction" until Fisher mentioned it in her courtroom. "I thought, well, that's funny, that's a good, funny term," she said. "I didn't realize that this is a serious—you know, that you are very serious about this. . . . I just don't think too much of your theory, Mr. Fisher." Repeatedly, the judge tried to remind Fisher that his case, in theory at least, involved his client's claim of employment discrimination, not psychobabble about the president's deepest urges. Fisher's evidence of a cover-up was even thinner. He said they wanted to depose Jack Palladino, a San Francisco private investigator who had worked for the 1992 Clinton campaign, and Sam Jones, a Little Rock lawyer, but Fisher couldn't say what relevant evidence they might provide.

Wright wound up talking to the lawyers nearly all day on Monday. The judge was torn. She wanted to limit the lawsuit to a fairly straightforward matter—"the issue is whether he sexually harassed Paula Jones and caused her damages—and that's really it." But the law did compel her to allow the plaintiff's lawyers to wander through Bill Clinton's sexual past. Though she held no especially fond feelings for the president, Wright had a sense of foreboding about the spectacle of a sexual cross-examination of him. But as the midwinter skies began to darken in Pine Bluff, Wright saw that Saturday's deposition was going to proceed. She agreed to remain on call at her home in Little Rock, so the parties could telephone her if any disputes arose at the deposition.

If she was called on Saturday, Bennett warned the judge, she should not use a portable phone, because her words might be intercepted. "I'll certainly try to, you know, remain close at hand," Wright said. "I'm already thinking what room in my house am I going to go that doesn't have those little phones. I do have one—my daughter has a telephone that's a teddy bear. It's a speakerphone, and the bear talks."

/ / /

Two days later, Bob Bennett made a call that might have saved Bill Clinton's presidency. Earlier in the proceedings, Bennett had said, in a spirit of business as usual, that he did not want Judge Wright to attend Clinton's deposition. She had not attended the depositions of other witnesses—federal judges almost never preside over these examinations—and the final pretrial conference had proceeded on the assumption that she would not attend Clinton's, either. But Monday's secret meeting had made it so clear that the Dallas lawyers were going to focus on sexual matters that Bennett felt he had to request an exception to the general rule. On Wednesday, January 14—the day after the Starr team made its "sting tape" of Lewinsky and Tripp—Bennett requested a telephone conference with his adversaries and Judge Wright. In its decision in *Jones v. Clinton,* the Supreme Court had said that the judge should give considerable deference to the office of the president in presiding over the case. Accordingly, Bennett argued, Judge Wright should travel to Washington and protect the office—not the man—in person. Wright was persuaded and made plans to come to Washington on Saturday, January 17.

Wright's decision to attend conferred an enormous advantage on Clinton. All other witnesses had to answer every question that was put to them, no matter how irrelevant or abusive. Paula Jones had to endure Bill Bristow's degrading inquisition about her sex life even though those questions would probably never have been allowed to be aired in open court. Bill Clinton would have no such problem. The judge would be available to rule on the questions to him *before* he was forced to answer them—which, as a practical matter, greatly narrowed the range of questions Fisher could ask.

So Susan Webber Wright and her clerk Barry Ward joined in the great convergence that was taking place in Washington in the days leading up to Bill Clinton's deposition. The events of Saturday, January 17, would change everything. The deposition, *Newsweek*'s deadline, Lewinsky's decision whether to cooperate secretly with Starr—all would be resolved on that day. As in the final act of a drawing-room farce, all the players—among them, the Dallas lawyers, Susan Carpenter-McMillan, George Conway, Michael Isikoff, Bob Bennett, Mitch Ettinger, Linda Tripp, Lucianne Goldberg, Monica Lewinsky, Jackie Bennett, Bruce Udolf, Paula Jones, Kenneth Starr, and Bill Clinton—took their places for the denouement.

/ / /

Fisher returned home to Dallas after the secret court session in Pine Bluff to complete the preparations for his historic encounter with the president. Fisher was no less conservative than his fellow partners at the firm, but he had a gentler, less confrontational manner than Campbell. Where Campbell served on the board of the Rutherford Institute, Fisher helped run a Christian ministry called the Art of Family Living. It hurt Fisher's feelings that Clinton's lawyer Mitch Ettinger referred to the Dallas firm as "the Branch Davidians," whereas Campbell took the jibe as a badge of honor. Because Fisher had smoother edges, and also greater experience with depositions, than Campbell, the Dallas lawyers had agreed from the beginning that he would examine the president.

But as Fisher sat down to make his plans, he had to confront the fact that he and his team had been consistently outmaneuvered by Bennett and his. (Indeed, Fisher was interrupted in his final preparations by the conference call in which Bennett asked the judge to attend the deposition.) Fisher knew that the president's lawyers had spent an enormous amount of energy portraying the Dallas lawyers as political extremists—"drooling monsters," as Fisher put it. So Fisher wanted to avoid any unnecessary prurience in the course of the deposition. Still, the entire focus of the plaintiff's case had been to show that the president was, in deed if not in name, a sexual addict. Fisher's dilemma was how to make that case without talking too much about sex.

Fisher's answer was to turn, as others did, to the definition of sex in Representative Susan Molinari's Violence Against Women Act. Fisher sat down with a copy of the definition and altered it slightly so that it would cover (he thought) consensual as well as unwelcome sexual advances by the president. By using this definition, Fisher believed, he could ask Clinton questions about his sexual activities but do so in a manner that would not offend the judge. The definition that Fisher labored to create at his word processor would turn out to be another event of Wednesday, January 14, that helped guarantee the president's survival in office.

Fisher's partners, on the other hand, were still conducting their dance with Linda Tripp in preparation for the deposition. On Thursday, the lawyers all flew to Washington. Their top priority, of course, was to get copies of Tripp's tapes. If they had the tapes, they could confront Clinton with them during his deposition. Fisher's partner Wes Holmes had been assigned to track the tapes down, and he wasn't making any progress. Several times on Thursday, Jim Moody, Tripp's lawyer, had canceled meetings with him. (Unknown to Holmes, Moody was just that day collecting the tapes from Kirby Behre, playing them for Isikoff and his colleagues at *Newsweek,* and then taking them to Ann Coulter's apartment to listen to them with George Conway.)

By Friday, January 16, Holmes was growing frantic. Lucianne Goldberg had been telling the Jones team for weeks about the existence of the tapes, but Holmes couldn't get Tripp's lawyer to give them to him. (In fact, this was the day that Moody turned them over to the Office of Independent Counsel.) And while Holmes was trying to reach Moody, the Starr lawyers were meeting with Lewinsky at the Ritz-Carlton and attempting to persuade her to wear a wire on Currie, Jordan, and perhaps the president.

Finally, late on Friday, Holmes and Moody did speak, and Tripp's lawyer proposed a deal. He wouldn't turn over the tapes (Moody didn't say that he had already given them to Starr), but Moody would allow one of the Jones lawyers to interview Tripp that evening. So Holmes picked up Moody in a rented car and they set off for Tripp's home in the distant Maryland suburb of Columbia. (Not surprisingly, because Holmes didn't know the area and Moody couldn't see, they got lost on the way.) The meeting lasted only half an hour, and Tripp mostly provided information that the Jones team already knew from their conversations with Goldberg. More disappointed than pleased, Holmes returned empty-handed to the Jones team's base at the Hyatt Regency Hotel.

There, the happiest woman was Susan Carpenter-McMillan. Paula Jones was delighted, too. At the Pentagon City Mall, Susan had surprised Paula by buying them matching Jones New York suits for the big day on Saturday. Susie would wear cream, Paula black. Paula's mentor bought two identical sets of earrings as well.

/ / /

By late Friday, the rumors were everywhere. An intern. Tapes. As the story reached the lawyers at Williams & Connolly, who were defending Clinton on Whitewater, there was an intern claiming an affair with the president, and there were tapes about something else. As with so many rumors, truth and fiction mingled in an unreadable tangle. On this day, Isikoff kept a lunch appointment with Lanny Davis, a White House lawyer who served as a spokesman on scandal issues. Davis found Isikoff distracted and preoccupied. In the course of a rambling conversation, Davis happened to say, "These womanizing stories are old hat and still haven't gone anywhere."

"They're more real than you think," the reporter replied cryptically.

By Friday afternoon, the circle of knowledge about Starr's sting was expanding. Frustrated that *Newsweek* hadn't yet committed to running a story in the next issue, Lucianne Goldberg tipped a reporter at the *New York Post* to call Isikoff and ask him about the big scoop he had in the works. Isikoff, meanwhile, was abiding by Jackie Bennett's request that he hold off on calling Vernon Jordan. But the reporter was itching to make the call, because *Newsweek* couldn't run a story unless he had at least tried to get in touch with Jordan.

And Bill Clinton was preparing for his testimony for one final day. After the session on Monday, the plans of the Jones lawyers could not have been clearer. They would begin by asking about Kathleen Willey and proceed to the woman whose name the judge didn't recognize—L-E-W-I-N-S-K-Y. Actually, as Bennett's team had their final meetings with their client, they received encouraging news. Frank Carter, Lewinsky's lawyer, faxed Clinton's lawyer a copy of Lewinsky's affidavit, so Bennett knew that Clinton and Lewinsky were allied in their denials.

Bennett and Ettinger arrived at the White House at four o'clock on Friday afternoon, and they didn't leave for six hours. Ettinger did most of the mock interrogation of the president, pelting him with the rudest questions he could imagine. Ettinger focused, as he knew Fisher would, on the other women: Willey, Lewinsky, and the like. Clinton's responses were unchanged from the moment that the lawyers had first told him these names were on the witness list. Settlement was off the table. Clinton was confident, instructing Bennett, "If Paula Jones wants a trial, go and give her one."

Bennett had a final word of advice for his client. "The only thing you have to worry about is if you lie in there," he said. "The crazies will come after you. They will try to impeach you if you lie. That's the only thing to worry about." Bruce Lindsey, who was also present, thanked Bennett for emphasizing that point.

Finally, at around ten o'clock on Friday evening, Ettinger said, "Okay, I think you're ready."

"No," the president replied. "Come back tomorrow morning, and let's do it again."

So, starting at about eight in the morning of Saturday, January 17, Bennett and Ettinger gave the president a final ninety minutes of preparation. Afterward, Ettinger made his way to the deposition on his own, but Bennett rode in the presidential limousine, along with Secret Service agent Larry Cockell, the short distance to the offices of Skadden Arps and their 10:30 A.M. appointment with their adversaries.

/ / /

On August 17, 1998, seven months later to the day, President Clinton testified at the White House in a videotaped presentation for Kenneth Starr's grand jury. By that point, of course, Starr was investigating whether Clinton had lied in the course of his deposition on January 17. Late in the tense day of questioning by Starr's prosecutors, Clinton provided a vivid picture of his state of mind at the time he confronted Paula Jones's lawyers.

"I think we might as well put this out on the table," Clinton said. "I will admit this, sir. My goal in this deposition was to be truthful, but not particularly helpful. I did not wish to do the work of the Jones lawyers. I *deplored* what they were doing. I *deplored* the innocent people they were tormenting and traumatizing. I *deplored* their illegal leaking. I *deplored* the fact that they knew, once they knew our evidence, that this was a bogus lawsuit—and that because of the funding they had from my political enemies, they were putting ahead. I *deplored* it.

"But I was determined to walk through the minefield of this deposition without breaking the law, and I believe I did."

In the Skadden Arps office on that Saturday in January, the lawyers and the judge gathered around the oval table promptly at ten-thirty. There were four lawyers from Bennett's firm; the White House counsel, Charles F. C. Ruff; Bill Bristow, representing Danny Ferguson; and a half-dozen lawyers from Rader, Campbell, Fisher & Pyke, of Dallas, Texas.

"Good morning, Judge," Bennett began—and he tried to get an edge right away. "The presidency is an important institution, Your Honor," Bennett said, "and it is very important that it not be held in disrespect or it be held up to be the laughingstock of the world."

He accused the Jones team of leaking information about Kathleen Willey's deposition, which had just been completed. He needled the six lawyers present from Donovan Campbell's firm about their plans to blanket the Sunday-morning news shows the following day. "My only point in raising this," Bennett went on, "is this just underscores the importance of Your Honor keeping restraints and controls on this deposition."

The judge shared Bennett's concerns, but she recognized her duty to proceed under the law. "I have agonized over this case and the very embarrassing nature of some of the issues in the case," she said, then added a sentiment that would be shared by many people before the year was out: "What was initially very shocking and embarrassing to the Court is not quite as shocking and embarrassing anymore."

After a little more preliminary discussion, Bennett said, "I'll get the president."

Clinton walked through the double doors and greeted Judge Wright warmly. The president also had a few words for Bill Bristow, who was attempting to follow in his footsteps into the Arkansas governor's mansion. He greeted the videotape operator and the court reporter. For Paula Jones and her counsel, Clinton had neither a handshake nor a smile.

This was more extraordinary than it seemed. Clinton prided himself on his courtesy toward adversaries, and he got a perverse sort of pleasure out of reaching out to even his most fervent enemies. During Starr's prosecution of the two Arkansas bankers in 1996, Clinton had given videotaped testimony at the White House, where he was sharply examined by Hickman Ewing, who was well known even then as a fierce opponent of the president. Following his testimony, Clinton went around the room to shake hands, and it appeared to several people that Ewing was trying to slip away before he had to exchange any greetings with the president. Clinton rushed to Ewing's side, put his hand on his shoulder, and practically spun him around in order to shake his hand. But on January 17, Clinton did not even display the pretext of civility with the Jones lawyers and their client. He deplored them—and he wanted them to know it.

"Sir," Fisher began, "I'd like to hand you what has been marked Deposition Exhibit 1. So that the record is clear today, and that we know that we are communicating, this is a definition of a term that will be used in the course of my questioning, and the term is 'sexual relations.' I will inform the Court that the wording of the definition is patterned after Federal Rule of Evidence 413 [the Molinari law]. Would you please take whatever time you need to read this definition, because when I use the term 'sexual relations,' this is what I mean today."

It was, in a peculiar way, a fitting way to begin the deposition. From its origins more than three years earlier, the Paula Jones case had never been about whether Paula Jones suffered employment discrimination, but whether Bill Clinton could be embarrassed about his sex life. Here, Fisher had begun this climactic part of the case not by asking about the nominal subject matter of the lawsuit, but rather about the obsession of Clinton's enemies—sexual relations as a general matter. As Fisher asked the question, he handed the judge, the president, and his lawyers a copy of the definition he had crafted back in Dallas earlier in the week. It read:

> For the purposes of this deposition, a person engages in "sexual relations" when the person knowingly engages in or causes—
>
> (1) contact with the genitalia, anus, groin, breast, inner thigh, or buttocks of any person with an intent to arouse or gratify the sexual desire of any person;
>
> (2) contact between any part of the person's body or an object and the genitals or anus of another person; or
>
> (3) contact between the genitals or anus of the person and any part of another person's body.
>
> "Contact" means intentional touching, either directly or through clothing.

Even by the low standards of legalese, this definition stood out for its complexity and incomprehensibility. With his complaints about prurience, Bennett had spooked Fisher into gumming up a fairly simple issue: What exactly had Bill Clinton done with these assorted women? The president's enemies would pay a heavy price for Fisher's blunder.

But at the moment the definition was being passed around the table, Mitch Ettinger was struck by another thought. A former prosecutor, he noticed the similarity of the language to the federal law of sexual assault. He leaned over to Bennett and whispered, "Bob, they're trying to get him to admit to a criminal act."

Bennett had still another thought. "Your Honor, as an introductory matter, I think this could really lead to confusion, and I think it's important that the record be clear," he said. "For example, it says, 'contact' means intentional touching, directly or through clothing." What if Clinton patted Bennett on the behind and said he could lose ten pounds? That would seem to be covered under the definition. Bristow jumped in on the same theme: "Frankly, I think it's a political trick, and I've told you before how I feel about the political character of what this lawsuit is about." Bennett had a point. A pat on the butt could have been covered under item 2 of the definition.

The issue put Judge Wright on the spot right away—and illustrated the importance of her presence at the deposition. Basically, she agreed with Bennett's argument that the definition was "too broad, too encompassing." So she struck items 2 and 3 and limited the definition to item 1—which she said covered "intentional sexual contact." (Curiously, Clinton's supporters, and Clinton himself, later argued that the definition was too narrow—that it covered sexual intercourse and nothing else; at the time, Bennett complained that it was too broad—that it covered any kind of contact.)

Fisher, feeling a little embattled before the president had even answered a question, tried to defend his original three-part definition. But Bennett cut him off. "Your Honor," he said, "I object to this record being filled with these kinds of things. This is going to leak. Why don't they ask—they have the president of the United States in this room for several hours. Why don't they ask him questions about what happened and what didn't happen? . . . He can ask the president, what did you do? He can ask him specifically in certain instances what he did, and isn't that what this deposition is for? It's not to sort of lay a trap for him, and I'm going to object to the president answering and having to remember what's on this whole sheet of paper, and I just don't think it's fair. It's going to lead to confusion."

This was a time for quick thinking by Fisher. He had come up with the convoluted definition because he wanted to avoid antagonizing the judge with explicit sexual questions. But now Bennett was inviting Fisher to make just those kinds of inquiries. With the benefit of Tripp's briefing, Fisher could have had Clinton on the spot immediately with straightforward questions like "Did Lewinsky perform oral sex on you?" But Fisher, in a classic lawyer's mistake, stuck with his plan. "What I'm trying to do is avoid having to ask the president a number of very salacious questions and to make this as discreet as possible," Fisher said. This prompted even more back-and-forth among the lawyers, and soon the deposition was twenty minutes old and the president hadn't been asked a single substantive question.

At one point, Wright sighed, "It's just going to make it very difficult for me to rule, if you want to know the truth, and I'm not sure Mr. Clinton knows all these definitions, anyway." That sentence alone might have crippled a perjury prosecution of the president, but Fisher let it pass uncontested. A full half hour into the proceedings, Fisher finally turned to his first subject. "Mr. Clinton," the Jones lawyer said, eschewing the honorific "Mr. President," "do you know a woman named Kathleen Willey?"

Clinton was primed and ready for the subject. His story was simple and believable. He had met Willey and her husband during the 1992 campaign, and after the election, Kathleen had worked as a volunteer in the White House social office. Once she had visited him in his private office at the White House to ask for a full-time job because her husband was having financial difficulties. (She would return home to Richmond and find that he had committed suicide that very day.) "I remember this very well," Clinton testified, "and she didn't stay long, but she was quite agitated, and that was the only meeting I had with her."

The president did not behave like a trained witness; he gave long answers, and often volunteered more information than was called for by the questions. At one point, he said, unbidden, "I embraced her. I put my arms around her, I may even have kissed her on the forehead. There was nothing sexual about it." But Clinton's windiness sometimes worked to his advantage, as when he added, "Let me remind you—Kathleen Willey asked for this meeting with me. I didn't ask for the meeting with her."

At about eleven forty-five, Fisher turned to a new subject.

"Now," he said, "do you know a woman named Monica Lewinsky?"

"I do," Clinton said.

Fisher began with a series of questions about Lewinsky's employment history—her internship, her service in the White House, then her move to the Pentagon. Throughout the deposition, Clinton suggested he knew Lewinsky because she was a friend of Betty Currie's. Accordingly, Clinton professed a vague familiarity with her progress through the ranks, and the questions didn't trouble either the president or his lawyers. (In truth, Clinton had played no role in Lewinsky's various job changes within the government, much to her dismay.)

After a short break, though, Fisher started to put his knowledge to work. "Mr. President, before the break," he said, "we were talking about Monica Lewinsky. At any time were you and Monica Lewinsky together alone in the Oval Office?"

"I don't recall," Clinton began. "I typically worked some on the weekends. Sometimes they'd bring me things on the weekends. She—it seems to me she brought things to me once or twice on the weekends. In that case, whatever time she would be in there, drop it off, exchange a few words and go, she was there." (This, of course, was the cover story Clinton and Lewinsky had constructed to explain her visits to him on the weekends. It was why Lewinsky always carried a folder when she visited Clinton for their assignations.)

"So I understand," Fisher continued gently, "your testimony is that it was possible, then, that you were alone with her, but you have no specific recollection of that ever happening?"

"Yes, that's correct," Clinton said. "It's possible that she, in, while she was working there, brought something to me and that at the time she brought it to me, and she was the only person there. That's possible." In the year to come, this series of questions about whether they were "alone" proved to be the nightmare of Clinton's defenders. The president's answers were unequivocal lies.

"Did it ever happen that you and she went down the hallway from the Oval Office to the private kitchen?" Fisher continued.

Bennett took the opportunity to jump in—and unveil what he regarded as his secret weapon on the subject of Monica Lewinsky. "Your Honor, excuse me, Mr. President," Bennett said, "I need some guidance from the Court at this point. I'm going to object to the innuendo. I'm afraid, as I say, that this will leak. . . . Counsel is fully aware that Ms. Lewinsky had filed, has an affidavit which they are in possession of, saying that there is absolutely no sex of any kind in any manner, shape or form, with President Clinton. . . ."

Perhaps understandably, the affidavit—and several conversations between Bennett and Frank Carter—had lulled the Clinton team into a false sense of security about Lewinsky. With both Clinton and Lewinsky on record as insisting that there was no sexual relationship between them, Bennett felt he had the right to be indignant about the "innuendo" in Fisher's questions. Bennett insisted, "I would like to know the proffer"—the basis for Fisher's questions about Lewinsky. "In preparation of the witness for this deposition, the witness is fully aware of Ms. Lewinsky's affidavit, so I have not told him a single thing he doesn't know, but I think when [Fisher] asks questions like this where he's sitting on an affidavit from the witness, he should at least have a good faith proffer."

But Judge Wright let Fisher proceed without a proffer, and he asked Clinton again about whether he and Lewinsky had gone down the private hallway to the kitchen behind the Oval Office.

At this point, as if in an instant, Clinton's demeanor changed. To answer this question, and all of the remaining queries about Lewinsky, the president assumed the posture in which he would spend much of the following year—one of abject self-pity, coupled with sustained dishonesty.

"Well, let me try to describe the facts first," Clinton began, "because you keep talking about this private kitchen. The private kitchen is staffed by two naval aides. They have total, unrestricted access to my dining room, to that hallway, to coming into the Oval Office. The people who are in the outer office of the Oval Office can also enter at any time.

"I was, after I went through a presidential campaign in which the far right tried to convince the American people I had committed murder, run drugs, slept in my mother's bed with four prostitutes, and done numerous other things, I had a high level of paranoia. There are no curtains on the Oval Office, there are no curtains on my private office, there are no curtains or blinds that can close the windows in my private dining room. The naval aides come and go at will. There is a peephole in the office that George Stephanopoulos and then Rahm Emanuel occupied that looks back down that corridor.

"I have done everything I could to avoid the kind of questions you are asking me here today, so to talk about this kitchen as if it is a private kitchen, it's a little cubbyhole, and these guys keep the door open. They come and go at will. Now that's the factual background here.

"Now, to go back to your question," Clinton said, at long last, "my recollection is that, at some point during the government shutdown, when Ms. Lewinsky was still an intern but working the chief of staff's office because all the employees had to go home, that she was back there with a pizza that she brought to me and to others. I do not believe she was there alone, however. I don't think she was. And my recollection is that on a couple of occasions after that she was there but my secretary, Betty Currie, was there with her. She and Betty are friends. That's my, that's my recollection. And I have no other recollection of that."

This extraordinary monologue, full of both fact and fiction, could serve as a useful template of Clinton's obsessions. He had conditioned himself to see the Jones suit, indeed the entire legal assault on his presidency, more as a metaphor than a reality. For him, the case served as a symbol of all of the outrageous accusations that he had fought off over the past six years. Their ends justified his means; his deceptions, the reasoning seemed to have gone, paled next to his enemies' offenses. He had indeed removed the curtains and taken those other steps to free himself from suspicion. (That was why Clinton limited his trysts with Lewinsky to the study, bathroom, and hallway, where they could not be seen through the windows.)

But thanks to Tripp's briefing, Fisher was not as easily dissuaded from pursuing the Lewinsky matter as he was about Willey. "At any time," Fisher asked, "have you and Monica Lewinsky ever been alone together in any room in the White House?"

"I think I testified to that earlier," Clinton said. "I think that there is a, it is—I have no specific recollection, but it seems to me that she was on duty on a couple of occasions working for the legislative affairs office and brought me some things to sign, something on the weekend. That's—I have a general memory of that." Another clear lie.

Then, a real surprise to his lawyers, if not to Clinton. Fisher asked about any letters that were sent by Lewinsky to Currie for Clinton. (On Thursday, two days earlier, Isikoff had called Currie to ask about these letters.) Clinton hedged, said it was possible. The questions grew more specific. Had Clinton met with Lewinsky at the White House between midnight and 6 A.M.? (This was based on faulty information from Tripp and Goldberg, because Lewinsky never claimed any such late-night encounters.) "I certainly don't think so," Clinton replied. Were any false records kept of his meetings with Lewinsky? Again, Clinton thought not.

"Have you ever talked to Monica Lewinsky about the possibility that she might be asked to testify in this lawsuit?" Fisher asked.

"I'm not sure, and let me tell you why I'm not sure. It seems to me the, the, the—I want to be as accurate as I can here. Seems to me the last time she was there to see Betty before Christmas we were joking about how you-all, with the help of the Rutherford Institute, were going to call every woman I'd ever talked to, and I said, you know—"

"We can't hear you, Mr. President," Bennett interjected. In his nervousness, Clinton had dropped his voice considerably.

"And I said that you-all might call every woman I ever talked to . . ." Clinton resumed.

This, too, was false. One month earlier, in the middle of the night of December 17, Clinton had called Lewinsky to tell her that Currie's brother had died and that she was on the witness list. "It broke my heart when I saw your name on the list," he had said.

Fisher moved now to ask about how much Clinton knew about Lewinsky's contacts with Vernon Jordan and Bill Richardson. Clinton parried, suggesting he had some vague knowledge of the meetings.

"Have you ever given any gifts to Monica Lewinsky?" Fisher asked.

Clinton paused for an excruciating ten to fifteen seconds. His lawyers were dumbstruck.

"I don't recall," Clinton said, then paused again. "Do you know what they were?"

"A hat pin?"

The previous night, Tripp had struggled to remember the gifts she had heard about from Lewinsky. Clinton had given Monica *Leaves of Grass*, by Walt Whitman, but Fisher asked if he had given her "a book about Walt Whitman."

Clinton waffled again. "I could have given her a gift, but I don't remember a specific gift."

What about anything from "the Black Dog store [actually a restaurant] in Martha's Vineyard?"

Clinton did remember such a gift. Currie had told him that Monica wanted something from the Black Dog. "I bought a lot of things for a lot of people," he said, "and I gave Betty a couple of the pieces, and she gave I think something to Monica and something to some of the other girls who worked in the office."

At this point, Bennett was getting nervous. Ettinger was also fidgeting a great deal. What was going on? Fisher obviously had a wealth of detail about contacts between Clinton and Lewinsky. The lawyers were hearing a great many of these things for the first time from their client, who was obviously laboring. There had to be a source who was feeding this stuff to the Jones lawyers.

Finally, Fisher came to the heart of his examination.

"Did you have an extramarital sexual affair with Monica Lewinsky?"

"No," said the president.

"If she told someone that she had a sexual affair with you beginning in November of 1995, would that be a lie?"

"It's certainly not the truth."

"I think I used the term 'sexual affair,'" Fisher went on. "And, so the record is completely clear, have you ever had sexual relations with Monica Lewinsky as that term is defined in Deposition Exhibit 1, as modified by the Court?"

At the judge's suggestion, Fisher handed the definition to Clinton so he could study it.

"I have never had sexual relations with Monica Lewinsky," Clinton said. "I've never had an affair with her."

A moment later, Clinton couldn't help but ask his own question.

"Mr. Fisher," he said, "is there something, let me just—you asked that with such conviction, is there something you want to ask me about this? I don't, I don't even know what you're talking about, I don't think."

Fisher replied elliptically, and accurately, "Sir, I think this will come to light shortly, and you'll understand."

The session broke for lunch. Ettinger whispered to Bennett, "Bob, they've got Linda Tripp," and bolted to a phone.

/ / /

Fisher had been questioning the president for a little more than two hours—about half the planned length of the deposition—and he had spent about three quarters of his time on Monica Lewinsky. In all, Fisher did an inept job. Given the information available to him, he could have locked Clinton into a dozen false statements in about five minutes. Did Lewinsky perform oral sex on you? Did she ever touch your genitals? Did you touch her breasts? Did you ever call her on the telephone? Clinton would have had to answer these simple questions categorically, and he certainly would have lied. Instead, Fisher stuck with his convoluted definition of sex and left Clinton an escape hatch that he later tried hard to use.

Still, the morning had left the Clinton team troubled, and Ettinger figured he had to do some investigating of his own. He knew that the Jones lawyers had subpoenaed Tripp, knew that she worked with Lewinsky, knew that she had been Isikoff's source on the Willey story, and knew that she was angry at Bennett about his quotes in that piece. She had to be their source. So Ettinger frantically dialed the phone number of the man he understood to be Tripp's lawyer—Kirby Behre. But it was Saturday, and there was no answer. Ettinger stewed on the issue for the remainder of the day.

The remainder of the deposition was anticlimactic. Fisher skipped around a variety of topics—Clinton's record-keeping as governor, his dealings with the Arkansas troopers, the events at the Excelsior Hotel on May 8, 1991.

"Now, seated to my right, two chairs down, is Ms. Paula Jones. Do you recall ever having met her before today?"

"No," Clinton replied. "I've said that many times. I don't."

The Jones team's vaunted examination of Clinton's sex life had produced relatively little except Lewinsky and some old Arkansas gossip. There was, however, proof that Little Rock was a small town. Fisher at one point asked if Clinton had ever bought presents for other women at a store there called Barbara Jean's.

"Her name is what?" Fisher asked. "The woman that owned it."

"Barbara—I don't know," Clinton said.

At this point, the judge jumped in. "I'm not here to testify. I believe it's Barbara Baber."

"I think that's right," Clinton said with a smile.

Fisher asked only a few harmless questions about Shelia Lawrence, Beth Coulson, and Marilyn Jo Jenkins. With Gennifer Flowers, Clinton admitted to a single sexual encounter, in 1977. Near the end of the day, Fisher asked two questions to which the judge sustained Bennett's objections: "Please name every person with whom you had sexual relations when you were either governor of the state of Arkansas or president of the United States" and "Please name every person with whom you sought to have sexual relations when you were governor of the state of Arkansas or president of the United States." If Judge Wright had not attended the deposition, Clinton might well have been forced to answer these preposterously broad and invasive inquiries, and his answers would certainly have been fodder for the Starr investigation that was already under way.

Bennett had only a few questions of his own. He showed Lewinsky's affidavit to Clinton, and he ratified once more its denial of any sexual relationship between the two of them. For his final question, Bennett followed up on something Fisher had asked about why Clinton had run for president in 1992, but not in 1988. The president said that he had been told in both elections that "the press" had decided he had no chance to win. Then he added, with his trademark sense of victimhood, "The press had to have somebody in every election, and I was going to be offered up, and they were so gullible about little states that they'd believe anything they were told about Arkansas, and if I ran, I'd be destroyed. That's what I was told. And for six years they've worked very hard at doing it. But I'm very glad I did it anyway."

13

The Richard Jewell File

With the president's deposition completed, the partisans on all sides sought to shape the public's perception of this consummately political event. The Jones team tried first.

Susan Carpenter-McMillan had waited not so patiently through the six long hours that Clinton was upstairs. She had promised the assembled throng of reporters that Jones would make a statement at the end of the day, but the lawyers hustled Jones back to their hotel. When McMillan tracked down her friend at the Hyatt Regency, she saw why. Jones was crying hysterically—just the weight of the accumulated tensions of the day, she told McMillan.

McMillan didn't like the image of Jones skulking away from the deposition, so she decided to make her own plan. "I don't care whether you want to or not, but you are going to dinner," McMillan told the lawyers. "You're in my courtroom now."

She had arranged for a table in the window of the Old Ebbitt Grill, a famous Washington restaurant around the corner from the site of the deposition. McMillan assembled Paula, her husband, Steve, Paula's hairdresser (who had traveled from California with them), and the legal team to make a quasi-public celebration of their success at the deposition. In truth, the lawyers were pleased. They had nailed down Clinton's denials about Lewinsky, and they had succeeded in putting him on the record about the other women as well. As McMillan hoped, news of the Jones dinner party was included in much of the next-day coverage—although one important detail was omitted. None of the reports mentioned the one unfamiliar face at the Jones table. Chris Vlasto, a dogged producer for ABC News, had been pursuing Clinton scandal stories for almost as long as Isikoff. McMillan had invited him along, and he even paid the tab—a wise investment, as it turned out.

Other Clinton enemies weren't as pleased that Saturday night. After extended deliberations, the *Newsweek* editors decided to withhold Isikoff's story from the issue that would be released the following day. As a courtesy, Isikoff let Goldberg, Moody, and Conway know that his story had been spiked. (Henceforth, Goldberg would enjoy teasing Isikoff with the nickname "Spikey.") On that Saturday, Moody took the news with his usual distracted air, but Goldberg and the elves were furious, and they decided to do something about it. Having failed to plant their story in the mainstream press, they decided to go to their favorite journalist of second resort—Matt Drudge.

/ / /

In the days after the Lewinsky story made him famous, there was much debate about whether thirty-one-year-old Matt Drudge was a "journalist"—as if something of importance turned on whether he deserved that dubious honorific. In truth, Drudge resembled what might be called a meta-journalist. He did journalism about journalism. For the most part, he relayed the scraps that were too sordid or too thinly sourced to make it into more conventional distribution channels. He was not always wrong—far from it—but he went faster, and with less compunction, than virtually anyone else with a wide audience. Drudge pushed stories in line with his proudly conservative orientation (at least in his politics), and he established contact early on with the elves and others associated with the pro-Jones and anti-Clinton cause.

Drudge came to stand, for better or worse, as an icon of the Internet age: born to liberal parents outside Washington, D.C.; a news junkie at home, a misfit at school; found work on the swing shift at 7-Eleven. "So, in the famous words of another newsman,

Horace Greeley," he said in a triumphant speech at the National Press Club, "I, still a young man, went west." To a dismal apartment in a crime-ridden section of Hollywood, employed folding T-shirts in the gift shop on the CBS lot. His father, in despair about his son's prospects, bought him a computer in 1994. Matt discovered e-mail, chat rooms, an electronic community. He started sending out news of this and that—ratings, movie grosses, gossip—he had picked up on the lot. (Sometimes literally; that is, by rummaging through the CBS garbage.) He called it the *Drudge Report* and moved it to the infant World Wide Web, including easy-to-use links with scores of other news sources. By 1998, the *Drudge Report* had six million visitors a month.

Drudge always walked the line between fame and notoriety, especially after he lobbed a false accusation of spousal abuse at the White House aide Sidney Blumenthal, in August 1997. But Drudge won a devout following among his own generation of conservatives—people like Ann Coulter and George Conway. In the summer of 1997, when Conway and others had grown frustrated that Isikoff was not reporting the Willey story as quickly as they would have liked, Conway leaked news of the story to Drudge. As was his custom, Drudge reported the Willey story as a press controversy—will *Newsweek* publish Isikoff's article?—rather than on its own merits—are Willey's charges true? As Conway had hoped, planting the Willey story with Drudge increased the chances that *Newsweek* would run it, which, of course, *Newsweek* did soon thereafter. Frustrated at the *Newsweek* editors' refusal to go with the story on January 17, the elves simply tried to run the Willey play once more. Again, it worked.

Drudge had heard rumors about the president and an intern for more than a month. In November 1997, he had received an anonymous e-mail with Lucianne Goldberg's telephone number, but he had never followed it up. On the night of Saturday, January 17, Drudge woke Goldberg from a deep sleep and read her the item that he had written based on what he had heard from the elves. Goldberg confirmed the story. Then at 2:32 A.M. on the East Coast (three hours earlier in Los Angeles, where Drudge was composing), Drudge hit the send button on his computer. At that moment, he later said, he had tears in his eyes because of the magnitude of the moment.

NEWSWEEK KILLS STORY ON WHITE HOUSE INTERN

Blockbuster Report: 23-Year-Old, Former White House Intern, Sex Relationship with President

World Exclusive
Must Credit the DRUDGE REPORT

At the last minute, at 6 p.m. on Saturday evening, NEWS-WEEK magazine killed a story that was destined to shake official Washington to its foundation: A White House intern carried on a sexual affair with the President of the United States!

The DRUDGE REPORT has learned that reporter Michael Isikoff developed the story of his career, only to have it spiked by top NEWSWEEK suits hours before publication. A young woman, 23, sexually involved with the love of her life, the President of the United States, since she was a 21-year-old intern at the White House. She was a frequent visitor to a small study just off the Oval Office where she claims to have indulged the President's sexual preference. Reports of the relationship spread in the White House quarters and she was moved to a job at the Pentagon, where she worked until last week.

The young intern wrote long love letters to President Clinton, which she delivered through a delivery service. She was a frequent visitor to the White House after midnight, where she checked in the WAVE logs as visiting a secretary named Betty Curry [*sic*], 57.

The DRUDGE REPORT has learned that tapes of intimate phone conversations exist.

The relationship between the president and the young woman became strained when the President believed that the young woman was bragging about the affair to others.

In retrospect, several things are notable about Drudge's report. After the first paragraph, the story is filled with errors. Reports of the relationship had not spread to others at the White House; Lewinsky did not write "long love letters" to Clinton; Lewinsky did not visit Clinton "after midnight"; Clinton did not break off the affair because he feared Lewinsky was bragging. Drudge falsely implies that the "intimate phone conversations" were between Lewinsky and Clinton; the calls were between Lewinsky and Linda Tripp. Still, the gist was true. *Newsweek* was working on a story about a sexual affair between the president and a former intern.

Drudge's initial account served as a useful snapshot of what Goldberg and the elves believed was important about the Lewinsky story. Drudge wasn't told of Lewinsky's status as a subpoenaed witness in the Jones case or of the unfolding Starr investigation related to her. There was no pretext that the affair between the president and the intern related to Clinton's truthfulness, his litigation strategy, or a criminal investigation. Drudge only had the sex—but that was enough for him and his sources. They knew the sex would make the story irresistible to the mainstream media. Once Drudge issued his first bulletin, it was foreordained that the story would leak into the political life of the nation.

It took only about eight hours, and the vehicle was a Sunday-morning talk show. Though little watched by most Americans, the network programs serve as useful benchmarks for the political class. Because the incumbent administration and its supporters are expected to put forth a more or less coordinated message each week, the Sunday shows are generally where that position is first made public. By early 1998, Matt Drudge was helping to set the Sunday agenda.

Bill Kristol, the editor of *The Weekly Standard* and a conservative panelist on the ABC News program *This Week,* heard about the Drudge story early on Sunday morning, January 18, and he made an effort to check it out. He spoke to the elf Porter (with whom Kristol had served on the staff of Vice President Dan Quayle) and satisfied himself that Drudge was on to something real. The former Clinton aide George Stephanopoulos, at that time still a defender of the president on the program, decided to make a discreet inquiry of his own. On Sunday morning, he called John Podesta, then the White House deputy chief of staff.

Podesta had been hearing ominous rumblings for about a day. On Saturday, while Clinton was still in his deposition, Podesta was called by a reporter for *Time* magazine who was nosing around about a possible scoop by his competitor Mike Isikoff at *Newsweek.* Podesta knew nothing about it, but he decided to call Isikoff, whom he knew vaguely. Isikoff said that he was working on a story about a woman named Monica Lewinsky and the Paula Jones case, but "it had nothing to do with the grand jury or Ken Starr."

In light of all this, the call from Stephanopoulos was not a complete surprise to Podesta. So he took a cautious route and, as Podesta later testified, told Stephanopoulos, "The only way you can respond to it is to say, 'This is Drudge, he's a rumormonger . . . and you can't believe what you read in the *Drudge Report.*'"

Kristol and Stephanopoulos were now briefed to do battle on the air. On Sunday's broadcast, Kristol said, "The story in Washington this morning is that *Newsweek* magazine was going to go with a big story based on tape-recorded conversations, which a woman who was a summer [*sic*] intern at the White House, an intern of Leon Panetta's—"

Stephanopoulos interrupted Kristol, saying, "And Bill, where did it come from? The *Drudge Report.* You know, we've all seen how discredited that is. . . ."

"No, no, no," Kristol replied. "They had screaming arguments in *Newsweek* magazine yesterday. They finally didn't go with the story. It's going to be a question of whether the media is now going to report what are pretty well-validated charges of presidential behavior in the White House." The story of the intern and the tapes had moved into general circulation.

/ / /

Like Susan Carpenter-McMillan, the president's team tried to shape public perceptions of the deposition. According to leaks from the Clinton camp, everyone was delighted by the way the day had gone. But that wasn't really the case. Bennett and Ettinger had been unnerved by the strangely specific questions about Lewinsky, and even in Clinton's answers, they sensed that their client had not told them everything about his relationship with the young woman. That evening, Clinton himself was uncharacteristically subdued as well. He made a handful of telephone calls and canceled his dinner plans.

The deposition seems to have evoked a clear sense of foreboding in the president. In one of those conversations that night, he called Betty Currie, whose name he had mentioned so often in response to the questions about Lewinsky, and asked her to come in to work the following day. It was unusual for the president to summon Currie on a Sunday—and this meeting was stranger still.

Inside of a month after the Lewinsky story broke, the public perception of Betty Currie was defined by a single image—that of a diminutive, overwhelmed African-American woman fighting through an unruly crowd of photographers after her first appearance before the grand jury. The truth about Currie was more complex. She occupied a distinctive niche in Bill Clinton's White House. In an atmosphere that was usually busy, even frenetic, Currie had little to do. She handled some of Clinton's private correspondence, placed some of his phone calls, and generally passed time with visitors who were waiting to be admitted to the Oval Office. She handed out candy to frazzled staffers and reminded them not to work too hard.

But Currie, who had long ago retired as a federal government secretary in Washington, was also a seasoned pol. At fifty-seven years old, she had worked in every Democratic presidential campaign since 1984, and even moved to Boston to work for Michael Dukakis in 1988, and then to Little Rock, to help Clinton, four years later. (During downtime she worked as an assistant to the celebrity biographer Kitty Kelley.) As it turned out, Currie was also Kenneth Starr's potentially most damaging witness against Bill Clinton.

Currie met Clinton on the White House putting green at about five o'clock on Sunday, and a few moments later they sat down together in the Oval Office. There, Currie testified, Clinton told her that he had been asked a number of questions at his deposition about Monica Lewinsky. "There are several things you may want to know," Clinton said, and then prompted her to agree with a rapid-fire series of statements:

- "You were always there when Monica was there."
- "We were never really alone, right?"
- "Monica came on to me, and I never touched her."
- "She wanted to have sex with me, and I can't do that."

Clinton had to know that these statements were false. In her testimony about this peculiar conversation, Currie put the most benign face possible on Clinton's behavior. First, she said she didn't know that all the statements were specifically false; second, she said she felt no pressure "whatsoever" to agree with the president's comments. As for Clinton, he later testified that he spoke to his secretary on Sunday because he was trying to "refresh my recollection" and because he figured a media storm was going to erupt and "I was trying to figure out what the facts were." Clinton gave basically the same rationale for having a second conversation with Currie along the same lines three days later—when the story had indeed broken in the press.

As a technical legal matter, Clinton's lawyers were probably correct that the president's behavior with Currie on these two occasions did not amount to a crime—neither obstruction of justice nor witness tampering. For one thing, Currie was not yet a witness in the Jones case (or before Starr's grand jury); for another, his secretary's very supportive rendering of Clinton's behavior suggested that she did not feel that she was being coerced to lie. Finally, it is possible, through tortured analysis, to conclude that not all of Clinton's statements to Currie were completely false. (In justifying his statements to Currie, in his grand jury testimony, Clinton made the infamous remark that "it depends how you define 'alone.'") In sum, then, most prosecutors probably would not have brought a criminal case against the president based on these facts.

But lawyers' excuses cannot obscure how contemptibly the president behaved with his secretary. Clinton had to live with the consequences of his dismal affair with Lewinsky. But here Clinton recruited another person into his circle of deceit—his secretary, who occupied a position at the opposite end of the spectrum of power and prestige from his own. A less loyal and savvy woman than Currie might have drawn a more sinister portrait of her boss's behavior. But still, the picture is bad enough. The president's willingness to use others to serve his own ends probably deserves greater condemnation than his sexual misadventures. Clinton's right-wing enemies had indeed leveraged the Lewinsky affair from a personal problem to a legal and political crisis. But instead of confronting the issue with candor and courage, Clinton hid behind lies and the skirts of his secretary.

And Currie—despite her brave words to the contrary—seems also to have panicked in response to the summons from the president. After her meeting with Clinton on Sunday, Currie began paging Lewinsky frantically. In the past, Lewinsky had responded instantly whenever Currie paged her; indeed, Currie spent a great deal of time ducking Monica's own pages. Currie tried four times on Saturday night. Monica called back once late, but Currie was too tired to talk. Then, on Monday morning, starting at 7 A.M., Currie paged Monica seven times in an hour, attaching increasingly alarmed messages each time. "Please call Kay [Betty's code name with Lewinsky] at eight this morning." "Please call Kay at home. It's a social call. Thank you." "Please call Kate [sic] re: family emergency." "From Kay. Please call. Have good news." No responses.

Monday was Martin Luther King Day, so Clinton was checking with Currie at home, to see if she had reached Monica. In the morning, the president spoke with Vernon Jordan, who had just heard from Frank Carter that Lewinsky had hired a new lawyer. The last time Clinton spoke to his secretary on Monday, he explained that the reason Monica hadn't called back was probably that her new lawyer had told her not to talk to anyone.

/ / /

The new lawyer was Bill Ginsburg. He had been drawn into the story late on Friday afternoon, when his old friend and client Bernie Lewinsky had tracked him down at a court appearance in Santa Monica. Bernie had sounded agitated on the telephone, telling Ginsburg that he had to see him right away but refusing to give the reason. It happened that two of Ginsburg's children were on airplanes that day, and he became consumed with the thought that Bernie was going to tell him that one of the flights (or both!) had crashed. Monica's father was the kind of old friend who might be trusted to deliver that kind of news. On the drive downtown to rendezvous with Lewinsky at the Biltmore Hotel, Ginsburg was so nervous that he wouldn't even turn on the radio for fear that he would hear of the crash.

Melodrama suited Ginsburg. Bearded and bespectacled, Ginsburg represented Lewinsky from January to June 1998 and through his incessant appearances on television became one of the most familiar faces in the country. Because of his ubiquity on the airwaves, Ginsburg made the transition from conscientious advocate to national joke faster than almost anyone in history. But if he mangled his role as a public spokesman—a business associate once described him as "an ego with a digestive system"—he also did a better job for his client than he was generally given credit for. Indeed, Ginsburg's epitaph might come out of Monty Python: "I may be an idiot, but I'm no fool."

At the time of the phone call from Bernie, however, Ginsburg had a nonexistent public profile. He defended medical malpractice cases at a quietly successful firm of about forty lawyers in Century City and lived in modest circumstances in the San Fernando Valley. Lewinsky had invited Ginsburg to speak on Friday evening at a radiologists' conference at the Biltmore. When the lawyer finally tracked down the doctor at the hotel, Ginsburg was so overwrought that he practically fell into Lewinsky's arms. But Ginsburg's family wasn't the problem.

"Monica's in some kind of trouble," her father said.

Ginsburg knew that she worked at the Pentagon, so a single thought flashed through the lawyer's brain.

Espionage! Monica's been arrested for selling state secrets!

Not exactly, said Bernie.

The two men commandeered one of the rooms at the Biltmore, and Bernie started to explain.

"Monica might be involved with the president of the United States," Lewinsky said.

Ginsburg figured this was the kind of news that entitled them to raid the minibar.

Bernie said Monica was with the FBI even as they spoke. The two men convinced themselves that even they might be subject to surveillance at that moment, so they decided to take their drinks and start walking around downtown Los Angeles, to foil wiretaps.

At last, they migrated to the Jonathan Club, a social club a few blocks away, where Ginsburg called the room at the Ritz-Carlton Hotel where Monica was being interrogated. He spoke to Michael Emmick, of Starr's staff. Emmick asked, "How do I know you're her lawyer?"

"Because, you miserable cocksucking motherfucker, I tell you I'm her lawyer!"

The exchange set the tone of Ginsburg's relationship with the Office of Independent Counsel for months to come.

Emmick told Ginsburg that Starr's office wanted Lewinsky to make controlled telephone calls as part of their investigation. Wisely, Ginsburg said he wanted immunity for his client—transactional immunity, which is the broadest kind. After Emmick and Ginsburg squabbled for a while about immunity, the prosecutor said there was another problem. He didn't have a word processor or a fax machine, so they couldn't make a deal right there. Ginsburg, who had stayed at the Ritz-Carlton and knew there were fax machines in the concierge lounge, said he would happily accept a handwritten agreement. Emmick wouldn't oblige.

Ginsburg persuaded Emmick to put Monica on the telephone, and her new lawyer instructed her simply to leave the hotel and go home. Along with her mother, who had arrived by that point, that was just what Monica did.

The following morning, Saturday, January 17, Ginsburg flew to Washington, and Monica picked him up at the airport. From there they drove to the Hay-Adams Hotel, across the street from the White House, where they spent three hours discussing Lewinsky's situation. One thing Ginsburg knew for sure was that Monica shouldn't talk to anyone—not the president, not Betty Currie, and not the prosecutors (at least before he obtained immunity for her). That evening, Monica ignored her lawyer's advice and did return one of Currie's pages, but that was when the president's secretary was too tired to talk. The following day, when Currie tried seven times to prompt a phone call from her, Lewinsky did not answer.

/ / /

The story percolated, just beneath the surface, for one more day, the King holiday on Monday. At this point, Drudge had basically turned over his site to Lucianne Goldberg, who was giving him new material every few hours. Drudge became the first person to go public with the name Monica Lewinsky, and then he reported that Lewinsky had filed an affidavit in the Paula Jones case denying a "sexual relationship with President Clinton." At one point, however, on that frenetic Monday, Goldberg and Drudge got their signals crossed.

The headline on one Drudge dispatch was CONTROVERSY SWIRLS AROUND TAPES OF FORMER WHITE HOUSE INTERN, AS

STARR MOVES IN. This was a major development, because it was the first suggestion that the Lewinsky matter had potential criminal ramifications and that Starr was investigating. Drudge was on to the story of his life, and though he wished Clinton ill, he was more interested in generating scoops than protecting Starr's investigation. Goldberg, on the other hand, had a broader perspective and a deeper political and personal animus.

"Take that goddamn story down!" Goldberg shouted at Drudge on the phone. The news that Starr was involved would deprive the prosecutor of the element of surprise. (Ginsburg, who was visiting the Starr offices on Monday, recalled prosecutors passing around printouts of the *Drudge Report* and despairing about the leak of their investigation.)

Drudge's news flash about Starr had been posted for only twenty minutes, so he did take it down overnight. But on Tuesday, Drudge saw that events were moving so fast that he said to himself, Fuck her—let's run it. Drudge's transmission actually anticipated the central controversy about the new area within Starr's jurisdiction. "'Starr is not on the bimbo beat,' one source close to the situation told the *Drudge Report* late Tuesday. 'He's looking at a potential for obstruction of justice charges.'.... The development has completely consumed high-level Washington, with Starr's investigators working past midnight in recent days.... Developing ..."

/ / /

At around nine in the evening on Tuesday, January 20, a White House lawyer named Lanny Breuer was sitting at his desk addressing invitations to his wife's fortieth-birthday party. Breuer was in charge of handling the legal aspects of the manifold congressional and criminal investigations of the White House—mostly on campaign finance (which was still a relatively hot topic) but also on the dying embers of the Starr investigation. The phone rang with a call from Wolf Blitzer, of CNN.

"Have you heard anything about an intern?"

Unlike many people at the White House, Breuer did not read the *Drudge Report*. (Drudge enjoyed pointing out that his site received 2,600 visits from White House staffers in the twelve hours after his first Lewinsky dispatch.) Breuer couldn't help Blitzer ...

but then about ten minutes later the White House lawyer's pager nearly overheated with calls.

The same thing was happening all over Washington. Scores of reporters had spent the day in a blind sprint to catch up to the disclosures that Goldberg had been feeding Drudge for the past three days. The prosecutors in the Starr office had been saying nothing, relying on the increasingly forlorn hope that they might still arrange for controlled telephone calls to their chief targets. But the Jones lawyers were emboldened by the possibility of an obstruction of justice investigation based on their lawsuit. Above all, they wanted Clinton destroyed, which a new criminal probe might accomplish. The Jones lawyers—not the Starr prosecutors—served as leakers-in-charge.

Chris Vlasto, the ABC producer who had dined with the Jones team on the night of the deposition, called Bob Bennett at home on Tuesday night and told him there were tapes of Lewinsky. At first, Bennett was so distraught he could scarcely mutter a single question: "How bad?"

When *The Washington Post* finally reached him later that evening, Bennett announced, "I smell a rat"—which was indignant but noncommittal. (*The Washington Post* and ABC News both posted their first reports about Lewinsky on their web sites just after midnight on Wednesday, January 21.)

As Tuesday night wore on, Lanny Breuer figured the news was big enough to summon his boss, Charles Ruff, back to the office for an emergency conference with the scandal management team, including Podesta, Bruce Lindsey, Cheryl Mills, and Lanny Davis (who would be leaving the White House staff in a few days). Ruff, who had attended Clinton's deposition, said he thought the questions about Lewinsky "came out of left field." Clinton's private lawyer, David Kendall, was brought in by speakerphone, and they decided to take the safest course—to say as little as possible.

Clinton himself spoke to both Kendall and Bennett on Tuesday night and persisted in his denial of any sexual relationship with Lewinsky, just as he had in the deposition. Ruff said White House spokesmen could repeat this denial in the morning, but no one should go into any detail, not until they knew more about the whole story.

The president left a wake-up call for 7:00 A.M. on Wednesday morning, and he called Kendall at 7:02. He then awakened his wife. Hillary Clinton later recalled that her husband woke her up with the words "You're not going to believe this, but . . ."

/ / /

The news prompted a press frenzy without precedent in recent American history. The anchors of the network news programs scrambled onto private jets to return from Cuba, where they were covering the pope's visit. Talk of resignation, impeachment, and an incipient political Armageddon enveloped Washington.

All through that Wednesday morning, Clinton met with his staffers and assured them that there was nothing to the allegations. Clinton began most days with a nine o'clock meeting with his chief of staff, Erskine Bowles, and his two deputies, Podesta and Sylvia Matthews. At the meeting on January 21, the president took the initiative as soon as the trio gathered before him in the Oval Office. "I want you to know that I did not have sexual relationships with this woman Monica Lewinsky," Bowles testified that Clinton said. "I did not ask anybody to lie. And when the facts come out, you'll understand." Others—including Mike McCurry, the press secretary—heard a similar recital from Clinton that day.

The president had three interviews scheduled for Wednesday, all timed to preview his State of the Union address, which was to be given the following Tuesday. In keeping with the fevered atmosphere, all three major broadcast networks broadcast the first interview, with PBS's Jim Lehrer, live. As Clinton walked into the Roosevelt Room at three-thirty, the atmosphere was funereal, and it leavened only slightly when his then new dog, Buddy, planted himself by the president's chair and refused to leave. The president had to get up from his seat and drag Buddy out of the room.

In answer to Lehrer's question about Lewinsky, Clinton said, "There is not a sexual relationship, an improper sexual relationship, or any other kind of improper relationship." Reporters immediately seized on the president's peculiar use of the present tense, and in his subsequent two interviews—with the newspaper *Roll Call* and National Public Radio—Clinton made his position clear that there had been no sexual relationship in the past, either. Still, as in the first interview with Lehrer, he looked and sounded tentative and unsure.

Only one member of the White House staff received a more thorough explanation of the Clinton-Lewinsky relationship on this tumultuous first day—or, as it turned out, ever. Sidney Blumenthal was only in his fifth month of government service, but he already occupied a special place in the firmament of people around the president and first lady.

Blumenthal had been born fifty years earlier in Chicago, and had worked his entire professional life as a journalist until he joined the president's staff. (For a few years early in Clinton's presidency, we were colleagues on the staff of *The New Yorker*.) Ironically, perhaps, in light of his previous career, Blumenthal quickly asserted himself as perhaps the most partisan member of the Clintons' circle. In a White House, and a capital, where people tried to slice issues into narrow, achievable objectives, Blumenthal saw the world in a broad sweep of ideological conflict between the Clintons and what he invariably called "the right wing." He shared his views by conducting unnerving Socratic dialogues to hint of the larger forces that underlay his worldview. "Starr, right?" Blumenthal might say. "Leaks, okay? You know? Money from the Rutherford Institute, right? Get it? Right?" The specifics were frequently obscure, and his colleagues at the White House generally viewed him with a sort of wary amusement. Blumenthal's predilection for conspiracy theories prompted his colleague Rahm Emanuel to nickname him "G.K."—for Grassy Knoll.

The first lady and Blumenthal talked often. After enduring six years of investigations about everything from the Whitewater investments to her health-care task force, Mrs. Clinton had grown bitter about the accusatory nature of politics in Washington. Blumenthal's Manichaean outlook—his sense of the world as divided between the Clintons' supporters and their implacable and obsessed enemies—had come increasingly to appeal to the president's wife. To her, the Lewinsky story simply looked like the latest chapter in the unrelenting war on the Clintons.

So it wasn't surprising that on Wednesday, January 21, Mrs. Clinton took Blumenthal aside and explained her view of what had happened—that is, what the president had told her about Monica Lewinsky that morning. Monica was a troubled young woman, Mrs. Clinton said, and her husband had "ministered" to her. "He ministers to troubled people all the time," she said. "He's done it dozens if not hundreds of times. He does it out of religious conviction and personal temperament.

"If you knew his mother," she said to Blumenthal, "you would understand it." (The first lady often attributed her husband's behavior to the influence of his mother, as she did in a much-publicized interview with *Talk* magazine, in 1999.)

The attack on the president from the Jones lawyers and the Starr prosecutors was simply political, Mrs. Clinton felt, and it was a shame that her husband was being punished for his good deeds.

Late in the afternoon, after the president had completed the three interviews, he summoned Blumenthal to the Oval Office. According to his grand jury testimony, Blumenthal began by saying he had spoken earlier to the first lady and she had explained his relationship with Lewinsky. Clinton knew that they had spoken, and then he began to tell the same story, almost word for word, that Blumenthal had heard from Mrs. Clinton. He told of how he was being punished for ministering to this troubled woman.

Blumenthal said he understood Clinton's compassion, but "you're president, and these troubled people can just get you in incredible messes, and you just—I know you don't want to, but you have to cut yourself off from them."

"It's very difficult for me to do that, given how I am," Clinton said. "I want to help people."

Clinton told Blumenthal that Dick Morris, his political consultant and on-and-off Svengali, had called him earlier and said, "You know, Nixon could have survived Watergate if he had gone on television and said everything he had done wrong and got it all out in the beginning."

"What have you done wrong?" Blumenthal asked.

"Nothing," Clinton said. "I haven't done anything wrong."

"Well, then, that's one of the stupidest ideas I've ever heard," said Blumenthal, who despised Morris in any event.

The president then gave Blumenthal an account of his relationship with Lewinsky. "Monica Lewinsky came at me and made a sexual demand on me," Blumenthal later testified that Clinton had said. He rebuffed her. "I've gone down that road before, I've caused pain for a lot of people, and I'm not going to do that again."

Lewinsky had responded to Clinton's rejection by threatening him. She said she was known as a "stalker" by her peers—she hated that—and if she said they had actually had an affair, she wouldn't be known as the stalker anymore.

"I feel like a character in a novel," Clinton said. "I feel like somebody who is surrounded by an oppressive force that is creating a lie about me, and I can't get the truth out. I feel like a character in the novel *Darkness at Noon*."

This remarkable conversation prompted a duel of literary analogies. Clinton thought of himself as Nicholas Rubashov, the hero (and victim) of Arthur Koestler's parable about Stalinist totalitarianism. Much later, Blumenthal would cast himself as Nick Carraway, who ferried messages between the doomed lovers in F. Scott Fitzgerald's *The Great Gatsby*. Yet these selections seem rather more pretentious than the circumstances warranted. Having damaged his relationship with his girl, then compounded his troubles by lying to her about it, the boy tries to work his way back into her good graces by bamboozling her best friend, too. It was a theme played out regularly in the pages of *Archie* comics.

But Clinton had a political, as well as romantic, crisis on his hands, and, as he told Blumenthal, he had turned for advice to Dick Morris. This garrulous New Yorker had flitted in and out of Clinton's life since 1977, advising on campaign strategy, wearing out his welcome, then being summoned again in moments of crisis. He was exiled again after his exposure, on the eve of the 1996 Democratic National Convention, as a patron of a Washington prostitute, but in this moment of great peril, Clinton turned to him once more.

"You poor son of a bitch," Morris told the president in their first conversation of the day.

"I didn't do what they said I did," Clinton replied, according to Morris's later testimony. "I've tried to shut myself down, sexually, I mean. But sometimes I slipped up, and with this girl, I just slipped up." Morris and the president then agreed that Morris should conduct a poll on public attitudes about the Lewinsky matter. Morris said he would call back late that night with the results.

Morris then typed up four single-spaced pages of questions and faxed them to Action Research, a polling operation in Melbourne, Florida. He knew few facts at this point and decided to do a poll based on a worst-case scenario. In the key questions in his survey, he asked the respondents to assume that Clinton had had the affair with Lewinsky, had lied about it himself, and had asked Monica to lie about it as well. In light of all this, only 47 percent would want him out of office. If Clinton pleaded guilty to the crime of obstruction of justice, only 56 percent would want him out of office. The questions were fairly garbled, but it appeared that adultery alone would pose relatively little problem for the voters—and lying about adultery would only make it somewhat worse.

Morris called Clinton at about 1:15 A.M. on Thursday morning to tell him about the poll. All in all, the news wasn't too bad for the president, but Morris seemed to misread the results. Morris said he thought the voters weren't ready for any kind of confession.

"Well," Clinton said, "we just have to win, then."

/ / /

In those first few days, Clinton marinated in his sense of victimhood. To a handful of close advisers, he mentioned a file that he kept in his desk in the Oval Office—what the president called his "Richard Jewell File," named for the Atlanta security guard who was falsely accused of the bombing at the Olympic Games in 1996. Clinton spoke often of Jewell. In November 1996, long before the Lewinsky story broke, Clinton compared himself to Jewell at a press conference in Australia. "I would urge you to remember what happened to Mr. Jewell, in Atlanta," Clinton said, "remembering what has happened to so many of the accusations over the last four years made against me that turned out to be totally baseless." Clinton's Jewell File contained some of the most outlandish accusations against him—and a handful of stories that pointed out the way he had been persecuted.

Clinton circulated one item from the Jewell File to at least one aide, an op-ed piece from *The New York Times* that the president had saved for more than three years. Written by H. Brandt Ayers, the editor of the local paper in Anniston, Alabama, the article was headlined "The Death of Civility." Ayers denounced "the hatred of unprecedented violence being directed at the White House . . . and the well-financed personal industries dedicated to destroying Mr. Clinton. . . . The unsubstantiated allegations of sexual misconduct by Mr. Clinton are nothing but a red herring." Ayers's theme was that while all presidents were criticized, the level of antagonism toward Clinton was unprecedented.

Clinton's complaints made interesting fodder for debate, but as the week ended, his staff in the White House faced a more immediate problem—what to say on the Sunday talk shows. Through Whitewater, Travelgate, Filegate, and campaign finance, White House aides had developed a fairly well-tuned strategy for scandal management. They did their best to stay in front of the stories, to release damaging material themselves, and to make sure there were no surprises.

But as Rahm Emanuel brought his baby son to the White House on Saturday, January 24, those options weren't available. Bruce Lindsey, John Podesta, Paul Begala, and others floated in and out of the West Wing asking the same questions. What can we say? If Clinton and Lewinsky did not have a sexual relationship, what kind of relationship did they have? What did the president say to her about her testimony in the Paula Jones case? And did he help her find a job in New York? No one knew the answers—and the lawyers, Kendall and Ruff preeminently, weren't letting anyone ask questions. James Carville, stuck in a hotel room in San Francisco and scheduled to appear on *Meet the Press,* struggled with the same question. What can we say? Should the message be contrition, caution, magnanimity, something else? *What can we say?*

But as Zach Emanuel was passed from one set of shoulders to another, his noisy presence a welcome distraction on a difficult day, the answer finally came into focus. It was obvious in retrospect, but it didn't seem that way at the time. In a narrow sense, their answer was the product of six years of defending Bill Clinton. They did what they knew. But from a broader perspective, the White House response to the Lewinsky allegations represented a logical culmination of changes in the political culture that had been occurring for decades. Politics had degenerated into litigation by other means. You push us, we push you. For the White House, the strategy would boil down to a single word.

Attack.

14

"I Guess That Will Teach Them"

As Harry Thomason cradled the television remote control in his office on the CBS lot—just downstairs from Jerry Seinfeld's digs and a few blocks from Matt Drudge's former enclave in the gift shop—he did not like what he saw. Thomason was watching Clinton's interview with Jim Lehrer, on Wednesday, January 21, and he thought the president looked tentative and unsteady. Thomason told his wife, Linda Bloodworth-Thomason, of his concerns, and she said, "You need to go to Washington." Harry then put a call through to the first lady, who had only one question for him.

"When can you get here?"

Harry took the first plane to Washington on Thursday morning. He moved into a third-floor bedroom in the residence area of the White House and didn't leave for thirty-four days. Linda joined him about halfway through his stay.

/ / /

The son of a grocer in a small town in southern Arkansas, Harry worked as a high school art teacher and a football coach, but he wanted to make movies, so one day he checked out a book on filmmaking from the local library. By the early 1970s he was making commercials and low-budget movies in Little Rock. In 1974, he obtained the rights to a *Reader's Digest* story about a terminally ill athlete and hitched a ride on a freight plane to Los Angeles; in time, he started producing for television. Linda's tale was only somewhat less unlikely. The daughter of a politically liberal lawyer who moved from Arkansas to southern Missouri, she also went west, taught school briefly in Watts, and discovered a gift for writing when she and a friend dashed off a script for the *M*A*S*H* TV series. At the time Clinton was elected president, the couple had three situation comedies on the air—*Hearts Afire, Evening Shade,* and, their biggest hit, *Designing Women.* With Linda doing almost all the writing, Harry directing, and both of them producing, they were reported to be making $300,000 a week.

Along the way, the Thomasons became devoted friends of the Clintons. They never had formal roles in any of the Clinton campaigns, but Harry had stage-managed several of the most important public moments in the president's career, including his walk to Madison Square Garden during the 1992 convention and his train ride across the Midwest before the 1996 convention, in Chicago. For her part, Linda produced *The Man from Hope,* a Capraesque documentary about Clinton that was shown at the 1992 convention, and a sequel that was shown at the convention four years later. The Thomasons had no political or social ambitions of their own in Washington—only a ferocious determination to protect their friends in the White House.

In this respect, then, it wasn't surprising that the first lady would summon Harry when her husband was in political extremis. But the move symbolized something larger, too. By early 1998, the Clintons had lived in Washington for more than five years and made precisely one close friend in the city. But that ally, Vernon Jordan, was himself implicated in the unfolding scandal, so the Clintons had to call across the country for shoulders to lean on. The leaders of the political and journalistic establishment never had much use for the Clintons (and vice versa), and this hostility contributed to the atmosphere that overtook the city almost overnight—that of a decorous lynching party.

Indeed, the Thomasons may have unintentionally contributed to the Clintons' social isolation. The couple had also served as impresarios of the president's first inauguration ceremony, in 1993, and as part of the proceedings, Linda produced a five-minute film for the evening gala. To the strains of Frank Sinatra singing the Gershwin tune "They All Laughed," the film featured a rapid-fire series of sound bites from Washington media figures during the 1992 campaign. One after another, Robert Novak, Fred Barnes, David S. Broder, and other journalists were shown dismissing Clinton as a "loser," "unelectable," and "dead meat." The Thomasons regarded the film as a harmless needle at some puffed-up egos, but several of the targets and their friends regarded it as an act of war. The lingering controversy about the film may have reflected the thin skins of the Washington press corps more than any initial hostility on the part of the Thomasons, but it helped to poison the ambiance for the Clintons almost from day one.

The Thomasons themselves had an even worse time of it. Harry stumbled into what became Travelgate, by suggesting that an aviation-consulting company in which he had a small interest might provide a better deal for the White House. Two civil suits against Harry for his role in Travelgate were dismissed, and Starr's prosecutors never even questioned him in the matter, but the issue further soured the Thomasons on Washington—and the city's establishment on them. The travel-office debacle broke in the press during the same week in 1993 as the infamous presidential haircut aboard Air Force One, in Los Angeles. It was Christophe, the hairdresser for the cast of *Hearts Afire,* who gave the haircut, and it was Thomason who introduced Christophe to the Clintons and hired the hairdresser under a "personal services contract." Contrary to press reports at the time, the haircut did not delay air traffic, and Harry was in Florida when it occurred. But placing Christophe in the president's entourage was a perfect opening for the president's critics to mock him as an elitist masquerading as a populist.

By 1998, the Thomasons were pretty thoroughly embittered about Washington, and like their friends in the White House, Harry and Linda shared a heartfelt contempt for the entire metropolis of prosecutors and pundits. Harry Thomason said not long after the story broke, "We've had a slow-motion assassination in process for some time. Once everybody on our side falls in, this is war. Never give them a break. Never give them one inch. Once you finally get that through your head, then you have to get out and fight this every way you can.

"My grandfather used to say that the Bible said when someone hits you, you turn the other cheek," Thomason went on, "but after that, you deck him."

/ / /

Thomason arrived in Washington on the rainy night of Thursday, January 22, and around midnight he and the president took Buddy for a long walk around the White House grounds. Thomason knew enough about criminal investigations to refrain from asking Clinton any direct questions about his involvement with Lewinsky, but the president conveyed the same message to his friend that he had to his staff—that he was being hounded for his fatherly interest in the girl. More than that, though, Clinton saw himself as the victim of an unparalleled effort at personal destruction. The conversation between the two men continued, on and off, for three more days, as Thomason accompanied the Clintons for a tense weekend at Camp David. There the Catoctin Mountain air was perfumed with the scent of old grudges, as Harry traced the current crisis to villains of their shared past. (For months, Thomason explained the president's troubles with the phrase "It's all Arkansas politics.") As the cabin fire crackled, they talked of Cliff Jackson, who had midwifed the Paula Jones suit and Whitewater investigations, and of Sheffield Nelson, Clinton's 1990 gubernatorial opponent, who had first nudged the stories about Juanita Broaddrick and other women toward a public stage.

By the end of the weekend, though, Thomason began to sense a shift in momentum. On the Sunday talk shows, Clinton's supporters began their effort to change the subject from the president's behavior to that of the prosecutor. James Carville, on *Meet the Press*: "This started out as a $40,000 land deal that lost money, and about $50 million and five years later, after nobody could find anything, we're wiring up people in hotels and feeding them whiskey trying to get them to talk and everything else. This is a scuzzy investigation." Rahm Emanuel, on *Face the Nation*: "The only thing that matters is the truth as it pertains to two questions. Did he have a sexual relationship? And did he ask her to lie? The answer to those questions is no and no."

Now all that remained was for Clinton himself to resume the offensive. On Sunday night, January 25, Thomason returned with the Clintons to their residence at the White House, where Harold Ickes, the equally combative former deputy chief of staff, joined them in the solarium. (A news junkie, Thomason was happiest with one eye scanning the all-news television stations and the other browsing the political web sites. Mrs. Clinton, on the other hand, refused to watch any television news during this period, so Harry was constantly turning the television in the solarium on and off depending on whether Hillary was in the room.) At this point, Thomason began leaning on the president to make a stronger denial than he had with Lehrer the previous Wednesday.

"You know, you shouldn't wait any longer," Thomason told Clinton. "You should make a strong statement at the first opportunity. There was nothing wrong with what you said last week. It was the way you said it." Ickes concurred—and aides were sent to search for the right moment in the president's schedule. Since the State of the Union message was just forty-eight hours away, and the frenzy showed no sign of abating, there wasn't much time.

It was after midnight, early Monday morning, when the phone rang in the Washington hotel room of Bill White, the president of the C. S. Mott Foundation. White was scheduled to speak at a ceremony in the Roosevelt Room, at ten-thirty that morning, to showcase an after-school child-care program that the president would be lauding before Congress on Tuesday. Earlier, White had been told that Vice President Gore and the first lady would be presiding.

"There has been a slight change in plans," White was told.

/ / /

"Thank you. Thank you and good morning," Hillary Clinton said, as the applause died down. "Please be seated. Welcome to the White House." There was a slight edge to her smile when she added, "And I'm especially pleased to see in the audience so many people who care so much about education and child care." As the first lady knew, few of the fifty or so people who had squeezed into the room were thinking much about child care on the morning of Monday, January 26.

True, the president's supporters had finally started to put up a fight, but the rain of new disclosures had continued to fall on the White House. On Saturday, ABC had independently confirmed, through other sources, what Goldberg had fed to Drudge earlier in the week: that "Lewinsky says she saved—apparently as a kind of souvenir—a navy-blue dress with the president's semen stain on it." On Sunday, there were the first broadcast reports that someone—unnamed—had witnessed an intimate encounter between Clinton and Lewinsky. This prompted both of the New York tabloids, the *News* and the *Post,* to trumpet the same headline across their front pages on Monday morning: CAUGHT IN THE ACT. On their Sunday shows, some network pundits had put Clinton's chances of survival in office at "fifty-fifty at best," while others wondered if the president would last out the week.

"This morning we come together to hear about the president's plans to strengthen education," Mrs. Clinton gamely went on. "This afternoon, I will be visiting a model program in Harlem. . . ." As the minutes passed with excruciating slowness, Mrs. Clinton turned the floor over to Richard Riley, the secretary of education, then to Bill White, of the Mott Foundation, then on to a local couple whose children had taken advantage of the after-school program, and then on to the vice president, who thanked everyone for coming—especially Senators Dianne Feinstein, Barbara Boxer, and Chris Dodd, who were seated directly in front of the lectern. Finally, after close to an hour, Vice President Gore said, "I am very pleased to introduce America's true education president and the greatest champion of working parents and working families that the United States of America has ever known: President Bill Clinton."

The small crowd jumped to their feet and offered a nervous, almost frantic cheer for the embattled president. Clinton said "Thank you" fourteen times before he could continue. The president then spoke easily for about ten minutes about the after-school program and the other education proposals he would be raising the following evening in the State of the Union address. He spoke of reducing class size; teaching every eight-year-old to read; hooking up classrooms and libraries to the Internet—the kind of popular, small-bore initiatives on which he had built the revival of his presidency. "Now I have to go back to work on my State of the Union speech," Clinton said, "and I worked on it till pretty late last night."

Then the president looked down and paused. No one—no

one—knew what he was going to say next. Not his wife, not the vice president, not Harry Thomason, who was watching Clinton's remarks on a video monitor in an office down the hall in the West Wing. Nine days earlier, he had given sworn testimony in the Paula Jones case that he did not have a sexual relationship with Monica Lewinsky. But according to the press, there were semen stains! Eyewitnesses! What was he going to say?

For the first time, Clinton leaned forward on the small lectern, inched closer to the microphone, and began in a soft voice that grew louder with each word: "But I want to say one thing to the American people. I want you to listen to me. I'm going to say this again."

At this moment, Clinton stood up straight and raised his right index finger nearly to his chin, and then pumped it four times as he uttered the following sentence: "I did not have sexual relations with that woman, Miss Lewinsky." Clinton blinked awkwardly after saying "that woman"; he later told Thomason he had used the phrase because, in the stress of the moment, he had momentarily forgotten Lewinsky's name.

Another jab of the finger, this time hitting the lectern in front of him: "I never told anybody to lie, not a single time, never."

Jab, again banging the wood: "These allegations are false."

At this point, Clinton was moving his arm so much that the camera operator had to widen the shot to make sure he remained in the frame.

One more: "Now I need to go back to work for the American people. Thank you."

As the president walked away, the applause was more stunned than joyous.

For her part, Mrs. Clinton left the Roosevelt Room to gather her belongings for her trip to New York to talk about child care. She planned to spend the night at the Waldorf-Astoria Hotel and then, the following morning, appear on the *Today* show.

/ / /

Clinton's statement had its biggest impact in newsrooms. Up to that point, the Lewinsky story had been careening as if down a hill, picking up momentum each day. Each new disclosure made Clinton look worse; every new story made it appear more likely that the president had been sexually involved with the intern and had obstructed justice in the Jones case. Clinton's forced departure from office seemed, in this moment, almost inevitable. On Saturday, Wolf Blitzer of CNN reported from the White House lawn that Clinton aides were "talking among themselves about the possibility of a resignation." Several aides promptly chased Blitzer across the grass to tell him he was wrong, but his report reflected the spirit of the moment. In the frenetic atmosphere of that first week, there appeared to be little risk to pushing the story as hard as possible. It seemed that if bad news for Clinton wasn't true yet, it probably was going to be true soon, anyway.

Suddenly, on Monday, Clinton had a simple message for the press corps: Prove it. That, it turned out, was going to be more difficult than it appeared. The president's finger-waving challenge occurred at just about the time the main sources for the previous week's disclosures—Paula Jones's lawyers—were tapped out. The Jones team basically knew only what Linda Tripp had told them; and by January 26, the lawyers had leaked all of her best material— the semen-stained dress, the phone sex, the exchanges of gifts. (Lucianne Goldberg had passed these same stories to the tabloids.) And Tripp, of course, knew only what Lewinsky had told her about the relationship. There wasn't much corroborative evidence in late January 1998. The infamous dress was still hidden and would not appear for seven more months. The reports about eyewitnesses to White House trysts were simply erroneous. In a purely cynical sense, it was precisely the right time for Clinton to tell this extraordinary public lie.

Like every other White House aide, Sidney Blumenthal did not know for sure that Clinton was lying about Lewinsky, but as a former reporter, Blumenthal did recognize the brief moment of opportunity that beckoned for the Clinton forces. Press and public interest in the embryonic scandal remained intense, but Clinton's enemies found themselves, for the moment, without new merchandise to sell to reporters. What would fill the void left by the stanched leaks from the Jones lawyers? Blumenthal had an idea, which he shared with the first lady as she spent Monday night at the Waldorf before her appearance on the *Today* show.

At that moment, no one was more important to Bill Clinton's political future than his wife. Much later, after the president admitted he had been sexually involved with Lewinsky, many of the Clintons' adversaries suggested that Mrs. Clinton knew all along that he had lied to the public about the relationship. According to this theory, Hillary had backed up her husband's lies so that they both might cling to power. The evidence suggests otherwise. People who spoke to her during this period recalled that she expressed only passionate support for, and belief in, her husband. Moreover, for Mrs. Clinton to believe that the affair had taken place would be to acknowledge an extraordinary betrayal, and a public humiliation on a grand scale. What human being, given the option, wouldn't try to avoid such a fate? In light of her husband's track record, of course, one can imagine that the first lady harbored suspicions about him. But no one glimpsed any hesitancy in those first few days.

Indeed, Mrs. Clinton's certainty about the falsehood of the accusations against her husband made her all the more receptive to Blumenthal's message. It was a version of a conversation the former reporter and the first lady had had many times. Since the Lewinsky story broke, Blumenthal said, the press had so far focused on the president's behavior to the exclusion of all other subjects. But he asserted the real story was something very different. The press had to see that "the right wing," not the president, bore responsibility for this scandal. As of the morning of January 27, Mrs. Clinton was the most important character from whom no one had heard. This was a sex scandal, and her posture as a wronged—or supportive—wife might make all the difference to her husband.

/ / /

The interview on the *Today* show had been scheduled for more than a month. The first lady's staff had booked her for the morning of the State of the Union address to talk about the "national treasures" initiative, a historic preservation project that her husband would be mentioning briefly in his speech that night. In the years since her health-care proposal had imploded, Mrs. Clinton had been relegated to softer, more traditional first-lady projects like this one. But with her husband embroiled in a sex scandal, Hillary Clinton would return to a pivotal role in his administration. She knew the stakes for this first interview, and she reveled in the action. By five-thirty on the morning of Tuesday, January 27, a squadron of television satellite trucks had set up outside Rockefeller Center merely to catch the first lady's arrival at the NBC studio.

In the makeup room, at about six-thirty, Mrs. Clinton was relaxed and confident as she was welcomed by Jeff Zucker, the executive producer of *Today*. "You must be the smartest producer in America to have booked me for today," she told him. She greeted Matt Lauer, the coanchor, with words of sympathy for Katie Couric, whose husband had died of cancer the previous weekend.

"On Close-Up this morning," said Lauer, at the top of the broadcast, "the first lady of the United States, Hillary Rodham Clinton." Lauer began by noting that the interview had indeed been scheduled several weeks earlier, and then said, "We appreciate you honoring the commitment, even in light of recent events. Thank you very much.

"There has been a question on the minds of a lot of people in this country, Mrs. Clinton, lately, and that is what is the exact nature of the relationship between your husband and Monica Lewinsky? Has he described that relationship in detail to you?"

"Well, we've talked at great length," she said. "And I think as this matter unfolds, the entire country will have more information. But we're right in the middle of a rather vigorous feeding frenzy right now. People are saying all kinds of things, putting out rumor and innuendo. And I have learned over the last many years being involved in politics, and especially since my husband first started running for president, that the best thing to do in these cases is just to be patient, take a deep breath, and the truth will come out. But there's nothing we can do to fight this firestorm of allegations that are out there."

Lauer said that Clinton had told the American people what the relationship was not. "Has he described to you what it was?"

"Yes," Mrs. Clinton said. "And we'll find that out as time goes by, Matt. But I think the important thing now is to stand as firmly as I can and say that, you know, that the president has denied these allegations on all counts, unequivocally. . . ."

Lauer turned to one of the specific allegations. Had the president given Lewinsky gifts?

Mrs. Clinton said it was possible. "I mean, I've seen him take his tie off and hand it to somebody, you know. . . . I've known my husband for more than twenty-five years, and we've been married for twenty-two years, and the one thing I always kid him about is that he never meets a stranger. He is kind, he is friendly, he tries to help people who need help, who ask for help." Here Mrs. Clinton was hinting at the explanation that her husband had given her and Blumenthal on the first day—that he was ministering to a troubled young woman. Then, in the course of the same answer, the first lady started to try to steer the conversation in the direction she wanted it to go. "So I think everybody ought to just stop a minute here and think about what we're doing," she said. "I'm very concerned about the tactics that are being used and the kind of intense political agenda at work here."

"I want to ask about Ken Starr in a second," Lauer replied, and then after a few questions about whether Mrs. Clinton knew Lewinsky ("No"), Vernon Jordan's role ("I just can't describe to you how outgoing and friendly" he is), and whether her husband would apologize for again causing pain in their marriage ("No. Absolutely not, and he shouldn't"), Mrs. Clinton had a chance to say what she felt about the investigation.

"This is what concerns me," she said. "This started out as an investigation of a failed land deal. I told everybody in 1992, 'We lost money.' People said, 'It's not true, you know, they made money. They have money in a Swiss bank account.' Well, it was true. It's taken years, but it was true. We get a politically motivated prosecutor who is allied with the right-wing opponents of my husband, who had literally spent four years looking at every telephone—"

"Spent $30 million," Lauer interjected.

"—more than that, now. But looking at every telephone call we've made, every check we've ever written, scratching for dirt, intimidating witnesses, doing everything possible to try to make some accusation against my husband."

"We're talking about Kenneth Starr," Lauer said, "so let's use his name, because he is the independent counsel."

"But it's the whole operation," she replied. "It's not just one person. It's an entire operation. . . . I do believe that this is a battle. I mean, look at the very people who are involved in this, they have popped up in other settings. This is the great story here, for anybody who is willing to find it and write about it and explain it, is this vast right-wing conspiracy that has been conspiring against my husband since the day he announced for president. A few journalists have kind of caught on to it and explained it, but it has not yet been fully revealed to the American public. And, actually, you know, in a bizarre sort of way, this may do it."

The phrase "vast right-wing conspiracy" created an immediate sensation and quickly became probably the best-known utterance by a first lady in the history of the United States. Yet there was nothing new about Mrs. Clinton's feelings on the subject. In February 1994, just as the Whitewater story was heating up, the first lady gave an interview to Meryl Gordon, of *Elle* magazine, in which she said, "Look, I know what this is about. This is a well-organized and well-financed attempt to undermine my husband and, by extension, myself, by people who have a different political agenda or have another personal and financial reason for attacking us." Four years later, she felt the same way.

But was it a fair critique of the president's adversaries, to call them a "vast right-wing conspiracy"? To the extent the word "conspiracy" suggested illegal behavior, Mrs. Clinton's remark was not warranted. At that point, there was no evidence that anyone around either Paula Jones or Kenneth Starr broke the law. Nor were the anti-Clinton efforts centrally coordinated. Many of the participants in Mrs. Clinton's conspiracy—say, Cliff Jackson and the elves, or Lucianne Goldberg and Starr himself—did not know one another at all. As for "vast," the central players in the effort to bring down Clinton could probably all have fit in a single school bus. Moreover, the claim ignored the fact that the president brought many of his problems on himself, especially by conducting his disastrous relationship with Monica Lewinsky. Parsed in this way, Mrs. Clinton's famous phrase did not exactly hold up.

But the charge had—and has—the unmistakable ring of truth. The Paula Jones and Whitewater investigations existed only because of the efforts of Clinton's right-wing political enemies. People who hated the Clintons initiated these projects and sustained them through many years. To put it another way, there was no one of importance behind either the Starr investigation or the Paula Jones case who was not already a dedicated political adversary of the Clintons. There was scarcely, say, a single prominent Democrat or Clinton supporter who was convinced by the evidence to change sides. The evidence simply reinforced existing political orientations. It was, above all, a story of political passions being played out on a legal stage. In this respect, there was indeed a "vast right-wing conspiracy" to get the president.

Still, Mrs. Clinton's view neglected an important, and troubling, point. Her outrage about the conspiracy presupposed a belief that there was something extraordinary about the use of the legal system to achieve political aims. In a world where, thanks largely to Democrats like the Clintons, the legal system had taken over the political system, the existence of this conspiracy was business as usual. At a time when lawsuits were replacing elections as weapons of political change, it was not surprising that Clinton's enemies chose to attack him the way they did. All they were doing was using the tools of the contemporary political trade.

Since Mrs. Clinton's phrase became a piece of Americana, the importance of her adjacent challenge to journalists had been largely forgotten. The reason she was talking about a "vast right-wing conspiracy" was to appeal to journalists to look into Starr's background and that of his associates. Sidney Blumenthal had not come up with the famous four words—Mrs. Clinton did that herself—but he had urged her to goad the reporters covering the story. The fever of first disclosures was breaking. Something else had to take its place. "This is the great story here," Mrs. Clinton had promised. Within a few days, Blumenthal made it his mission to midwife that story to life.

After her appearance on *Today*, though, Mrs. Clinton had to return to Washington and join her husband for the State of the Union address that evening. Her defense of her husband and attack on his pursuers had electrified the Clintons' staff and friends—and, it appeared, the first lady herself. On the subject of the investigation, the president had been muzzled by his lawyers, reduced, during a photo opportunity with the Palestinian leader Yasir Arafat, to asserting vaguely that "the American people have a right to get answers. I'd like for you to have more rather than less, sooner rather than later." Mrs. Clinton, on the other hand, had for the moment replaced him as the political soul of the family—the combatant, the savior, the indispensable ally in the strategy for survival. Mrs. Clinton was still flush from her triumph in New York when she returned on Tuesday afternoon to join Harry Thomason's vigil in the solarium.

"I guess that will teach them to fuck with us," the first lady said.

The president's spirits didn't respond as quickly as his wife's. Thomason continued to coach the president, exhorting him to keep after his adversaries. When Thomason walked Clinton to the door of the White House as he was leaving for Capitol Hill to give the State of the Union address, he told him, "Just remember—you've got the biggest balls over there. Just go over and kick their butts."

Which was, more or less, what Clinton did. His pollster, Mark Penn, was standing just out of camera range in the House chamber, waiting for the first thirty seconds of the speech. Penn knew that the president was prepared to deliver a poised and polished address, full of the moderate, poll-tested initiatives that were the trademark of his presidency. Once Penn saw that the legislators would react to Clinton the way they had in previous years, he exhaled. He knew then that Clinton was going to make it.

Unaccountably to many in the scandal-crazed capital, as the story approached its one-week anniversary, independent public opinion polls registered little change in the president's already high approval ratings. In the year ahead, those polls would provide no end of succor to the White House. Yet there was another key to Clinton's deliverance, one that also began to emerge on the same tumultuous day that saw the first lady discoursing to Matt Lauer and the president orating before Congress. However, this other favorable augury for the president was visible only to those who had access to the secret proceedings of Kenneth Starr's grand jury.

/ / /

From the moment that Starr's investigators first interviewed Linda Tripp, they knew that Betty Currie would be a central witness in their investigation. She served as the intermediary between all of Starr's principal targets—between Clinton and Lewinsky, Lewinsky and Jordan, and even, to a lesser extent, Clinton and Jordan.

As Lewinsky described her relationship with the president in the conversations that Tripp tape-recorded, Currie had served as enabler in chief for the commander in chief. Everyone on Starr's staff knew they had to have Currie as a witness. So, on Saturday, January 24—when Harry Thomason was fortifying the Clintons' spirits at Camp David—Starr's investigators took Currie to Room 618 of the Residence Inn Hotel, in Bethesda, Maryland, to begin debriefing her.

Who should lead the questioning of Currie? Not surprisingly, in an investigation that seemed to go from irrelevant to omnipotent in about a week, issues of turf quickly arose for the prosecutors. But Starr had no doubt about which lawyer he wanted in charge of the president's secretary—Bob Bittman. After all, along with Jackie Bennett and Hick Ewing, Bittman was one of Starr's three top deputies in 1998. Indeed, while Bennett supervised the work of the independent counsel's entire Washington office, Starr placed Bittman in direct charge of the first criminal investigation of the president of the United States since Watergate.

Perhaps no lawyer in American history had been given an assignment for which he was less qualified. One of Starr's original top deputies, Mark Tuohey, had hired Bittman in 1994. At the time, Bittman was thirty-two years old, and his legal career consisted of six years as an assistant state attorney in Maryland's Anne Arundel County. There Bittman mainly prosecuted street crime in Annapolis. In his most noteworthy case, he tried a high school teacher for having had consensual sex with one of her students. She was acquitted. In Annapolis, as later in Starr's office, Bittman was renowned for his devotion to his golf game, and he would often stay at his parents' home, adjacent to the grounds of the storied Congressional Country Club, so that he could squeeze in a game around work. Bittman was also a stalwart Republican.

Bittman worked his way through the ranks of the Starr office. Though hired as a third-level prosecutor, he had stayed long enough to see virtually all of the seasoned veterans who started with him move on to other opportunities. Bittman took over as the sort of chief administrative officer of the Starr operation, running meetings and keeping tabs on various investigations. In office debates about strategy, Bittman (like his fellow deputy Jackie

Bennett) invariably took the toughest line with the office's adversaries. This impressed Starr, who gave Bittman the nickname "Bulldog."

Bulldog Bittman spent parts of both days over the weekend at the hotel in Bethesda with Currie, her two lawyers, and a pair of FBI agents. The mood was tense, urgent. The FBI had chosen the obscure location so that no one would know Currie was cooperating with Starr. Bittman told Currie's lawyers that he wanted to bring Currie before the grand jury that very week. Currie's lead lawyer, Larry Wechsler, an experienced Washington hand and former prosecutor, wondered about the rush. Federal prosecutors usually devote many painstaking hours to preparing key witnesses to testify in the grand jury. But Bittman had talked to Currie for only four hours on Saturday and less than two on Sunday. He wanted her to testify on Tuesday.

By any standard, Currie wasn't ready to testify. She was emotional; her memory was not good; her dealings with the principal players occurred over many months and involved many separate conversations; the Starr office had yet to analyze her telephone or pager records; Bittman didn't have any important documents to refresh her recollection. Currie was giving the Starr prosecutors all the time they wanted. They could have taken days, even weeks, to nail down her story. What was the hurry?

The answer revealed a great deal about the future course of the investigation. Bittman argued that calling the president's secretary as the first witness before the grand jury would be a sign that Starr's office meant business. He wanted to "lock her in" to her story right away. Starr, who of course had no prosecutorial experience of his own, put much stock in purported "signs" of "strength" and "weakness." Besides, Bittman argued, the longer Currie remained outside the grand jury, the greater the chance that she would be "love bombed" by the Clinton forces and her testimony spun in ways favorable to the president. Starr wanted the White House to see how fast his investigation was moving. Currie would be his first witness. So much the better that it was Tuesday morning, January 27, 1998, the day of the State of the Union address.

/ / /

"Mrs. Currie, that water in front of you is yours," Bob Bittman began at 10:19 A.M., three hours after Mrs. Clinton's appearance on the *Today* show and eleven hours before her husband's speech to Congress. As he stood before the witness, Bittman had never prosecuted a single case in federal court.

"Thank you," the president's secretary said.

Currie moved haltingly through her background and her responsibilities as the president's secretary. She gave a complex description of the routes in and out of the Oval Office, but because Bittman had not arranged for a diagram, Currie's recital was almost incomprehensible. Quickly, Bittman moved to the subject of Monica Lewinsky. Currie said that she had had some vague awareness of Lewinsky when she worked at the White House, but had become friendly with her only after Lewinsky went to work at the Pentagon.

"How many times since Ms. Lewinsky left the White House has she visited the West Wing of the White House, in the immediate area of the Oval Office, approximately?" Bittman asked.

"I'd only be guessing. I cannot—" Currie sputtered.

"Would it be fair to say that is several times?"

"That would be a good one, sir—several."

Bittman went on to ask about how often Currie had cleared Lewinsky into the West Wing, and how often the former intern actually saw the president. With more preparation, and with the benefit of White House records that had not yet been produced, Currie might have been prodded to provide a more specific picture of the relationship between Clinton and Lewinsky, but Bittman was left with Currie's vague disavowals.

After Lewinsky left the White House staff, Bittman asked, did her relationship with the president change?

"I was unaware, sir—not to my knowing," Currie replied, in another damaging (and rather preposterous) answer for the prosecutor. If she had been confronted with all the phone messages, pager calls, records of visits, and gifts between them, Currie might have changed her mind. But in this rushed appearance, Bittman was stuck with the answer.

The examination meandered to the topic of Lewinsky's private meetings with the president. Currie could remember only two, though there were more. Bittman then asked a convoluted series of questions about Currie's phone calls to Lewinsky. He wanted to know whether Currie was calling for herself or for Clinton. But he asked like this: "On the several occasions that you called Ms. Lewinsky at the Pentagon, you told us that you called more than half the time for the president or on behalf of the president?"

In answer to this bewildering statement, Currie could say only, "I don't know."

Asked why she and Lewinsky used code names for their messages to each other, Currie said, "I don't know. It was suggested. Fine." Bittman left it at that.

Still, the real disaster in Bittman's examination concerned the president's single most legally incriminating act in the aftermath of his affair with Lewinsky. Currie testified about how, on the day after Clinton's deposition in the Jones case, the president had summoned her and made his series of leading statements—"You were always there when Monica was there," "We were never really alone," and so on.

But the greatest potential risk to Clinton concerned his second round of leading statements to Currie—and this was where Bittman blundered. This climactic moment in Currie's grand jury testimony began with a question about a late-night phone call to her from the president on the night of Tuesday, January 20.

"And I was sound asleep at the time," Currie replied. "And he told me that apparently—let's see—what story that broke on Wednesday—I think, tapes maybe, whatever—"

Bittman broke in to say, "The story broke on Tuesday morning, in *The Washington Post.*"

"It was Tuesday morning?" Currie asked.

"It was Tuesday morning that the story broke in the print media. It was on Monday that it broke in a report called the *Drudge Report.*"

"Then he may have called me Monday night," Currie said.

But Currie was right and Bittman was wrong. The story had broken on Wednesday morning, not Tuesday. Bittman was so ill prepared to examine Currie that he was polluting the transcript with his own errors and confusing an already perplexed witness.

"Okay," Bittman went on. "Did there come a time after that you had another conversation with the president about some other news about what was going on? That would have been Tuesday or Wednesday, when he called you in the Oval Office?"

"It was Tuesday or Wednesday," Currie said. "I don't remember which one this was, either. But the best I remember, when he called me in the Oval Office, it was sort of a recapitulation of what we had talked about on Sunday—you know, 'I was never alone with her'—that sort of thing."

"Did he pretty much list the same—?"

"To my recollection, sir, yes."

Here Bittman was questioning a witness about an event of potentially enormous significance, yet he could scarcely have confused matters more if he had tried. If the conversation between the president and Currie took place on Wednesday, as seems likely, that would have been of great importance, because on that day Clinton knew for certain that a criminal investigation was under way. If it was Tuesday, Clinton's lawyers might have put a more benign spin on it. Bittman didn't even try to sort it out. And what exactly did Clinton say? That, too, could make or break a case against him for obstruction of justice. But Bittman never even asked, and instead left Currie's vague characterization—"sort of a recapitulation"—without asking for elaboration. If Bittman had devoted adequate time to preparing his witness, not to mention himself, he might have avoided these problems.

If Bittman's bad morning had been an isolated act of incompetence in an otherwise flawless investigation, it might have loomed smaller than it eventually did. Instead, it established a pattern that Starr's team would follow straight through the following year—an obsession with meaningless atmospherics and tendentious "signs" to their adversaries, an unhealthy interest in using the media to send messages, and a predilection for canine zeal over solid prosecutorial judgment. As Starr himself often pointed out, he relied on what he called his staff of "career prosecutors." But the ones Starr listened to were the country-club tough guys (and the whole staff was, almost without exception, guys) like Bittman, whose faux sophistication led them all to oblivion.

Indeed, for all the attention they lavished on the media, Starr's staff couldn't even manage the easy stuff. For Currie's grand jury appearance on January 27, the prosecutors had arranged for Currie and Larry Wechsler to enter the courthouse through a side door so they would not have to battle their way through the unruly crowd of photographers by the main entrance. But Starr's team made no provision for Currie's departure, so she and her lawyer had to run that gauntlet on their way home. The resulting photographs of Currie in that maelstrom became a lasting metaphor for an excessive and blundering investigation (and press corps). Sooner rather than later, there would be other such symbols, too.

15

"Words of Assent"

In the days after Bill Ginsburg settled in Washington to begin representing Monica Lewinsky, he had a single priority: to keep his client from killing herself.

Lewinsky had been confronted by Starr's investigators on Friday, January 16, at the Ritz-Carlton, and Ginsburg had arrived to join her the following day. In those first few days, Ginsburg saw his role as as much family friend as lawyer. The lawyer regarded himself, in essence, as Bernie Lewinsky's proxy, and as Monica began to tell him the story of her relationship, Ginsburg grew furious at the president. Ginsburg had known Monica as a child, and he still thought of her that way. It revolted him that Clinton, in his view, had taken advantage of her. Still, in the matter of a few days, Starr's prosecutors managed to redirect Ginsburg's fury away from their chief target, the president, and toward the Office of Independent Counsel.

For their part, in those last few days before Lewinsky's name became public, Monica and her mother, Marcia Lewis, lived in a kind of suspended animation at their apartment in the Watergate complex. Their place was already in desolate shape. Marcia had more or less moved to New York, to live with her fiancé, a wealthy former broadcasting executive named Peter Straus. And Monica was well along in her packing for her own move to the city, where she would be starting her job with Revlon. Now, with the threat of arrest hanging over at least Monica and perhaps Marcia as well, the two women kept the doors locked and shades drawn, fearful that the Starr forces would descend at any moment. They ate little and spoke softly, to avoid the listening devices that they assumed had been installed. For several days, Marcia even saved the household trash, as a gesture to persuade the FBI that they had not tried to destroy any evidence.

When Ginsburg first went to the Starr office, on Saturday night, January 17, the prosecutors—on this day, Jackie Bennett, Bob Bittman, and Mike Emmick—still wanted Lewinsky to make controlled phone calls to their targets. Ginsburg said no—such betrayals were un-American, he asserted. Besides, he thought that in Monica's precarious mental state, the prospect of becoming an undercover operative was simply too overwhelming. Ginsburg promised that his client would tell prosecutors everything she knew, but she wouldn't go to work for them. At this point, Ginsburg wanted to see Clinton exposed—as a "misogynist," even as a "molester." But the prosecutors were greedy. They wanted Monica first to enter a guilty plea in connection with the filing of her affidavit in the Jones case and then to testify against the president. The prosecutors said that if Monica cooperated with them after her plea, they would make a motion to the sentencing judge that would virtually guarantee her no jail time. Ginsburg was bewildered. Who ever heard of prosecuting a twenty-four-year-old for lying about an affair?

After his meeting with the prosecutors, Monica and Marcia picked up Ginsburg at the independent counsel offices, and together they drove to the Ritz-Carlton. An excitable trio in the best of circumstances, Ginsburg, Lewinsky, and Lewis spent the rest of the evening—indeed, much of the following week—in a prolonged bout of group hysteria.

Ginsburg had known Monica's version of her relationship with the president only since earlier that day—that they had had a consensual sexual affair since November 1995. However, in the car to the hotel, Ginsburg declared he was going to denounce Clinton as a child molester. In other words, even after the prosecutors' initial round of threats, Ginsburg was still more angry at Clinton than Starr. But Monica, ever protective of what she called, in her Senate testimony, "my relationship," bellowed, "That's not true!" For the moment, Ginsburg backed off his threat, but his anger at the president remained.

When Lewinsky, Lewis, and Ginsburg reached the hotel, they commandeered a conference room. Lewinsky and her mother remembered that Ginsburg said they had only two options—for Monica to make the controlled phone calls to Currie, Jordan, and perhaps the president, or for Monica to face trial and possible jail. Ginsburg told them that the trial alone would cost Monica's father half a million dollars in legal fees and possibly bankrupt his practice. Ginsburg asserted that he presented a third possibility to Lewinsky, that he would keep fighting for immunity, but conceded that things looked pretty dire at this point. Soon, both women were wailing, and Ginsburg was screaming—at them, at the Starr forces, at the president, at the heavens. Monica said she couldn't take it anymore and asked to be checked into a psychiatric hospital. Instead, the two women returned to their darkened, box-strewn apartment at the Watergate.

Realizing he was in over his head, Ginsburg placed a late-night phone call to an old acquaintance, Nathaniel Speights, an experienced, if low-profile, Washington criminal lawyer, to assist him with the legal work. In their dealings with the OIC over the next several months, Nate Speights would play the good (or at least the sane) cop to Ginsburg's erratic bad guy.

On Sunday, Ginsburg and Monica spent most of the day at Speights's house, in Chevy Chase, and Lewinsky gave another operatic rendition of her relationship. The first thing Speights did was rule out a plea deal. Few people were ever prosecuted for filing a false affidavit in a civil case, and the lawyer saw many avenues of defense if Lewinsky actually was charged. Besides, Speights could see that the prosecutors were bluffing. They needed Monica more than she needed them. Starr needed her testimony to prosecute the people he really wanted—Clinton, Jordan, Currie, anyone connected to the White House. Speights called Mike Emmick at the OIC to say that if his office was considering prosecuting Monica, they could forget about any kind of cooperation. He wanted immunity for her or there would be no further discussions. Emmick called back and said that immunity was a possibility, but they needed to hear more of Monica's story before they made a decision. He invited the three of them—Ginsburg, Speights, and Lewinsky—to the independent counsel offices the following day, January 19.

On that next morning—which was the Martin Luther King holiday—Lewinsky's day began with Betty Currie's series of messages to her pager: "Please call Kay re: family emergency," "Please call, have good news," and so on. Vernon Jordan and Frank Carter called, too. At her lawyers' insistence, Lewinsky returned none of the calls. Then, rattled by the pages, the phone calls, everything, Lewinsky was summoned by her lawyers to join them for the day's negotiating session at the Starr suite.

Ginsburg spent most of the day shuttling between two conference rooms—one with the prosecutors and the other with a weeping, writhing Monica Lewinsky. Ginsburg and Speights wouldn't let the prosecutors speak directly to Lewinsky, but she was answering their questions, through the lawyers. The awkward setup was what lawyers call a proffer session, in which a witness previews what he or she will say if the prosecutors grant immunity. Her message to the prosecutors would never change over the following year. Yes, she had had a sexual relationship with the president. No, Clinton had not asked her to lie or otherwise obstruct justice. The three-way conversation was tedious, but the prosecutors were getting some answers to their questions.

In the middle of this back-and-forth, on Monday afternoon, the prosecutors were called away to study some important news that had just arrived: the *Drudge Report,* which contained the first public reference to Lewinsky's name. "It's too late now," Jackie Bennett announced. "She's radioactive." Suddenly Monica's value as a covert operative dropped to zero. The disclosure soured an already testy mood.

Still, even with Lewinsky's undercover work off the table, Ginsburg and Speights felt they were approaching a deal. It was hard to tell. For one thing, though Starr himself was present in the office suite, he refused to participate in the negotiations. When Ginsburg left the conference room to talk to Monica, prosecutors Bennett, Emmick, and Bittman would consult with Starr. (Ginsburg met Starr only when they found themselves in adjoining urinals in the men's room.) The setup displayed Starr's lack of confidence in his own judgment. He decided everything after consulting with his full complement of prosecutors, so no one person could say for sure what the Starr team even wanted from Monica. Once Speights showed up, the guilty plea was off the table. But the prosecutors were making noises about offering limited-use immunity, not the broader, transactional grant of immunity; about forcing Monica to take a lie detector test; about examining her face to face, rather than through attorneys. Finally, Ginsburg asked for a dinner break for his exhausted and overwrought client. They'd go to the Hard Rock Café, across the street, eat dinner, then call to see whether the Starr team were ready to resume negotiations.

After Ginsburg, Speights, and Lewinsky finished their burgers, they called over to the office, only to be told to call back later. Two hours passed. Finally, Jackie Bennett told them to return and announced that he had toughened the conditions for a deal. She needed to come in and make an oral proffer, known as a "Queen for a Day" arrangement. If the prosecutors believed her story, they would give her limited-use immunity, not the broader transactional immunity being sought for her.

Ginsburg said no to the oral proffer. For one thing, he didn't trust the Starr people. He thought Monica would tell them everything they needed to know, and then they would turn on her and prosecute her anyway. Something like this had happened to Webb Hubbell in the Whitewater cases, and he didn't want to take that risk. More important, though, Ginsburg wouldn't agree to an oral proffer because he didn't think Monica was in any mental state to deal directly with the prosecutors. He was in the process of arranging psychiatric care and medication for her. A confrontation with prosecutors might push her over the edge.

At first, Bennett was just patronizing. "It would be malpractice if we entered into an immunity agreement without talking to her first," he said.

Malpractice—this was Ginsburg's turf. And he knew that in technical legal terms, government lawyers had no clients. He removed his glasses and shot back, "So who the fuck is going to sue you?"

Bennett tried another tack. He said there was information on the Tripp tapes that suggested that Monica's mother, Marcia

Lewis, might have been party to Monica's scheme to obstruct justice.

"Bullshit," said Ginsburg. "You have nothing on her."

The conversation went on along these lines for some time, until the dispute between the two men was distilled into a single issue. Bennett demanded an oral proffer before they gave Monica immunity. Ginsburg wanted the immunity deal before she said anything to them. Finally, at around ten-thirty on Monday night, Bennett tried one last gambit to shake up the Lewinsky team.

"I'd like you to accept service of a subpoena for her mother," said Bennett, handing Ginsburg the document summoning Marcia Lewis to the grand jury. Reluctantly, Ginsburg accepted it.

Moments later, with nothing resolved, Ginsburg collected Monica to leave. As Monica tried to walk to the elevator with Ginsburg and Speights, she fell to the floor, weeping and wailing. The two lawyers almost had to carry her out of the office.

Still, for Monica Lewinsky, Monday was pretty good compared to Tuesday, to say nothing of Wednesday.

/ / /

During the negotiations on Monday, Ginsburg and Speights had agreed to allow Starr's investigators to search Monica's apartment at the Watergate the following day. (It wasn't much of a concession, because Starr could have obtained a search warrant with little difficulty.) But in the chaotic conclusion to Monday's events, Emmick thought that Ginsburg had withdrawn permission for the search. So Emmick was surprised to get a grumpy phone call from Ginsburg the next morning. Where are the agents? he asked. Why aren't they doing their search? In this way the OIC learned that Ginsburg was willing to allow the agents in Lewinsky's apartment at the Watergate and that her lawyers wanted to continue negotiations.

When the agents finally arrived at Lewinsky's apartment, one of them called Speights to ask about some pictures and photographs that they had been led to believe were on the walls. Now, it appeared, there were only blank spaces. Where were the pictures?

As patiently as he could, Speights asked the agent whether he saw any cardboard boxes directly below the spaces on the wall. Did you look in the boxes? Speights asked.

No, the agent hadn't gotten around to it.

You're searching the apartment and you haven't looked in the moving boxes? Speights was incredulous.

The agents did rouse themselves to look through the boxes, and they also collected Lewinsky's computer and most of her dresses. They were, of course, looking for the semen-stained dress that Tripp had told them about, but it had been moved earlier to Monica's mother's new apartment, in New York. All in all, then, the search yielded little useful evidence, but it left Lewinsky with almost nothing to wear.

In any event, the true life-changing event for Lewinsky took place on Wednesday, January 21, when she confronted a double blow. First, of course, she remained a suspect in a criminal investigation. But the big news on Wednesday was that her name had finally surfaced in the mainstream press, and she became the object of the most intense media surveillance since O. J. Simpson's Bronco ride across Southern California. For the next several months, camera crews established round-the-clock surveillance in front of her building in the Watergate complex. (One day, Monica's next-door neighbor, former senator Bob Dole, brought doughnuts to the crews.)

The public disclosure of Monica's name transformed Ginsburg's behavior, and even his personality. At this point, Ginsburg shut down virtually all contact between Monica and the outside world. He basically forbade his client to speak with anyone except her mother. He even directed his friend Bernie to cease speaking to his daughter for the time being. Monica moved upstairs to the fifth floor of the Watergate, where Marcia's mother had an apartment, and she began spending virtually all of her time staring at her own image on the television and relying on her attorney to keep her apprised of her fate. Outside of her mother, her lawyer, and her newly recruited team of psychiatrists, Lewinsky had almost no contact with the world.

In one sense, Ginsburg was just being cautious. As the subpoena to Marcia Lewis illustrated, the prosecutors were obviously willing to question those closest to Lewinsky in order to build their case. Limiting contact with Monica restricted the amount of evidence that could be assembled against her. But the move was also a power play. Ginsburg quickly developed a taste for being the center of attention, and his exclusive access to his client guaranteed him a ready audience whenever he wanted one. His first public comment on the case suggested that his anger at Clinton still trumped his distaste for Starr. "If the president of the United States did this—and I'm not saying he did—with this young lady, I think he's a misogynist," Ginsburg told the press on the day the story broke. "If he didn't, then I think Ken Starr and his crew have ravaged the life of a youngster." Since Ginsburg at that point knew that Clinton "did this"—that is, conducted the affair with Lewinsky—Ginsburg did regard the president as a misogynist. But the Office of Independent Counsel was taking steps to make sure that their putative star witness, and her lawyer, would transform their allegiances.

/ / /

It is no exaggeration to say that the next two weeks determined the fate of Bill Clinton's presidency, and the critical behind-the-scenes drama of that period was the negotiation between William Ginsburg and the Office of Independent Counsel. The president himself raised the stakes to this level with his finger-wagging denial of January 26. In the clearest, most emphatic way, Clinton denied that he had had "sexual relations with that woman, Miss Lewinsky." Ginsburg's client could give the testimony—and provide the physical evidence—that would prove definitively that the president had lied. Could Ginsburg and Starr cut a deal that would let the prosecutor make his case?

Starr's team convened on this and other issues twice a day, at eight in the morning and five in the afternoon. Dozens of people—prosecutors, agents, paralegals, as many as fifty of them at a time—would gather around the large conference table to chew over the matters before the office. (Often, Starr's team of a dozen or more people in Little Rock would join in the conversations by speakerphone.) Starr believed in giving everyone a chance to talk, and the result was a maddeningly slow way to do business. But the group dynamics had a substantive impact, too. Over and over, Starr spoke of the need for "toughness," and he relished those comments that called for confrontation and conflict. The independent counsel not only recognized that he lacked experience but hated that the public saw him as a fleshy, Milquetoast kind of person. One day he mentioned how angry he was that some of his adversaries in Little Rock were spreading the false rumor that he was having an affair on his visits there; what really teed him off was that everyone—everyone!—thought the rumor was inconceivable.

After months, even years, of irrelevance, it was suddenly a heady time for Starr's prosecutors. The Jones lawyers wanted to piggyback on the OIC's investigation, so they started to send their own subpoenas to everyone Starr was calling before the grand jury, starting with Betty Currie. The Starr team objected, filing a motion before Judge Wright to stop the Dallas attorneys. "After serious consideration," the brief stated, "we respectfully submit that the pending criminal investigation is of such gravity and paramount importance that this Court would do a disservice to the Nation if it were to permit the unfettered—and extraordinarily aggressive—discovery efforts currently under way to proceed unabated. The criminal matter raises issues of the gravest concern, and their resolution may moot many of the discovery questions pending." This last line demonstrated the confidence in the Starr camp. It suggested that Clinton might soon leave office, and thus his departure would moot some of the issues before Judge Wright.

But the Arkansas judge was one of the few people to remain calm and focused in the excitement of the first week of the scandal. She noted that discovery was already scheduled to close at the end of January, so she was disinclined to cancel the last few days. Then Judge Wright did something even bolder. She simply ruled that all "evidence concerning Monica Lewinsky should be excluded from the trial of this matter." From the beginning, Wright had clung to the idea that the Jones case was about one lone woman's claim of employment discrimination, not an open-ended inquiry into Bill Clinton's sex life. Judge Wright concluded that Clinton's relationship with Lewinsky in 1998 had nothing to do with whether Paula Jones was sexually harassed in 1991. The decision was both an astute resolution of a legal quandary and a subtle message to Starr—that his investigation had steered off into areas remote from anything except his determination to land the president.

If that was Wright's message, few in Starr's camp were in the mood to hear it. They believed they had Clinton on the ropes, and their confidence leeched into arrogance with everyone they dealt with—especially Bill Ginsburg. True, Ginsburg seemed to be doing his best to alienate Starr's people as well. In public, he had become a one-man interview machine, providing reporters with often inaccurate accounts of his negotiations with Starr. In private, Ginsburg was even more unhinged. During one session with Jackie Bennett, the prosecutor mentioned darkly that successful doctors like Bernie Lewinsky often found themselves in trouble with the IRS and then asked Ginsburg to accept service of a subpoena to Monica's father, just as he had earlier accepted one for her mother.

It was a ghoulish, entirely inappropriate threat by Bennett, and Ginsburg—jet-lagged, emotionally overwrought, and a little loony—responded by losing his composure completely.

"You motherfucking, cocksucking cunt," he remembered saying, "I will kill you before I accept service for a subpoena to Bernie."

Bennett stood up across the conference table.

"If you want to take a cut at me," Ginsburg went on, "I'll whip your ass." Ginsburg collected Speights and left with the issue of immunity for Monica still unresolved. (Bennett denies mentioning the IRS.)

At last, the OIC hit on the strategy of leaving the negotiations with Ginsburg to the two most experienced public corruption prosecutors in the office, Mike Emmick and Bruce Udolf. (Ginsburg and Bennett couldn't get along, and Bittman, preoccupied with Betty Currie, popped in and out of the discussions.) In their own ways, Emmick and Udolf were renowned for their toughness in their respective parts of the country. But they quickly came to the conclusion that it was self-defeating to go on quibbling with Ginsburg about immunity for Lewinsky. They had, at best, a one-witness case against Clinton for lying and obstruction of justice, and Monica was the witness. Sure, Ginsburg was behaving like a clown, but the needs of the case required that Starr give the lawyer what he wanted.

By January 27—the day of the State of the Union address—Ginsburg and the prosecutors were exchanging drafts of an immunity agreement. Each day, Emmick and Udolf would haggle with Ginsburg and then return to the conference room, where their work would be critiqued by the committee of fifty. The invariable consensus there: Emmick and Udolf weren't being tough enough. Why wouldn't she take a polygraph? In response, Udolf added a line to the agreement: "It is understood and agreed that upon request by the United States, Ms. Lewinsky will voluntarily submit to polygraph examination." What if she told her shrink about her relationship with Clinton? Another new line: "Upon request, she will waive all privileges, without limitation, except as to your representation of her." This meant the prosecutors could interview Lewinsky's therapists.

Finally, the committee persisted on the issue of the oral proffer. Why should they give her immunity if they didn't get to talk to her first? They wanted the "Queen for a Day" agreement before they committed themselves to immunity. Here, Ginsburg, fearing for Monica's sanity, wouldn't budge. But he hit on a compromise with Emmick and Udolf. In her own hand, Monica would write out a proffer, which would summarize her testimony, and the prosecutors could decide whether it was sufficient.

So on January 30, Ginsburg sent Monica to an empty room at the Cosmos Club—the city club in downtown Washington where he was now staying—and told her to write a summary of her relationship with the president. The resulting ten-page document, written in Monica's girlish scrawl, is above all a poignant summary of a young woman's crush. She summarized all of the key issues in the relationship—her transfer to the Pentagon, her dealings with Vernon Jordan, her job hunt, the subpoena from the Jones team—but the first sentence gave the clearest picture of Monica's conception of the relationship. The first two paragraphs isolated the key legal issues as well.

1. Ms. Lewinsky had an intimate and emotional relationship with President Clinton beginning in 1995. At various times between 1995 and 1997, Ms. Lewinsky and the President had physically intimate contact. This included oral sex, but excluded intercourse.

2. When asked what should be said if anyone questioned Ms. Lewinsky about her being with the President, he said she

should say she was bringing him letters (when she worked in Legislative Affairs) or visiting Betty Currie (after she left the WH). There is truth to both of these statements.

The ten pages were good enough for Emmick and Udolf. The handwritten proffer merely repeated what Monica had been saying through her lawyers all week, and it was undoubtedly the best they were going to do. On Sunday, February 1, Emmick wrote back to Ginsburg that "after evaluating your draft, we hope to meet with you this evening and, if we succeed in bridging what I believe are relatively small differences between us, negotiate a binding agreement." The deal, in other words, was just about cut.

/ / /

If Bill Ginsburg is remembered for anything in future years, it may be for a dubious bit of history he made on the same day that Mike Emmick wrote to him about his client's immunity. On February 1, Ginsburg appeared on all five major Sunday-morning talk shows. From the day Lewinsky's name became public, Ginsburg had reveled in the attention of the television news aristocracy. Months after the stars lost interest in him, Ginsburg still pined for them. "Mike Wallace is like a father to me," he said. "Barbara, Wolf, and Cokie kept me sane."

February 1 marked the high point of his logorrhea. Yet Ginsburg didn't just talk a lot, he seemed to go out of his way to offend the very prosecutors with whom he was trying to close a deal. For one thing, Ginsburg simply lied in the interviews about what Monica's testimony would be—denying, for example, that she and the president had engaged in phone sex when he knew that they had. Sometimes he undercut his own client's credibility. When the reporter Gloria Borger asked him, on *Face the Nation,* whether "your twenty-four-year-old client might have a tendency to exaggerate a bit," he replied, "I'm saying that every twenty-four-year-old, and we were all once twenty-four, except for you—you still look twenty-four. Seriously, all twenty-four-year-olds . . . tend to embellish." Altogether, it was a baffling performance. Worse still was what Ginsburg was saying off-camera. While his public posture was that Lewinsky told the truth in her affidavit, he was admitting to any number of journalists, off the record, that his client and the president had indeed had a sexual relationship. These remarks filtered back to the prosecutors, further enraging them about Ginsburg's media campaign.

Still, on Monday, February 2, Emmick and Udolf pressed forward on closing the deal with Lewinsky. The heart of Starr's planned case against Clinton was that he had obstructed justice by persuading Lewinsky to lie about their relationship. Udolf wanted to strengthen that portion of the written proffer, so he and Ginsburg negotiated two new, final paragraphs for Monica's statement. After several phone calls, the two lawyers settled on the following language, which Lewinsky approved and then wrote out in her own hand:

> 11. At some point in the relationship between Ms. L and the President, the President told Ms. L to deny a relationship, if ever asked about it. He also said something to the effect of if the two people who are involved say it didn't happen—it didn't happen. Ms. L knows this was said some time prior to the subpoena in the Paula Jones case.
> 12. Item #2 above also occurred prior to the subpoena in the Paula Jones case.

The statement, even with the additions, did not give the prosecutors everything they wanted. Lewinsky's position all along was that Clinton always wanted her to lie about their relationship, not just when asked about it by the Jones lawyers. As Ginsburg and Lewinsky recognized—indeed, as a clear majority of the country came to recognize—lying is simply an integral part of such relationships, with or without a pending lawsuit.

In any event, Monica's written proffer was enough for Udolf. "There does not seem to be any purpose in prosecuting this woman," he told Ginsburg. "If you, Nate, and your client will sign and return it with the one change, we have a deal. . . . If that's what it says, I think we have a deal." (Udolf, Emmick, and Ginsburg have substantially identical recollections of what Udolf said on this occasion.) As Emmick later testified, he heard Udolf give "words of assent" to Ginsburg that they had concluded an immunity deal for Lewinsky.

In this conversation late on Monday night, Emmick asked Lewinsky's lawyers when his team could start debriefing Monica. Ginsburg said that he was taking Monica home to Los Angeles, to see her father, on the following day, but that they could start talking out there on Wednesday, February 4. They even agreed on a schedule for her debriefings: ten in the morning to three in the afternoon for weekdays, eleven to three on weekends.

With that, Bob Bittman faxed a formal immunity agreement to Ginsburg. Written on OIC letterhead and dated February 2, 1998, the three-page document began, "This letter will confirm the agreement reached between Monica Lewinsky and the United States, represented by the Office of Independent Counsel." In the key provision, the agreement said that if Lewinsky testified truthfully, "the United States will not prosecute her for any crimes committed prior to the date of this agreement arising out of the facts summarized in [Lewinsky's handwritten] proffer." The agreement also stated that in return for Monica's truthful testimony, the OIC would not prosecute Bernard Lewinsky or Marcia Lewis, either.

At the bottom of the last page were spaces for five signatures: Bruce L. Udolf and Mike Emmick, for the OIC; and Monica Lewinsky, William Ginsburg, and Nathaniel H. Speights III. Monica and her two lawyers signed their names, faxed the document back to Bittman, and completed their plans to fly west in the morning. Monica Lewinsky had every reason to believe that she was hours away from beginning her career as a witness for the prosecution.

/ / /

"It's a sign of weakness," said Jackie Bennett.

On February 3, the prosecutors assembled around the big conference table for a postmortem on the negotiations that had led to the grant of immunity to Lewinsky. Bennett thought that his colleagues Bittman and Udolf had wimped out.

She was still holding back, Bennett asserted. They needed to get her in there and examine her themselves. The written proffer was inadequate. It was true that prosecutors, in general, rarely gave immunity without insisting on face-to-face proffers—that is, without "Queen for a Day" interviews with witnesses. Monica didn't deserve any special treatment. They were giving away the store to Monica . . . and to Ginsburg.

The mention of Ginsburg set off a round of groans and denunciations around the table. His five-show television onslaught had enraged everyone on Starr's team. On *Meet the Press,* Tim Russert had asked Ginsburg, "How is this all going to wind up?" In response, Ginsburg had waxed elegiac. "It'll pass," he said. "The president will remain in office. He'll do a good job. We'll all hopefully have a sound economy, keep our jobs, and I think everything's going to be fine."

The president will remain in office. This guy was obviously in the tank to Clinton. The prosecutors should give him nothing.

By the time the meeting began, everyone in Starr's office had seen a front-page story in *The Washington Post,* written by Ruth Marcus and Bob Woodward. Under the headline AS GINSBURG BROADCASTS, COLLEAGUES AIR DISBELIEF, the story catalogued the attorney's extraordinary media offensive. "The airwaves have become a virtual Ginsburg News Network, with up-to-the-minute bulletins about the progress of his negotiations with Starr over whether Lewinsky should receive immunity from prosecution in return for cooperating with Starr," the story noted. "Ginsburg's media whirlwind has astonished and perplexed those with more experience in criminal matters. It has also—by Ginsburg's own admission—infuriated prosecutors in Starr's office."

Indeed it had. Bennett, joined by Bittman, challenged Starr, who sat through the commentary of his subordinates in silence. Were they going to let this clown push them around?

Emmick and Udolf, who had negotiated the immunity deal with Ginsburg, said little at first. Then, gradually, they began to defend their work. Emmick, the smooth Californian, spoke of the need for them to keep their eye on the ball. Monica would be a good witness for the prosecution. She would prove conclusively that Clinton had lied under oath about the sex—and, in time, she might turn into a valuable witness on obstruction of justice as well. Forget Ginsburg, Emmick urged. The point was how best to help their investigation, and Lewinsky was the witness who could do the most for them.

Udolf, in contrast to his glib ally, was so angry he could barely speak. He loathed the macho posturing of his colleagues, most of whom had a fraction of the experience that he and Emmick did. So what if they hated Monica's lawyer? How in the world were they proposing to make a case against Clinton without Lewinsky's testimony? It was foolish to pretend they didn't need her. And anyway, they had a deal. They had sent her the immunity agreement, and she and her lawyers had signed it.

That may be, someone pointed out, but the agreement had only been signed by the defense. The spaces for Emmick's and Udolf's signatures were still blank. There was no contract until both sides signed.

Udolf was incredulous. As a technical matter of contract law, it might have been true that no formal contract existed. But in U.S. Attorney's Offices around the country, when a prosecutor faxes an immunity agreement to a defense lawyer on government letterhead, that's a deal.

"I gave my word as a man and as a lawyer," Udolf said.

In the end, of course, the decision was up to Starr. He said he was going to go with the clear majority view on his staff: he would veto the immunity deal with Monica. Ginsburg was behaving horribly, Starr said. He thought Bennett was right. Monica should have to give an oral proffer. She was probably holding back information damaging to Clinton. In short, the independent counsel wasn't yet ready to authorize an immunity deal.

Starr's decision on February 3 marked the precise moment when Bill Clinton's survival in office became assured. It was made just seven days after Bill Clinton gave the American people his finger-wagging denial of a sexual relationship with Lewinsky. If Starr had agreed to the immunity deal on that day, he would have had the ammunition—in testimony and in conclusive genetic evidence—to prove that Clinton had lied. He could have had an impeachment report for Congress in a month or less. Instead, Starr's obsession with toughness and devotion to the Washington conventional wisdom led him to disaster. In attempting to punish Ginsburg, he merely damaged himself. In believing the reports about Ginsburg's incompetence, he only established his own.

The Lewinsky immunity debacle in February illustrated a larger truth about Clinton's enemies, too. Starr and his team rejected the deal for Lewinsky because they were convinced she was withholding additional evidence of Clinton's criminality. This belief was pervasive among those who tried to drive the president out of office—that some grander conspiracy was sure to be uncovered, just over the horizon. Of course, this evidence was never located because it didn't exist. The persistence of this myth proved more about the fanaticism of those who believed in it than about the evidence against the president. And it was to such zealots that Starr increasingly turned to direct his investigation.

Emmick and Udolf refused to put their names to the letter informing Ginsburg that the immunity deal was off. Indeed, after he had humiliated Emmick and Udolf, Starr made it clear that he now preferred someone else to run the Lewinsky investigation. So it fell to the new boss to inform Ginsburg and Speights that their client was not getting immunity after all. On February 4—the day that Lewinsky's debriefing was scheduled to begin in Los Angeles—Ginsburg instead received a fax from Washington. (Speights had even traveled to Los Angeles to assist in the prosecutors' first interviews with Monica.) "Dear Messrs. Ginsburg and Speights," the letter began. "Thank you for your proposed modifications to the draft agreement and the amendments to your client's written proffer," it said, employing an Orwellian redesignation of the signed government contract that Ginsburg had returned to the OIC. "After carefully considering them," the letter continued, "we must respectfully decline to enter into an agreement on the proposed terms." The letter was signed "Robert J. Bittman."

/ / /

In her famous appearance on the *Today* show, Hillary Clinton had goaded journalists to explore the "vast right-wing conspiracy" that was out to get her husband. Less than forty-eight hours after Starr voided Lewinsky's immunity deal, the fax machine whirred to life next to Sidney Blumenthal's office in the former White House barbershop. The messages he received would help Blumenthal assist his former colleagues in the news media to find the "great story" that he and the first lady had touted. Blumenthal would focus on Starr's staff.

The faxed message was a clip from the front page of the *Los Angeles Daily Journal,* a newspaper that serves the legal community in Southern California. STARR AIDE NO STRANGER TO SEX TAPE INQUIRIES, the headline read, and the story mentioned Mike Emmick. A little while later, Blumenthal received another fax, this one an op-ed piece in the *Atlanta Constitution.* STARR'S TAINTED

LIEUTENANT, the headline to Martha Ezzard's story read. "Georgians remember Bruce Udolf as a man who trampled a citizen's rights; now he's investigating the President."

The concept of "opposition research" was a fairly old one in politics but something new in American law—and its deployment by Blumenthal offered a classic illustration of how law and politics merged over the course of the Jones and Lewinsky cases. With "oppo," as it is often called, a political candidate attempts to learn embarrassing information about an opponent and uses the news media to spread the bounty to a wider public. In more genteel days, even as recently as the Iran-Contra affair, no one thought to go after prosecutors in this way. But in this "war," to use Harry Thomason's description, there were new rules of engagement, and Blumenthal decided to put them to work against Emmick and Udolf.

Blumenthal's oppo was such an organic process that it didn't even require a formal mobilization. The troops simply knew their roles and went to work. The article about Emmick came to Blumenthal from Stanley K. Sheinbaum, a veteran liberal activist and fund-raiser in Brentwood; the piece about Udolf was sent by Jack Bass, a journalist and historian based in Atlanta. Blumenthal hadn't asked them to conduct research for the defense of the president, but Sheinbaum and Bass assumed that Blumenthal was going to try to multiply these local stories into broader and more sustained critical attention to the Starr team—which was exactly what he did. Blumenthal sent the clips to Doug Kelly, the research director of the Democratic National Committee, as well as to some of the reporters Blumenthal spoke to on a regular basis. His faxes bore the heading FROM: SIDNEY BLUMENTHAL but omitted any specific reference to their origin in the White House.

Blumenthal took greater precautions when he was handling videotapes. At around this time, Nicole Seligman, a member of Clinton's defense team at Williams & Connolly, passed Blumenthal a cassette of a local television report from Los Angeles about Emmick's controversial case. Instead of using government facilities, Blumenthal asked a friendly political consultant, Robert Shrum, to make copies for distribution. Shrum's firm made ten copies for Blumenthal, who passed one to the DNC and shared others with individual journalists. At the Democratic Party headquarters, Blumenthal's media research was distilled into talking points, and Blumenthal, in turn, directed reporters to the resulting product. By his own account, Blumenthal shared the reports about Emmick and Udolf with "news organizations ranging from CNN, CBS, ABC, *New York Times,* New York *Daily News, Chicago Tribune, New York Observer, L.A. Times.*"

For Blumenthal, the timing of his oppo assault was propitious. By mid-February, many of the reporters covering the story needed a new angle, and the professional background of the president's pursuers made an ideal sidebar. Calls from reporters about the prosecutors flooded into Starr's offices, and not just about their job histories, either. Journalists dredged up rumors about drug use, sexual orientation, divorces, and school records, which the stunned prosecutors tried to shoot down as best they could. As Blumenthal later described his role, he was like the sorcerer's apprentice. All he meant to do was raise a few questions about some controversial cases on the public record, and he couldn't help it if those legitimate issues spiraled into something much more vicious and personal. He was, he explained, very sad about what happened to the prosecutors.

/ / /

Blumenthal's leak about Mike Emmick never bothered the prosecutor very much. It concerned a case that he hadn't even prosecuted, so he dismissed the tempest as "water off a duck's back"—a phrase he used often in those days.

Bruce Udolf, on the other hand, was taking it harder. For one thing, Udolf had a bigger skeleton in his closet. He had become an elected district attorney in a suburban Atlanta county at a young age, and on March 17, 1985—when he was thirty-three years old—he made a big mistake. Agents of the Georgia Bureau of Investigation mixed up some registration numbers and arrested a carpenter named Ronald Reeves for possessing a stolen gun—which was not, it turned out, stolen at all. Still, Udolf and the agents held him for twenty-four hours before they even arranged for bail to be set, and then they had it set at an unconscionable $100,000. In the end, the interrogation of Reeves went on for five days, until he was finally allowed to go home, with no charges filed against him. Two years later, Reeves sued Udolf in connection with the incident, and Georgia taxpayers were obligated to cover a $50,000 judgment.

It was a costly and embarrassing lesson, and the Georgia voters turned Udolf out of office. He decided to move to Miami and, in effect, start his legal career over again. This Udolf did, with some help from one of his adversaries in the Reeves case, who thought the prosecutor behaved honorably in sorting out the mess. However, in the fevered atmosphere in which he found himself in Washington, Udolf knew that his decade of impeccable service in the U.S. Attorney's Office would count little against this black mark. The crush of press phone calls about the Reeves case grew to such a point that he felt he had to say something, so he issued a brief statement: "I accept responsibility for that, and I regret it."

The unwanted attention Emmick and Udolf were receiving in the news media had a subtle but real impact back in the Starr office as well. As such things often do, an office joke revealed a great deal about the tensions roiling the office. Not long after the Lewinsky scandal broke, someone on Starr's team put up a hand-scrawled chart in a normally vacant office in which each prosecutor was supposed to rate the chances that Clinton would survive in office and the reasons why. The trick was, no prosecutor wrote down his own views, but instead guessed at what others believed. The chart thus became a kind of stock market for perceived manliness. At the top of the list—at about 80 percent chance of removal—someone wrote the names of David Barger and Sol Wisenberg, who were close allies of Bennett and Bittman and were described on the chart as the "Likud." (Among his Jewish colleagues, Wisenberg was sometimes referred to as "the most conservative Jew in America.") Emmick and Udolf ("commie wimps," said the chart) were at the bottom, at around 25 percent. As for the purported reason for Udolf's lack of confidence, someone wrote "lawsuit." In other words, the perception was that Udolf had backed down because he was intimidated by the disclosure of the Reeves case.

For Udolf, unlike his friend Emmick, this was not water off a duck's back. Rather, it was torture. At the same time he was berated in the press as a thug, he was scorned by his colleagues as a coward. Udolf didn't think either of the descriptions was fair, and he certainly didn't think both could be true. And his internal exile in Starr's office came about only because he wanted to give Monica Lewinsky immunity, which was, Bennett and Bittman notwithstanding, the only real way to get to Bill Clinton. If that made him a wimp, so be it.

Udolf had another responsibility—to help put Marcia Lewis in front of the grand jury. On February 10 and 11, Udolf brought several excerpts from the Tripp tapes to play for Marcia Lewis in the grand jury—in hopes of forcing her to admit that she indeed did know that her daughter and the president were having an affair.

But Lewis wouldn't quite admit it. She testified that Monica told her she was "in love" with the president, but as a mother, she didn't want to know the details of her daughter's sex life. It was a degrading, awful two days in the grand jury, and the office was pummeled for forcing a mother to testify against her daughter. Late on the second afternoon, Emmick asked a series of questions about the word "Babba," which was how Monica, in her conversations with Tripp, had referred to Hillary Clinton.

"Has your daughter ever referred to Hillary Clinton as 'Babba'?"

"I don't remember that . . ." Lewis said.

"All right," Emmick went on. "Then let me ask you this. Is there a Yiddish phrase for grandmother that sounds something like 'babba' or 'bubba' or something like that?"

"I think there is, yes."

"All right. What is that phrase?"

"I think it's 'bubba'?"

"'Bubba.' All right," said Emmick.

"But I'm not sure," Lewis went on. "I don't speak Yiddish."

Wisenberg—the most conservative Jew in America—took over the questioning at this point.

"Have you ever referred to anybody to your knowledge as Babba or the Babba?" he asked.

"Yes," Lewis replied.

"Okay, who would that be?"

"Oh, it's just a silly family thing we say," Lewis replied. "It's not—it has nothing to do with this. It's just—like our grandmother. We used to call her Babba."

"Okay," Wisenberg plowed on. "But it's your family's—different families have variations of Grandma, Grandmother, Granny, and, as I understand it, this was your family's variation of the grandmother? Is that correct?"

"I think so, yes," Lewis said, but then she simply broke down in tears and couldn't go on.

Udolf stepped in and walked Marcia Lewis out of the grand jury room. He delivered her to her lawyer, and went back to his colleagues and said, This is it. She can't continue. "Let's shut this down," Udolf said, and the questioning of Lewis was suspended.

But to Udolf, it had all gotten so absurd. This office would rather torment this woman about bubbas and babbas and grannies than do the one thing that would bring the case to an expeditious conclusion: make a deal with Monica and move on. Udolf's health was not perfect, and the stress of the past month had made everything worse. Within a few days of Lewis's grand jury testimony, Udolf found himself in the hospital with pneumonia.

Udolf never really made it back to Starr's office. Bob Bittman absorbed most of his responsibilities. There was, Udolf decided, more to life than this case. Back in Florida, he had a wife and daughter he adored, and he was sick of commuting to see them. No one called it a resignation in protest, but that, basically, was what it was. Technically, Udolf stayed on the payroll until the end of April, but he was really gone much earlier. After spending his entire legal career as a prosecutor, he signed up as a partner in a private law firm in Miami. He and his wife even thought about adopting a child, and Udolf brought his résumé to meet with a counselor.

"The Starr office," the counselor mused as she studied Udolf's qualifications to be a father. "You weren't involved in the abuses there, were you?"

16

"Eighteenth-Hand" Rumors

On February 5, *The Washington Post* disclosed the breakdown of negotiations between Ginsburg and the prosecutors in an article headlined STARR REJECTS LEWINSKY PROPOSAL ON IMMUNITY. The newspaper story, by Susan Schmidt and Peter Baker, showed how the mindless aggressiveness of the Starr lawyers carried over to their strategy with the news media, too. The article began by disclosing—accurately—that "Independent Counsel Kenneth W. Starr yesterday rejected a proposed cooperation agreement with Monica S. Lewinsky's lawyers." The reporters then went on to repeat several falsehoods that the Starr team fed to them. To be sure, the *Post* reporters and editors did not intentionally mislead their readers; they merely put their trust in the wrong sources. (Lewinsky's lawyer Nate Speights recalled with amusement how, after his daily phone call with Jackie Bennett, the *Post*'s Schmidt would call him and invariably repeat what Bennett had just said to him.)

Most of the article concerned Lewinsky's handwritten proffer, which Ginsburg had submitted to try to close the immunity deal. "Sources" told Schmidt and Baker that a "written statement from Lewinsky was not solid enough to form the basis of an agreement because it contained inconsistencies and contradictions." This was false. The statement, which was later released by Starr, has no significant flaws of this kind. "In her statement," the article went on, "sources said, Lewinsky asserted that she was not urged to lie to Jones' lawyers, for example, but said that she was told to tell a certain version of events—one that did not actually happen." This was a fantasy. The statement said no such thing.

The article went on to characterize the famous "talking points," which were, in the press at least, long perceived as a linchpin of a criminal case against someone close to Clinton and perhaps against the president himself. "Individuals who have spoken to Tripp," Schmidt and Baker wrote, "have said that . . . the talking points discuss how Tripp should deny any knowledge that Lewinsky had any sexual relationship with the President." In fact, the talking points, which were also released later, said nothing at all about how Tripp should testify about Lewinsky. Finally, the article raised the rumor of the movie theater tryst. "Starr's office this week questioned a Justice Department lawyer, who had told colleagues that he was aware of an agent who reportedly had said he guarded the door of the White House movie theater last summer while Clinton was inside alone with a young woman," the *Post* story said.

All of this misinformation had a distinct purpose—to persuade official Washington, and Lewinsky herself, that Starr had a strong case. At the very least, the reporters seemed convinced. "Starr's decision to reject the proffer may reflect confidence in the rest of the case he is building," Schmidt and Baker wrote. "In recent days, his office has moved to find witnesses who may have seen Clinton and Lewinsky together, including White House valets and Secret Service agents." But these leaks would ultimately redound to Starr's detriment, when his evidence failed to deliver on the implicit promises in news stories like this one. Lewinsky's written statement was both internally consistent and exculpatory for Clinton on the issue of obstruction of justice; the talking points did not counsel Tripp to lie about anything, much less about the president and the intern; there were no eyewitnesses to a presidential grope, in the movie theater or anywhere else.

Notwithstanding the tone of news reports like this one, the failure to close an immunity deal with the former intern left Starr's prosecutors—not Lewinsky's team—with the real problems. The entire OIC investigation was based on the premise that Clinton and Lewinsky had been sexually involved with each other. In order to bring any of the possible charges against the president—including perjury and obstruction of justice—the Starr investigators first had to establish that the sex had taken place.

It was unusual enough to have a criminal case based on a consensual sexual relationship between two adults. But here the prosecutors had to prove the sexual liaison without the testimony of either participant in it. As of early February, thanks to the breakdown of negotiations with Ginsburg, Lewinsky would not be testifying anytime soon. No one in Starr's office held out much hope that Clinton would be a witness in the immediate future, either. Characteristically, the Clinton forces made this position clear in a provocative, disdainful way.

On February 2, Bittman wrote the first of a series of letters to Clinton's lawyer David Kendall "inviting" the president to testify before the grand jury. The word was chosen with care. Starr did not want, at this point, to set off a constitutional confrontation over the unsettled issue of whether a president could be formally subpoenaed before a grand jury. Knowing that Bittman's letters lacked the legal force of a subpoena, Kendall replied by stringing him along. For months, Bittman and Kendall exchanged letters about Clinton's possible testimony, their correspondence a symphony of passive aggression on both sides. Kendall carefully avoided saying anything that could be construed as Clinton taking the Fifth, which would have been a political disaster for him. But he didn't say yes, either.

Instead, the defense lawyer sent replies to Bittman that radiated his client's contempt for Starr. "I was unable to respond to your February 4 invitation by the Friday deadline you had indicated in your letter because I was in the process of dealing with prejudicial and false leaks of information about your investigation," Kendall wrote in one such letter. "However, under the circumstances, it is impossible to accept this invitation. The situation in Iraq continues to be dangerously volatile, and this has demanded much of the President's time and attention." Bittman kept pursuing Kendall ("The situation in Iraq has, thankfully, eased," the prosecutor noted on one occasion), but Kendall always came up with new reasons to say no. Notwithstanding his early promise of cooperation with the investigation—"more rather than less, sooner rather than later," as Clinton had said at the Arafat photo opportunity—the president was not going to help make Starr's case for him.

/ / /

As always, the priority in Starr's office was projecting toughness, even more so after the White House–sponsored attacks on the integrity of the prosecutors. Jackie Bennett had handled most of the fallout from the press inquiries—the phone calls from reporters, the staffers weeping in his office, the offers to resign from nervous prosecutors—and he, as always, favored a direct response. "If the Gambino family was using contacts in the press to intimidate prosecutors, we'd go after them, and that's what we should do here," he told his colleagues. Bennett often used the metaphor of the White House as an organized crime family, and on those terms the prosecutors' next move made a lot of sense.

On February 20, Bennett orchestrated a subpoena of Sidney Blumenthal, so the prosecutors could ask him about his opposition research strategy. Bennett meant the subpoena as a signal that the Starr team would not be cowed by Blumenthal's leaks. But like so much the Starr team did to make public statements, the subpoena to Blumenthal backfired.

Starr himself explained the rationale for the Blumenthal subpoena during one of his morning strolls to deposit the garbage by the curb of his modest home in suburban Virginia. From the day the Lewinsky story broke, camera crews camped out on the front lawn of Starr's house, and the independent counsel answered a few questions almost every day. If Starr had simply refused to talk, the networks would have pulled their crews after a few days. But Starr couldn't resist trying to ingratiate himself with the Washington press corps, and he regularly commented on the day's developments during these trash runs. For starters, these Hefty-bag press availabilities were simply a ludicrous way of imparting information on a matter of national importance; more important, Starr's professorial style did not translate well in the curbside setting. For example, when asked about the Blumenthal subpoena, Starr said, "It's not in the interest of the First Amendment for distortions, lies about civil servants to be spread about. . . . Lies and distortions have no place in our First Amendment universe."

As a judge, Starr had written eloquently on the values underlying the First Amendment, so even his admirers found it baffling that he so mangled the freedom-of-speech issue. According to long-settled constitutional law, the First Amendment exists to prevent the government from deciding what the truth is, not to empower some prosecutor to determine what is true or false. To be sure, Blumenthal's press offensive had been distasteful, but he had every legal right to conduct it; a White House communications aide, regardless of his motives, has the right to distribute newspaper clippings to anyone he chooses. Jackie Bennett may have thought that Blumenthal was a gangster, but he was actually a White House aide whose job involved talking to reporters— whether the OIC liked it or not.

Ironically, there was a perfectly legitimate, independent reason for Starr to call Blumenthal before the grand jury. Blumenthal's conversation with Clinton on the day after the story broke constituted important evidence about the president's state of mind. But by defending the subpoena in the inept way he did, Starr succeeded only in making the White House aide a martyr for the First Amendment. Out of all the options available to Starr—which included defending the subpoena as a way to gather relevant evidence, or better yet, saying nothing at all, or, better still, hiring prosecutors who did not send subpoenas out of macho posturing— the independent counsel made the worst choice. Here, Starr's obsession with toughness, and with the press, led to more self-inflicted wounds.

Blumenthal took advantage of this blunder by Starr—and then some. In a press conference on the courthouse steps after his grand jury appearance on February 26, Blumenthal said, "Today, I was forced to answer questions about my conversations, as part of my job, with—and I wrote this down—*The New York Times,* CNN, CBS, *Time* magazine, *U.S. News,* the New York *Daily News,* the *Chicago Tribune,* the *New York Observer,* and there may have been a few others I don't remember right now. Ken Starr's prosecutors demanded to know what I had told reporters and what reporters had told me about Ken Starr's prosecutors."

This was a considerable distortion of what actually went on in the grand jury. Blumenthal was asked generally about his contacts with reporters, but it was he, not his interrogators, who volunteered the names of the news organizations. Moreover, before they turned to Blumenthal's press contacts, prosecutors first asked him in the grand jury about his conversation with the president about Lewinsky on the day the story broke in the news media. On February 26, Blumenthal refused to answer questions on that subject, citing executive privilege. Blumenthal did not choose to mention that subject on the courthouse steps.

/ / /

The Blumenthal controversy, which occupied much of late February, was not only a public relations disaster for Starr; it also gave the Starr team no assistance at all in proving the sexual relationship between Clinton and Lewinsky. As it turned out, Starr's task was much like that of a matrimonial lawyer, hired in a divorce case, who needs to prove adulterous conduct. So, first, the prosecutors began to look for admissions—people in whom Lewinsky might have confided about her relationship. Drawing on names taken from her computer, her e-mails, and her phone book, they made some good progress in this area. They started with her mother, of course, but then moved on to her friends. FBI agents fanned out around the country to interview these young women, and the prosecutors brought some of them back to the grand jury.

The first one they found was a woman named Neysa Erbland, a friend of Lewinsky's from Beverly Hills High School. Sol Wisenberg put her before the grand jury, and she introduced the jurors to the kind of sexually explicit testimony that they would be hearing over the next several months.

"She told me that she had given him a blow job," Erbland said, "and that she had had all of her clothes off, but that he only had his shirt off and that she had given him oral sex and they kissed and fondled each other and that they didn't have sex. That was kind of a little bit of a letdown for her." (In retrospect, it is amazing that the secret of this relationship held for as long as it did. Erbland testified that even though Lewinsky swore her to secrecy about the affair, she had told her husband, her parents, her mother-in-law, and a friend named Charles, who was "a booking agent on a TV show." Other friends of Lewinsky's had similar difficulty in refraining from sharing what was, admittedly, very good gossip.)

Shortly thereafter, the Starr investigators located Catherine Davis, a college friend of Monica's, and she was brought from

Japan, where she was living, to testify before the grand jury. Like Erbland, Davis recounted Lewinsky's version of the relationship, but this time the indefatigable Wisenberg had new details he wanted to impart for the record.

"When Monica was describing the physical relationship with the president," the prosecutor asked, "did she ever mention any objects that were used as an aid to that physical activity?"

"Yes," said Davis.

"All right. Tell us about that."

"She mentioned the use of a cigar."

"All right," Wisenberg went on. "And what did she say was done with the cigar?"

"She said that he used it and put it inside of her."

The statements to friends corroborated what Lewinsky had told Tripp on the tapes. Given Lewinsky's emotional instability, however, Clinton's defenders had enough ammunition to dismiss the young woman as an obsessed fan, a fantasist, or a stalker. Starr needed Lewinsky herself—or, better still, eyewitnesses.

Here the prosecutors took the investigation into the White House itself. They worked meticulously, identifying all of the people who kept track of the president's whereabouts. They ranged from former top advisers like Leon Panetta, Evelyn Lieberman, and George Stephanopoulos to his secretary, Betty Currie, and her supervisor, Nancy Hernreich, whose title was director of Oval Office operations. They questioned Stephen Goodin, the president's personal aide, whose job it was to make sure Clinton had the papers he needed and that he made it to meetings on time. (In her conversations with Tripp, Lewinsky immortalized Lieberman, Hernreich, and Goodin as the "meanies" who did their best to keep her away from Clinton.) The investigators tracked down two of the Navy stewards, Bayani Nelvis and Glen Maes, who served Clinton his food and took care of his clothes. In the early part of 1998, Starr's investigators also talked to some of the uniformed Secret Service agents who controlled access to the Oval Office. In all, the prosecutors proved the wisdom of the adage describing the White House as the crown jewel of the federal prison system. The picture of Clinton was of a man monitored, probed, scheduled, coddled, catered to, and controlled virtually twenty-four hours a day.

And despite all that, no one saw anything—at least not directly. Almost all of the sexual encounters had taken place on weekends when Monica was still on the White House staff. For most of their trysts, Clinton had simply arranged to run into Lewinsky "accidentally" in the hallway and then invite her to the study. Often, no one saw her go in. (And since they were intimate fewer than a dozen times, there were not many opportunities to be discovered.) Starr's best witness was a former uniformed Secret Service agent named Lewis Fox, who testified about a weekend afternoon in late 1995, when he was on duty outside the Oval Office. On that day, Clinton had poked his head out of the office door and said to Fox, "I'm expecting a young lady, a congressional staff member. Would you please let me know when she shows up?" Moments later, Lewinsky arrived, and Fox admitted her to the Oval Office. "You can close the door," Clinton then said. "She'll be here for a while." About forty minutes later, Lewinsky left. To be sure, the incident was suggestive, but it didn't prove a sexual affair. And it was the best direct evidence Starr had.

So the prosecutors, imbued with the macho culture of the Starr office, pressed their witnesses for any sliver of information about Clinton and Lewinsky's relationship. Grand juries operate under different, looser rules of evidence than criminal trials. Most important, hearsay evidence is admissible before grand juries, so witnesses can be asked what they heard from other people about the issues in the case. But as weeks and then months passed with little visible progress, the prosecutors grew frustrated, and they began searching farther afield to find something—anything—that might substantiate Lewinsky's tales to Tripp. The testimony of a uniformed Secret Service agent named John Muskett provided a characteristic, and disturbing, example of the Starr office in action.

Muskett testified about how he saw Lewinsky enter the Oval Office alone on Easter Sunday in 1996—similar testimony to Fox's, about a different occasion. The prosecutor Sol Wisenberg then asked, "Now, were there to your knowledge before the April 6, 1996, incident, were there any rumors about Monica and the president that you were aware of before that incident? . . ."

"Not that I was aware of, sir," Muskett said.

"Okay, and were there any rumors about why she was transferred?"

"Yes, sir."

"And can you tell us briefly what those rumors were?"

"Briefly, Monica was seen by someone, and I believe to the best of my ability today, someone from the White House or the first lady's staff walked in on the president and Monica in the family theater located in the East Wing," Muskett explained.

"All right," Wisenberg went on. "Walked in and then what?"

"I guess in a compromising position."

"Okay, that's the rumor that was going around?"

"Yes, sir."

There was nothing technically improper about this kind of questioning by Wisenberg, but it was an extraordinarily shabby way to conduct a criminal investigation. "Rumors" have no legal significance. Like Isikoff years earlier, the prosecutors were having trouble nailing down "rumors" of Clinton's amorous adventures, and like the reporter, Starr's investigators were expanding the definition of relevance in an effort to pin something on the president.

But Wisenberg wasn't finished with Muskett. The prosecutor went on to ask about what he called an "outlandish version" of a rumor: "Was it ever expressed to you as you having witnessed Monica with her head in the president's lap?"

"The only time I ever heard that side of the story or that rumor was in the independent counsel," said Muskett, "when I came down here to have a talk a couple of weeks ago." In other words, Wisenberg was polluting the minds of the grand jurors with "rumors" that appear to have been manufactured in Starr's office. (False rumors at that; not even Lewinsky ever claimed to have had a sexual encounter with Clinton in the White House theater.)

This kind of zeal and desperation bred questions like this one from Wisenberg to Navy steward Glen Maes: "Did you ever hear anything from any source, firsthand, secondhand, eighteenth-hand . . . ever hear anything that led you to believe that there may have been some kind of social or physical relationship between Monica Lewinsky and the president?"

The reply was as succinct as the question was tendentious: "No."

/ / /

As the Lewinsky investigation moved into its third month, in March, the Starr forces and Paula Jones's lawyers moved into an imperfect alignment. In the first days of Starr's Lewinsky investigation, the Jones forces had made trouble for the prosecutors by trying to subpoena people who were also witnesses in the criminal case. But after January, when Judge Wright had cut off further depositions in *Jones v. Clinton,* the priorities of these two centers of anti-Clinton activity merged. Each one, in its own way, put aside all other priorities to try to drum the president out of office. For his part, Starr began assembling staff to write an impeachment report to Congress. The Jones lawyers took a less decorous and, for them, more familiar route—that of public humiliation.

Ever since Judge Wright's candid remarks in the secret court hearing before Clinton's deposition, the Jones lawyers had known she was strongly tempted to throw the case out on summary judgment. Thus, the lawyers recognized that if they were going to hurt the president politically, they had to use the process of what was probably the final legal proceeding in the case to dump damaging material into the public domain.

Bob Bennett, too, spent much of the previous month seething at Bill Clinton. The lawyer quickly came to the conclusion that the president had at least misled him about his relationship with Lewinsky, if not outright lied. (Later, it became apparent that Clinton did lie.) But the existence of Starr's Lewinsky inquiries made it all the more important for Bennett to win his summary judgment motion. In filing such a motion, a defendant says, in effect, that in light of all the evidence collected in the discovery process, the plaintiff has no case. Winning a motion for summary judgment would thus serve a crucial double purpose for Clinton. It would, on a simple level, rid him at last of the Jones case; and in a more atmospheric way, it would also undermine Starr's efforts by showing that his obstruction of justice case was, in effect, created out of thin air—that there was never a genuine case to obstruct.

Bennett had studied Wright carefully during the long years that the case had been pending, and he knew the argument that would appeal most to her. He recognized that Wright had no special fondness for Clinton, but he could tell that the judge resented how the Dallas lawyers used her court to press their political agenda. In ordinary circumstances, a he said/she said case like this one might not be dismissed on summary judgment; judges usually let juries decide whom to believe. But in a brilliant, power-ful brief written by Bennett's colleague Amy Sabrin, the Clinton lawyers argued that even if the then governor had propositioned Paula Corbin at the Excelsior Hotel, she had never suffered any on-the-job harm that amounted to legal sexual harassment.

The brief included a damning recital of the way Jones's lawyers neglected the facts of their client's case in favor of their investiga-tion of Clinton's sex life. "Plaintiff spent 99 percent of her discov-ery efforts attempting to substantiate rumors that President Clinton made sexual advances to *other* women," Sabrin wrote. "But she has failed to establish that she personally has a cause of action." In a small but revealing fact about the way the Jones case was pursued, Clinton's brief noted that the plaintiff admitted during her deposition that she had never examined her own employment records at the Arkansas Industrial Development Commission—neither before she filed the suit nor before she gave her deposition. Those records revealed that Jones had always re-ceived raises and satisfactory job reviews. In short, there was no evidence of any kind of retribution for the purported incident at the hotel. What was the only "tangible job detriment" that Jones could point to as a supposed result of her encounter with the gov-ernor? "The only specific act of rudeness to which plaintiff pointed was that she did not receive flowers on Secretary's Day in April 1992, nearly one year after the purported incident," the brief ob-served.

The Dallas lawyers used their reply brief, which was submitted to Judge Wright on March 13, to disgorge the sexual research they had gathered over the past six months. As exhibits to their brief, the plaintiffs attached hundreds of pages of excerpts from the de-positions of Kathleen Willey, Gennifer Flowers, and Dolly Kyle Browning—the most salacious material they had. (In light of the fact that the husband-and-wife team of Rick and Beverly Lambert had interviewed more than two hundred women in search of dirt on Clinton, their yield of useful material was rather small.) All of this sexual evidence was, of course, irrelevant to the summary judgment issue before Judge Wright, but the Dallas team still la-dled it into the public domain.

In the relatively small portion of their brief devoted to the actual issues in the case, the Jones lawyers betrayed their desperation to prove that Paula had suffered some kind of legal injury because of the incident at the hotel. So they attached a deposition they had obtained just a week earlier from one Patrick J. Carnes, the editor in chief of a publication called *Sexual Addiction and Compulsivity,* in Wickenburg, Arizona. Carnes said that he had met Jones in February 1998, nearly seven years after the alleged incident. Based on this single meeting, Carnes concluded that Jones was still suffering from post-traumatic stress disorder and that Clinton had caused her to experience "extreme anxiety, intrusive thoughts and memories, and consequent sexual aversion." The precise nature of her sexual aversion was not disclosed. Her lawyers asserted in their brief, "Mrs. Jones continues to feel ashamed and horrified and is unable to watch Mr. Clinton on television, talk about the incident, or even think about it without experiencing emotional trauma and stress." (A few weeks later, Jones was apparently able to put aside these feelings and attend the president's speech at the White House Correspondents' Dinner, where she and Susan Carpenter-McMillan were guests of Sun Myung Moon's *Insight* magazine.) On March 20, the Clinton team responded to this torrent of irrelevancies by asking, in a rather perfunctory way, for Judge Wright to strike them from the record, itself a rather meaningless remedy because the documents were already public.

What followed, however, was a signal moment in the whole long saga—one of the most irresponsible acts by Clinton's adversaries, ever. It is considered professional misconduct for a lawyer to distribute a legal filing to the news media before it is submitted in court. So, on Saturday, March 28, the Jones lawyers deposited a brief in a twenty-four-hour drop box in the federal courthouse in Pine Bluff, many miles from Judge Wright's chambers in Little Rock. This sham filing allowed the Dallas team to distribute copies of the document all over the country, in time for the Sunday papers.

The real outrage, however, was what the document said. The centerpiece of this brief was a new claim in the case: that "significant evidence suggests that Defendant Clinton and his agents have exerted great efforts to suppress and obstruct testimony by

Juanita Hickey Broaddrick that Defendant Clinton in the past forcibly raped and sexually assaulted . . . her and then bribed and/ or intimidated her and her family into remaining silent about this outrage." The claim had no relevance to any issue in the brief (or even in the case), but rather it was meant to float one more example of the president's alleged inhumanity. Not incidentally, the disclosure of her name also violated Judge Wright's rules on privacy; Broaddrick was supposed to be identified only as Jane Doe Number Five. Jones's lawyers also failed to inform the judge that Broaddrick had, just weeks earlier, given a sworn affidavit and deposition *denying* any untoward conduct by the president. This final brief by Jones's team of Dallas lawyers—an improper, immoral act, which was as unfair to Broaddrick as it was to Clinton—epitomized the lawlessness at the heart of the legal offensive against Clinton.

Far worse for the lawyers, and especially for their client, they had riled Susan Webber Wright. Two days later, Judge Wright gave the first sign of her displeasure. In an order dated March 31, she repeated her admonition that "no party should make public any pleading, past, present or future, which reveals the identity of any 'Jane Doe.'" Further, she noted frostily, "No future pleadings should be made public before they are filed in Little Rock or otherwise in the hands of the judge. The Court has not yet seen the pleadings filed by the plaintiff in a drop box in Pine Bluff, Arkansas. . . ." The following day, she took her revenge—not merely against this final transgression by the lawyers, but against the abuse of the legal process that the entire Paula Jones case represented. In a lucid, understated thirty-nine-page opinion issued on April 1, 1998, Judge Wright granted summary judgment to Clinton and (apparently) ended the case of *Jones v. Clinton* just short of the fourth anniversary of its commencement. True to her role as an isolated beacon of sanity in the darkness around her, Judge Wright ruled that nothing in the case showed that "plaintiff's reaction to Governor Clinton's alleged advances affected tangible aspects of her compensation, terms, conditions, or privileges of employment."

On a state visit to Senegal, Clinton celebrated the news by smoking a cigar and banging on an African drum. But just as

Judge Wright's order did not entirely end the Paula Jones case, the president still had so much trouble ahead that he might have come to regard his apparent liberation as an April Fool's joke.

/ / /

Twenty-three days later, on April 24, Monica Lewinsky stood on a Malibu beach wearing plumy magenta feathers and not much else. In the photographs from that day that were eventually published in *Vanity Fair* magazine, Lewinsky looked as if she were alone on the windswept sand, but there was actually a sizable crowd watching Herb Ritts take the pictures. Bill Ginsburg was supervising, and Nate Speights came west for the occasion, and Monica's father, a serious amateur photographer himself, and his wife were on hand, too. Counting makeup artists, lighting designers, and a security guard watching over $600,000 in borrowed jewelry, there were more than a dozen people observing Monica striking one suggestive pose after another. In one, she posed with the American flag. (After the shoot, Lewinsky had a brief fling with one of Ritts's assistants, which would account for a cryptic phrase about the photo session in Andrew Morton's authorized book about her: "She treasures the friendships she made . . .")

When the photos were published, the magazine introduced them this way: "In the spirit of open government, and also for the heck of it, Monica Lewinsky permits HERB RITTS to remove her first veil." As should have been apparent to anyone (but especially her lawyers), the *Vanity Fair* photo extravaganza was a terrible idea. At the time, Lewinsky remained a subject of Starr's criminal investigation. In his public statements, Ginsburg was portraying his client as less a vamp than a victim—of Starr, of the media, and even of her former paramour, the president. But the Monica before the camera reveled in her notoriety and her sexuality. Ginsburg and the family justified the photo shoot in the New Age babble that was the Lewinsky lingua franca; Ritts's attentions were said to boost the young woman's "self-esteem." When the photographs from the session were published, and the inevitable condemnations of Monica followed, Marcia Lewis and her ex-husband blamed Ginsburg for allowing the project to go forward, but plainly the photographs were encouraged by Mom and witnessed by Dad, and, in fact, they served as an apt expression of Lewinsky family values.

Still, fairly or not, Monica and her parents added the *Vanity Fair* fiasco to a lengthening bill of particulars against Ginsburg. After the immunity negotiations with Starr broke down in February, Ginsburg had actually engaged in some clever lawyering. He and Speights filed a motion before Chief Judge Norma Holloway Johnson demanding that she intervene in the investigation and order that Lewinsky be granted immunity. The defense lawyers' theory was simple. They asserted that the February 2 letter—the one with the blank signature spaces for Emmick and Udolf—amounted to a valid contract between Lewinsky and the OIC, and she had the right to sue to enforce it. Judges rarely intervene in a prosecutor's decision to grant or withhold immunity, but Johnson took Ginsburg's demand seriously enough to conduct a hearing about it.

So, on March 12, Ginsburg, Emmick, and Bittman testified in secret sessions before the judge about what had been said in the course of their negotiations. No prosecutor enjoys testifying, and the experience was especially awkward for Emmick, because he was forced to admit that Udolf had told Ginsburg that they had a deal. (Fortunately for the OIC, Udolf himself was unavailable at the time, and thus was spared giving his version of the events.) Ironically, it might have been better for the Starr forces to lose this particular motion; if the judge had forced them to grant Lewinsky immunity, they could finally have started using her as a witness. But the notoriously pro-government Judge Johnson came through for Starr, albeit on extremely narrow grounds. She ruled that because Udolf, not Starr himself, had made the deal with Ginsburg, the immunity contract was not valid, and she would not enforce it. As the judge put it, "Mr. Udolf did not have actual authority to bind the OIC to such a contract." So, as March moved into April, Ginsburg and Starr remained at odds—and Lewinsky, neither a defendant nor a witness, remained in limbo.

Notwithstanding Ginsburg's commendable legal efforts, the *Vanity Fair* photographs, plus the lawyer's continued sniping at Starr in the press, began to crystallize the doubts that Monica and her parents were having about him. All through the spring, both sides of the Lewinsky family began relying increasingly on a different lawyer—Billy Martin, whom Nate Speights had recruited to represent Marcia Lewis. Martin had spent fifteen years as a federal prosecutor, including seven in Washington, and he projected a silky proficiency, a notable contrast to the frequently overwrought Ginsburg. Martin regarded the Starr prosecutors as just obsessed enough to bring a case against Lewinsky. He told the family that they had better make a deal or face the possibility that Monica would be indicted.

Ginsburg, oddly enough, was thinking much the same thing, except, in his megalomania, he was looking forward to it. In May, without telling Monica or Bernie, Ginsburg published "An Open Letter to Kenneth Starr," an extended attack on the prosecutor, in *California Lawyer* magazine. "Congratulations, Mr. Starr!" he wrote. "As a result of your callous disregard for cherished constitutional rights, you may have succeeded in unmasking a sexual relationship between two consenting adults." At this point, Ginsburg really did seem to be trying to provoke Starr into charging Lewinsky, a point the lawyer did not really deny. "I didn't want to make any deals with the devil, because I was angry," Ginsburg said. "I got to the point where I wanted to have a trial. I wanted to take them down in court."

Lewinsky, understandably, did not. Prodded by Martin, Monica started interviewing replacements for Ginsburg. Martin had two top candidates—Plato Cacheris and Jacob Stein. To Washington insiders, the mere mention of their names explained why they were being considered. Cacheris was sixty-nine and Stein was seventy-three, and they were Starr's peers in the upper echelon of Washington law practice. In the course of their eminent careers, Cacheris had represented John Mitchell in Watergate, Fawn Hall in Iran-Contra, and Aldrich Ames in the CIA spy scandals; Stein had represented Kenneth Parkinson, the only major Watergate figure to be acquitted, and served as an independent counsel himself, to investigate former attorney general Edwin Meese III. Both men had basically stopped trying cases and instead cut deals for their clients. That was what Lewinsky and Martin wanted them to do now—get her immunity at long last.

When Lewinsky and Martin interviewed Cacheris—in a secret meeting in an obscure hotel on Capitol Hill, on June 1—the lawyer made a great show of saying he would never negotiate a guilty plea for Lewinsky. "If you want to plead guilty," the lawyer told his prospective client, "you should hire someone else." In fact, this bravado was a form of marketing. As any competent attorney would recognize, Cacheris saw that Lewinsky made an unappealing target for Starr. Even the reviled Ginsburg recognized from the start that Monica should demand immunity. All Lewinsky and her advisers were doing (probably wisely) was changing the messenger but not the message.

Cacheris and Stein were old friends who worked in the same office building, and when they heard they were both interviewing for the job, they decided to join forces. On June 2, the two lawyers returned to the Washington Court Hotel and signed on officially as Lewinsky's new lawyers. Ginsburg later made a great show of insisting that he had not been fired—"I Didn't Get Dumped" was the headline of an op-ed piece he wrote for *The Washington Post* later that week—but instead he asserted that he volunteered to leave the case. The truth was somewhere along the lines of a job departure once described by Casey Stengel: "We call it discharged because there is no question I had to leave."

For their part, still on June 2, Cacheris and Stein decided to make a courtesy call on the prosecutors before they publicly announced that they were replacing Ginsburg. Seated around a conference table before Bittman, Bennett, and Wisenberg, the two new defense lawyers said they were looking forward to a new chapter in the relationship between Lewinsky and the OIC. Bittman, however, was anxious to make one of his characteristic "shows of strength."

"You know," he said, "we have a strong case against her."

Cacheris raised his hand and said this was not the time to debate the merits of the case. They just wanted to say hello and clear the slate. A couple of days later, however, Cacheris and Stein returned to the OIC for a more formal negotiating session, this one with Starr in attendance.

Bittman again began by announcing that Lewinsky had much to fear from an indictment. They had the evidence to convict her.

This time Cacheris answered, saying, "We are not here to discuss a disposition." There would be no guilty plea. Stein, the quieter of the defense pair, muttered, "I have one good trial left in me."

From there, the conversation turned to the issue of immunity, and it quickly bogged down on the question of an oral proffer. Bittman said Monica had to provide one before the OIC would consider granting immunity. Cacheris said he wanted immunity before Monica made any oral statement to the prosecutors. Through it all, Starr was silent, and neither side changed its position.

In all, this conversation was nearly identical in substance to those Ginsburg and Speights had conducted with the OIC four months earlier. A quick rejection of a guilty plea; a standoff about an oral proffer. Without Ginsburg's theatrics, the tone was more civilized, but Lewinsky's status remained unchanged. The two sides had returned to the stalemate that had charcterized their relations during the Ginsburg era. After June 12, Cacheris and Stein heard nothing from the other side.

Inside the OIC, Starr was obsessing—still—about toughness. In the daily meetings around the big conference table, the prosecutors mused like teenagers planning dates: Should we call them or wait for their call? If we call first, does that make us look weak? Days passed, then weeks. In the summer, Starr was feeling energized. Several witnesses, like Blumenthal, had asserted executive and attorney-client privileges during their grand jury testimony, and Starr was leading the fight to force them to answer questions. These were purely legal questions, and as such they represented one of the few areas where Starr, the former solicitor general, could stand on equal footing with his staff. The White House ultimately backed down on most of the privilege issues, but this battle in particular invigorated Starr. More than many on his staff, Starr thought he had a strong case against the president, even before he had the testimony of Lewinsky or Clinton himself. It was a circumstantial case, to be sure, but Starr had thought since early spring that it was strong enough to file an impeachment report to Congress. Maybe, he thought, they didn't even need Monica.

The prospect of the 1998 midterm congressional elections preyed on Starr's mind. At first, he wanted to send his report to Congress by the end of July; that date was sufficiently before November that he couldn't be accused of trying to affect the outcome. But that deadline proved unrealistic. Linda Tripp, the prosecutors' star witness, didn't even begin testifying in the grand jury until

June 30, and Bittman was still asking questions of Betty Currie well into July. Then there was Clinton's own testimony. Bittman had basically given up on his pas de deux with David Kendall in April. The prosecutor's increasingly forlorn letters ("Yet since this matter arose, the President has—with all respect—found time to play golf, attend basketball games and political fund-raisers, and enjoy a ski vacation . . .") continued to be met with dismissive replies.

At last, Starr decided to call Kendall's bluff. With the end of summer bearing down, Starr authorized Bittman to send, on July 17, 1998, a grand jury subpoena calling for the testimony of William Jefferson Clinton—the first such subpoena to a president of the United States in American history. Clinton would need more than Kendall's cute evasions now.

/ / /

From almost the day the scandal broke, the key members of the White House political operation—among them John Podesta, Rahm Emanuel, and Paul Begala—recognized that the chances for Clinton's survival in office rested principally on the shoulders of congressional Democrats. As long as the White House could portray Starr's investigation as a partisan vendetta, impeachment and removal—not to mention resignation—appeared to be remote possibilities. But the political team thought frequently of the delegation of Senate Republicans who came calling on Richard Nixon in the first week of August 1974. When this group, which included such party stalwarts as Barry Goldwater and Hugh Scott, told Nixon he had to go, they—more than any Democrats—forced the first presidential resignation. It was the possibility of a similar mission by their heirs across the aisle that obsessed Clinton loyalists.

So John Podesta was especially attentive when he was summoned to Steve Elmendorf's office one afternoon in May. As the top aide to Richard Gephardt, the leader of the Democrats in the House, Elmendorf served as the principal day-to-day emissary between the White House and its most important constituency. (The frenetic Emanuel would sometimes call Elmendorf almost hourly for briefings on Clinton's status among House Democrats.) Gephardt had told Elmendorf to pass an emphatic message to his counterparts on Clinton's staff. "John," Elmendorf told Podesta, "you cannot let him take the Fifth. He has got to know that that's just not an option. He has got to testify. You'll lose the Democrats up here if he doesn't." Podesta, who had worked on Capitol Hill for many years, did not disagree, but David Kendall did—vehemently.

Fifty-three years old, Kendall was an odd amalgam—a Quaker and a zealot. After growing up in a small Indiana town, he had discovered the civil rights movement—he was jailed in Mississippi during the Freedom Summer of 1964—and eventually moved into private law practice at Williams & Connolly. If the Quaker values of tolerance and nonviolence shaped Kendall's political conscious-ness, the very different spirit of Edward Bennett Williams forged his approach to the law. Williams believed in litigation, and espe-cially criminal law, as total war—a ceaseless battle in which a law-yer should never yield on even the smallest points. (In this, Kendall's outlook clashed with that of Bob Bennett, who took a more accommodating approach, and the two men shared a rich contempt for each other.) Kendall did mostly civil work at the firm, and he long represented the *National Enquirer*. In his office, he possessed perhaps the only leather-bound sets in existence of not only the *Enquirer* but its wackier sister tabloid, the *Weekly World News*.

In representing criminal defendants, Kendall had absorbed the central lesson of Williams's catechism—that a suspect should al-ways, *always* take the Fifth Amendment. But this was, as even Kendall had to recognize, a political matter more than a legal issue, and ultimately Clinton's political advisers—and, of course, the president himself—had their way. On July 24, in a letter marked CONFIDENTIAL, Kendall wrote to Bittman, "The President is willing to provide testimony for the grand jury. . . ."

/ / /

The subpoena to Clinton had another effect, one that was not yet visible to the lawyers in the president's camp. The prospect of Clinton's testimony had prompted Starr to call Jake Stein and sug-gest that they meet for breakfast at the home of Sam Dash, the Georgetown law professor who served as Starr's ethics adviser. The call came as a surprise to Stein, because he and Cacheris had not heard anything from the OIC in nearly six weeks. Of course, Lewinsky's lawyers did not know that Starr had just subpoenaed Clinton and it appeared that the president was actually going to testify. Even the hard-liners in Starr's office now recognized that they needed Lewinsky's testimony more than ever. If they were going to examine Clinton properly, and especially if they were going to prove that he lied, they were going to have to hear Monica's side of the story first.

The meeting at Dash's house on Friday morning, July 24—the same day that Kendall told Bittman that Clinton would testify at long last—didn't even last long enough for anyone to touch the bagels that had been laid out. Starr and Dash agreed that if Monica gave what they regarded as a truthful proffer under a "Queen for a Day" agreement, the OIC would give her full and complete immunity from prosecution. Starr said they wanted to meet with Monica right away. Because she was in California, they settled on Monday morning, July 27, in New York, where there would be less press scrutiny than in Washington. They would meet in what Starr called "Grandma's apartment"—his mother-in-law's place—on East 56th Street. Wearing a blond wig, baseball cap, and sunglasses, Monica flew to New York on Sunday night. Tell the truth, Lewinsky's lawyers instructed her, and you're home free.

Starr spent Sunday night at Grandma's place, but left first thing in the morning to teach his class at NYU Law School. From Ginsburg, Starr knew how Lewinsky loathed him, and he thought it better to stay out of her sight on this traumatic day. At around ten-thirty, Lewinsky arrived with her team—Stein, Cacheris, and Sydney Hoffmann, a part-time colleague of Cacheris's whom he had brought on to handle the detailed debriefings of his client. ("I didn't want to hear about who blew who," Cacheris said later.) The Starr team was already in place—Bittman, Sol Wisenberg, Mary Anne Wirth, Sam Dash, and an FBI agent to take notes. In order to make Monica more comfortable, the prosecutors allowed Hoffmann to lead the questioning for the first half hour.

So, in Grandma's small living room, Lewinsky told what would soon become a very familiar tale: the first encounter during the government shutdown, the furtive visits to the study, the phone sex, her forced departure from the White House staff, the job search from the Pentagon, the gifts from the president that she hid with Betty Currie. Lewinsky's memory was dazzling. When she discussed having breakfast with Vernon Jordan, she remembered where and what they ate—and the name of the waiter! There was only one moment of tension.

"What about a dress?" Bittman asked.

"We're not talking about that item today," Cacheris interjected. He knew that the blue Gap dress was still in Marcia Lewis's New York apartment. Cacheris was worried that the Starr team might give Lewinsky or her mother something called "act of production" immunity, force them to produce the dress, and then prosecute them for hiding it. (That might have been a clever strategy, but it apparently never occurred to anyone at the OIC.) Better, Cacheris thought, simply to wait until Monica had full immunity and then produce the dress without any fear of reprisal. On this occasion, Bittman didn't press the issue.

The core of Lewinsky's story would never change. Yes, there was a sexual relationship (short of intercourse). No, neither the president nor anyone else ever told her to lie or withhold evidence in the Paula Jones case. In the argot of those closest to the case, Monica gave them the sex but not the obstruction.

At about two-thirty, Cacheris saw that Monica's energy was starting to flag, and he said he thought they should stop. The lawyers on both sides retreated into a bedroom to discuss their next steps.

"We need another day to question her," Bittman said.

Cacheris exploded: "If you don't have the story by now, you'll never have it." He said they could talk to her again only if they gave her a full immunity agreement.

Bittman smiled and said, "You mean a *signed* agreement?"—a joking reference to the unsigned February 2 document that had caused both sides so much aggravation. They parted on friendly terms.

That night, Starr called Stein and asked him to come to the independent counsel offices the following morning. He had an immunity agreement waiting, and the defense lawyers found little to quibble with in the wording. By that afternoon, Lewinsky had signed, making her officially a government witness, and Cacheris announced the deal to the public. The following day, Monica would begin a grueling round of all-day debriefings.

It was July 28, 1998, precisely 176 days since Bruce Udolf had made his immunity agreement with Bill Ginsburg. That delay of nearly half a year earned Starr and the Office of Independent Counsel precisely nothing—and cost them a great deal. Lewinsky's recitation in Grandma's living room was substantively identical to the version she wrote out by hand in the Cosmos Club. But if Monica's testimony did not waver, the political and legal terrain had been transformed since those frenzied first days of the scandal. By and large, the months had allowed the country to come to terms with the fact that the president probably did have the affair with the intern—but that he had managed to do a pretty good job anyway. Starr had used the time to prove that his ineptitude was exceeded only by his zeal.

Like so many enemies in Clinton's past and future, Starr had held out with Lewinsky in the hope that something would turn up to cinch the case against the president. But it didn't and it wouldn't, because the case was never anything more than it appeared to be—that of a humiliated middle-aged husband who lied when he was caught having an affair with a young woman from the office.

17

"I Don't Care If I'm Impeached . . ."

Starr spoke frequently to his staff about their need to insulate themselves from the political currents swirling around their work. He was particularly preoccupied by the November 1998 elections. His initial insistence on submitting his report to Congress in July, more than three months before the voting, suggested how much Starr worried about the perception that he was trying to help the Republicans and hurt the Democrats. In public and private, Starr's statements on this issue never changed.

There is, however, ample evidence that the independent counsel protested too much about his desire to veer clear of politics. Indeed, the negotiations between Bob Bittman and David Kendall about the president's grand jury testimony admit to almost no other interpretation. The OIC's position about Clinton's testimony suggested that far from seeking distance from the electoral fray, Starr's office did have a political agenda—specifically, to humiliate the president and damage his party.

On July 24, Kendall told Bittman that Clinton would testify, but the lawyer didn't lay out his conditions until three days later. On that day Kendall wrote to the prosecutor saying that Clinton would testify only "in a way that is consistent with the obligations of the office." Kendall demanded withdrawal of the subpoena, meaning Clinton could testify voluntarily; testimony at the White House, not in the grand jury room; strict time limits; and "adequate time to prepare"—which the lawyer interpreted as no testimony before September 13 or 20. Kendall and Bittman spent many hours hashing out these points between July 27 and 29. (The announcement of Lewinsky's immunity deal, on July 28, made the stakes for Clinton's testimony even higher.)

To Kendall's astonishment, Bittman caved on almost everything. He agreed to withdraw the subpoena, so Clinton would not have to suffer the indignity of being the first president compelled to appear before a grand jury. Bittman agreed to allow Clinton to testify at the White House, in the presence of his lawyers—which was something denied to all other grand jury witnesses, who had to face their interrogators alone. And in the most important concession, Bittman quickly surrendered his demand for two days of testimony from Clinton and settled for just four hours. The OIC spent that much time on minor witnesses and dozens of hours with people like Tripp, Jordan, and Currie. Kendall believed that with no judge present to limit how much Clinton talked, a mere four hours would pass in a flash. Such accommodations were nearly without precedent in the rancorous relationship between the president and the independent counsel.

But Bittman did not yield on two points. The first was the date. The prosecutor said the middle or end of September was simply too late. In his letter, Kendall admitted that the Clintons had planned a two-week vacation starting on Saturday, August 15. A trip to Ireland and Russia would immediately follow. The letter had all but invited a compromise date in lieu of the first few days of the president's vacation, and Kendall settled on Monday, August 17, for Clinton's testimony. But Bittman's other demand was more surprising. Kendall had agreed that the grand jurors could come to the White House or, alternatively, watch a live closed-circuit feed of Clinton's testimony, but Bittman insisted that the testimony be videotaped as well. Kendall asked why.

"Someone on the grand jury might be absent that day," Bittman said.

This was preposterous. First, it is hard to imagine that any of the twenty-three grand jurors could have had more pressing business on August 17 than listening to the president of the United

States testify. Second, even if someone was absent, he or she could read a transcript or listen to a reading of one; that was how grand juries usually worked. Still, in light of all of Bittman's other concessions, Kendall decided to give in on this one as well.

But why did Bittman insist on only these two points? Testimony in August allowed Starr to release his report in early September—at the beginning of the campaign season, but not so late as to expose him to criticism for interfering in the races. In fact, one could not have chosen a more politically incendiary moment to release the report than the time Starr eventually did select. The videotape demand was even more suspicious. At this point, Starr knew that he would be turning evidence over to Congress; he understood that the legislators would face enormous pressure to release it, especially in the middle of their campaigns. Though Starr, Bittman, and his staff denied it, the only reasonable interpretation of their insistence on videotape was to embarrass Clinton—to display him to the public answering the kind of questions that no president, and scarcely any American, had ever been required to address.

The videotaped grand jury testimony was, it appeared, the independent counsel's form of payback for four years of Clinton's hostility and disdain. Yet like so many of Starr's plans during his long tenure, this one, too, did not have the results he may have expected.

/ / /

Both sides spent the next fortnight in frantic preparations for Clinton's grand jury testimony. Starr gained a psychological edge with a brief, understated letter that Bittman sent to Kendall on July 31. "Investigative demands," he wrote, "require that President Clinton provide this Office as soon as possible with a blood sample to be taken under our supervision." That could only have meant one thing. On the day after Lewinsky signed her immunity deal, she handed Mike Emmick a "GAP dress, size 12, dark blue," as the FBI report put it, in a brief meeting in Cacheris's office. A test the next day showed the presence of semen, giving Bittman the justification for his letter. Though Kendall was not told the results of the DNA tests before Clinton's testimony, the lawyer had a pretty good idea why Bittman was asking. (The president provided the blood sample on August 3, and preliminary tests that night showed a match. More refined tests later put the odds at 7.87 trillion to one that the semen on the dress came from someone other than Clinton. In a reflection of the tense atmosphere in the Starr office before the president's testimony, Bittman lied to several colleagues about the results of the DNA test, suggesting there was no match.)

At around nine on the morning of August 6, Lewinsky made her way past the phalanx of television cameras in front of the United States Courthouse and settled down to her first day of grand jury testimony. At 11:06 A.M., President Clinton appeared in the Rose Garden of the White House at a ceremony to mark the fifth anniversary of the gun control legislation known as the Brady Bill. That night, Monica's mother knew how tired her daughter would be after her big day, so she brought home her favorite Chinese dinner, chicken chow mein, and the two women ate in front of the television. As they were watching, Monica was startled to see the blue-and-gold necktie Clinton was wearing on the occasion.

"I gave that to him," she told her mother, of the Ermenegildo Zegna design. "I bet it's a signal to me."

Thus began one of the story's more peculiar byways—the saga of the "love tie," as it was sometimes called. The next day, Lewinsky passed her hunch to the prosecutors. She said that she had mailed Clinton the tie for his fiftieth birthday, in August 1996, and told him, "I like it when you wear my ties because then I know I'm close to your heart." (It was at Clinton's fiftieth birthday party, at Radio City Music Hall, that she surreptitiously grabbed his penis.) Some of Starr's staff believed that the tie was another sign of Clinton's perfidy—that he was dressing to obstruct justice. By wearing the tie, they thought, he was instructing Lewinsky to remain faithful to him.

This was a fairly absurd notion; Clinton appeared in public only after Lewinsky began testifying. But Jackie Bennett took the tie issue seriously enough to ask Clinton several questions about it during his grand jury testimony. Within a week of Clinton's testimony, the tie issue leaked in the press, to much public merriment. Surprisingly, the tie-signaling story made sense to some of Clinton's closest friends. Unlike most people, they knew Clinton was actually a superstitious man, a collector of rabbit's feet and lucky pennies, which he meticulously placed in his pocket each day. (Some of these same friends were convinced that Clinton had had an affair with Lewinsky only when they heard that she had given him a wooden frog letter opener; small frog sculptures were another one of his private hobbies.) It would be like Clinton, they thought, to seek some sort of cosmic alliance with Lewinsky by wearing her tie on the day of her debut before the grand jury.

After Clinton's own grand jury testimony, Starr avoided the tie controversy in his report to Congress, so the issue largely faded from view. But had the prosecutors pursued the issue, the president might have been saved by a suitably bizarre deus ex machina regarding the love tie. In December 1996, the president's brother, the singer Roger Clinton, had traveled to Italy. His agent had told him to look up another one of his clients, a woman named Marina Castelnuovo, who made her living as Italy's foremost Elizabeth Taylor impersonator. In Rome, Castelnuovo took Roger shopping for Christmas presents for his brother, an expedition that was tape-recorded by the RAI television network. Almost two years later, when Italian television broadcast photographs of the Zegna tie in question, the Italian entertainer instantly realized that she and Roger, not Monica Lewinsky, had purchased that tie for the president. Castelnuovo tracked down the RAI videotape and passed the proof triumphantly to David Kendall.

In truth, the matter could never be resolved definitively. Clinton received many ties from different people and cycled through them quickly, and he swore he couldn't remember the origin of the blue-and-gold number he had worn on August 6. It was even possible that Roger and Monica had both given him the same tie; Zegna distributed this model only in 1996. Perhaps there was an innocent explanation. But as Clinton prepared to face his inquisitors at the Office of Independent Counsel, he could be sure that they, if not the American people, were always ready to believe the worst about him.

/ / /

Clinton had survived decades of rumors about his sex life either by denying them or refusing to address them. In spite of this strategy—or, perhaps, because of it—he had twice been elected president of the United States. As the August 17 date approached, all of the people around the president knew how difficult it would be to persuade him to change his ways. But Lewinsky had been in the grand jury; the DNA tests were under way. Though no one in the Clinton camp said it directly, the mission in preparing the president was to save him from himself.

Only two people were in a position to know what he was going to say. In the days leading up to his testimony, Kendall and his partner Nicole Seligman spent many hours with Clinton, and even they were not entirely sure how he was going to address the issue of his relationship with Lewinsky. On many issues, Clinton's positions were clear. He didn't ask Vernon Jordan to find Monica a job in return for her silence; he didn't ask her to retrieve the gifts to avoid the Jones subpoena; he didn't obstruct justice. That was the easy stuff. But as for the issue at the core of the case, Clinton wouldn't commit one way or the other. This was, of course, a personal as well as political and legal dilemma. For seven months, he had told his wife nothing more than he had on the first day—that he had only "ministered" to the troubled Monica Lewinsky.

As the final weekend before his testimony approached, the White House moved into the same kind of crisis mode that had prevailed just after the story broke. Harry Thomason and Linda Bloodworth-Thomason returned from California. Mickey Kantor, the former trade representative and commerce secretary, began spending virtually all his time at the White House, in his role as an additional personal lawyer for the president. A genuine foreign policy crisis further rattled the atmosphere. Saddam Hussein evicted United Nations weapons inspectors from Iraq, and the administration was threatening to resume air strikes.

Finally, the logjam was broken in a manner distinctive to Washington. In the Friday, August 14, edition of *The New York Times,* a front-page story bore the headline CLINTON WEIGHS ADMITTING HE HAD SEXUAL CONTACTS. Citing a member of Clinton's "inner circle," the story suggested that Clinton was thinking of changing his story to admit that he had had "intimate sexual encounters" with Lewinsky. In a way, the story could be seen as a proactive leak—designed more to shape Clinton's testimony than to disclose his plans for it. Most people around the president felt that he had more to lose from lying than from admitting the affair; thus, this leak. In private as well as public, all of those in the "inner circle" denied being the source of the story. However, close observers were drawn to one of the four bylines on the *Times* story—that of David E. Sanger. An international economics specialist, Sanger had not covered the Lewinsky story. On the other hand, he had spent several years chronicling Mickey Kantor's career.

The leak to the *Times* had its intended effect. On that Friday, Clinton said gravely to Harry Thomason, "I've got to talk to Hillary." Indeed, that same day, the president went to Linda Bloodworth-Thomason, who was especially close to the first lady, and asked if she might soften the blow a little bit. She refused. She didn't want to get in the middle of a situation like this one. Bill had gotten himself into this mess, and she wasn't going to help him get out of it—at least not with his wife. Almost as a form of therapy, the president on Friday began handwriting a draft of a speech that he would deliver to the nation after his grand jury testimony on Monday. It was little more than an angry diatribe about the invasions of privacy he had had to endure, but it made Clinton feel better—a little.

Paul Begala would be responsible for shepherding the Monday-night speech through to completion, so over the weekend, he called Robert Shrum, a veteran Washington speechwriter and author of several Clinton State of the Union addresses, to do a draft. Shrum was on vacation in Sun Valley, and he received no special instructions. He simply worked off the *Times* leak and wrote what he thought Clinton should say. On Sunday night, he faxed his draft to Begala and to the president's pollster, Mark Penn. "My fellow Americans," Shrum wrote:

> No one who is not in my position can understand fully the remorse I feel today. Since I was very young, I've had a profound reverence for this office I hold. I've been honored that you, the people, have entrusted it to me. I am proud of what we have accomplished together.
>
> But in this case, I have fallen short of what you should expect from a President. I have failed my own religious faith and values. I have let too many people down. I take full responsibility for my

actions—for hurting my wife and daughter, for hurting Monica Lewinsky, for hurting friends and staff, and for hurting the country I love. None of this ever should have happened.

I never should have had any sexual contact with Monica Lewinsky. But I did. I should have acknowledged that I was wrong months ago. But I didn't. I thought I was shielding my family, but I know that in the end, for Hillary and Chelsea, delay has only brought more pain. Their forgiveness and love, expressed so often as we sat alone together this weekend, means far more than I can ever say.

What I did was wrong—and there was no excuse for it. I do want to assure you, as I told the Grand Jury under oath, that I did nothing to obstruct this investigation.

Finally, I also want to apologize to all of you, my fellow citizens. I hope you can find it in your heart to accept that apology. I pledge to you that I will make every effort of mind and spirit to earn your confidence again, to be worthy of this office, and finish the work in which we have made such remarkable progress for the last six years.

God bless you and goodnight.

Begala read it and thought—No way. Too much groveling. Like many White House aides, Begala was a student of the presidency, and he was familiar with the high point of presidential apologies. In 1987, Ronald Reagan conceded, in a famous use of the passive voice, that "mistakes were made" in the Iran-Contra affair. Saddam Hussein would be listening to Clinton's speech. He couldn't sound like a weakling. So Begala went to work on his own draft, which he and Emanuel fiddled with on Sunday night. An apology; an acceptance of responsibility; and a firm insistence on reclaiming a measure of his own privacy—a point that was especially important to Clinton. Erskine Bowles, the chief of staff, had charged Begala with taking responsibility for shepherding the speech to completion on Monday night. Neither man knew that their boss had his own plans.

/ / /

When Starr arrived at the White House just after noon on Monday, Kendall intercepted him and pulled him aside for what he would later call a "walk in the woods." He told the independent counsel that the president would concede an inappropriate sexual relationship with Lewinsky, but he wouldn't talk about the details. Kendall was really packaging a threat as a concession. If Starr and his people demanded the details, Kendall would fight him every step of the way.

Starr had planned for this contingency. For the prosecution's rehearsals of the examination, Hickman Ewing had come up from Little Rock to play Clinton. Compared to denying the sex outright or simply refusing to answer any questions about it, a third option of a limited confession made the most sense. The absence of the element of surprise made the failure of the Starr team that afternoon all the more striking.

The questioning began at 1:03 P.M., with Kendall keeping time, to make sure that the prosecutors would have exactly 240 minutes. Starr had awarded his three favorites with the historic opportunity to question the president—Bob Bittman, Jackie Bennett, and Sol Wisenberg. After Wisenberg asked a few questions to establish that Clinton understood the meaning of his oath, he turned the interrogation over to Bittman.

"Mr. President, we are first going to turn to some of the details of your relationship with Monica Lewinsky," Bittman began. "The questions are uncomfortable, and I apologize for that in advance. I will try to be as brief and direct as possible.

"Mr. President, were you physically intimate with Monica Lewinsky?"

Bittman had begun with admirable candor. In an investigation about sex, he had asked the only question that really mattered. Clinton was ready for it. He asked permission to read a statement—which would, he said, "perhaps make it possible for you to ask even more relevant questions from your point of view." This last remark reflected the spirit with which Clinton sparred with the prosecutors in the grand jury. He knew—as did they—that the president had a very different notion of what was "relevant" to their investigation than they did.

"When I was alone with Ms. Lewinsky on certain occasions in early 1996 and once in early 1997, I engaged in conduct that was wrong," Clinton recited. "These encounters did not consist of sexual intercourse. They did not constitute sexual relations as I understood that term to be defined at my January seventeenth, 1998, deposition. But they did involve inappropriate intimate contact.

"These inappropriate encounters ended, at my insistence, in early 1997. I also had occasional telephone conversations with Ms. Lewinsky that included inappropriate sexual banter. I regret that what began as a friendship came to include this conduct, and I take full responsibility for my actions.

"While I will provide the grand jury whatever other information I can, because of privacy considerations affecting my family, myself, and others, and in an effort to preserve the dignity of the office I hold, this is all I will say about the specifics of these particular matters. . . .

"That, Mr. Bittman, is my statement."

Though Kendall and Seligman had applied their gloss, the statement was vintage Clinton—a quivering dance on the edge of falsehood. He put the start of the relationship in 1996, when Monica was a staffer, not in 1995, when she was still an intern; he said their relationship "began as a friendship," whereas in fact it commenced after she showed him her thong, just a few hours before his pants came down in his study; he coined the prim phrase "inappropriate sexual banter" to replace the indignity of "phone sex." Still, in spite of it all, Clinton had made a clever tactical move. In a single paragraph, he had neutralized months of grand jury testimony and investigation by Starr—the DNA test, the Secret Service witnesses, the accounts of the relationship provided by Monica to her friends and family. Yes, they had had an affair. What else could Starr's team establish in the four hours that were available to them?

The answer was clear: not much. The hapless Bittman began by sparring with the president about the definition of sexual relations that had been used in the January deposition. But Clinton knew the tortured definition better than the prosecutor did, and they debated such vague phrases as "causes contact" and "intent to gratify." Bittman wasted more than an hour and a half, until Kendall called a break, and then Wisenberg took over the questioning. The prosecutor asked the president about Bob Bennett's assertion in the Paula Jones deposition that "there is absolutely no sex of any kind in any manner, shape or form, with President Clinton."

"That statement is a completely false statement," Wisenberg said. "Is that correct?"

Clinton's almost comic literalism landed him in trouble. "It depends on what the meaning of the word 'is' is," he said, smiling, realizing a little too late how foolish he sounded. Still, despite the absurdity of the remark, Clinton's larger point was a fair one. Bennett was his lawyer; Clinton wasn't Bennett's. It wasn't the client's job to monitor what his lawyer said. And anyway, Starr had the admission about sex. What else did he want?

Kendall had done his best to make sure that Starr got as little as possible. As part of the cynical calculus that the defense lawyer had employed in preparing Clinton, the president had about a dozen set-piece speeches he could deploy at various times during the session. Without a judge present, there was no real way that Clinton could be stopped from running down the clock in this manner. So, in Wisenberg's portion of the examination, the president inveighed at length against the motives of the Jones lawyers, the weakness of their case, the burdens of his job, his fading memory. And other than on the questions about sex—that is, the details of what he and Lewinsky did with each other—Wisenberg made no more progress than Bittman had.

The other two prosecutors took so long that Jackie Bennett was cheated out of most of his time. Unlike the others, Bennett had a strategic approach to this work—a sense of the larger structure of the attempt to bring Clinton down. After three-plus hours, it was clear that the Lewinsky line of questions had produced little of use for the prosecutors. So instead of meandering over the same topics as the others, Bennett asked Clinton a series of specific questions about Kathleen Willey, eliciting the categorical denials that the OIC potentially could use for a separate perjury charge against him. As Clinton enemies did throughout his presidency, Bennett tried to lay the plans for the next battle—in this case, staking his office's credibility behind Willey's allegation that the president had groped her on November 29, 1993.

After Kendall warned the prosecutors that only twelve minutes remained, Starr himself asked a handful of questions about the invocation of executive privilege, and then Wisenberg used several of those last precious seconds on the matter of the love tie. He had gone to the trouble of locating photographs of the president wearing the Zegna model on August 6, the day of Lewinsky's appearance before the grand jury.

"Were you sending some kind of signal to her by wearing a tie that she had given you on the day that she appeared in front of the grand jury?" Wisenberg asked.

"No, sir," Clinton said, for the first time in the long afternoon breaking into a smile at the peculiarity of the question. "I don't believe she gave me this tie. . . . I don't, I don't want to make light about this. I don't believe she gave me this tie. . . . And I had absolutely no thought of this in my mind when I wore it."

With almost no time left on the clock, Bennett made a pitch to lengthen the session, but Kendall cut him off. Ever the politician, Clinton interjected that he was sorry he could not have addressed the grand jurors' questions face to face. He noted that Kendall had tried to arrange for the grand jurors to be brought to the White House for the session.

This was a touchy topic for the prosecutors. "Just for the record," Wisenberg jumped in, "the invitation to the grand jury was contingent upon us not videotaping, and we had to videotape because we have an absent grand juror." (One grand juror did fail to attend court on August 17.)

Suspicious—for good reason—of this explanation for preserving this awful moment in Clinton's presidency for posterity, Kendall shot back, "Is that the only reason, Mr. Wisenberg, you have to videotape?"

Clinton, too, saw the political dimension to the videotaping issue. "Well, yes," he said. "Do you want to answer that?"

But Bittman decided it was time to go. At 6:25 P.M., he said, "Thank you, Mr. President."

/ / /

There is nothing political people hate more than enforced ignorance, but the top people on the White House staff spent the afternoon of August 17 in a state of brittle anticipation. Like everyone else, they knew nothing about what was going on in the Map Room, so they worried and traded gossip. Given the stresses that the Lewinsky matter imposed on the staff, Clinton's advisers managed to get through the year without taking out too much of their anger on each other—with a single exception. Mickey Kantor's ill-defined duties, his boasting about his closeness to the Clintons, and his officious manner made him a favorite target of the full-timers on the staff. Late in the afternoon of the seventeenth, Kantor poked his nose in Chuck Ruff's office, where press secretary Mike McCurry, his deputy Joe Lockhart, the lawyer Lanny Breuer, and a handful of others were waiting out the final moments of the testimony.

"I want you to know," Kantor announced to the group, "that the president appreciates everything you have done for him."

The recipients nodded at this unctuous expression of gratitude, and when Kantor closed the door, they erupted in a cheerful chorus of "Fuck you!" and "Who the fuck do you think you are?" The invective cheered everyone up, if only for a little while.

Kantor had issued one decree about the White House on August 17. Mark Penn could not be allowed on the premises. Kantor didn't want any news stories saying that the president's pollster had told him how to testify. In fact, Penn had been intimately involved in planning the testimony. He had even polled on whether Clinton should take the Fifth; the public was highly negative. Penn had tested the phrase that the White House invariably used to describe how the president was handling the crisis—by focusing on "the people's business." The expression scored very high, and it was used often.

Later in the afternoon, James Carville arrived from a trip to Brazil, and he posted himself in Rahm Emanuel's office. Clinton's team figured the president would want to see a friendly face when he walked out of the Map Room, so they stationed Carville by the door. When Clinton and his lawyers stepped outside the room, they were still chuckling quietly about the questions about the Zegna tie. For Kendall, Seligman, and Chuck Ruff, the tie issue symbolized the pointlessness of so many of the inquiries about Clinton. A tie signal? Carville joined in the amusement, but the president seemed subdued, tired—and, it quickly became apparent, full of rage.

Clinton often operated in an atmosphere of barely controlled chaos, but the hours after his grand jury testimony and before his speech to the nation set a new standard for tense improvisation. The plan to leave the speech to the political team—led by Begala, Emanuel, and Doug Sosnik—quickly evaporated as volunteers, chiefly Kantor, injected themselves into the process. The political people, the lawyers, and outsiders like Carville and Linda and

Harry Thomason all milled around the solarium—the big room on the top floor of the White House—and contributed thoughts and phrases. "A cluster fuck," in Clinton White House argot.

After a shower and a quick meal, Clinton himself took charge of the process. Begala and Emanuel had three touchstones for the speech: responsible, accountable, and apologetic. Begala and Linda Bloodworth-Thomason had spent the day refining his draft from the weekend. But the president had a different priority—his outrage at the Starr investigation itself.

"I did wrong—and so did he," Clinton said. "Dammit, somebody has to say these things. I don't care if I'm impeached. It's the right thing to do."

As the clock inched toward nine, drafts of the speech multiplied. Eventually, though, the controversy centered on how much criticism of Starr the president should include. Kendall and Kantor backed strong words against the prosecutor; the political people, along with the Thomasons, favored a more conciliatory approach. With less than an hour to go, the first lady arrived in the solarium.

Everyone gave her a wide berth, knowing the humiliation to which her husband had just subjected her. On the Starr issue, Mrs. Clinton didn't take a strong position. At last, she told her husband, "It's your speech. You should say what you want to say." Her anger at him flashed when she added, "You're the president of the United States—I guess."

When Carville left the solarium to race to the studio for *Larry King Live,* the dispute had narrowed down to whether the speech would include one critical adjective of Starr or two. At around that time, Linda Bloodworth-Thomason told the president that she didn't like his tie, so he invited her to go up to his closet with him to select another one. There Thomason picked out a bright blue one—and that prompted a smile from Clinton. He might have thrown out a lot of his ties, but this one he had kept. "I wore that one at my inauguration," he said. (His first, in 1993.)

Clinton kept working on the text until the last minute. In the last half hour, the president posted himself at a small round table, and Kantor started waving his arms to keep everyone else away from him. The speech simply wasn't finished, and Kantor thought the president himself deserved the final say on the text. With minutes to go, Begala took care of getting the speech on the Tele-PrompTer. Less than five minutes before the speech was to begin, Clinton walked into the Map Room with Harry Thomason and Linda Bloodworth-Thomason standing on either side of him. Linda took a seat in a chair, and Harry sat cross-legged on the floor, just out of camera range.

"Good evening," Clinton said.

> This afternoon, in this room, from this chair, I testified before the Office of Independent Counsel and a grand jury. I answered their questions truthfully, including questions about my private life, questions no American citizen would ever want to answer. Still, I must take complete responsibility for all my actions, both public and private. And that is why I am speaking to you tonight.
>
> As you know, in a deposition in January, I was asked about my relationship with Monica Lewinsky. While my answers were legally accurate, I did not volunteer information.

Kendall had demanded this last sentence. He was not going to allow Clinton to make a public admission that Starr could later use in a prosecution for perjury.

> Indeed, I did have a relationship with Miss Lewinsky that was not appropriate. In fact, it was wrong. It constituted a critical lapse in judgment and a personal failure on my part for which I am solely and completely responsible.
>
> But as I told the grand jury today, and I say to you now, that at no time did I ask anyone to lie, to hide or destroy evidence, or to take any unlawful action.
>
> I know that my public comments and my silence about this matter gave a false impression. I misled people. Including even my wife. I deeply regret that.

At this point in the speech, Linda Bloodworth-Thomason had inserted a straightforward apology to the American people. But after she went to change Clinton's tie, she never followed through on inserting it into the final draft. That night, no one ever considered an apology to Lewinsky or her family.

I can only tell you I was motivated by many factors. First, by a desire to protect myself from the embarrassment of my own conduct. I was also very concerned about protecting my family. The fact that these questions were being asked in a politically inspired lawsuit, which has since been dismissed, was a consideration, too.

Clinton had rewritten almost the entire remainder of the speech in the last half hour or so before delivering it—that is, after Carville left the room.

In addition, I had real and serious concerns about an independent counsel that began with private dealings twenty years ago—dealings, I might add, about which a federal agency found no evidence of any wrongdoing by me or my wife over two years ago.

The independent counsel investigation moved on to my staff and friends. Then into my private life. And the investigation itself is under investigation. This has gone on too long, cost too much, and hurt too many innocent people.

Now this matter is between me, the two people I love most, my wife and our daughter, and our God. I must put it right. And I am prepared to do whatever it takes to do so.

Nothing is more important to me personally, but it is private. And I intend to reclaim my family life for my family. It's nobody's business but ours.

At this line, sitting in front of Clinton, Harry Thomason pumped his fist in agreement.

Even presidents have private lives. It is time to stop the pursuit of personal destruction and the prying into private lives and get on with our national life.

Our country has been distracted by this matter for too long, and I take my responsibility for my part in all of this. That is all I can do. Now it is time—in fact, it is past time—to move on. We have important work to do, real opportunities to seize, real problems to solve, real security matters to face.

And so tonight I ask you to turn away from the spectacle of the past seven months, to repair the fabric of our national discourse, and to return our attention to all the challenges and all the promise of the next American century.

Thank you for watching and good night.

The Thomasons hugged Clinton after he finished the four-and-a-half-minute speech, and the three of them stepped out of the Map Room together. The president went for a brief walk outside, and when he returned, he was met by Rahm Emanuel, who had the early returns from the television pundits.

"It's getting panned," he said.

The frustrations of the day welled up in Clinton's red face. "I said what I wanted to say," he yelled at his aide, "and I don't care what those people say—and I don't care what happens now!"

To an almost unprecedented degree in the history of presidential oratory, Clinton's speech on August 17 drew unanimous derision in the news media—and for good reason. On a day when he admitted he had "misled" the entire country—in fact, he had outright lied—he chose to devote much of his speech to attacking Kenneth Starr. Even among those who found much to criticize in Starr's work, many believed that this was a moment for contrition, not calumny, by the president. On this occasion, Clinton was blinded by his self-pity, unable to recognize that this was a day to discuss his own sins rather than those of his enemies. He had never displayed his flaws more clearly or in front of a bigger audience.

And yet two other points stand out about his performance on August 17. First, though he was often accused of being guided more by polls than principle, the president spoke out of conviction on this night. The public never saw greater candor or honesty from Bill Clinton, albeit in service of earlier lies. Second, and more important, Clinton displayed on this evening the skills that made him the most extraordinary politician of his generation. The press rejected his speech; the public embraced it. Notwithstanding the torrent of criticism in the news media, Clinton's poll numbers hung steady at their high level following his speech. (Mark Penn, who arrived at the White House moments after Clinton finished his speech, did a quick poll that showed clear majorities believed that the speech was "presidential" and that Clinton had apologized; two-thirds thought he was "sincere.") He had an almost preternatural sense that the public agreed when he said, "It's nobody's business but ours." In an intuitive way, he understood what the journalists, for all their prattle about character, did not—that the American people believed there was a difference between his public and private life. Clinton didn't have a lot of company in this view, even among his own staff, but in this he was defiantly, even courageously, correct.

/ / /

For all the condemnation of Clinton's speech in the news media, the prosecution team didn't take any false optimism out of the events of August 17. In his grand jury testimony, the president had been more careful than in his deposition, seven months earlier. Increasingly, the savvier members of the prosecution staff recognized that their entire case came down to the sex—whether the president had lied about it in his deposition and then in his grand jury testimony. In light of Clinton's refusal to answer certain questions, Bittman and Wisenberg had pinned him down as best they could. Before the grand jury, Clinton had repeated his position that as he understood the definition of sexual relations provided to him on January 18, he had not had such contacts with Lewinsky. Clinton had admitted to "inappropriate intimate contact," which he declined to spell out, but by a sort of process of elimination, he had said he had not "directly" touched Lewinsky's breasts or vagina with his hands or mouth "with intent to arouse" her.

It was a slender basis on which to make a case. Since Clinton had admitted intimate contact, what difference did it make whether he acknowledged precisely how and where he had placed his hands and mouth? A big difference, according to the clear consensus at the Office of Independent Counsel. If they could prove a falsehood—any falsehood—they were going to make a case, regardless of the subject matter. In a United States Attorney's Office, where judges and prosecutors were lied to with regularity, prosecutors would weigh the significance of the false statements and consider whether the government's resources might be better deployed in another way. But in an independent counsel's office, especially this one, this kind of thinking was anathema. As Starr said in one of his curbside news conferences, "Okay, you're taking an oath . . . under God, that you will—'so help me, God, that I will tell the truth.' That's awfully important. Now that means we attach a special importance to it. There's no room for white lies. There's no room for shading. There's only room for truth. . . . You cannot defile the temple of justice."

So Starr would pursue the perjury about sex, and that raised a different issue. In her testimony before the grand jury on August 6, Lewinsky had spoken in a general way about her sexual relationship with the president. Now, in light of how the Starr team wanted to parse Clinton's answers in the grand jury, there would be a need for a great deal more specificity about the mechanics of their encounters. How they chose to conduct that next examination of Lewinsky would itself turn out to be a landmark in the history of American law enforcement.

/ / /

Women who met Starr for the first time often remarked on his courtliness—opening doors, pulling out chairs, and generally behaving as he was taught in San Antonio. He was a good listener, too, and his pet phrase "the deliberative process" almost became a joke around the OIC because things sometimes moved so slowly. But no matter how long it took, Starr believed in hearing everyone out. At the end of the process, though, one thing remained the same in any organization Starr had led: he followed the advice of men.

During the three decades of Starr's career, the legal profession integrated many women into positions of responsibility. This was especially true in criminal law. But in the Justice Department, at Kirkland & Ellis, and in the Office of Independent Counsel, Starr invariably chose deputies who looked and sounded like him. As someone who had benefited enormously from powerful mentors like Warren Burger and William French Smith, Starr, too, had a series of protégés in the law—all young white men. Starr's refusal to delegate power to women was especially striking at the OIC. All of his deputies were men. Twenty-nine prosecutors represented the OIC in the grand jury—twenty-five men and four women. There were 121 sessions with witnesses before the grand jury—and women prosecutors led the questioning six times.

Starr's history with women made the OIC's solution to its Lewinsky problem all the more striking. Who would ask Monica Lewinsky about the gory details of the caresses in the presidential study? Mary Anne Wirth and Karin Immergut. Ironically, they were two of the more experienced federal prosecutors in the group, and they had compiled admirable records on opposite sides of the country, Wirth in New York and Immergut in Los Angeles. In light of their accomplishments, it was all the more poignant that they agreed to be used in this manner, because the session they conducted with Lewinsky on August 26 was a disgrace—to the prosecutors themselves, to Starr, to Lewinsky, and, indeed, to the criminal process. It was also a monument to the absurdity of the entire Starr investigation, that an inquiry about a land deal in the 1970s had come down to . . . this.

/ / /

"We are on the record," Karin Immergut began. "Ms. Lewinsky, could you please state and spell your full name for the record?"

It was 12:35 P.M. on August 26. Immergut, Wirth, and Lewinsky were gathered with a female court reporter in a conference room in the independent counsel offices on Pennsylvania Avenue. In light of the questions Lewinsky was going to be asked, the prosecutors thought she would find it easier if they conducted a private deposition rather than confront her in front of the grand jurors. For her earlier grand jury appearances, the prosecutors had prepared a chart listing each of Lewinsky's sexual encounters with the president. On this day, Immergut handed the chart to her and said, "What I would like to do is go through the events that are written in bold, which deal with the private encounters you had with the president."

Immergut started with the first one, the thong-induced intimacies of November 15, 1995. Lewinsky recounted that in the president's study, "I know that we were talking a bit and kissing. I remember—I know that he—I believe I unbuttoned my jacket and he touched my, my breasts with my bra on, and then either—I don't remember if I unhooked my bra or he lifted my bra up, but he—this is embarrassing."

"Then he touched your breasts with his hands?" Immergut offered.

"Yes, he did."

"Did he touch your breast with his mouth?"

"Yes, he did."

"Did he touch your genital area at all that day?"

"Yes," Lewinsky said. "We moved—I believe he took a phone call in his office, and so we moved from the hallway into the back office, and the lights were off. And at that point, he, he put his hand down my pants and stimulated me manually in the genital area."

"And did he bring you to orgasm?"

"Yes, he did."

Immergut was just getting started. She asked, "Was there any discussion during the November seventeenth encounter about sex during the encounter?"

"I don't know exactly what you mean. . . ."

"Well, either about what he wanted or what you wanted, or anything like that, in terms of sex?" Immergut asked.

"No," said Lewinsky. "I mean, I think that there were always things being said, but not necessarily in a conversational form. Does that make sense?"

Both Lewinsky and Immergut were kind of struggling at this point. "Okay," the prosecutor resumed. "And when you say there were always things being said, do you mean kind of chatting while you were having sex, or things that felt good? I don't mean that. I mean—"

"Okay," Lewinsky said, trying to rescue the floundering prosecutor.

"—trying either implicitly giving you direction about what he wanted, or why he wouldn't ejaculate, anything like that?"

"I believe why he wouldn't ejaculate was discussed again," Lewinsky said.

As the prosecutor and witness continued their desultory march through the "encounters," certain themes emerged. Lewinsky was defensive about the brevity of the trysts. (She generally removed her underwear before going to the Oval Office, which moved things along.) About the third one, Immergut asked, "Do you know how long that sexual encounter . . . lasted . . . ?"

"Maybe ten minutes. Not, not very long. We would always spend quite a bit of time kissing. So."

"And kissing and talking and just . . . being affectionate?" Immergut interjected helpfully.

"Yes."

Lewinsky was also baffled by the president's insistence on not ejaculating. "The two excuses he always used were, one, that he didn't know me well enough or he didn't trust me yet," she said. "So that it sort of seemed to be some bizarre issue for him."

As this surreal proceeding continued, Immergut at times sounded more like a sex therapist than a prosecutor. "On that occasion," she said at one point, "you mentioned that he did not touch your genitals at all. Was there any discussion about that?"

"No," said Lewinsky.

And:

"At that point, sex was sort of the more dominant part of the relationship?"

"Yes."

"Rather than as it became—" Immergut continued.

"There was always a lot of joking going on between us," Lewinsky said. "And so we, you know, I mean, it was fun. . . . We were very compatible sexually. And I've always felt that he was sort of my sexual soul mate, and that I just felt very connected to him when it came to those kinds of things."

Always, though, Immergut returned to the sweaty minutiae. "And again, just with respect with bringing you to an orgasm, did he touch you directly on your skin on your genitals, or was it through underwear?"

"First it was through underwear, and then it was directly touching my genitals," said Lewinsky, who did display remarkable recall.

Immergut kept after Lewinsky for nearly two hours, and like any drama, this inquisition built, as it were, to a climax. On February 28, 1997, Clinton and Lewinsky had not been alone together in nearly eleven months, but after attending his Saturday radio address, she wangled an invitation to his study. There, she testified, "I was pestering him to kiss me." One thing led to another, and then, "I continued to perform oral sex and then he pushed me away, kind of as he always did before he came, and then I stood up and I said, you know, I really, I care about you so much; I really, I don't understand why you won't let me, you know, make you come; it's important to me; I mean, it just doesn't feel complete, it doesn't seem right.

"And so he—we hugged. And, you know, he said he didn't want to get addicted to me, and he didn't want me to get addicted to him. And we were just sort of looking at each other and then, you know, he sort of, he looked at me, he said, okay. And so then I finished."

"How did the meeting then end, or the encounter?" Immergut asked.

"We, well, we kissed after—"

"The ejaculation?" asked the prosecutor.

"Yes...."

There was really only one more important question.

"The dress that you were wearing on this occasion, is that the blue dress from the Gap?"

Monica Lewinsky's sigh was almost audible on the transcript. "Unfortunately, yes," she said.

Kenneth Starr's case for impeachment of the president was ready to go to Congress.

18

Winning by Losing

When it became clear that Henry J. Hyde, the chairman of the House Judiciary Committee, would be running the first presidential impeachment process in a generation, he received a rapturous greeting in the press. He was "a man of courtliness and character" (*Time*) who was "too intellectually honest to throw his weight around for partisan reasons" (*USA Today*). The praise was well deserved—and about ten years out of date. In 1998, Hyde remained a principled conservative, but he was also a tired and sick man who lacked the energy that statesmanship required. His challenge was to turn a rancorous political battle years in the making into a moment of dignity and honor for himself and for the House. Hyde's tragedy was that he saw how to do it, but he just didn't have it in him to lead the way.

Hyde was seventy-four in 1998, a congressman first elected in the face of the Democratic landslide of 1974, after eight years in the Illinois house. In his twenty years in the minority party in Congress, he was best known as an abortion opponent—the author of the Hyde Amendment, which barred government funding of abortions. He represented a solidly Republican suburban Chicago district, and he had, in the past, frequently reached out to Democrats on issues like adoption and gun control. In the early nineties, though, his wife died, and he endured a serious bout of prostate cancer, which left a painful and inconvenient legacy in his life. He didn't work as hard as he had formerly, and he had less patience, too. In every respect, as Hyde turned to face impeachment, his best years were behind him.

Late in the spring, Hyde turned to an old friend as his chief counsel, David Schippers, a Chicago defense lawyer and former prosecutor. He was a safe, familiar face for Hyde, but Schippers could not have been less suited for this kind of delicate political assignment. As news reports invariably noted, the sixty-eight-year-old Schippers was a Democrat, but the designation was misleading. Having grown up during Chicago's days as a one-party state, Schippers had a sort of genetic predisposition for the Democratic Party, but he was in fact a ferocious conservative. Schippers had almost no legal experience outside of the Chicago city limits and none at all in Washington. His staff consisted almost entirely of former prosecutors and investigators from Chicago, none of them terribly distinguished. In the best Chicago tradition, Schippers, the father of ten children, also hired one of his sons.

In the months leading up to the release of the Starr report, Hyde often said that any impeachment had both to be and to be perceived as bipartisan. Yet during these critical months, Hyde did nothing to reach out to John Conyers, Jr., the ranking Democrat on the committee, or any other Democrat. In part, Hyde was the victim of the independent counsel law. Because the law in effect gave Starr the exclusive right to initiate an impeachment proceeding, Hyde might have looked overaggressive if he had started any impeachment work on his own. Still, there was much Hyde could have done, such as ask Conyers to have their staffs work together on some issues or allocate the number of staff members in an equal way. But Hyde lacked the energy for this kind of forward thinking. The chairman basically drifted through the summer without a plan for what to do when Starr finally made his case. In the months before September, Schippers spent most of his time in Chicago.

The Republicans did accomplish one thing. In an obscure corner of Capitol Hill, Hyde directed the construction of what amounted to a small chapel dedicated to the contemplation of whether President Clinton should be impeached. In ordinary circumstances, only a hodgepodge of congressional staffers, and no actual members of the House of Representatives, worked in the Gerald R. Ford House Office Building. Until September, the newly renovated first-floor suite called H2-186 sat empty. There was a combination lock on the front door and a motion-detecting alarm system inside. There were two codes to disable the alarm—one for the majority Republicans on the Judiciary Committee and the other for the Democrats. This ecumenism also informed the interior design of the suite: flanking a little administrative area in the middle were separate offices for each party. Within these small rooms, the plan went, members of the Judiciary Committee would read and review the report on impeachment that Kenneth Starr was going to submit to them . . . someday.

/ / /

Like so much that happened in Starr's office, the content of his report to Congress was determined more by many small decisions than by a single conclusive step. The law offered almost no guidance to Starr about how to proceed. The independent counsel law said that the counsel "shall advise the House of Representatives of any substantial and credible information . . . that may constitute grounds for an impeachment." In the two decades that the law had been in effect, no independent counsel had ever found such information. In 1974, Leon Jaworski, the Watergate special prosecutor, had turned over some of his evidence to the Judiciary Committee, and he had done so in a dry and understated way, drawing no conclusions and making no arguments. That kind of report was one kind of report Starr could have written.

Starr rejected the Jaworski model. From the beginning, Starr had divided the report in a way true to his roots as an appellate court judge—in two parts, the facts (called the "Narrative") and the law (dubbed "Grounds for an Impeachment"). Separate teams of lawyers worked on each section for months, continually expanding the text as the investigators developed more evidence. Practically since the day he started examining Tripp's allegations, even when his evidence consisted only of the tales from Lewinsky's confidantes, Starr had believed Clinton had lied under oath about the sex. The new evidence, especially Clinton's and Lewinsky's testimony, simply reinforced his prior views. The authors of the report added new material as it came in, but they didn't remove the old stuff—and the size of the report kept increasing.

So did the staff's passion for the destruction of Bill Clinton. Instead of following the just-the-facts style of the Jaworski report, Starr directed the creation of a sustained attack on the president in which every inference about Clinton's behavior was drawn in the most negative possible way. In contrast to the custom at the Justice Department for "prosecution memos"—outlines of possible cases, which the Starr report roughly resembled—the independent counsel's staff excluded exculpatory information. In terms of the substance of the report, nearly every dispute about whether an embarrassing detail should be included was resolved in the affirmative. Not surprisingly, then, by far the most important piece of evidence, certainly the one relied on most heavily in the footnotes of the report, was the sexual autobiography that Lewinsky provided for Karin Immergut on August 26. There was almost a tug-of-war between the authors of the Narrative and those of the Grounds for an Impeachment to make more use of Immergut's work. Indeed, in the giddy rush to complete the report in the two weeks after that deposition, the Narrative and the Grounds started to resemble each other more and more.

This similarity meant that every sexual encounter between Clinton and Lewinsky was described in the Starr report at least twice—and some three or four times. Though Starr originally envisioned the Grounds as a sort of legal brief for impeachment, it wound up with even more sexually explicit detail than the Narrative. The Grounds was principally the work of Brett Kavanaugh, a lawyer from Kirkland & Ellis and a former Supreme Court law clerk, who was perhaps the most favored of Starr's young male protégés. In one amazing stretch of the Grounds, Kavanaugh cited Lewinsky's sex deposition in thirty-four consecutive footnotes, and he included some material that even the Narrative's authors judged too viciously unnecessary to mention. For example, after the description of the December 31, 1995, tryst, Kavanaugh's team dropped the following deadpan footnote: "After the sexual encounter, she saw the President masturbate in the bathroom near the sink." Such details had no conceivable relevance to Congress's duty, but were rather designed to humiliate Clinton. The men (and the principal authors were all men) who wrote the Starr report were so confident of the historical importance of such work that some of them had themselves photographed hunched over their word processors, just for posterity.

For his part, Starr was so afraid of being accused of collaborating with the House Republicans that the independent counsel did not give anyone in Congress notice of when, or even if, the report might arrive. Indeed, Hyde had the suite built in the Ford building solely on the basis of news leaks and guesswork. But the guesses were right, as the House sergeant at arms learned at 3:45 P.M. on Wednesday, September 9. At that moment, Jackie Bennett announced that the report and its supporting material were being placed in vans for delivery to the Ford building. There were two copies of everything—one for the Democrats, one for the Republicans. The report itself totaled 452 pages, with 1,660 footnotes and 18 boxes of supporting material—FBI interviews, grand jury testimony, and other evidence. In a cover letter, Starr wrote: "The contents of the referral may not be publicly disclosed unless and until authorized by the House of Representatives." In the roiling political environment of that moment, Starr's cryptic message amounted to an invitation to the House to make the report public.

Indeed, Newt Gingrich, the speaker of the House, had made certain that the report would be released almost immediately. He gave jurisdiction over the report first to the House Rules Committee, which the speaker controlled. On Thursday, September 10, the day after the report arrived on Capitol Hill, the committee voted to release the report before anyone had read it. Democrats made a brief fuss about allowing the president's lawyers some advance opportunity to examine the contents before it was released to the public—an idea that was voted down along party lines—but in the end, all the members of the president's party on Rules agreed to the immediate release. This was the beginning of a true disaster scenario for the president's allies—a looming bipartisanship, even civility, on the question of impeachment. The next day, September 11, the full House took up the question of releasing the Starr report.

On that Friday morning, it became apparent that Clinton's own influence on the impeachment process would be limited, if not nonexistent. As it happened, a national prayer breakfast was scheduled for the morning of September 11 at the White House, and Clinton always worked hard to prepare for it. On this day, he told his aides that he had stayed up until four o'clock in the morning writing what he was going to say. "I may not be quite as easy with my words today as I have been in years past," he told the hundred or so assembled clerics of many faiths assembled in the East Room. "I was up rather late last night thinking about and praying about what I ought to say today. And rather unusually for me, I actually tried to write it down. So if you will forgive me, I will do my best to say what it is I want to say to you, and I may have to take my glasses out to read my own writing.

"First, I want to say to all of you that, as you might imagine, I have been on quite a journey these last few weeks to get to the end of this, to the rock-bottom truth of where I am and where we all are. I agreed with those who have said that in my first statement after I testified, I was not contrite enough. I don't think there is a fancy way to say that I have sinned.

"It is important to me that everybody who has been hurt know the sorrow I feel is genuine: first, and most important, my family; also my friends; my staff; my cabinet; Monica Lewinsky and her family; and the American people. I have asked all for their forgiveness. But I believe that to be forgiven, more than sorrow is required, at least two more things.

"First, genuine repentance: a determination to change and to repair breaches of my own making. I have repented.

"Second, what my Bible calls a broken spirit: an understanding that I must have God's help to be the person that I want to be, a willingness to give the very forgiveness I seek, a renunciation of the pride and the anger which cloud judgment, lead people to excuse and compare, and to blame and complain. . . ."

Clinton's remarks—at once passionate, earnest, and humble—demonstrated a kind of eloquence rarely seen in American life. Yet their impact reflected how much he had squandered his gifts. When it came to the Clintons' personal life, who could believe anything he said? Eight months earlier, he had spoken with just as much conviction when he denied having sexual relations with "that woman." In the coming battle over his impeachment, he would turn out to be a discredited, even useless witness in his own behalf. His supporters on the Hill preferred him as a symbol—of prosecutorial excess—rather than as the flesh-and-blood real thing.

Ignoring the president's latest words of contrition, the members of the full House turned on that Friday morning to debate disclosure of the Starr report. The result was a bipartisan rout, a vote of 363 to 63 to release the report. In a little-noticed, but ultimately important, provision of the resolution, the House also voted to release all of Starr's underlying evidence by September 28, unless the Judiciary Committee voted to the contrary. The chief backer of opening all the files was John Dingell, the veteran Michigan Democrat, who had a special loathing for Clinton's behavior, if not for all of his policies. Only the Congressional Black Caucus, which accounted for twenty-nine of the sixty-three votes against the resolution, and a handful of other urban liberals stood with the president on release of the report. The House leadership, including Gephardt, voted for disclosure. Another senior Democrat, David Obey, a passionate liberal, turned to Gephardt amid the voting and said, "We have to get rid of this guy. He will destroy the Democratic Party for a generation, Dick. You and [Senate Democratic leader Tom] Daschle have to go tell him to get out."

Shortly after two o'clock in the afternoon, technicians in the House clerk's office threw a switch and posted the full text of the report on Congress's internal intranet. From there, moments later, it was copied on virtually all of the major news web sites—and devoured by a fascinated public. America Online said its thirteen million users spent a record 10.1 million hours logged on to AOL on that Friday. The single file containing the Starr report was downloaded 750,000 times during the first twenty-four hours. Congressional staffers remembered a strange stillness on Capitol Hill that Friday afternoon. The phones did not ring. People everywhere sat at their computers, reading. Many major newspapers printed the full 112,000-word text of the report the following day.

Amid all the excitement, Gephardt found time to summon Abbe Lowell, the Democrats' chief counsel to the Judiciary Committee, to his office for a brief conversation. From Obey, and from his own political instincts, Gephardt knew that he would have to make a fast decision. "Tom Daschle and I would like to meet with you on Sunday at one o'clock," Gephardt said. "And I know you're going to be under a lot of time pressure, but we'd like you to go through the evidence by then and tell us what you think. We'd like you to tell us whether you think the president has committed an impeachable offense. Because if he has, we'll have to go to the White House next week, and it will be our sad duty to say that he has to resign."

For most of the summer, as Lowell waited for Starr to complete his report, the defense lawyer had relatively little to do. At forty-six, the Bronx-born Lowell had spent most of his career in street fights with prosecutors on behalf of clients, often congressmen in ethical trouble. But he also had a scholarly bent—he'd worked on human rights issues for the United Nations—and so Lowell set out to learn everything he could about the history of impeachment. The subject had come up just rarely enough that this was a manageable assignment. Before Clinton, there had been a total of fifteen impeachment proceedings in Congress—of twelve judges, one cabinet member, one senator, and one president. The most recent had been in 1989, when the federal judges Walter L. Nixon, Jr., of Mississippi, and Alcee L. Hastings, of Florida, were impeached and then removed from office. Judge Nixon had been convicted of perjury, and Hastings lost his trial in the Senate even though he had been acquitted of bribery charges in a criminal trial. (Following his expulsion, Hastings won election to Congress, where he applied his novel form of expertise to the subject of Clinton's impeachment.)

In light of the modest number of precedents, impeachment was one of the few subjects in constitutional law where the answers to most questions were relatively clear. Lowell found most of these conclusions in the leading work on the history of impeachment, a report prepared by the staff of the House Judiciary Committee during the Nixon investigation, twenty-five years earlier. Among its authors had been a young lawyer named Hillary Rodham, who had joined the committee staff shortly after her graduation from Yale Law School. Like many liberal lawyers of her day, Rodham had helped engineer the legal system's takeover of the political world. Now she and her husband were living with the consequences.

The final wording of the provision for impeachment in the Constitution emerged from a brief debate among some of the greatest of the Framers, on September 8, 1787, in Philadelphia. The working draft of the document allowed Congress to remove the president only for bribery and for treason, but George Mason, fearing an unduly powerful chief executive, proposed that "maladministration" be added as another basis. His fellow Virginian James Madison objected, because "so vague a term will be equivalent to a tenure during pleasure of the Senate." Gouverneur Morris added a similar point, noting that "an election of every four years will prevent maladministration." As an alternative, Mason offered instead to add a phrase that had been used in English law as early as 1386—"high Crimes and Misdemeanors."

By the twentieth century, the word "misdemeanor" had come to suggest a minor or trivial offense, but the Framers had a different understanding. In eighteenth-century England, high misdemeanors referred to offenses against the state, as opposed to those against property or other people. In *Federalist no. 65,* Alexander Hamilton put forth the most famous explication of this view. Impeachable offenses, Hamilton wrote, "are of a nature which may with peculiar propriety be denominated POLITICAL, as they relate chiefly to injuries done immediately to the society itself." In 1974, the Judiciary Committee rejected an article that sought Richard Nixon's impeachment for cheating on his income taxes. Even among most Democrats, the consensus had been that this kind of offense was too personal—and insufficiently POLITICAL—to merit the sanction of impeachment.

For all its august beginnings, the early history of impeachment unfolded largely by negative example. In 1805, Justice Samuel Chase, a Federalist on the Supreme Court, was impeached on politically motivated charges of judicial bias raised by his Jeffersonian adversaries; he then narrowly avoided conviction in the Senate. The low point in impeachment history took place in 1868, when a bitter Reconstruction Era political battle nearly drove President Andrew Johnson from office. Radical Republicans, who controlled the House and despised Johnson, had passed, over his veto, a plainly unconstitutional restriction on the president's power to fire members of his cabinet. Johnson tested the law by firing his secretary of war, Edwin M. Stanton, and the House responded by voting to impeach the president. Johnson avoided conviction in the Senate by a single vote. The lesson of these failures was plain: the more that political imperatives, rather than actual high crimes, were seen to have driven the impeachment process, the more damning the judgment of history.

Still, as Lowell and everyone else who studied the subject came to recognize, it was impossible to conduct an impeachment in a kind of politics-free zone. For all that the labors of Congress would be guided by the text of the Constitution, there was also a rough-hewn truth in the most famous contemporary utterance on the subject. On April 15, 1970, then representative Gerald R. Ford took to the well of the House to speak in favor of the impeachment of Justice William O. Douglas, of the Supreme Court, on the ground of supposed financial conflicts of interest. "An impeachable offense," Ford said, "is whatever a majority of the House of Representatives considers it to be at a given moment in history." So, for better or worse, it was.

Still, in the hours leading up to the report to his superiors in the Capitol, Lowell did his best to judge the evidence against Clinton under the general standards set down over the previous two centuries. To do this, he spent those two days cloistered in the Democrat quarters of the impeachment suite in the Ford building. Like the rest of the world, Lowell could read the Starr report on the Internet or in the newspapers, but the lawyer wanted to examine the underlying evidence before reporting his conclusions. Working until the guards threw them out after midnight each day, Lowell and his colleagues started marking up the evidence with Post-it notes—yellow for primary evidence against the president, blue for prosecutorial misconduct, and pink for exculpatory evidence.

In this process, Lowell discovered early what the rest of the world would see when the evidence was released over the next several weeks. Through leaks to favored journalists like Schmidt at *The Washington Post,* Starr's team had oversold their case. The famous "talking points"—the supposed instructions from Lewinsky to Tripp about how to testify falsely—fizzled completely as an issue. Lewinsky said she wrote them without help, and in any event they called for truthful testimony. Lewinsky's job hunt was a far more complex undertaking than the Starr leakers had led anyone to believe; most important, Clinton and Vernon Jordan had started helping Monica well before she was subpoenaed in the Jones case. Similarly, there was no direct evidence that Clinton had asked Currie to retrieve his gifts from Monica. Clinton's lies, on the other hand, were real. In his deposition in the Paula Jones case in particular, Clinton had clearly given false testimony.

When Lowell made his report on Sunday morning, he didn't resort to any cute legalisms to describe the president's deposition. Surrounded by Gephardt, his staffers Elmendorf and Laura Nichols, the Democrats' spokesman on impeachment, Jim Jordan, and Bob Bauer, an aide to Daschle, Lowell ran down each of Starr's allegations against Clinton.

"Perjury in the deposition," Lowell began. "No question that he lied.

"Perjury in the grand jury," he said. "Closer call.

"The rest of it is not there," Lowell continued. "Vernon probably lied through his teeth about what he knew, but there's no way to prove otherwise. They can't make the case on obstruction of justice. There's no smoking gun."

As far as the false statements were concerned, Lowell asserted that they were clearly not impeachable offenses. "It was all about sex," he said. "It had no bearing on his public duties." Lowell was applying the standard that Hamilton had set down in *Federalist no. 65*. With his lies about whether he had been alone with Monica Lewinsky, Clinton had done no injury to "society itself."

Gephardt had no love for Clinton—he was not at all surprised to hear that the president had lied under oath—but the minority leader was relieved to hear Lowell's report. He did not want to have to call on a president of his own party, or of any party, to resign. Besides, Gephardt was a ferocious partisan himself—a true man of the House of Representatives, where Democrats and Republicans live in a state of constant, rattling warfare. So Gephardt had recoiled at the notion of driving a fellow Democrat out of office.

Like everyone else, though, Gephardt was not beyond a certain bewildered fascination with the evidence. Well into his sixth decade, Gephardt retained his boyish looks (and his first wife), and his staff regarded him as an almost comically straight arrow—still the milkman's dutiful son from St. Louis. Yet toward the end of the meeting, Gephardt couldn't contain his curiosity about one subject.

"Abbe," Gephardt asked, "is the cigar thing real?"

/ / /

In the first weekend after the release of the Starr report, the Clinton presidency teetered. Far more than when he was actually impeached by the House or tried by the Senate, this brief period was the closest the president came to being forced from office. During these frantic couple of days, James Carville happened to make a speech in northern Virginia, where he ran into James Moran, a moderate Democratic congressman from the area. Moran was furious at Clinton, and he all but asked Carville to pass along the message that the president should resign. A stampede for resignation from within the president's own party—the kind that finally drove Nixon to quit—seemed a real possibility. A disastrous appearance by David Kendall on the Sunday program *This Week* failed to halt the momentum against Clinton. Kendall's lawyerly insistence that his client had not committed perjury further inflamed even the president's defenders. Gephardt promptly denounced Kendall for resorting to "hairsplitting" and "legalisms," but in fact, even with his critical comments, the House minority leader was beginning the counterattack.

The point, Gephardt believed, was to shift the focus from the president to his accusers. That was the way for Clinton—and more important, the Democrats—to win. Gephardt believed he couldn't be seen as Clinton's lapdog; thus his criticism about Kendall's "hairsplitting." But when Lowell came to him the following week to complain about how the Republicans on the Judiciary Committee were treating the Democrats unfairly, Gephardt replied with the words that would define his party's strategy for the next six months.

"Abbe," Gephardt promised, "we're going to win by losing."

Gephardt believed that Democrats would win the impeachment battle by showing that the process was a partisan vendetta. By this reckoning, Democrats, the minority party in the House, could triumph in the wider public arena by being consistently outvoted, along party lines. Then, in theory, public opinion would drive the Republicans to retreat on impeachment. In this, Gephardt was taking a big chance. His adversaries could preempt this strategy at any moment, just by displaying a little flexibility. And if the Republicans wanted to try some political jujitsu, they quickly had their chance.

/ / /

The gentleman from South Carolina had a motion.

Along the upper tier of the great wooden rostrum that dominated Room 2141 of the Rayburn House Office Building, Representative Bob Inglis of South Carolina sat to the extreme right of Chairman Henry Hyde. On September 18, the Judiciary Committee convened for the first time in connection with the impeachment of President Clinton, but the seats before them were all empty. Hyde had called his committee in executive session to address the one issue left open by the overwhelming vote in the House of the previous week. How much of the supporting evidence that Starr had sent over to Capitol Hill should remain secret from the public?

The Democrats had planned carefully for this moment. Lowell and Julian Epstein, who was Conyers's chief aide, wanted to use this first hearing to test Gephardt's strategy of winning by losing. The majority and minority staffs had met well into the previous night and come to some consensus on the material to be deleted from the documents—home addresses and telephone numbers, certain national security matters, details relating to Secret Service protection. From Lowell's perspective, this era of good feelings was bad. He had to pick a fight—and lose.

Then, not long after the hearing began, Inglis asked to be recognized. Intelligent, articulate, and ferociously conservative, Inglis wore the contented smile of a rising star in his party. After two terms in the House, he was engaged in a close and spirited campaign for the Senate seat held for decades by the Democrat Ernest Hollings. Partisans on both sides looked to him as a bellwether of Republican thought.

As befit his self-confident manner, Inglis was the first Republican on the committee to make a motion about the evidence. As he began to speak, it became clear that he thought that Schippers and his colleagues had given away too much in their negotiations with

Lowell. The two sides had agreed to black out some of the most graphic sexual material, but Inglis thought that was wrong— about one sex act in particular. Instead of just redacting the material, Inglis thought that the committee should insert a message: "Reason for redaction," the Inglis message would read, "description of oral-anal sexual contact between the President and Monica Lewinsky."

The proposal evoked a kind of mute awe from Inglis's colleagues on the committee. The idea was so mad, so completely deranged—the notion that the House of Representatives needed this information to fulfill its constitutional duty on impeachment— that not even Inglis's Republican colleagues could summon the nerve to speak about it. (Lowell and Epstein had to flee the committee room in haste because they were laughing so hard.) Inglis himself muttered a few words on behalf of his proposal, asserting that disclosure of this detail would help evaluate Lewinsky's credibility. But the proposal itself was voted down by the full committee, twenty-nine to five.

Still, notwithstanding his defeat, Inglis had set the tone for the committee's deliberations. The Republicans would not give in on anything. By the day of this hearing, a week had passed since the disclosure of the Starr report, and a public backlash against the report was building. Starr had included so many gratuitous details about Clinton and Lewinsky's misadventures that the prosecutor had generated a certain degree of sympathy for the president. Characteristically, the Republicans missed these signals from the public. In an odd way, the president's accusers, like Clinton himself, were blinded by lust—in their case, for one man's downfall.

By the end of the first day of secret deliberations in the committee, the Judiciary panel had taken twelve roll-call votes, and virtually all of them were decided along party lines. More than anyone, Hyde understood how the Democrats were trying to win by losing, but he lacked the will to fight back. To be sure, there was a cynical core to Gephardt's strategy of provoking fights and then crying partisanship; it was the rough legislative equivalent of the man who murders his parents and seeks sympathy as an orphan. But the Democratic strategy illustrated a truth about the impeachment fight, too—that Clinton's opponents were indeed obsessed with his humiliation, with his ouster, and with his sex life.

/ / /

The tableau of the full Judiciary Committee in session resembled a caricature of the contemporary Republican and Democratic parties. The twenty-one Republicans included twenty white Christian males, plus Mary Bono, Sonny's newly elected widow. The sixteen Democrats included five African-Americans, six Jews, three women, and one openly gay man. This was no coincidence. Judiciary attracted the hard core of both parties, the kind of representatives who cared more about taking stands than bringing home pork. To a great degree, the members of the committee had safe seats—thirty of the thirty-seven members had been last elected with at least 60 percent of the vote—so they had little reason to fear retaliation at the polls for taking controversial stands.

It was ironic, then, that the single member of the committee who had the most important, if least publicized, role in the impeachment debate fit none of the stereotypes about the Judiciary Committee. With his starched white shirts, thick glasses, thinning hair, and formal manner, Rick Boucher was the one Democrat on the committee who looked like a Republican. He represented the poor and rural southwestern corner of Virginia, and his legislative concerns focused on economic issues dear to his constituents in Appalachia. In light of his legislative priorities, Boucher was not looking for this fight. Instead, in the best American tradition, this soft-spoken congressman came from, and largely returned to, obscurity—but not before emerging as one of the few admirable characters in the whole sordid drama.

Opposing impeachment did Boucher no particular good in his district, but he brought fervor to the cause. A Wall Street lawyer before he returned home to the small city of Abingdon, Boucher was offended by the lynch-mob atmosphere he sensed among the Republicans. Moreover, as a congressman since 1982, Boucher had watched the House descend into more or less permanent partisan rancor. Boucher determined to do whatever he could to stop the process, which was fortunate, because Gephardt had plans for him as well. From the beginning, the minority leader fixed on Boucher as the one Democrat on Judiciary who could reach out to his more moderate colleagues in the full House.

But before Boucher could do anything, the president had one

more important hurdle to pass. On September 21, thanks to the vote of the Judiciary Committee in executive session, the videotape of Clinton's grand jury testimony was released. As with each major development in the case, this one was preceded by predictions from pundits that it was finally—finally!—going to change public opinion about the president. And like all the others, the release of the tape prompted no meaningful change in the polls. No matter what question was asked, the polls stuck at where they had been since January—about 60 percent support for Clinton, 30 percent opposition, and 10 percent undecided. Though many questioned Kendall's agreement to the taping procedure, the release of the tape did prove he was right about one thing. Kendall had insisted that the camera remain fixed on Clinton, with no provision for pictures of the questioners or their reactions. This pitiless shot, unchanged over four hours, generated sympathy for Clinton, as viewers identified more with his discomfort at answering these questions than with his interrogators' struggle to get him to tell the truth.

The videotape of the president's grand jury testimony, much more than the transcript, demonstrated something else that seemed strangely unexpected after all this time. In a peculiar way, one could see that Clinton cared for Monica Lewinsky. He generally gave an embarrassed smile when he spoke of her, but there was, if not gallantry, a kind of affection as well. At one point during his testimony, he said that he recognized that Lewinsky would tell others about their affair. "Not because Monica Lewinsky is a bad person," he went on. "She's basically a good girl. She's a good young woman with a good heart and a good mind. I think she is burdened by some unfortunate conditions of her, her upbringing. But she's basically a good person." These were the words of a man who had listened to Monica complain about her parents, and Clinton's demeanor as he discussed his former girlfriend illustrated a seldom-noticed key to the president's enduring popularity, especially among women. It has often been observed that some philandering men love women, and some hate them. Perhaps Clinton behaved as he did out of loneliness, lust, or simple neediness, but he was not a misogynist. Many women sensed the peculiar form of Clinton's neuroses and they recognized, in other circumstances, his clear respect and admiration for women; thus many, as a consequence, tolerated his wayward ways.

/ / /

With the release of the president's grand jury testimony safely in the past, Boucher turned to the next big date on the impeachment calendar. On October 8, the House would vote on whether to authorize the Judiciary Committee to begin a full impeachment investigation. Could the Republicans maintain the bipartisan spirit that characterized the first, full House vote on impeachment? Or could Gephardt win by losing, and thus demonstrate that impeachment was a Republican plot to get the president?

Gephardt put Boucher in charge of crafting the Democratic position. Boucher realized that the country was tiring of the whole Lewinsky story, so he came up with the idea of placing a time limit on the impeachment inquiry. In the same spirit, Boucher sought to limit the scope of the investigation to Starr's referral to Congress—that is, to the Lewinsky allegations only. This restriction would keep the Republicans from turning the impeachment hearing into the meandering search for wrongdoing that Clinton's opponents in Congress had been conducting for years. On September 29, Boucher put his proposal to Gephardt, who approved it and then directed the Virginian to unify the Democrats on the Judiciary Committee around the proposal.

This wasn't easy. These Democrats were a fractious, opinionated bunch, and all of them wanted their fingerprints on a piece of American history. The hard-core liberals on the panel—including Zoe Lofgren and Maxine Waters of California, Bobby Scott of Virginia, Mel Watt of North Carolina, and Jerrold Nadler of New York—didn't like Boucher's idea at first. They wanted the committee to set down the standards for an impeachable offense, and only then to establish limits on the time and scope of hearings. Gradually, though, Boucher wore down his colleagues and convinced them of the political appeal of his proposal. On October 1, in a meeting in Gephardt's office, Boucher reported that the committee Democrats were united on the issues of time and scope.

But Boucher's work was only half done. Having persuaded the liberal Democrats that he wasn't being too tough on the president, he then had to convince the conservative Democrats that he wasn't being too easy on him. There wasn't much time, either, because Gephardt wanted the Democratic position announced at a press conference on Friday morning, October 2, at 10:30 A.M. So Boucher asked the "Blue Dogs"—the collection of the two dozen or so most conservative Democrats in the House—to meet with him at 8:30 A.M. that Friday. At half past ten, Boucher would meet the rest of his Judiciary colleagues and let them know if there was a unified Democratic position or not.

The Blue Dogs gathered in the office of their leader, Gary Condit, of California. At a meeting like this one, a Maxine Waters or Jerry Nadler would have been out of place, but Boucher spoke the moderates' language. Condit said he could live with a time limit on the impeachment hearings, but it had to be long enough for a reasonable examination of the evidence. "If it's only forty-five days, that sounds like a cover-up," Condit said. Boucher said around ninety days, or until the end of the year, would be fine. All of the congressmen present wanted to talk, and the time of the press conference was drawing near, but Boucher didn't want to break away.

At the "swamp," the triangle of grass on the Senate side of the Capitol where congressional press conferences took place all day long, the other Judiciary Democrats waited impatiently for Boucher. At last, Conyers started without him. At about ten forty-five, Boucher jogged up to the gaggle of his colleagues and gave them a satisfied nod. By the time it was Boucher's turn to speak, most of the reporters had lost interest, but he knew, as did just a handful of others, what he had accomplished.

/ / /

Every day at 7:30 A.M., Henry Hyde would meet his chief of staff, Thomas E. Mooney, at the Hyatt near Capitol Hill, eat breakfast, and mope. From the day the Starr report arrived, Hyde had hated everything about the process—not least what had happened to him. On September 16, the on-line magazine *Salon* had reported a story about an extramarital affair Hyde had had during the 1960s. He had made peace about the issue with his wife, who had died in 1992, but none of his children or grandchildren had known about it. Hyde recognized that the source of the story was probably the woman's cuckolded husband, but he blamed the White House for its scorched-earth method of dealing with adversaries. He was right to worry. Sidney Blumenthal had shifted the target of his "oppo" campaign from the Starr prosecutors to Clinton's pursuers in Congress. One day around this time, Blumenthal, who is from Chicago, told me his mother had recently been reminiscing about how Hyde used to bring his girlfriend to the Sherman Hotel.

Such an environment put Hyde in no mood to compromise. Hyde was in a political vise. As the reaction to the release of Clinton's grand jury videotape illustrated, there was little public support for impeachment. But Hyde's Republican colleagues on the Judiciary Committee desperately wanted to press forward. And overriding all other motivations was the belief that had sustained Clinton's enemies for years: Hyde believed that there were more shoes to drop. Starr had tantalized the Republicans on the committee with his pregnant warnings that his investigation was continuing. Whitewater, Travelgate, and Filegate remained within his jurisdiction, as did the separate inquiry about whether Clinton had lied about his encounter with Kathleen Willey. The supposed campaign finance scandal, with its vague intimations of a connection to Communist China, beckoned Hyde as well. In light of all this, what really worried the chairman about Boucher's proposal was the limitation on the scope of the hearings to Lewinsky alone.

But Boucher had put Hyde on the defensive, as became apparent when the chairman appeared on *Meet the Press* on Sunday, October 4. Hyde rejected the Boucher plan's limitations on time and scope of the hearings, but the chairman wanted to show that he was being reasonable, too. So Hyde volunteered, "I have a New Year's resolution and that is we finish by New Year's. Now, you know how New Year's resolutions sometimes get broken, but it's my hope and prayer that we could finish by New Year's." Democrats rejoiced. By limiting his schedule to the end of the year, with the November election intervening, Hyde had essentially admitted that he would not have time to call any witnesses about Clinton's behavior. (If Hyde started calling fact witnesses like Lewinsky and Vernon Jordan, Democrats would have had the right to call their own witnesses, and that would have taken the hearings well into 1999.) Hyde's New Year's resolution meant that he would be relying exclusively on the evidence collected by Starr. Whether

Hyde liked it or not, he was now the unpopular Starr's permanent teammate.

On Tuesday, October 6, Hyde had one last chance to thwart the Democrats' strategy. At a committee hearing to determine the measure that would be sent to the House floor, Howard Berman, an unpredictable liberal from California, surprised everyone with a proposal that seemed to split the difference between Boucher's limited approach and Hyde's open-ended mandate. Berman proposed that the committee simply assume that the allegations in the Starr report were true and then move to a determination whether such conduct by the president amounted to an impeachable offense. It was simple and straightforward, and Barney Frank, the Massachusetts iconoclast who was the best tactician on the committee, saw that the Republicans might embrace it. This possibility of an outbreak of civility worried Frank, because he believed in Gephardt's winning-by-losing strategy.

Frank sat near Berman in the hearing room, and he leaned over and whispered to Berman that he knew just how to kill his proposal—by endorsing it wholeheartedly. Frank knew that many Republicans on the committee were simply against anything he was for, on principle. Frank's gambit worked, and Berman's idea was voted down on a party-line vote. So was Boucher's proposal. And Hyde's open-ended, no-formal-deadline approach was passed by committee, also by a straight party-line vote, twenty-one to sixteen.

The Boucher and Hyde proposals, both slightly modified, came to the floor on October 8, the first time that the full House had considered impeachment since September 11, when Clinton was thrashed in the vote to release the Starr report. This time, though, the atmosphere was different. Buoyed by polls that suggested continued support for the president, nearly all the Democrats had come home. That didn't stop a last-minute bout of panic from hitting the White House—when James Carville bellowed at Rahm Emanuel that the Republicans were going to undercut Gephardt's strategy and agree to Boucher's proposal. The contagion of worry even spread to Abbe Lowell, who burst in on Gephardt to ask, "What if they accept the deal? What if the Republicans call our bluff and agree with our proposal?"

But Gephardt, at this point a veteran of the Gingrich Republicans' kamikaze style, promised that the GOP would stand unified behind Hyde's proposal, even if it meant being branded as a partisan lynch mob. "They can't help themselves," Gephardt said. "They will never do it. They will be against it because we are for it."

Gephardt was right. Hyde's plan passed by a vote of 258 to 176, with all of the Republicans in the House and just thirty-one Democrats voting with the majority. At the end of the day, Rick Boucher's proposal came to the floor and the gentleman from Virginia rose with a request for Newt Gingrich. "Mr. Speaker," he said, "on that I demand the yeas and nays."

The tabulations found 236 against and 198 for the plan that limited the impeachment hearings to the Lewinsky allegations and called for their conclusion by the end of the year. The vote had run almost entirely along party lines. No loser ever left the House floor more content than Rick Boucher did on that day. And like the rest of his colleagues, he fled the Capitol following the vote and returned home to campaign.

19

Mr. Genitalia and the Perjury Ladies

On Wednesday, November 4, the day after the elections, Henry Hyde summoned his aide Tom Mooney to the place they always went when they wanted secrecy: a conference room at the O'Hare Hilton, just outside Hyde's district in Illinois. The chairman's mood had evolved from misery to despair. The elections of the previous day had been an epic disaster for the Republicans. In the sixth year of a two-term presidency, the party controlling the White House had traditionally lost many, sometimes dozens, of seats in Congress. With the Lewinsky scandal roiling, Democrats had feared losses of that magnitude. (Vice President Al Gore told Mark Penn, the president's pollster, that he thought the Democrats would lose between thirty and forty seats.) Though many polls tightened in the final days, almost no political observer predicted the scale of the Democratic comeback. The Senate stood unchanged, at fifty-five Republicans and forty-five Democrats. Republicans actually lost five seats in the House, and their advantage there was shaved to a bare 223 to 212.

Every election was subject to varying interpretations, but Hyde joined in the consensus that the voters were expressing their displeasure with the Republicans' obsession with the scandal. Gingrich's last-minute decision to spend $10 million of party money on advertisements that attacked Clinton had flopped. If there was any good news for Hyde, who loathed Gingrich, it was that the election would clearly cost the speaker his job. (By the end of the week, Gingrich announced plans to resign.)

But the question of impeachment remained. What should Hyde and his committee do now? Late on that Wednesday afternoon, Hyde and Mooney convened a gloomy conference call with the other twenty Republicans on Judiciary. Jim Rogan, who had expected an easy coast to reelection, was still waiting for the last votes to be counted, to make sure that he had won. Bob Inglis had lost his Senate race in South Carolina. Their experiences provided vivid examples of the political cost of association with their cause. Hyde said that he wanted to discuss two issues. First, he said he was completing work on written questions for Clinton to answer. The president had refused invitations to testify before the committee, but Hyde thought that he could at least put Clinton on the spot by forcing him to address some of the embarrassing questions raised by his conduct.

Second, the chairman said, he believed they ought to call Kenneth Starr as a witness. Previously, it had been mostly Democrats who were agitating to hear from Starr. They said they wanted to confront him about the alleged improprieties in his investigation, but basically the Democrats had wanted Starr as an exhibit—a physical embodiment of the most unpopular man in American politics. But Hyde now saw Starr as a final opportunity to see if there really was something more to the scandals than Lewinsky. If anyone knew of the elusive other shoe, it was Starr—so they ought to hear what he had to say.

Hyde's colleagues didn't agree or disagree as much as listen in grumpy silence. The chairman sensed their dismay, so he offered words of gentle encouragement. "What can we do?" he asked. "Can we sweep it under the rug?" No, he answered for them, they had a duty to continue, regardless of the political consequences. Later, Hyde would joke privately that he gave this speech twice a week to his fellow Republicans on Judiciary. In a strange way, Hyde was invigorated by the futility. Like Clinton, he reveled in self-pity. Indeed, the less popular he and his inquiries became, the more he was persuaded that he was on the right course. The chairman promised he was leading his troops to certain failure, to public ridicule, to political calamity even greater than the one they had just endured.

Onward!

/ / /

"Point of order, Mr. Chairman," said Mel Watt, an imperious Democrat from North Carolina.

"I don't yield for any points of order," Henry Hyde responded. "I would like to make my statement."

It was November 19, the day that Starr was going to testify, and the Judiciary Democrats were observing their custom of opening each hearing with a little procedural torture for the chairman. Watt was protesting the amount of time that Hyde had allotted David Kendall to question Starr. "Now," Hyde continued, "you are disrupting the continuity of this meeting with these adversarial motions."

"We are disrupting a railroad, it seems like, Mr. Chairman," Watt shot back.

Everyone was on edge, because Starr was the one person who could, in theory, transform the impeachment debate. The Democrats were particularly worried. In the typical congressional manner, they had demanded that he appear—and then panicked when it became clear that he would. For days, the Democratic members had badgered their counsel, Abbe Lowell. "What should we ask him? What should we do?"

Starr also recognized the stakes, both for his investigation and for his own reputation. He had prepared for his appearance as he used to rehearse for Supreme Court arguments, with staff members peppering him with questions. As a former solicitor general, Starr was well suited for this kind of interrogation, and he wore a confident smile when he sat down at the witness table, with his diminutive wife behind one shoulder and the stolid Bob Bittman behind the other.

"Thank you, Mr. Chairman," Starr began. "I welcome the opportunity to be before the committee."

"Would you pull the mike up?" Hyde interrupted.

"I was just told to push my mike away," Starr replied.

"By a Democrat, I am sure," Hyde said, drawing a laugh.

"The person did not identify his affiliation in saying that," Starr answered, displaying, in contrast, his leaden wit.

The previous night, the OIC had given the prepared text of Starr's two-hour presentation to members of the Judiciary Committee, so there were no surprises. His remarks basically recapitulated the highlights of the Starr report. Following the lunch break, the Democrats had their chance to have at Starr for the first time. Abbe Lowell took the first shot, and he employed the clipped, contemptuous tone of a veteran cross-examiner. "Mr. Starr, isn't it true that . . ."; "Mr. Starr, you have to agree, I take it . . ."; "Mr. Starr . . . the key word in your title 'Independent Counsel' is 'independent'? . . . Part of being 'independent,' I think you would agree with me, is being free of conflicts of interest that might bias your investigation, correct?"

The consistent theme of the Democratic critique, articulated first by Lowell and then by the committee members themselves, was that Starr himself had broken laws—that he and his staff had violated Lewinsky's rights in the Ritz-Carlton, had illegally leaked information to the press, had conflicts of interest in the Jones case. Starr handled these accusations with aplomb. Ironically, with respect to Starr, the Democrats fell into the same trap as the Republicans did throughout the Clinton years. The problem with Starr was not that he was a lawbreaker, as the questioners consistently tried to imply, but rather that he lacked judgment and reason when it came to this case. Neither Starr nor Clinton was a criminal. The errors of both Starr and his critics illustrated the perils of a world where the legal system had taken over the political system. It was never enough to prove that your adversaries were mistaken; you had to prove that they were evil as well.

On most of the issues that Starr addressed, the prosecutor also had the advantage of being right. When Lowell pressed him about the alleged mistreatment of Lewinsky on January 16, Starr calmly and appropriately rejected the charge. "We did, in fact, use a traditional technique that law enforcement always uses," he said in his fussy diction. "We made it clear to the witness that she was, in fact, free to leave. The Ritz-Carlton, shall I say, is a fairly comfortable and commodious place. We will show you . . . telephone records that indicated she reached out to Mr. Carter, her attorney. . . .

She called her mother. She went for a walk. . . . We conducted ourselves professionally." And so, Democratic accusations notwithstanding, they had.

/ / /

As usual, though, Barney Frank was operating a few steps ahead of everyone else. Listening to Starr's opening presentation, Frank noticed that, in passing, the prosecutor had conceded that he had found no evidence of impeachable offenses in the Travelgate and Filegate areas within his jurisdiction. This admission dashed the Republicans' central hope in summoning Starr—that he had some new bombshell to drop. But Frank, characteristically, was thinking of a further implication of this disclosure by Starr. Frank noted that Starr had said he sent the information about impeachable offenses to Congress "as soon as it became clear." But when, the congressman asked, had he decided that there was no information incriminating to the president in Travelgate?

"Some months ago," Starr conceded.

"Let me just say, here is what disturbs me greatly," Frank replied. Starr had filed his report about Lewinsky before the election, but his office had actually been studying the Filegate and Travelgate affairs for much longer than they had been scrutinizing Lewinsky, "yet now, several weeks after the election, is the first time you are saying that.

"Why did you withhold that before the election when you were sending us a referral with a lot of negative stuff about the President and only now . . . you give us this exoneration of the president several weeks after the election?"

Starr mumbled a meager answer that began, "Well, again, there is a process question"—but it was more than a process question. Starr and his team had worked to exhaustion to get their Lewinsky allegations in front of Congress and the public at the most politically perilous moment for Clinton's party. But they felt no rush to reveal their exoneration of the Clintons on Filegate and Travelgate. Again, there was nothing illegal about Starr's priorities, but they did reveal a great deal about the "process" that was under way in his suite on Pennsylvania Avenue.

The questioning from that moment forward consisted mostly of alternating harangues and homages, depending on the party of the interrogator. The back-and-forth took so long that it wasn't until eight-thirty in the evening that the most important confrontation of the day took place, between Starr and David Kendall, who began by saying, with characteristic bombast, "My task is to respond to the two hours of uninterrupted testimony from the independent counsel, as well as to his four-year, $45 million investigation, which has included at least twenty-eight attorneys, seventy-eight FBI agents, and an undisclosed number of private investigators, an investigation which has generated by computer count 114,532 news stories in print, and 2,513 minutes of network television time, not to mention twenty-four-hour scandal coverage on cable, a 445-page referral, 50,000 pages of documents from secret grand jury testimony, four hours of videotape testimony, twenty-two hours of audiotape, some of which was gathered in violation of state law, and the testimony of scores of witnesses, not one of whom has been cross-examined.

"And I have thirty minutes to do this."

After this introduction, Kendall began simply. He called Starr's attention to a press release that the OIC had issued in February regarding the immunity negotiations with Lewinsky. "We cannot responsibly determine whether she is telling the truth without speaking directly to her," Starr had said. "We have found that there is no substitute for looking a witness in the eye, asking detailed questions, matching answers against verifiable facts," and so on.

Clinton's lawyer then noted that during Starr's testimony before the committee, he had been asked many questions about the credibility of witnesses, including Lewinsky. "It is true," Kendall then asked Starr, "that you were not present when Ms. Lewinsky testified before the grand jury?"

"That is true," Starr replied.

"And you were not present at her deposition?"

"I was not present."

Then Kendall went through all of the interviews that Starr had not seen firsthand, including all of them with Lewinsky (whom Starr never met), as well as the interrogations of Betty Currie, Vernon Jordan, and literally hundreds of other people questioned by the OIC.

Kendall's point was clear—and devastating. Starr was the only witness to testify about the facts of the allegations against the president. Yet Starr had neither seen the events in question nor interviewed anyone who had. In other words, the Judiciary Committee was considering the impeachment of the president of the United States based on, at best, a thirdhand recitation of the evidence against him. Even by the low standards of congressional hearings, it was a remarkably shabby practice.

Having made this elegant point, however, Kendall promptly turned to the same kind of name-calling as the rest of the Democrats. "Mr. Starr," Kendall intoned at one point, "in fact there has been no case remotely similar to this in terms of the massive leaking from the prosecutor's office. I think we know that." This kind of speechifying by Kendall allowed Starr to offer some righteous indignation of his own. "I totally disagree with that," Starr said, and the examination descended into a decorous spat.

Kendall even left an opening for Hyde to make a telling joke at his expense. Shortly after nine at night, with everyone in the room growing punchy, Hyde announced, "Mr. Kendall, your time is up. You may want to get into the facts. Do you need additional time?"

As the chairman pointed out, Kendall had not asked Starr a single question about Clinton's conduct, preferring to belabor Starr about his. It was probably a wise strategic choice on Kendall's part, but it also opened a revealing window on the legal case for the president. By implication, Kendall's priorities suggested that even Clinton's own lawyers found his conduct indefensible—not impeachable, to be sure, but repugnant in every other way. In any event, Kendall devoted the remaining minutes that Hyde granted him to hectoring Starr about the treatment of Lewinsky at the Ritz-Carlton.

With the clock passing ten, Schippers finally took over, and he brought his mannered, regular-guy persona to Starr's defense—and to Hyde's. Unfortunately, Schippers also brought a nearly total ignorance of constitutional law. For example, stung by Kendall's criticism of the process in the Judiciary Committee, Schippers pointed out that "the sole power to try an impeachment resides in the Senate."

"That is true," said Starr.

"So if this House were to permit cross-examination and to hold a mini-trial here, they would be usurping the constitutional duties of the United States Senate, isn't that correct?"

Much as Starr welcomed Schippers's softballs, the former judge knew too much about the Constitution to embrace this absurd idea. "Well," Starr stuttered, "I am not sure I would necessarily agree with that"—and then the Democrats began groaning at the absurdity of Schippers's idea that the House had no right to call witnesses. Except for this impeachment, that was how it was always done.

"I hear the moaning of the left," Schippers snarled, then moved on to his remaining questions. He had planned his peroration carefully. "Judge," Schippers wound up, "you have been pilloried and attacked from all sides, is that correct?"

"I would hope not all sides, but yes, that's—"

"How long have you been an attorney, Judge Starr?"

"Twenty-five years."

"Well, I have been an attorney for almost forty years, and I want to say I am proud to be in the same room with you and your staff."

With that, to close the day's events, Schippers led a Republicans-only standing ovation for the independent counsel.

Starr had borne up with dignity during his nearly twelve hours of testimony, but he wasn't allowed even a day's grace to savor the accomplishment. The following morning, November 20, Starr's "ethics adviser," Samuel Dash, resigned from the OIC in protest. A law professor at Georgetown and a former aide to the Senate Watergate committee, Dash charged that Starr had impermissibly become an "advocate" for impeachment during his testimony before the Judiciary Committee. In truth, Starr's remarks differed only in degree, not in kind, from his report to Congress two months earlier. The only thing that had changed in the interim was that Starr's popularity had continued to plummet. A prodigious egomaniac even by Washington standards, Dash no longer found it useful to be associated with the office that had paid him $400 per hour in taxpayer money for his advice on lawyerly virtue. Dash's eleventh-hour abandonment said more about his own character than Starr's ethics, but the White House savored the news, just the same.

/ / /

Hyde thought Starr had been a superb witness, even though he had not delivered any bombshells to change the political dynamic surrounding the impeachment. (Indeed, the only "news" in Starr's appearance had been his revelation that the Clintons had been cleared on Travelgate and Filegate.) Still, the chairman was frustrated by what he regarded as hostile press coverage of Starr's appearance. He wanted the Republican members of the House to know that the independent counsel had made a powerful case for Clinton's impeachment. Fortunately, to Hyde's thinking, there was a volunteer to spread the news among the Republican faithful.

Tom DeLay agreed to keep everyone posted. In the months that followed the House vote on impeachment, several myths flourished about the role of the former exterminator who went on to become the third-ranking Republican in Congress. It was said that DeLay, the majority whip, browbeat fellow Republicans into voting yes, that he threatened to take away their subcommittee chairmanships, that he promised conservative primary challengers to any moderates planning to vote the other way. With everything from his slicked-back hair to his well-cultivated air of menace, DeLay practically encouraged the legends about his own ferocity. But in truth, DeLay did less than many people thought. At a time when Gingrich had surrendered and his designated successor, Robert Livingston, had refused to play a public role in the impeachment controversy, DeLay made sure the process continued. He vowed that the House leadership would deliver a prompt vote on any articles of impeachment—and, most important, he promised that no vote on censure would be allowed. By depriving fence-sitters of the appealing middle ground of censure, DeLay forced his fellow Republicans to make a straight up-or-down vote on the president's conduct.

DeLay's role began after Starr's testimony. He ordered his whip organization to put out summaries of Starr's main arguments, and from that point forward DeLay kept his deputies churning out anti-Clinton material to the members. In an atmosphere in which many members often feel neglected by their leadership, De-Lay's attentions were much appreciated by the rank and file. After November 27, when Clinton gave heavily lawyered answers to the eighty-one questions Hyde had submitted to him, DeLay helped spread the official Republican line of indignation.

DeLay's priorities were noted by his nominal superiors as well. During the week after Starr's testimony, Gephardt went to Livingston's office for a private one-on-one meeting with the speaker-designee about impeachment. Earlier, just after the election, Livingston had suggested to Gephardt that he might be amenable to allowing a vote on censure in the House. But by later in the month, Livingston had a different message for the Democratic leader. Now he wasn't going to allow an alternative to impeachment to reach the floor. DeLay's view had become Livingston's.

Notwithstanding the backstage machinations, though, Hyde was still left with the problem of what to do with the rest of the hearings. In this he was guided by one of his most energetic and determined fellow Republicans, Bill McCollum, of Florida, the third-ranking member of the panel. McCollum had represented an Orlando district for nearly two decades, but he retained a boyish enthusiasm for his work. Actually, McCollum was mesmerized by one part of the case in particular, and it earned him a secret nickname among Republican staff members: "Mr. Genitalia." McCollum dwelled obsessively on the fact that Clinton had lied about where and how he placed his hands on Monica Lewinsky's body. McCollum did have a point. Lewinsky had testified that the president had touched her breasts and vagina, and Clinton had denied it, or at least denied that he had employed his hands and lips "with intent to arouse" her. McCollum had carefully placed tabs on the sections of Lewinsky's sex deposition where she had described how Clinton had stimulated her. "If he fondled her breast or messed around with her in the other way, it's perjury," he told visitors to his office.

The issue actually made a useful proxy for the whole impeachment debate. On the one hand, the president's position that his gropings with Lewinsky amounted to a sexual one-way street was fairly absurd on its face. But on the other, one could scarcely imagine less significant falsehoods than those concerning the mechanics of the Clinton-Lewinsky frolics. The question came down to how seriously to take the issue of "lying about sex," as Clinton's perfidy was often described. McCollum and his allies asserted that lies on this subject, as much as any other, amounted to high crimes and misdemeanors; the public—with the history and meaning of the Constitution on its side—was never convinced.

The obsession of McCollum and others with pumping up outrage over this kind of misdeed led to the unintentional comic high point of the impeachment hearings. On December 1, Hyde convened a hearing on what he called, rather grandly, "the consequences of perjury and related crimes." Hyde and his staff located the two witnesses around whom the day's testimony would resolve—"the perjury ladies," as some would come to call them.

After his sonorous introduction, Hyde turned the questioning over to McCollum, who promptly demonstrated why many congressmen leave this sort of thing to the staff.

"Ms. Parsons," McCollum intoned, addressing the younger of the two women at the witness table before him, "am I correct that you were basketball coach at the University of South Carolina when the occasion of this perjury that you were convicted of arose? Am I right about that?"

"No," the witness corrected gently. "I had resigned."

"You had resigned, but you had been previously."

"I had been previously," Pam Parsons agreed.

"Am I correct that the subject of your perjury was consensual sex?"

"No," she said. Wrong again.

"What was the subject of the perjury, then?" the ill-prepared McCollum went on. "Please clarify that."

"Well, it is really kind of funny," the languid and somewhat spacey Parsons answered. "There is a gay bar called Puss in Boots in Salt Lake City, Utah. It wasn't easy to say. I have been there. That occurrence was two years after, then, the things that I was suing *Sports Illustrated* for. It wasn't a pretty picture for me. I thought I had many reasons for why I could say no, but it was an out-and-out lie. I had been there."

At this moment, there was scarcely a person in the packed hearing room who had any idea what Parsons was talking about. Puss in Boots? *Sports Illustrated*? Who was this woman, and what did she have to do with the impeachment of the president?

To McCollum, apparently, she was both an expert witness and an exhibit on the wages of perjury. "You were in a position at one time of leadership."

"Absolutely," Parsons said. "I was also an athletic director."

"There you go," McCollum encouraged. "The president of the United States is the top leader in this country. What kind of message do you think it sends if we conclude that he committed perjury and do not impeach him and he gets away scot-free . . . ?"

"Please let me give this answer. I am ready," Parsons said dreamily, "Mixed message. We cannot raise our young people with mixed messages. There are no secrets, but the discretion of when to tell them things is what maturity is about. But secrecy doesn't cut it when we are raising young children."

Bewildered as everyone else by this answer, McCollum turned to the next witness, an older, demurely attired woman with a more earthbound manner. "Dr. Battalino, what is your thought about the double standard we might be creating if we conclude the president committed perjury and we don't impeach him, with respect to people such as yourself are convicted and sent to jail or put in house arrest for perjury regarding consensual sex? Is this fair?"

Barbara Battalino understood her role better than Parsons, and she gave the answer McCollum wanted. "I believe that we as a people, as a country, must not give the impression . . . that we are indeed a country that does not take seriously the rule of law and liberty and justice for all."

Few could quarrel with this admirable sentiment, but neither McCollum nor anyone else explained who these women were or why they were testifying. From 1977 to 1982, Pam Parsons had been a successful women's basketball coach at the University of South Carolina, but then *Sports Illustrated* ran a story that described her as a predatory lesbian who had "sex in mind" when she recruited players. Parsons sued the magazine for libel. During that civil case, she lied about many different subjects, including her familiarity with the establishment known as Puss in Boots. After her civil case was thrown out, the judge demanded that she be criminally investigated for her false statements. In the end, she pleaded guilty to perjury and was sentenced to four months in prison and five years of probation, which she completed in 1990.

Battalino's tale was even more peculiar. A patient had sued Battalino for malpractice based on her work as a psychiatrist at a Veterans Administration hospital in Idaho. The suit was dismissed, but then Battalino, who was a lawyer as well as a doctor, went to court to force the government to pay her legal fees. In the course of that proceeding, she was asked in a deposition whether she had ever had sex with the patient in question. She said no—a lie. (She had performed oral sex on him at the hospital.) She pleaded guilty to obstruction of justice and was sentenced to six months of home detention. She also lost her medical and law licenses.

As was apparent to almost any reasonable viewer, these women's sad stories bore little relevance to whether Bill Clinton should be impeached. For one thing, both women initiated the legal proceedings in which they lied—Parsons with her libel suit and Battalino with her fee application. The legal system looks especially askance at those who drag others into court on false pretenses. Moreover, Battalino's act of sex with a patient was misconduct in and of itself. Most important, though, the legal decision to bring a criminal charge differed fundamentally from the political choice to impeach an elected president. Regardless of Congress's decision on impeachment, Clinton could still have been prosecuted. The crude parallelism of McCollum's argument—these women didn't get away with it so neither should Clinton—was simply wrong. For the perjury ladies, the question was never whether they had committed high crimes and misdemeanors; for Bill Clinton, that was all it was.

This daylong perjury debacle was just one symptom of the disarray in Hyde's investigation. As the chairman knew better than most, the public had no interest in an impeachment based on the Lewinsky allegations. Thanks to Starr's testimony, Travelgate and Filegate had flamed out as possible grounds for impeachment. So, prodded by Schippers, Hyde announced plans to open an investigation on yet another front—the alleged campaign finance scandal. In the midst of the perjury hearing, Hyde confirmed that the committee would subpoena records from the Justice Department about its inquiry into the matter. "We are trying to find some things and we have good reason to believe they may be there," he said, adding that the committee was "duty-bound to explore" the campaign finance issues.

This exploration took less than forty-eight hours. Hyde quickly recognized that in the less than a month remaining before his stated finish line for the investigation, he couldn't accomplish more than his Republican congressional colleagues had in months of hearings about campaign finance. Schippers continued to mosey around other corners of the investigation—interviewing Kathleen Willey, trying to question Juanita Broaddrick—but Hyde, at least, confronted the fact that Lewinsky was all he had. In the end, Hyde resorted to a crude desperation to invest that sorry little tale with a significance it did not possess.

"Have you been to Auschwitz?" the chairman suddenly asked during the session with the perjury ladies. "Do you see what happens when the rule of law doesn't prevail?"

/ / /

After midnight on the day of Starr's testimony before the Judiciary Committee, Abbe Lowell, the Democrats' counsel, had gone for a late supper in Georgetown with three of the younger Republicans on the panel, Steve Buyer, Mary Bono, and Lindsey Graham. Over their beers, Lowell and Graham discussed the outline of a possible deal to avoid impeachment.

With his down-home demeanor and easygoing style, Graham came to enjoy a reputation as a sort of moderate on the committee. This wasn't really deserved. As a first-term representative from South Carolina, Graham had helped lead the first, abortive coup against Gingrich—the one based on the speaker's alleged undue moderation. In 1997, Graham had joined about a dozen extremists like Bob Barr in calling for impeachment hearings against Clinton even before the Lewinsky allegations arose. Still, Graham liked being the center of attention as much as he cared about ideological purity, so he told Lowell about an idea he had.

"If the president would only admit this," Graham told Lowell, "we could do this deal."

Thus was born, in theory at least, the last hope for Clinton to avoid impeachment. In the days leading to the committee vote, Graham and a handful of others floated the idea that if Clinton would only come clean, they would agree to some lesser punishment than impeachment—a censure, perhaps. Graham said he wanted Clinton to admit to "lying" and "perjury," which the president would never do, for good reason. For one thing, it was far from clear that his conduct did fit the technical meaning of perjury; for another, with Starr able to indict Clinton at any moment, it was madness to expect the president to admit to a crime. In fact, the whole Graham proposal resembled a sucker's game for Clinton—a floating standard of contrition that invariably found his remorse inadequate.

Certainly, as a constitutional matter, Graham's idea was laughable. The president's behavior either amounted to high crimes and misdemeanors or it didn't, and his subsequent statements should not have made any difference. But in the week leading up to the committee vote, Clinton's backers were willing to try anything, and the idea did succeed in getting Graham attention from White House aides—and even more interest from CNN and MSNBC.

For his part, Clinton had largely surrendered to his increasingly inevitable fate. On December 8, after a charity dinner in Washington, he met in the hotel basement with Peter King, the conservative Republican congressman from New York who had committed himself to fighting impeachment. King told the president that the combination of DeLay and Clinton's answers to the eighty-one questions had made it hard for Republicans to vote no. Clinton defended his answers, saying they were "true and misleading, but not true and complete."

"With all respect, Mr. President," the gruff King said, "I know you believe this, but most members of Congress think it's bullshit."

Clinton grew emotional. "Don't people in Congress realize what I have gone through the last three months?" he said. "Do they think it's been a walk in the park? I'm not just trying to save my ass. Just because I come to work every day doesn't mean this isn't tearing me apart. I have to act this way because I am the president."

Then Clinton allowed himself to speculate about his own trial in the Senate. "Bob Byrd has been waiting for this all his life," the president said bitterly, referring to the long-tenured senator from West Virginia. "He can give long speeches about the Constitution and impeachment. I can just see him walking around the Senate. He'll love it."

/ / /

The negotiations over Clinton's statement actually stretched right up to the time the committee voted. The debate in the committee's Rayburn building chamber had begun on December 10, but it wasn't until four o'clock on the following afternoon, just minutes before the actual vote, that a grim-faced Clinton left the Oval Office and walked the few steps to the White House Rose Garden to read his text.

Many on the committee took a break to listen to Clinton. It was a tense moment in the Republican staff office, as several representatives gathered around the television. As they listened to the five-minute presidential statement, Graham was seated directly in front of the screen—waiting to pass judgment. At one point, earlier, Graham and Bob Barr had almost come to blows when Barr denounced Graham for trying to write Clinton's words for him. Barr didn't want Graham giving Clinton any help in avoiding impeachment.

In the speech, Clinton acknowledged that he must be held accountable. "Should [Congress and the American people] determine that my errors of word and deed require their rebuke and censure, I am ready to accept that," he said. Clinton said he was "profoundly sorry" for misleading "the country, the Congress, my friends, and my family. Quite simply, I gave in to my shame."

Graham just laughed. "Not even close," he said, and then he and his colleagues returned to the committee room to vote.

/ / /

The desultory last day of debate on the four articles of impeachment added little to what had already been said many times. Members on both sides of the aisle congratulated themselves for their open-mindedness about the evidence—and then all the Republicans spoke for impeachment and all the Democrats came out against it. Democrats spent most of the day following up on an idea first expressed by Jerry Nadler of New York—that the articles unfairly failed to specify precisely which of Clinton's statements were false. This criticism was valid. The article charged that Clinton gave false testimony about "the nature and details of his relationship with a subordinate Government employee," but did not, as a perjury indictment would, identify the offending testimony. Out of all the reasons to oppose impeachment, this was a rather minor one, but Barney Frank caught the significance of this Republican omission.

In an exchange with George Gekas of Pennsylvania, Frank challenged him, "You are embarrassed to try and unseat a twice-elected president on this degree of trivia and you have therefore used obfuscatory language to suggest a set of offenses that don't have specific support." This was exactly right. The Republicans left out the details because the actual statements only dealt with the minutiae of the Clinton-Lewinsky encounters. To his credit, though, Bill McCollum at least had the courage to answer Frank's challenge. As his colleagues and staff cringed, McCollum said to the television cameras, "If you remember, that it was a very specific definition and it included in it touching of breasts and genitalia." Then the congressman hefted one of the volumes of Starr evidence and directed everyone's attention to "page 547 of the big document that we have got published here." He began quoting from Clinton's grand jury testimony.

> CLINTON: You are free to infer that my testimony is that I did
>   not have sexual relations as I understood this term to be used.
> QUESTION: Including touching her breasts, kissing her breasts,
>   or touching her genitalia?
> CLINTON: That's correct.

After this recitation, McCollum said, "That is specifically, if anybody wants to know, where the president committed perjury."

The votes began with an article alleging that Clinton gave "perjurious, false, and misleading testimony" before the grand jury, which passed in a straight party-line vote of twenty-one to sixteen. Article two charged "perjurious, false, and misleading testimony" in his deposition in the Paula Jones case. (In an especially bravura touch, the articles—and later the House managers—always referred to *Jones v. Clinton* as "a Federal civil rights action." After a fashion, this manufactured grandeur was accurate. Jones filed her suit under the civil rights laws only because she had missed the statute of limitations for Title VII, which is the usual vehicle for sexual harassment cases.)

One member broke party lines on article two. Lindsey Graham voted no, which meant that it passed by a vote of twenty to seventeen. Graham had sound reasons for voting against it. A former prosecutor himself, he thought no criminal case would ever have been brought based on an irrelevant matter in a dismissed civil lawsuit. But Graham's vote contributed to the impression that article two was weaker on the facts than article one—that is, that Clinton's lies were more easily proved in the grand jury than in the deposition. In fact, the reverse was true, which had important implications as the case proceeded. Partisan form returned on article three, which alleged obstruction of justice in the Jones case, and in article four, which was a much-amended melange that basically wound up charging Clinton with lying in his answers to the committee's eighty-one questions.

As the hour grew late on December 11, the members began to ramble more and give in to the occasional unguarded remark. Hyde's were the most revealing. After the first article passed, the chairman suddenly announced, "The chairman yields himself two minutes.

"I just want to say people watching on television might get the wrong idea that if we pass these articles of impeachment, we're throwing the president out of office. That's exactly not true. . . . What we do is we find whether there's enough evidence to warrant submission to the Senate," Hyde explained. "That's the process. And our Founding Fathers were very wise to have the accusatory body not be the adjudicatory body." The chairman returned to this theme several more times in the waning moments of the committee's deliberations—that impeachment was somehow no big deal, that the Senate could clear everything up. Hyde later denied this interpretation, but it wasn't difficult to find in the chairman's words a hint of remorse, a belated recognition that this process had spun out of control. In any event, by this point it was too late. The full House would consider impeachment in just eight days, on Friday, December 18.

/ / /

Hyde's mixed feelings came through even more clearly the following week. He knew that Howard Berman, his favorite Democrat on the committee, was interested in pushing a censure proposal. Hyde knew that several of Washington's old wise men, including the lawyers Lloyd Cutler and Robert Strauss and the recently retired Bob Dole, were pushing for a censure option to be allowed on the House floor. Hyde told Berman he had no objection to a censure vote on the floor, but Cutler and Strauss had to get Livingston and the Republican leadership to change their minds.

Berman said he would see what he could do, but the idea went nowhere.

The idea offered a window in Hyde's knowledge of Washington—which was extensive, circa 1985. Tom DeLay lived in an entirely separate universe from the fat-cat lawyers who could once privately broker deals in line with their idea of the national interest. DeLay answered to the Christian right activists who controlled the Republican Party at the grass roots. No overture from a Bob Strauss, or even a Bob Dole, was going to change their minds—or DeLay's.

By that final week, there was almost nothing left for Clinton to do. The much-discussed if seldom seen Republican moderates were simply carried along in the momentum generated by DeLay. In the Republican cloakrooms, there was much discussion of a recent election in California. In October 1997, the congressman for the district around Santa Barbara, a Democrat named Walter Capps, had died suddenly. Many national Republicans rallied behind the candidacy of Brooks Firestone, a wealthy moderate, but conservatives, including Tom DeLay, backed Tom Bordonaro. Bordonaro won the primary—and promptly lost the general election to Capps's widow. Bordonaro's primary triumph sent a chill through many moderate Republicans. DeLay's people could mobilize the party's base, and if they could topple the tire heir, they could bring down any number of moderates. DeLay didn't make explicit threats; none were necessary. But the moderates all knew that nothing mattered more to their party's base than impeachment.

Once again Gephardt asked Rick Boucher to serve as Clinton's emissary to moderates of both parties. Peter King, the conservative Long Island Republican, kept trying to help out, but with little success. Shortly before the vote, Mike Castle, a bellwether moderate Republican from Delaware, asked King to float a censure proposal that also included a fine for Clinton. The next thing King knew, Castle was saying publicly that he couldn't support "King's" censure proposal. In a sign of the desperation in the White House, aides to Clinton allowed some congressmen a rare look at their internal polling numbers from Penn, Schoen & Berland, which showed, according to the cover memo, that "voters are overwhelmingly against impeachment of the President and that the

Republicans' partisan drive for impeachment is causing their party's ratings to plummet." It moved no one.

On the Wednesday before the vote, Boucher finally realized that the battle to which he had unexpectedly devoted the last three months of his life was lost. Late in the afternoon, he decided to take a run along the great mall in front of the Capitol. He hadn't expected to feel so strongly. He had no love for Bill Clinton. But Boucher hadn't seen this kind of passion and anger in the country since Vietnam. He knew America was the strongest country in the world. No other country could threaten us. The only people who could hurt us were ourselves. He sat down by a tree near the Washington Monument and cried.

/ / /

As Boucher was taking his run, the president was making a brief televised address from the Oval Office. He had once again sent planes to attack Iraq, to ensure compliance with the settlement terms of the Persian Gulf War. It was the second time that Clinton had ordered a military strike at a crucial moment in the Lewinsky scandal. Just after the Starr report was released, in September, he had ordered bombing raids in retaliation for terrorist attacks on American embassies in Africa. On that occasion, Republicans had been generally supportive. This time, Trent Lott, the Republican leader in the Senate, said, "Both the timing and the policy are open to question." Gerald B. H. Solomon, the Republican chairman of the House Rules Committee, was even more explicit in his criticism. "Never underestimate a desperate president," he said in a news release issued on Wednesday afternoon. "What option is left for getting impeachment off the front page or maybe even postponed?"

That night, the House Republicans held a raucous meeting of their full conference to discuss what to do about the impeachment vote. A large screen was set up, so that the legislators could watch Clinton's remarks on Iraq. When his image appeared, the room erupted in hoots and boos. In the end, the House leadership agreed to delay everything one day. After two days of debate, the vote would take place on Saturday, December 19.

Hyde had directed a few of the abler Republicans on the Judiciary Committee to serve on what he called the "fact team" for the

House debate. These members would commit to staying on the floor at all times, to remain available to answer questions about the facts of the case. Jim Rogan had taken the job seriously, spending several late nights cramming for the assignment, so he wasn't especially interested when the Republican leadership called another meeting of the full conference for Thursday night.

In the early part of the meeting, the most notable statement came from Steve Buyer, an Indiana representative on the Judiciary Committee. In this quasi-public setting, Buyer made an argument that had been circulating privately among Republicans for several weeks. If you have any doubt about impeachment, Buyer said, you should go into the Ford building and look at the reports about Jane Doe Number 5. Schippers had devoted a good deal of his investigative efforts to tracking down the story of Juanita Broaddrick, the Arkansas woman who claimed that Clinton had raped her in 1978. This was an astonishingly unfair argument, but an effective one. The Republicans lacked the courage to raise this issue in public—and let the president's defenders respond to it—but they were willing to mutter their dark insinuations and display their secret evidence. Forty-five Republicans made the trek to the Ford building to examine the Broaddrick allegations. All of this group—including Michael Castle and Mark Souder, who had indicated they were going to vote no—wound up voting yes.

After about an hour in the meeting room, Rogan sidled up to Bob Livingston, the speaker-designee, to ask if he could leave early and return to his preparations.

"Bob," Rogan asked, "I'd like to get back to work. Is there anything else going on?"

"Yeah, there is," Livingston whispered. "Hang around for five minutes."

/ / /

On October 4, Larry Flynt, the publisher of *Hustler* magazine, had taken out a full-page advertisement in *The Washington Post* to announce that he would pay as much as $1 million to any woman who was willing to go public about her affairs with government officials. At the time, Flynt's ersatz political protest against the pursuit of President Clinton attracted little more than amusement from official Washington. But Flynt later said that his offer drew about two thousand calls to his 800 number. Flynt hired private investigators, who narrowed the original list down to forty-eight possibilities, and then took a closer look at about a dozen. Some of these tales concerned Bob Livingston.

A Louisiana congressman from a distinguished New York family, Livingston was relatively unused to attention from the press, much less from a notorious wheelchair-bound pornographer. Gingrich had handpicked Livingston over several members of greater seniority to chair the Appropriations Committee, and he had then emerged as a compromise choice among the many factions that wanted to evict Gingrich from the speakership. But as recently as a year earlier, Livingston had nearly quit the House to become a highly paid lobbyist. Short-tempered and haughty, Livingston had little experience with the public abuse that a true national public figure, like Gingrich or Clinton, absorbed on a daily basis.

A few minutes after Livingston told Rogan to hang around for the end of the meeting, he rose to speak to his Republican colleagues. "I've been outed by Larry Flynt," he said. He then reached into his pocket to read a statement that he said he would be releasing immediately. "I have decided to inform my colleagues and my constituents that during my thirty-three-year marriage to my wife, Bonnie, I have on occasion strayed from my marriage. . . ." (Flynt later said that four women had come forward to allege affairs with Livingston.)

"I want to assure everyone that these indiscretions were not with employees on my staff," Livingston said, "and I have never been asked to testify under oath about them."

Among his Republican colleagues, Livingston received three standing, if ultimately misleading, ovations in the course of delivering his news.

/ / /

Henry Hyde began the proceedings in the well of the House the following morning, Friday, December 18. "Mr. Speaker," he said, "I call up a privileged resolution . . . and ask for its immediate consideration. The clerk will read the resolution, as follows."

At that moment, a dark-haired man of medium height named Paul Hays walked to the podium in the middle of the floor and began reading.

"Resolved," Hays said, "that William Jefferson Clinton is impeached for high crimes and misdemeanors, and that the following articles be exhibited to the United States Senate. . . ." It took him five minutes to read through all four articles, and it was, oddly, the most chilling moment of the whole proceeding, the visible manifestation of the machinery of presidential removal. Such words had not been uttered in the House of Representatives in 130 years, since the impeachment of President Andrew Johnson.

Only a handful of people in the chamber knew of a small irony in Hays's recitation on that day. Hays, who was installed in his job by Gingrich, was the husband of Cindy Hays, the chief fund-raiser for the Paula Jones legal defense fund. In the early days of the lawsuit that led to this impeachment proceeding, Jones would stay at the home of the man reading the charges against the president.

The debate—mostly in two- or four-minute snippets from both sides—was especially bitter and angry. Members of Congress are used to fighting on the merits of issues, but they place a special value on procedural fairness. The failure of the House leadership to allow a vote on censure—to permit a "substitute," in the congressional argot—was especially galling. The House minority always received a vote on a substitute, but DeLay had shut down this option, and had made sure the Democrats knew it. Again, no one said anything especially memorable through twelve long hours of debate on Friday, and no one expected anything more in the moments leading up to the vote on Saturday.

When Bob Livingston rose to speak on Saturday morning, he hadn't given any sign that his words would differ much from those of any other impeachment supporter. The floor was not even half filled. Given his stature, he was allowed more time than most of the other members, but he ambled through the early part of his remarks, which were mostly devoted to defending the decision to take the vote while American bombers were still in harm's way.

"But to the president I would say:

"Sir, you have done great damage to this nation over this past year, and while your defenders are contending that further impeachment proceedings would only protract and exacerbate the damage to this country, I say that you have the power to terminate that damage. . . ."

This caused a stirring. People could tell what was coming next. On the Democratic side, John Conyers, Abbe Lowell, and Maxine Waters, who were seated together in front, snapped their heads forward.

"You, sir, may resign your post," Livingston continued, and the reaction was swift. Waters vaulted out of her chair, pointed at Livingston, and shouted, "You resign! You resign!" Boos cascaded down from other Democrats.

Livingston raised his hand for quiet. "And I can only challenge you in such fashion if I am willing to heed my own words," he said, and the room again fell silent.

"To my colleagues, my friends, and most especially my wife and family, I have hurt you all deeply, and I beg your forgiveness.

"I was prepared to lead our narrow majority as speaker, and I believe I had it in me to do a fine job. But I cannot do that job or be the kind of leader that I would like to be under current circumstances. . . ."

Now there was anger, except from the other side. Republicans were shouting at Democrats, "Are you fucking happy?" "Is this what you motherfuckers wanted?" Even House veterans could not recall an uglier, or more surprising, turn of events. Peter King, the Republican impeachment opponent, who was on the floor at the time, recalled later that the moment reminded him of when Jack Ruby shot Lee Harvey Oswald—the sense of national vertigo, of events spinning out of control.

". . . I will not stand for speaker on January 6 . . ." Livingston continued through the buzz around him. "I thank my wife most especially for standing by me. I love her very much.

"God bless America."

Standing ovations notwithstanding, Livingston's admission of adultery had cost him support among hard-core Republicans—"the perfection caucus," as they were sometimes called. If Livingston lost only half a dozen Republican votes, as he well might have, he could not have won the speakership. The Louisianan bowed to the inevitable.

Moments after Livingston finished his remarks, Richard Gephardt came to the floor and uttered a heartfelt invitation to his adversary to change his mind. "I believe his decision to retire is a terrible capitulation to the negative forces that are consuming our political system and our country," Gephardt said. "We are now rapidly descending into a politics where life imitates farce, fratricide dominates our public debate, and America is held hostage to tactics of smear and fear." In this, the Democratic leader was wrong. The politics were already there.

/ / /

In one respect, Livingston's announcement achieved the impossible: it rendered the impeachment of the president an anticlimax. Article one, perjury in the grand jury, passed by 228 to 206. For all the talk about party defections, only five Democrats voted for impeachment and five Republicans against it. Lindsey Graham's opposition to article two, perjury in the deposition, made it a safe way for Republicans to appear reasonable, so twenty-eight members voted with the Democrats. The article lost, 229 to 205. Article three, obstruction of justice, passed by just 221 to 212. (If the vote on this article had been delayed until January, when the Democrats would have five more seats, it almost certainly would have lost.) The garbled article four, ultimately based on Clinton's written answers to the Judiciary Committee, failed by a wide margin, 285 to 148.

As ever, the great fear of people around Clinton was that there would be a stampede of Democrats calling for his ouster. So in the days leading up to the inevitable, the president's advisers gently encouraged House members to make a postimpeachment show of support. Immediately after the vote, about fifty Democrats walked down the great steps of the Capitol and into buses that were waiting for them.

Clinton was subdued, almost embarrassed, on meeting the delegation from Capitol Hill. But the Democrats weren't faking their outrage at the proceedings that had just ended, and soon the president was savoring their encouragement. In a few moments, as Clinton chatted in the East Room, his spirits began to revive, and then, standing around with a group of members and staffers, the president said, "Anybody want to hear a dirty joke?"

It was suddenly very, very quiet.

There's this guy, Clinton recounted, and he's caught on a cliff in a storm. As the wind and rain rages around him, he grabs on to a branch and he's just about to fall off the cliff when he looks up and says, "Why me, God?"

And God looks down on him and says, "I just don't like you."

There was nothing dirty about the joke, and Clinton told it often, once even at a press conference. It is always possible to read too much into a joke, but one can see Clinton's attitude toward the entire swirling scandal contained in this little story. Clinton saw little difference between the man on the cliff, Richard Jewell, and himself—all victims of forces beyond their control. To be sure, he will be remembered as the target of an unwise and unfair impeachment proceeding. But just as certainly, history will haunt Clinton for his own role in this political apocalypse, and for that, despite his best efforts, this president can blame only himself.

20

These Culture Wars

The trial of the president in the Senate had relatively little to do with Clinton himself. With only fifty-five Republicans sitting in the upper chamber, there was never any real chance that the president's accusers could muster the two-thirds vote—sixty-seven senators—necessary to remove him from office. Clinton's poll ratings had actually improved during the undignified proceedings in the House of Representatives, so it was inconceivable that all the Republicans plus twelve Democrats would vote for Clinton's ouster. Barring sensational new disclosures—which remained, as ever, the great Republican hope—the president's job was safe.

Rather, the real drama of the Senate trial concerned the efforts of all the participants to avoid making bad situations worse. The Lewinsky story had diminished everyone it touched. The scandal had indirectly cost two speakers of the House their jobs, driven the Republican Party to new depths of unpopularity, and, of course, led to Bill Clinton's impeachment. In light of this sorry history, senators were united as they prepared to take up their constitutional duty. They wanted the whole thing to . . . just go away.

For a brief moment, Trent Lott tried to makes those wishes come true. The former Ole Miss cheerleader had worked his way through the ranks in Washington, as a congressional aide, a congressman for sixteen years, a senator for ten more, and majority leader since 1996. Like many Republican senators who had come up through the House, Lott was a strong conservative and resolute partisan. But he had been forced to adapt to his new surroundings. Unlike most House members, who effectively run unopposed, all senators run statewide, often in competitive races. They ignore public opinion at their peril. Lott didn't like Clinton any better than his House colleagues, but he knew a losing fight when he saw one.

Lott spent much of the Christmas break on the telephone with his Republican colleagues in the Senate, and he learned that they viewed the approaching trial with dread. This round of phone calls yielded a plan bearing the name of Slade Gorton, a Republican from Washington State, and Joseph Lieberman, a Connecticut Democrat. Under their scenario, which was leaked around Christmas, the Senate would hear opening statements and then take a preliminary vote. If none of the three articles drew the support of two-thirds of the senators—as, surely, none would—then the trial would end, without the managers having called a single witness. It was a way of shuffling the impeachment controversy out the door of the Senate in about week.

/ / /

Hyde's chief aide, Tom Mooney, had never seen his boss so angry. Gorton-Lieberman was a slap in the face, Hyde said, a sign of disrespect to the entire House. Like many veteran House members, Hyde resented the institutional condescension of the senators, who regarded their House counterparts in both parties as unreflective zealots, and none too bright either. But Hyde was damned if he was going to let those arrogant bastards push impeachment under the rug. Hyde ordered Mooney to write Lott a stinging letter to this effect, which they would promptly release to the press. In the key passage of the letter, dated December 30, 1998, Hyde used the patronizing tone that he expected from senators. "As you know, the constitutional duty of the House of Representatives as the *accusatory* body differs greatly from the Senate's constitutional duty as an *adjudicatory* body," Hyde instructed. "As the entity granted the sole power to try an impeachment—i.e., to determine the guilt or innocence of President Clinton—the Senate should hear from live witnesses." This intraparty dispute among Republicans formed the core drama of the Senate trial: Hyde and his band of true-believing managers against Lott and his election-minded colleagues.

Hyde's complaints about witnesses enraged senators in both parties. As they all knew, "live witnesses" in the context of this trial meant Monica Lewinsky. Given the nature of the charges, for her testimony to be at all meaningful, Lewinsky would have to provide anatomical details of her encounters with the president. Paul Sarbanes, the Maryland Democrat who, like Lott, had served on the House Judiciary Committee during Watergate, made the point repeatedly during his party's caucuses. "They didn't call witnesses in the House because they didn't want to be embarrassed with that kind of testimony," Sarbanes said. "But now they say that we have to call witnesses? That's outrageous."

Sarbanes was exactly right—and many Republicans agreed with him. The Constitution said nothing about how either body should conduct its impeachment inquiry. As Clinton's enemies always did, Hyde was simply hoping that the drama of live testimony would shake public opinion in a way that the words of the Starr report had not. But Hyde had no right to be sanctimonious about the rights of the House of Representatives. This was a political process, and just as he was representing the desires of the Republican base, Lott was speaking for the broader interests of the party. The Constitution, which Hyde invoked so promiscuously throughout this process, had nothing to say about whether Lewinsky should recite her tale from the well of the Senate.

The trial was scheduled to begin on Thursday, January 7, but no one had any clear idea how it would unfold. In a characteristic example of his passive management style, Hyde had essentially allowed any Judiciary Republican who wanted the assignment to become a "manager," or prosecutor, on the Senate floor. That left him with an unmanageable group of thirteen, all of whom had to be given something to do. Over the New Year's weekend, Hyde asked three of the more experienced prosecutors on the panel, Rogan, Asa Hutchinson of Arkansas, and Ed Bryant of Tennessee, to draw up a battle plan for a full-fledged trial. Rogan took the lead and came up with fifteen to twenty witnesses he regarded as essential. A couple of days before the trial was to begin, Lott came to the managers' headquarters to talk about plans for the trial.

In deference to Hyde's protests, Lott didn't push Gorton-Lieberman, but he didn't promise live witnesses, either. Lott chose a young first-term Republican senator named Rick Santorum, a former House member from Pennsylvania, as his unofficial deputy in dealing with Hyde and the managers. You know these people, Lott suggested to Santorum, maybe you can talk some sense to them. Not surprisingly, perhaps, Lott's choice of Santorum succeeded only in uniting the managers in contempt for their former colleague.

"So," Lott said to the managers, "how many witnesses do you need?"

Rogan explained his plan and mentioned the number twenty. Lott blanched.

"That's too many," the majority leader said. "How many do you *really* need?"

Thus began a haggling process that lasted more than a month. On the surface, it appeared that Lott and the Senate completely controlled the outcome, but the managers weren't without political muscle. From that first day, several of them, including Rogan and Chris Cannon of Utah, made clear that they would quit as managers rather than participate in a trial that gave them no chance to win. Several times in the next month the managers came close to a mass resignation. As the managers knew, such an exodus would have been a disaster for Lott—the nominal leader of the Republican Party—so the majority leader avoided categorical commitments of any kind. On a deeper level, this pas de deux over witnesses revealed what a sham the trial was. Both sides—Lott and his people and Hyde and his—paid far more attention to the number of witnesses than to the substance of what any of them might say.

/ / /

"Gentlemen, shall we?" said Ed Bryant.

Shortly before ten on January 7, the House manager from Tennessee asked his fellow managers to bow their heads in prayer. This had become a tradition of sorts for the Republicans on Judiciary. Before they voted the articles in the committee, and before the full House began its impeachment debate, Bryant had led the group in asking God's help. ("Gentlemen" was apt; the thirteen managers were all male.)

With that, Hyde directed the group in a solemn procession from the House to the Senate side of the Capitol. In this the managers were following the precedent laid down in the trial of Andrew Johnson in 1868. Lott was a stickler for tradition, and he directed his staff to choreograph the trial in line with the historical record. These solemn formalities, including an honor guard of senators for Chief Justice William H. Rehnquist, who presided, pleased Lott's tradition-minded colleagues but also sent a message to the public. The Senate believed in fairness and order. In other words, the Senate wasn't the House. (The managers, for example, had asked to sit to Rehnquist's left, in front of the Republican senators. Lott refused, reminding them that the managers in the Johnson trial had sat on the other side. As a result, the managers spent the entire trial under the grumpy stares of some of Clinton's biggest supporters, like Barbara Boxer of California and Charles Schumer of New York, who happened to sit up front.)

January 7 marked only a ceremonial start to the trial, with a reading of the charges by Hyde and then a cavalcade of senators to sign a book recording their roles as "jurors." They were each presented with a special pen for the occasion, but it somehow fit the seedy nature of the inquiry that the writing instruments were mistakenly imprinted with the words "Untied States Senate." With those brief formalities completed, the full complement of one hundred senators—who, in ordinary circumstances, rarely gathered together—found themselves assembled with little to do. The senators began chatting with one another and the idea took hold that they should meet informally, to try to set some ground rules for the trial.

Lott and Daschle agreed that the full Senate should march down the hall to the Old Senate Chamber. Some Democrats were reluctant. The image of impeachment as a partisan donnybrook had served the party well in the House. But "winning by losing" wasn't going to work in the Senate. The institutional self-image of the Senate called for a more dignified resolution, and even most Senate Democrats thought a little high-mindedness wouldn't hurt their cause—or the president's.

So, the following morning, the one hundred senators gathered in the room that had last been used for official business in 1859. Lott and Daschle presided jointly, and they began by recognizing Robert Byrd, the eighty-one-year-old West Virginia Democrat who was second in seniority to Strom Thurmond. Byrd had built his career as the custodian of the Senate's traditions, writing much-admired if little-read histories of the place. "The House has fallen into the black pit of partisan self-indulgence," he said. "The Senate is teetering on the brink of the same black pit."

Byrd had one suggestion at the outset. "We can start by disdaining any more of the salacious muck which has already soiled the gowns of too many," he said. Translated from Byrd's fussy diction, this was actually an important substantive point. Since the case against Clinton was based on "salacious muck," Byrd was obviously hoping that the gory details—and Monica Lewinsky—would be kept off the Senate floor.

Most of the comments followed in this vein—paeans to the glories of the Senate and attacks on the predations of the House. On the critical point of contention, the issue of live witnesses, the group quickly agreed on a most Senate-like solution: to put the decision off. They would allow the trial to start with opening statements from both sides, then allow the senators to ask questions of the lawyers, and only then would they turn to a vote on whether to allow witnesses. They were giving life to a favorite expression on Capitol Hill: "Let's see how it plays out." Democrats were betting that the managers would fail to shift the momentum, and Republicans were hoping they could play statesman without too much angering their political base.

Lott cleverly dubbed their plan the "Kennedy-Gramm solution," making it a joint project of Ted Kennedy and Phil Gramm, perhaps the greatest ideological foes in the entire Senate. It passed unanimously.

/ / /

During the opening statements by the managers, the trial quickly settled into a sort of routine, and the members of the Senate managed, even under a regime of enforced silence, to establish distinctive presences in the chamber. Joseph Biden of Delaware kept a diary of the impeachment experience, and he proved himself the

Senate's most aggressive notetaker, scribbling almost continuously into a leather-bound volume. In contrast, Dianne Feinstein of California was the most zealous multitasker, jotting notes to her staff on a yellow legal pad, glancing at the stacks of evidence in the case, and balancing her calendar book on her lap. Kennedy, the Senate veteran from Massachusetts, sagged in a resigned heap in his chair in the back row, making no effort to conceal his dismay at being compelled to participate in the process. John Kerry fidgeted; Paul Sarbanes guzzled water; Jesse Helms, among others, dozed. Throughout the long days, only a single senator emerged as a perfect model of unwavering attentiveness—ninety-six-year-old Strom Thurmond of South Carolina.

The "Kennedy-Gramm" proposal allowed the managers twenty-four hours of Senate time to make their case, and they used nearly all of it over three days. Hyde made a nominal effort to divide up the presentations into topics like "evidence," "law," and "precedents," but they all wound up sounding remarkably similar. (For example, during the opening statements, the senators heard no fewer than five accounts of Betty Currie's stashing Lewinsky's gifts under the bed.) In a peculiar way, the repetitiveness of the managers' opening statements underlined the weakness of the case. Multiple tellings could not invest the tawdry facts with a significance they did not possess. Bill McCollum, aka Mr. Genitalia, did maintain a distinctive presence, informing the senators, "In her sworn testimony, Monica Lewinsky described nine incidents of which the president touched and kissed her breasts and four incidents involving contact with her genitalia." Mark Penn's daily tracking polls for the president showed increased support for the managers after their first day of presentations, but a quick falloff after the repetitions of days two and three.

On Saturday, January 16, Hyde concluded the managers' opening statements with an oration of his own. "One hundred and thirty-six years ago," Hyde began, "at a small military cemetery in Pennsylvania, one of Illinois's most illustrious sons asked a haunting question: whether a nation conceived in liberty and dedicated to the proposition that all men are created equal can long endure."

What followed was a kind of quasi-military survey of American history. "We must never tolerate one law for the ruler and another for the ruled," he said. "If we do, we break faith with our ancestors from Bunker Hill, Lexington, Concord, to Flanders Field, Normandy, Hiroshima, Panmunjom, Saigon, and Desert Storm." Moments later, he said, "If across the river in Arlington Cemetery there are American heroes who died in defense of the rule of law, can we give less than the full measure of our devotion to that great cause?" Finally, he said, "On June the sixth, 1994, it was the fiftieth anniversary of the American landing at Normandy, and I went ashore at Normandy and walked up to the cemetery. . . . How do we keep the faith with that comrade at arms? Well, go to the Vietnam Memorial and the National Mall and press your hands against a few of the 58,000 names carved into that wall and ask yourself how we can redeem the debt we owe to those who purchased our freedom with their lives."

This was Hyde's solution—a kind of rhetorical excess that led him to invoke twelve battles in less than fifteen minutes. The effect was the opposite of what he intended. He was talking about war in a case about sex, which made the contrast all the more striking. In one way, though, Hyde seemed to recognize the intellectual and moral gulf that separated him from his fellow citizens on this issue, and he made at least a token effort to address it. The catalyst was, of all things, the Iran-Contra affair.

Throughout the impeachment battle, Clinton supporters pointed out how Hyde had served as a principal defender of President Reagan and his administration during the Iran-Contra affair. (For example, Hyde was the only member of Congress to attend the verdict in Oliver North's criminal trial. When North was convicted of making false statements and obstruction of justice, Hyde rushed to embrace him.) In an elliptical passage in the same battle-strewn speech, Hyde alluded to what some viewed as this contradiction in his views. "Morally serious men and women can imagine the circumstances at the far edge of the morally permissible when, with the gravest matters of national interest at stake, a president could shade the truth in order to serve the common good," Hyde said. "But under oath for private pleasure?"

In the end, the question was, what kind of lies were excusable? In preparing for his August 17 speech, Clinton and his advisers discussed the Reagan precedent—and reached precisely the opposite conclusion to Hyde's. To the Clinton team, the fact that Reagan's lies concerned matters of national importance made them more, not less, significant than Clinton's false statements about a personal matter. The Reagan and Clinton precedents thus neatly posed the issue of public vs. private morality, and Hyde, better than anyone, recognized that the country was not going his way. By this point, even the haughty moralists in the Washington press corps saw that no amount of puffing from them (or Hyde) could persuade most people to change their minds about the magnitude of the charges.

Near the end of the opening statements, Chief Justice Rehnquist gave the senators a signal that the Constitution permitted them to consider the views of their constituents. After perhaps the third or fourth reference by the managers to the senators as "jurors," Senator Tom Harkin of Iowa rose to object. (It would be the only objection from the floor during the entire trial.) "Mr. Chief Justice," Harkin said to the hushed audience, "I object to the use and continued use of the word 'jurors' when referring to the Senate sitting as triers in the trial of the impeachment of the president of the United States."

Harkin briefly pointed out some of the differences between the senators and ordinary jurors. Unlike courtroom jurors, the senators were all familiar with the defendant; they knew each other, too; and the senators had the right to establish the procedures in the trial and even to overrule the chief justice in his rulings. As Harkin acknowledged, it was to a certain extent a semantic point, but still an important one. "What we do here does not just decide the fate of one man," he said.

As Harkin suggested, impeachment was indeed more a political than a legal process, and senators had the duty, not just the right, to consider the views of the country. Under the Constitution, it mattered that Hyde, for all his effort, could never recruit more than a small group of already devoted Clinton-haters to his cause.

In his phlegmatic way, the chief justice indicated that he saw Harkin's point. "The Chair is of the view that the objection of the senator from Iowa is well taken," he said. "Therefore, counsel should refrain from referring to the senators as jurors."

Harkin was delighted. Moments after the ruling, he whispered to Pat Moynihan, "I just won my first Supreme Court case!"

/ / /

The atmosphere was brittle and tense as the White House prepared to begin its defense after the long Martin Luther King Day weekend, on Tuesday, January 19. The managers had not said anything that appeared to jeopardize Clinton's survival in office, but there remained, as ever, a sense that something unpredictable could still happen. What Clinton needed was a messenger of reassurance that the managers' cries were nothing more than hyperbole.

Fortunately for the president, he had the right advocate in waiting. Chuck Ruff wore his ferocity lightly. Unlike, say, David Kendall, the White House counsel projected statesmanship rather than partisanship, and though no one around him liked to admit it, Ruff's wheelchair helped. He had lost the use of his legs three decades earlier, after he contracted a mysterious illness on a charitable mission to Africa. The disability somehow added to Ruff's air of rectitude, but it also camouflaged his intensity. At the age of fifty-nine, Ruff had enjoyed one of the most distinguished legal careers of his generation, even before he came to the White House. He had served as the final Watergate special prosecutor, as U.S. attorney for the District of Columbia, and as a high-priced private litigator at the Washington powerhouse of Covington & Burling. As much as anyone at either counsel table, Ruff liked to win—and to that end he had hidden a secret weapon within his opening remarks.

Ruff began with a recital of the facts leading up to the impeachment. In his caution and deference, Ruff's very person marked a contrast to the zealots who spoke for the House. Ruff repeatedly made mention of someone whose name had scarcely passed the managers' lips over the past three days—Linda Tripp. Ruff's intensity built gradually as he showed how this impeachment was built on an incomplete record, a faulty understanding of the law, and a distorted view of the evidence. "I want you to have in mind throughout our presentation, and indeed throughout the rest of the proceedings, this one principle. Beware of it," he said gravely. "Beware of the prosecutor who feels it necessary to deceive the court."

Ruff had the facts to back up this bold charge. The crucial moment in Ruff's presentation concerned what he called "the magic date of December 11," 1997. On that day, two events of importance occurred. Judge Wright ruled that the Jones lawyers could ask witnesses about their sexual contacts with Clinton. Also, Vernon Jordan met with Lewinsky and made several calls to help her find a job. Ruff quoted from the opening statement to the Senate by Asa Hutchinson, the manager from Arkansas: "The judge's order came in, that triggered the president into action, and the president triggered Vernon Jordan into action." Extending the torture, Ruff even brought out a chart that Hutchinson had used in front of the senators, to show how the managers described a cause-and-effect relationship between the judge's order and the intensified job search.

Then Ruff lowered the boom.

"Let me show you the official report of the judge's discussion with the lawyers in the Jones case on that date," he said. The conference call began at 5:33 P.M. central standard time, or 6:33 P.M. in Washington. Where was Vernon Jordan at that time? According to his testimony (borne out by documentary evidence), "I left on United flight 946 at 5:55 from Dulles airport and landed in Amsterdam the next morning." (The president, it turns out, was out of town at that moment as well.) In other words, Jordan had left the country by the time Judge Wright issued her order. It was physically impossible for the order to have "triggered" the phone calls. Jordan had stepped up the job search without knowing how Lewinsky could be questioned in her deposition.

"Oh, I see," Ruff said, disposing of the accusation with grim satisfaction. "Well, never mind."

It was the kind of Perry Mason moment that few lawyers ever have the opportunity to savor, much less in such an important setting. Of course, that one fact did not refute all of the charges against the president, but it served as a useful example of the excessiveness of Clinton's pursuers. Ruff's charge that Hutchinson and company "deceived" the Senate was unfair; the truth was more banal. The managers never learned the facts as well as Clinton's defenders did, and guided by the ineffectual Schippers (who had made the same mistake about December 11 in his own testimony), they spun everything against Clinton whether or not the facts justified it.

After Ruff's statement, Lott called for an early conclusion to the trial day because the senators would soon have to march to the House chamber for another important ceremony, the president's State of the Union address. This was a milestone under any circumstances, but the evening's festivities would mark Clinton's second such speech in the age of Lewinsky. A year earlier, on the day that his wife denounced the "vast right-wing conspiracy" on the *Today* show, Clinton had spoken as a man whose presidency stood in desperate peril. So it was, in a way, again on this day. No president had ever addressed the Congress and nation while on trial for high crimes and misdemeanors.

In truth, though, the president and his party came to this day in a state of near euphoria. They had triumphed in the election beyond their greatest hopes. The Republicans' endless pursuit of Clinton was ending in political calamity for the hunters rather than their prey. Most important, Clinton was able to say in his speech, "My fellow Americans, I stand before you to report that the state of our union is strong." His address served as a triumphant accounting of an extraordinarily prosperous moment in American life. Democrats whooped; Republicans like Tom DeLay and Dick Armey sat, arms crossed, in grumpy silence. By the end of the address, at least thirty Republican House members had fled the chamber; to avoid a public backlash for this disrespectful gesture, they had their congressional pages fill the empty seats.

The strange best-of-times, worst-of-times atmosphere continued even after the president's speech. In a receiving line at the Capitol, the president and first lady greeted Strom Thurmond with smiles and handshakes. As they later described the scene to a friend, they heard Thurmond say, "You're two turds."

"Pardon?" said the president.

"You're two turds," the senator repeated.

As Thurmond moved through the line, the Clintons exchanged perplexed looks with each other, baffled by the hostility they engendered, and continued shaking hands. It wasn't until late in the evening that they realized that they had failed to understand the ancient senator through his soupy South Carolina accent.

412 / JEFFREY TOOBIN

They'll never get two thirds, Thurmond had said. *They'll never get two thirds.*

"I have seen the look of disappointment on many faces," Dale Bumpers said to the men and women he had counted as colleagues just three weeks earlier, "because I know a lot of people really thought they would be rid of me once and for all."

From the beginning, the White House defense strategy had been to play on the senators' exalted sense of themselves. Who better, then, to make Clinton's case than one of their own? At first, the president's team had tried to recruit George Mitchell, the former majority leader, who had recently played an important role in bringing peace to Northern Ireland. But Mitchell backed out at the last minute, leaving the defense team scrambling for another ex-senator. In desperation, they turned to Bumpers, Clinton's fellow Arkansan, who had just retired after twenty-four years in the Senate.

Kendall and Greg Craig of the president's defense team exchanged nervous looks as Bumpers began, because until the last minute, the former senator had been making indecipherable scrawls on a yellow legal pad. "Don't worry, boys," he told them, "I got it under control."

Bumpers's speech marked the high point of the trial—at once folksy and eloquent, funny and wise, heartbroken and heartfelt—in all, a great moment in the history of Senate oratory. He made no effort to disguise his affection for the man with whom he had dominated the politics of their state for a generation. Bumpers thus had a special credibility to make a point that had largely escaped notice as Clinton had moved toward his acquittal. "You pick your own adjective to describe the president's conduct. Here are some that I would use: indefensible, outrageous, unforgivable, shameless. I promise you the president would not contest any of those or any others. But there is a human element here that has not even been mentioned. That is, the president and Hillary and Chelsea are human beings," Bumpers said. "The relationship between husband and wife, father and child, has been incredibly strained, if not destroyed. There has been nothing but sleepless nights, mental agony for this family"—and so there was.

But the heart of Bumpers's remarks concerned the charges against Clinton. "We are here today because the president suffered a terrible moral lapse of marital infidelity—not a breach of the public trust, not a crime against society," he said. "It is a sex scandal. H. L. Mencken one time said, 'When you hear somebody say, This is not about money—it's about money.'" The audience laughed. "And when you hear people say, This is not about sex—it's about sex."

In this regard, Bumpers called on his long-ago experience trying hundreds of cases as the only divorce lawyer in tiny Franklin County, Arkansas. "In all those divorce cases, I would guess that in eighty percent of contested cases, perjury was committed," he said. "Do you know what it was about? Sex. Extramarital affairs. But there is a very big difference between perjury about whether there was marital infidelity in a divorce case, and perjury about whether I bought the murder weapon. . . . And to charge somebody with the first and punish them as though it were the second stands our sense of justice on its head.

"There is a total lack of proportionality, a total lack of balance, in the thing. The charge and the punishment are totally out of sync." No one ever put the case against Clinton into clearer perspective—and no one ever used a more apt word than "proportionality" to sum up the excessive nature of the attack on the president. With this word, Bumpers recognized Clinton's misdeeds but placed them in a wise man's sense of context and perspective.

As Bumpers turned to close, he began wandering the aisles he knew so well and delivered an elegant rebuke to Hyde's invocation of the nation's military history. Bumpers, too, spoke of the rule of law and how men had sacrificed for it. "If you want to know what men fought for in World War II," he said, "ask Senator Inouye," who was seated in the middle of the chamber. "He left an arm in Italy. . . . Certified war hero. I think his relatives were in an internment camp. So ask him, what was he fighting for? Or ask Bob Kerrey"—seated to Bumpers's right—"certified Medal of Honor winner. What was he fighting for? Probably get a quite different answer." Bumpers then turned to the Republican side. "Or Senator Chafee, one of the finest men ever to grace this body and certified Marine hero of Guadalcanal, ask him."

It was, in the end, a plea for tolerance, for reason—for a sense of proportionality. "The people have a right, and they are calling on you to rise above politics, rise above partisanship. They are calling on you to do your solemn duty, and I pray you will." For a moment, the senators broke the etiquette of the trial, and rose as one in applause. Not Daniel Inouye, though. He remained seated, and with tears running down his cheeks, used the one arm he brought home from his service to his country to pound his chair in appreciation.

/ / /

On the following morning, Friday, January 22, Trent Lott held a brief press conference in a Capitol hallway. He was asked if anything might change the momentum toward the president's acquittal.

"That depends on what NBC broadcasts on Sunday," the majority leader said.

In the shared code of Washington insiderdom, everyone caught the reference. For the past three weeks, many of the reporters covering the story had spent as much time gazing at web browsers as at the Senate floor. In a way, it was fitting that Clinton's trial would end with a backstage drama orchestrated by Matt Drudge—two of them, actually. It was appropriate, too, that the stories dated back to even before Bill Clinton was president. The tales about him recirculated endlessly, with each failure of proof serving merely to goad later pursuers. So, with the trial winding down in Clinton's favor, his enemies turned to their last hopes for the elusive lightning bolt that would finally strike him down.

The first story had its origins in a rumor that dated back to Clinton's days as governor of Arkansas—that he had fathered a child with a black prostitute. On February 18, 1992, the *Globe* tabloid had run a story with the headline GOV. CLINTON HAD ORGIES WITH 3 BLACK HOOKERS—IN HIS MOTHER'S HOUSE! A few weeks later, with the supermarket tabloid spread out in front of him, the Chicago financier Peter Smith had offered to pay David Brock to investigate this allegation, but Brock refused. Later, the writer did accept Smith's money to underwrite the article in *The American Spectator* that mentioned "Paula."

As the Senate trial was beginning, Drudge brought the black prostitute story back to life. In a series of reports beginning with his familiar tag "**World Exclusive**," Drudge announced, WHITE HOUSE HIT WITH NEW DNA TERROR; TEEN TESTED FOR CLINTON PATERNITY. In connection with the DNA tests that tied Clinton to Lewinsky's dress, the Starr report had disclosed the genetic makeup of the president's blood. As Drudge recounted, the rival tabloid the *Star* was planning to test the blood of one Danny Williams, son of the prostitute named in the *Globe* story, to see if there was a genetic match to his putative father, the president. "He looks just like him!" Drudge quoted the mother's sister as saying. Alas, a few days later, Drudge had to report that the *Star's* tests had ruled out Bill Clinton as the father of the young man.

Still, by this time, Drudge was on to a bigger story, one that had already damaged Clinton—the tale of Juanita Broaddrick, who was known as Jane Doe Number Five in the Jones case. This story dated to Clinton's last gubernatorial campaign, in 1990, when his opponent, Sheffield Nelson, had tried to put the rape accusation into public circulation. During the House impeachment inquiry, Schippers's team had tried hard to prove the charge, and the investigators assembled a secret store of evidence about it in the Ford building. Forty-five House members examined the evidence in the days before the impeachment vote. In January, shortly after his DNA "scoops," Drudge disclosed that NBC's Lisa Myers had interviewed Broaddrick for the network's *Dateline* broadcast. NBC SAID TO BE HOLDING INTERVIEW WITH "JANE DOE," according to Drudge's headline. As usual with Drudge, his reports consisted of meta-journalism—journalism about other journalists' stories.

Understandably, the network was taking its time to verify, as best it could, a twenty-year-old allegation of this kind. However, Drudge's increasingly frantic reports suggested that NBC was giving in to White House pressure not to broadcast the story during the trial. (BROADDRICK EXPLOSION: CALLS FOR NBC NEWS PRESIDENT TO RESIGN, went one typical headline.) The Broaddrick interview thus became the last great crusade of Clinton's enemies. With his comment at the press conference, Lott was, in effect, daring NBC to run Lisa Myers's interview on Sunday, while the trial would still be continuing. As Drudge chronicled the debates within NBC about when to broadcast the interview, a new collectible appeared on the Washington scene: lapel buttons bearing the words FREE LISA MYERS (Charles Grassley, a Republican from

Iowa, wore one on the Senate floor.) By the end of the trial, the Broaddrick interview became perhaps the most famous nonpublic work of journalism in American history, its propriety and fairness debated ad nauseam by a world of people who had not seen it.

In any case, despite the pressure from Lott, Drudge, and others, NBC did not broadcast the interview until after the trial. In the broadcast, Broaddrick came across as poised and articulate, and NBC did manage to determine that she and Clinton had apparently been in Little Rock on the date in question. In public, Clinton refused to address the allegation, leaving it to David Kendall to deny that he had raped anyone. In private, though, Clinton suggested to one friend that he had slept with Broaddrick, but that it had been a "consensual deal." An allegation like this one served mostly as a reminder of the reason behind statutes of limitations. Two decades later, it was simply impossible to determine what, if anything, had occurred between these two people.

As it turned out, Lott's challenge came on a day when even the most remote chance for Clinton's conviction disappeared altogether. At 3:45 P.M., on the afternoon of January 22, Senator Robert Byrd handed Tom Daschle, the Democratic leader, a copy of a press release he was issuing. Byrd said that he would "offer a motion to dismiss the charges and end this impeachment trial." It was clear to him, he said, that there would never be two-thirds support for Clinton's removal, so there was no point in continuing. From the beginning, both sides had recognized that Byrd was the most likely leader of a Democratic stampede against the president. His support of acquittal sealed the result. Byrd didn't want to hear from witnesses, either. All he wanted to do was "end this sad and sorry time for our country."

/ / /

A curious transformation overcame many of the managers as their task became more conspicuously hopeless. The more unpopular they became—in the Senate chamber and in the country at large—the more certain they became of their rectitude. Indeed, in a curious way, some of the managers seemed to take repudiation as proof of their righteousness. This trial isn't helping us politically, they said, so we must be pursuing it because we are right.

Hyde certainly expressed that view, with a characteristic dollop of self-pity as well. When the time came to debate Byrd's motion to dismiss, the chairman had taken full-time to playing the victim of the Senate's disdain. The motion to dismiss, he said on January 25, was worse than unwise; it was an insult to the dignity of the House of Representatives. "I sort of feel that we have fallen short in the respect side because of the fact that we represent the House, the other body, kind of blue-collar people, and we are trying to survive with our impeachment articles."

Hearing Hyde portray himself as "blue-collar" was too much for two veteran Senate Democrats, and Joe Biden and Paul Sarbanes stormed out of the chamber.

Hyde ignored them and continued with mock humility. "However you vote," he said, "we will collect our papers, bow from the waist, thank you for your courtesy, and leave and go gently into the night. But let us finish our job."

Despite all this, Hyde's ambivalence persisted. At around this time, the chairman called his old friend Howard Berman, the California Democrat on the Judiciary Committee, and asked him to make an overture to Joseph Lieberman, the Democratic senator from Connecticut. Berman was to tell Lieberman that Hyde would be amenable to a motion to end the trial with some sort of censure of the president. This conclusion would offer the managers something other than the embarrassment of a full acquittal. Berman passed the message to Lieberman, who in turn came back with an obvious question. When I propose this idea, can I say that Hyde authorized it—indeed that he came up with it? Hyde said no; he wouldn't stand behind the idea in public. So, predictably, without Hyde's promise of support for his own idea, the proposal fizzled.

All fifty-five Republicans (and one Democrat, Russ Feingold) voted against Byrd's motion to dismiss, which meant that the trial would continue—albeit with no chance for the managers to obtain the sixty-seven votes they needed to remove Clinton from office. The tortured negotiations between Lott and Hyde allowed the managers a shred of dignity on the witness issue. They could take videotaped depositions of three witnesses, and then argue to the Senate that further, live testimony was necessary. So the managers had to decide which three witnesses to call.

Given their central roles, Lewinsky and Vernon Jordan were automatic choices. By this reasoning, the third selection should have been obvious as well: Betty Currie. Indeed, there was an actual unresolved issue relating to the evidence that Currie could address. Because Bob Bittman had so botched Currie's examination in the grand jury, back in the previous January, the record was unclear on an important point. Had Clinton asked Currie leading questions about her recollections a second time? Did the president really try to persuade her to testify falsely either in the grand jury or in the Paula Jones case? And what of the transfer of gifts from Lewinsky to Currie? Who initiated that transaction?

The way the managers addressed the Currie issue underlined just how preposterous the Senate trial had become. Weighing the question back in the committee's offices, Hyde said he didn't want to confront a sympathetic African-American woman. He didn't want to compound the political damage the Republican Party had already suffered. (Indeed, for the same reason, Hyde didn't want to call Jordan either, but his managers talked him out of that view.) The issue of Currie's testimony thus provided a kind of laboratory demonstration of the way politics trumped truth-seeking in the trial.

Besides, Lindsey Graham gave Hyde a convenient excuse to avoid calling Currie. Graham had become obsessed by the role of Sidney Blumenthal in the case. With his fervent partisanship and refusal to give interviews, Blumenthal became a figure of some mystery, which only whetted the right's curiosity about him. Graham wanted to explore what he thought was a sinister plot by Blumenthal to discredit Lewinsky at the beginning of the investigation. The charge had nothing to do with the case against Clinton, but Hyde still decided to make the former journalist the managers' third witness.

/ / /

For the most part, the examinations only demonstrated the ineptitude of the managers. Lewinsky's lawyers advised her, above all, to remain consistent with her prior testimony. This wasn't difficult, because she knew the facts far better than Ed Bryant, the Tennessee congressman assigned to conduct the interrogation. In the videotaped session, held in a suite at the Mayflower Hotel on February 1, Lewinsky confidently breezed through her version of the events, and Bryant lacked both the knowledge and the intensity to challenge her. (McCollum, who was also present, nearly bolted out of his chair in irritation at Bryant's meandering style.) By the end of the interview, Lewinsky was treating the congressman like a silly schoolboy.

"Do you still have feelings for the president?" Bryant asked.

"I have mixed feelings," Lewinsky replied coolly.

"What, uh—maybe you could tell us a little bit more about what those mixed feelings are."

No, thanks, said the witness. "I think what you need to know is that my grand jury testimony is truthful irrespective of whatever those mixed feelings are in my testimony today," she said.

A day later, Vernon Jordan faced a more prepared questioner, Asa Hutchinson. On the evidence, Hutchinson obtained some concessions from Jordan—that he knew the president, not Betty Currie, was behind the request for the job search, and that Clinton had withheld from him the fact that Lewinsky's name had appeared on the witness list in the Jones case. Neither disclosure transformed the case, but both added to the air of unseemliness around the president's behavior.

More striking than what Jordan said was how he said it. Unlike his friend the president, Jordan had enjoyed the embrace of the Washington establishment (and press corps) throughout the Lewinsky story. Clearly, the lawyer believed the wonderful things that had been written about him, and so he spoke with breathtaking arrogance. The nadir came in an answer to David Kendall, who fed Jordan a softball about "the job assistance you have over your career given to people."

Jordan replied with a speech about the civil rights movement. When he graduated from law school in 1960, he said, "it was very clear to me that no law firm in Atlanta would hire me. It was very clear to me that I could not get a job as a black lawyer in the city government, the county government, the state government, or the federal government." So, he said, his high school bandmaster got him a job with a fraternity brother as a civil rights lawyer.

"I have never forgotten Kenneth Days's generosity," Jordan intoned. "That's always been etched in my heart and my mind, and as a result, because I stand on Mr. Days's shoulders and Don Hollowell's shoulders, I felt some responsibility to the extent that I could be helpful or get in a position to be helpful, that I would do that. . . ."

By Jordan's astonishing reasoning, then, it was the civil rights movement that taught him to assist the likes of Monica Lewinsky. In truth, the best that can be said of Jordan's role was that he behaved with a stunning lack of curiosity about why his friend the president was so interested in helping this particular twenty-four-year-old woman. Instead of displaying his heretofore legendary savvy, Jordan spoke couth to power and did Clinton's bidding. A more fitting lesson about Jordan's conduct was that black plutocrats behave a lot like their white counterparts.

/ / /

On February 3, Senator Arlen Specter, a Pennsylvania Republican, presided over the deposition of Sidney Blumenthal, and the senator promptly established that he hadn't even bothered to learn the House managers' names. Specter's repeated references to Lindsey Graham, who was conducting the questioning, as "Congressman Lindsey" weren't the only things that caused muffled laughter in this absurd examination.

Graham went into the deposition trying to prove that Blumenthal had orchestrated a vindictive and false press campaign to portray Lewinsky as a stalker. Blumenthal denied spreading any stories about Lewinsky, but on its face, Graham's allegation made no sense. The notion of Lewinsky as a stalker had been present in the case from the beginning, and Blumenthal had nothing to do with it. Isikoff's original story, which was posted on the web the day the story broke, mentioned stalking. Not surprisingly, the stalker issue surfaced in much of the early press coverage. More important, Lewinsky *was* a stalker. The young woman used Currie and the Navy stewards to monitor Clinton's schedule, and she even shadowed him around Washington, sometimes staking out his route to and from church. Her own aunt, Debra Finerman, told the FBI that "Lewinsky was known by some as the 'stalker.'" (After Blumenthal's testimony was released, the writer Christopher Hitchens and two other friends of Blumenthal's came forward to say that the White House aide had, in private conversations, called Lewinsky a stalker. These comments bore on Blumenthal's credibility, but could not assist Graham's futile campaign to prove a White House conspiracy against Lewinsky.)

Graham's lack of preparation irritated the pompous Specter. In response to the senator's chidings, Graham promised, at one point, "We'll try to be laserlike in these questions." An hour later, Specter twitted him, "We're still looking for that laser."

On Saturday, February 6, the managers had a day to play the videotapes and explain their significance, but the senators—bored and restless after a full month of trial—paid little attention. By this time, the managers all shared Hyde's incessant pout, and during the last break of the day their frustrations boiled over. Rick Santorum, Lott's unwanted emissary, made a trip to the managers' war room, off the Senate floor, and sought to buck up the troops.

"You're doing great," he said to the managers. "You're really having an impact on us."

Rogan called out in response, "So make a motion to let us call more witnesses."

"Oh, no," Santorum said, reverting to Senate form. "I can't do that."

"Then get the fuck out of here!" one manager called out, and a rain of obscenities fell down on the senator.

"I was just trying to help you guys!" Santorum said, and then he skittered away.

The exhausted lawyers droned through their closing statements, with the Republicans' Mr. Malaprop, George Gekas, thundering to the senators about "the bald-faced naked phrase of sexual relations." Even Ruff lost his touch at this point, making the mistake of playing an excerpt from Clinton's grand jury testimony on the Senate's television monitors. The mere sight of the president injected a jolt of adrenaline into the Republicans in the chamber. Senators Phil Gramm and Bob Smith had been sitting drowsily through Ruff's remarks, but when they saw Clinton on the screen, they sat up and began rolling their eyes and rubbing their faces in irritation. Such was Clinton's effect on his adversaries.

Hyde had the chance to speak one more time, and he resumed his posture of self-pity. "We are blessedly coming to the end of this melancholy procedure," he began. "But before we gather up our papers and return to the obscurity from whence we came"—laughter—"permit, please, a few final remarks."

There was little new—fewer battles (just Agincourt), and more references to the rule of law. Hyde despaired that he had failed to persuade the Senate—and the country—of the magnitude of Clinton's misdeeds. "Once in a while I do worry about the future," he said, almost as an aside. "I wonder if, after this culture war is over, this one we are engaged in, an America will survive that is worth fighting for to defend." In this final utterance, Hyde had abandoned any pretext about the nature of this fight. A scaffolding of law had been built around the conflict in this case, but the core was indeed cultural and political. It had been almost five years since Randall Terry's bus (SHOULD CLINTON BE IMPEACHED?) pulled into the parking lot of the Rose Law Firm in Little Rock. The battles of those years had been fought with the tools of the legal trade, but the argument had really been about what kind of country this was going to be. Bill Clinton might not have won that argument, but Henry Hyde had certainly lost it.

/ / /

The temperature in Washington reached an improbable seventy-four degrees on February 12, 1999, and the balmy air invested the proceedings with an even greater sense of relief and liberation. The Senate had spent the last two days in closed-door debate about the articles of impeachment, so there was little suspense about the final result. Still, at four minutes past noon, when the chief justice announced that voting would begin, the magnitude of the moment settled heavily in the Senate chamber. No living American had ever seen the Senate vote on whether to remove the president of the United States from office. For the only time in the trial, Rehnquist had a nervous catch in his voice as he read the script before him.

"The Chair reminds the Senate that each senator, when his or her name is called, will stand in his or her place and vote 'guilty' or 'not guilty' as required by Rule XXIII of the Senate rules on impeachment," he said. "The Chair also refers to Article I, Section 3, Clause 6, of the Constitution regarding the vote required for conviction on impeachment. Quote: '[N]o Person shall be convicted without the Concurrence of two-thirds of the Members present.'

"The question is on the first article of impeachment. Senators, how say you? Is the respondent, William Jefferson Clinton, guilty or not guilty?"

On count one, which charged perjury in the grand jury, the vote was forty-five guilty, fifty-five not guilty. All of the Democrats and ten Republicans voted against the article.

The managers had devoted most of their energy to proving count two, which accused Clinton of obstruction of justice. When they knew any hope of removal was gone, they had placed their hope on winning a simple majority. But five moderate Republicans, all from the Northeast—Susan Collins and Olympia Snowe of Maine, John Chafee of Rhode Island, Jim Jeffords of Vermont, and Arlen Specter—joined the Democrats in voting not guilty. A vote of fifty to fifty, which somehow fit the sour sense of irresolution hanging over the entire affair, left Clinton to serve out his term.

With the senators seated solemnly before him, the chief justice announced, "It is, therefore, ordered and adjudged that the said William Jefferson Clinton be, and he is hereby, acquitted of the charges. . . ."

/ / /

As the Senate engaged in a perfunctory debate over a censure of Clinton—the idea promptly died because Phil Gramm and others had vowed to filibuster it to death—the president's lawyers returned to the White House to report to their boss. Once the House voted in December, Clinton had largely withdrawn from day-to-day involvement in the case. The quasi-judicial setting made it improper for him to lobby the senators, and in any event, Clinton's best strategy had always been to concentrate on the nation's business. His spokesmen reveled in telling a disbelieving press corps that the president had not watched this or that important moment in the impeachment debate. But for the most part, those claims were true.

In the Oval Office with Ruff, Kendall, and the other lawyers, Clinton expressed his gratitude and set about analyzing the votes.

Several of those present were hoping that the president might reflect a little on the meaning of it all, but Clinton only wanted to talk politics. They talked of the splits among the Republicans, the difficulties that Lott had in keeping his party together. To Clinton, this was just like any other tough vote on the Hill.

By the end of the short gathering, the chatter of strategy and tactics had revived the president's spirits, and he was downright chipper.

"We got five Republican votes," he said. "That's not bad!"

EPILOGUE

Private and Public

Judge Wright's dismissal of the Paula Jones case, on April 1, 1998, turned out to be a less definitive conclusion than might otherwise have been expected. The Dallas lawyers appealed, and the case was assigned to the same panel of judges who had already ruled against Clinton on the issue of whether a president could be sued while in office. By summer, it was clear that Starr was going to file a report and Congress would debate impeachment. This meant that Donovan Campbell and the Rutherford Institute had largely achieved their political objectives. Pursuing the lawsuit, even if they won their appeal, would only cost the plaintiff's lawyers more money. From Clinton's perspective, a loss on appeal meant the nightmare of a trial. By early fall, it was apparent that a settlement could benefit everyone.

In the first days after the Starr report came out, in September 1998, Don Campbell called Bob Bennett and said that his client would no longer demand an apology. All she wanted was $1 million. The amount was too high for Bennett, but the withdrawal of the apology demand showed that Campbell was serious. On September 30, Bennett called back with a counteroffer of $700,000. Campbell expressed some interest and promised to be back in touch, but then the phones went silent.

At this point, Bennett thought the case had run out of surprises, but then Campbell's partner, Jim Fisher, telephoned on October 6. He said that Gil Davis and Joe Cammarata—the lawyers who had taken the Jones case to the Supreme Court—were making life very difficult about their fee. Fisher wondered how Bennett felt about a solution they were considering.

"Would you object," Fisher asked, "if, as part of the settlement, Abe Hirschfeld paid Gil and Joe's fee?"

The name vaguely rang a bell for Bennett, but then he didn't live in New York. As it happened, the Polish-born seventy-nine-year-old Hirschfeld had just lost a libel suit against the New York *Daily News* for calling him a "wacky indicted wanna-be politician," which was actually pretty apt. Hirschfeld made millions in the fifties and sixties as the developer of indoor parking garages and then became a kind of local legend with his half-baked runs for political office and doomed investments in Broadway shows and, once, the *New York Post*. Nothing, however, surpassed the plan he presented to Paula Jones's attorneys. "I will give Paula Jones a million dollars myself," he said at the time. "Then, after the release of her case is signed, I recommend that the president resign, and Mr. Gore becomes president, and he immediately names Bill Clinton the honorary president of the United States. And it is agreed that Roger [*sic*] Starr will get the first available seat on the Supreme Court. It's as easy as apple pie." Incredibly, the Dallas lawyers took Hirschfeld seriously, especially after he put the $1 million on deposit in a bank. Campbell's team spent weeks trying to structure a deal with Hirschfeld and his lawyer.

At this point, the whole Paula Jones community was in the process of imploding. Steve Jones had been fired from his job at Northwest, under disputed circumstances, and his acting career was going nowhere. He and Paula were still stuck in the same one-bedroom apartment in Long Beach and getting along poorly. Steve took to badgering Campbell and the other lawyers so much that they stopped accepting his calls. Susan Carpenter-McMillan prevailed upon her husband, Bill McMillan, a personal injury lawyer, to speak to the Dallas team on Paula and Steve's behalf—but Susan and Bill's marriage was in the process of breaking up, too. The one thing all these people had in common was their hatred for Davis and Cammarata, who were still insisting on being paid for their years of work on the case.

After Bennett did a little checking—and learned that, among

other things, Hirschfeld was under indictment for state tax evasion—he told the Dallas team that the president could not be party to any settlement that involved the colorful New Yorker. On November 5, Campbell called Bennett and lowered his demand to $950,000, but he added a new condition: "each party has to pay all costs." As Campbell told Bennett, "Barbra Streisand can't write a check." Bennett told Campbell it was none of his business how Clinton funded the settlement. In the meantime, Hirschfeld announced, for characteristically obscure reasons, that he was taking his money off the table. (He was also later indicted in a separate, murder-for-hire plot against a former business partner; both criminal cases against him ended in hung juries.)

On November 11, the deal finally came together at $850,000. In one sense, this was an astonishing amount of money for Clinton to pay. Jones's lawsuit had asked for only $700,000 in damages, and it had already been thrown out of court. Yet it will remain one of history's great understatements that the president should have settled the case earlier. Of course, no one could have predicted the precise nature of the calamity that this lawsuit would visit upon Clinton and his family. But the case did bear warning signs that the president should have heeded. For this failure, Clinton will pay in the most valuable currency that any president possesses—in the first paragraph of his obituaries, when reference is made to his impeachment. (Clinton came up with the money to pay Jones from his insurance policy with Chubb and a trust fund established by Hillary Clinton's father.)

The settlement hardly qualified as much of a victory for Paula and Steve Jones. Their final share of the proceeds came to about $200,000—less than half of what they would have received if they had agreed to the $700,000 settlement that Davis and Cammarata had negotiated in August 1997. Donovan Campbell's firm received $283,000, Davis and Cammarata $260,000, and the Rutherford Institute $100,000. In a distant echo of the original contract that Cliff Jackson drafted, the final settlement also stipulated that Davis and Cammarata were to receive up to $90,000 from any book or movie deals that Jones may make in the future. (Danny Traylor, the Little Rock lawyer who took the phone call that began the case, asked for and received nothing.)

In March 1999, Paula and her two boys moved back to Arkansas. She found a house not far from her hometown of Lonoke, and she signed on as a client of Jack Gordon, the former husband of LaToya Jackson and a self-described "celebrity promoter." Gordon brokered a deal for the former plaintiff to open the Paula Jones Celebrity Psychic Network, a telephone hot line where she and a staff of other psychics predicted the future for callers at $3.99 per minute. Gordon also arranged a paid interview with *OK!* magazine, a British publication. Jones told the magazine that she expects to become even more fearful for her safety after Clinton leaves office, because "he may think, 'well, since I'm not the president, now I can do whatever I want to—I can get rid of her and her family.'"

/ / /

The Starr investigation ended in ignominy. In the last three trials conducted by the Office of Independent Counsel—against the Arkansas bankers Herby Branscum, Jr., and Robert M. Hill, against Susan McDougal, and against Julie Hiatt Steele—the prosecutors failed to win a conviction on a single count. (Jurors acquitted on some charges and hung on others.) Starr's prosecutors filed a second and then a third indictment against Webster Hubbell, the Clintons' close friend and former associate attorney general. In one of these cases, a tax prosecution, Starr also charged Hubbell's wife, his lawyer, and his accountant with felonies. The trial judge threw out one of these cases, and though that ruling was subsequently reversed, the appellate court decision made it impossible for the prosecutors to proceed to trial. Consequently, both cases were resolved in a joint plea bargain that essentially imposed no new punishment on Hubbell. Starr dropped the cases against Suzanna Hubbell, the lawyer, and the accountant.

The decisions to bring the McDougal and Steele cases demonstrated the distinctive forms of bad judgment that were the hallmarks of the Starr prosecutorial style. Susan McDougal, one of the Clintons' former business partners in the Whitewater project, served eighteen months in prison for her still-inexplicable refusal to testify before Starr's grand jury. Even though McDougal made clear she would never cooperate with Starr, his Little Rock office used her failure to testify as the basis for filing another case against her, this one charging criminal contempt and obstruction of justice. This did not technically qualify as double jeopardy, but Hickman Ewing, Starr's deputy in Little Rock, was clearly trying to punish her a second time for precisely the same behavior. The Arkansas jury rejected this vindictive and unnecessary case.

If the McDougal case displayed the vengefulness of Starr's prosecutors, the prosecution of Steele, a minor figure in the whole imbroglio, displayed their unhealthy obsession with getting the president. Steele had been a close friend of Kathleen Willey's in 1993, at the time when Willey said Clinton had groped her. Four years later, in July 1997, when Michael Isikoff began investigating the story, Willey cited Steele to the reporter as a corroborating witness. In her first interview with Isikoff, Steele backed up Willey's story, saying that her friend had complained at the time about the president's crude pass at her.

When Isikoff decided to go ahead with his story, later in the summer of 1997, Steele told him that she had lied in their earlier conversation. In truth, Steele said, she had never heard Willey complain about Clinton in 1993. She had told the original falsehoods as a favor to Willey. In the months that followed, Steele stuck to the second version of her story—that Willey had asked her to lie in her behalf. On one level, the whole Willey vs. Steele controversy could be seen as much ado about relatively little. Two witnesses told conflicting stories, which is something that often happens in criminal investigations.

But the Steele prosecution grew out of the central obsession of Starr's investigation. Jackie Bennett, Starr's chief strategist, had questioned Clinton closely about Willey's charges in his grand jury testimony on August 17, 1998. The president categorically denied Willey's account of a groping. Bennett wanted to build another perjury case against Clinton—this one based on the word of Kathleen Willey. Steele's account made Willey out as a conniving liar herself, so the OIC set out to build up Willey and destroy Steele. Thus this prosecution.

As so often happened with the OIC, things did not go as the prosecutors hoped. Willey had to answer hard questions about the financial misdeeds that led her husband to commit suicide; she had provided, at best, dodgy and evasive testimony during her deposition in the Jones case. She had also made the customary inquiries about selling her story of Clinton's alleged sexual come-on.

In light of all this, Willey's attorney wisely insisted on a grant of immunity before she agreed to cooperate with Starr's office.

Then, after Willey received immunity, she told the Starr office a series of flat-out lies about her relationship with a man named Shaun Docking. After her husband's death, she had become sexually involved with this younger man, and the affair had ended badly, in 1995. As part of their breakup theatrics, she told him a false story about having gotten pregnant. In Steele's trial, Willey was asked, "Why did you not tell the United States" the truth about Docking?

"I was embarrassed, and I was ashamed of that," she said.

Willey's lies put Starr's prosecutors in a dilemma. Her immunity agreement stated clearly that if she didn't tell the truth, her immunity could be withdrawn and she could be prosecuted for all her crimes—including the lies that broke the agreement. But she was also their last, best hope to make another case against Clinton. Starr had to choose: hold fast to his oft-repeated insistence on the truth and void Willey's immunity deal, or ditch the principle and save a witness who might finally bring down Bill Clinton.

The prosecutors gave Willey a second immunity agreement, which served to excuse her latest round of lies. After all, Willey had only lied about sex.

/ / /

In a broad sense, Starr's team made the right call about Willey's immunity. On this most private subject in her life, she had lied out of shame and regret. There was no need to make a federal case out of it. But this reasoning should have been applied to Bill Clinton as well. The actions that led to his impeachment were rooted in his embarrassment about how he had conducted his sex life. Of course, prosecutors and the nation at large should hold the president to higher standards. But even by the stern measure a nation should apply to its leaders, Clinton's enemies staged a banquet of excess—in the tactics they used, in the judgments they made, and in the remedy they sought.

One person saw the case for what it was, and when the heat of the impeachment fever had passed, Judge Susan Webber Wright offered a cool final assessment. On April 12, 1999, the judge found Clinton in contempt of court for violating her orders in *Jones v.*

Clinton—that is, by lying about his relationship with Monica Lewinsky. After a brief, sober review of the facts, Wright concluded that "there simply is no escaping the fact that the President deliberately . . . undermined the integrity of the judicial system. Sanctions must be imposed, not only to redress the President's misconduct, but to deter others who might themselves consider emulating the President of the United States. . . ." In an especially bitter pill for Clinton, Wright ordered him to pay the Jones lawyers' expenses in connection with Clinton's deposition in the case. (After a final bit of rancorous litigation, Wright set that amount at $90,000.) The judge imposed a punishment that was no more, and no less, than Clinton deserved. The legal system may have taken over the political system elsewhere, but in one Little Rock courtroom, the basic rules of fairness still applied.

One more party also had the case right from the start—the American people. The Lewinsky saga abounded in fatuous judgments about the alleged sentiments of this great inert beast. But even employing due caution, one can only marvel at the quiet wisdom of the vast majority of Americans, especially in the face of nonstop hysteria from the political and media classes. These opinion leaders announced that long-established distinctions—between public and private, between personal and political—no longer mattered in American life. And the people replied, evenly, that they certainly did. This battle, of course, did not conclude with the verdict in the Senate. The self-appointed arbiters of moral fitness moved on to new targets—candidates instead of presidents—and new subjects—drug use instead of adultery—and insisted on passing judgment. Again, apparently, the public disdained these assessments from on high. But with the legal system showing no sign of relinquishing its hold over the nation's politics, the language of accusation and investigation will continue to dominate the nation's discourse.

/ / /

Bill Clinton responded to the end of the Lewinsky story with the same maddening concatenation of qualities that got him into, and out of, trouble in the first place. As he indicated in reviewing the trial with his lawyers on February 12, the president regarded the whole adventure, bottom line, as a victory. He thought this was a totally political attack on him from the beginning, and on those terms, he won and his enemies lost. For Clinton, the moral and personal implications of his behavior remained private and, apparently, not unduly troubling.

Indeed, on balance, the first family saw fit to turn trauma into opportunity. Back in the president's first term, when Hillary Clinton had formal political responsibilities of her own, she quickly became one of the least popular first ladies in memory. Her defense of her husband during the Lewinsky scandal, however, drove her to great heights of popularity. Her character and ambition had changed little in the interim, but she and her husband decided to try to capitalize on the good feelings toward her. With the same tenacity that led Bill to reach the presidency and then to cling to it, they began to invest in Hillary's nascent political career. The obstacles were large, but so were the Clintons' ambitions. As their friend Linda Bloodworth-Thomason liked to say, "When they're dead and gone, each one of them is going to be buried next to a president of the United States."

And at some point in the distant future, Americans will likely regard this entire fin de siècle spasm of decadence with incredulity—at the tawdriness of the president's behavior, at the fanaticism of his pursuers, and at the shabbiness of the political, legal, and journalistic systems in which this story festered. Mostly, though, these baffled future citizens will struggle with the same question about Bill Clinton. He was impeached for *what*? The answer will honor neither the president nor his times.

ACKNOWLEDGMENTS

My thanks begin with my terrific colleagues at *The New Yorker*. David Remnick has made the transition from *consigliere* to *capo di tutti capi* with characteristic grace, and my debt to him is vast—for his work on this book, for his leadership of the magazine, and for his incomparable friendship. Many thanks, also, to Dorothy Wickenden, for keeping a wary eye on me for several years now; to John Bennett, for hauling my words across the finish line; and to Amy Tübke-Davidson, for knowing the story better than I do. My gratitude also goes to my fellow writers on the Clinton beat: Rick Hertzberg, Joe Klein, and Jane Mayer. Also, I will always be grateful to Tina Brown for giving me a chance in journalism and for guiding my coverage of the early part of this case.

I also shared this story with many friends and colleagues at ABC News, and I am delighted to thank them all—especially the beat reporters, Jackie Judd and Linda Douglass. Chris Vlasto and I saw much about this case differently, so it is especially gratifying to thank him for his generosity to me while I wrote this book. I am grateful for the research assistance (and merciless criticism) of Josh Fine of ABC News and Sarah Smith, formerly of *The New Yorker*.

I am privileged, once again, to be published by Random House. Ann Godoff has guided this book with her trademark enthusiasm and savvy. The copy-editing team of Beth Pearson and Ted Johnson accomplished a great deal in a short time. Thank you also to Mary Bahr, Caroline Cunningham, Greg Durham, Richard Elman, Liz Fogarty, Kate Niedzwiecki, Tom Perry, and Carol Schneider. My agent, the great Esther Newberg, simply reigns.

I was blessed with an on-site focus group to address a much asked question in this case: What will the children think? At the age of eight,

Ellen Toobin is herself a veteran news analyst, and I treasure her insights. Her brother, Adam, two years her junior, wisely took the high road about the details of the president's difficulties, and I was delighted to explore other parts of the world with him. The mother of these great kids, Amy McIntosh, provides a living reminder of all that is best in our world. In return for the joy of sharing her life, the dedication of this book is the least I can offer her.

New York City
November 1999

SOURCE NOTES AND BIBLIOGRAPHY

This book is based principally on my observations and interviews during the two years I covered the Jones and Lewinsky cases. During this time, I interviewed more than two hundred people for this book. All quotations from private conversations come from one (or both) of two sources: my interviews with participants in the conversations, or a participant's testimony in the course of the Starr investigation. The House of Representatives chose to release an unprecedented amount of material from Starr's investigation, including thousands of pages of grand jury transcripts and FBI summaries of interviews. Though the wisdom of that decision remains open to question, that material stands as an extraordinary resource for journalists and historians, and I drew upon it heavily. All quotations from court proceedings come from the official court transcripts.

In addition to my own efforts, I have steeped myself in the voluminous media coverage of the case. I followed the continuing coverage in *The New York Times* and *The Washington Post*. I am especially grateful to the *Post*'s superb web site, which maintains a useful archive of its coverage (www.washingtonpost.com/wp-srv/politics/special/clinton/clinton.htm).

I drew upon the following books and articles in my analysis of the case and its context.

BOOKS

Aldrich, Gary. *Unlimited Access: An FBI Agent Inside the Clinton White House.* Washington, D.C.: Regnery Publishing, 1996.

Bennett, William J. *The Death of Outrage: Bill Clinton and the Assault on American Ideals.* New York: The Free Press, 1998.

Berger, Raoul. *Impeachment: The Constitutional Problems.* Cambridge, Massachusetts: Harvard University Press, 1973.

Black, Charles L., Jr. *Impeachment: A Handbook.* New Haven, Connecticut: Yale University Press, 1974.

Brock, David. *The Seduction of Hillary Rodham.* New York: The Free Press, 1996.

Brummett, John. *High Wire: The Education of Bill Clinton.* New York: Hyperion Books, 1994.

Clinton, Roger. *Growing Up Clinton: The Lives, Times and Tragedies of America's Presidential Family.* Arlington, Texas: Summitt Publishing Group, 1995.

Coulter, Ann. *High Crimes and Misdemeanors: The Case Against Bill Clinton.* Washington, D.C.: Regnery Publishing, 1998.

Davis, Lanny J. *Truth to Tell: Notes from My White House Education.* New York: The Free Press, 1999.

Dershowitz, Alan M. *Sexual McCarthyism: Clinton, Starr and the Emerging Constitutional Crisis.* New York: Basic Books, 1998.

Drew, Elizabeth. *The Corruption of American Politics: What Went Wrong and Why.* Secaucus, New Jersey: Birch Lane Press, 1999.

Flowers, Gennifer. *Passion and Betrayal.* Del Mar, California: Emery Dalton Books, 1995.

———. *Sleeping with the President: My Intimate Years with Bill Clinton.* Carson City, Nevada: Anonymous Press, 1996.

Gabler, Neal. *Life the Movie: How Entertainment Conquered Reality.* New York: Alfred A. Knopf, 1998.

Gerhardt, Michael J. *The Federal Impeachment Process: A Constitutional and Historical Analysis.* Princeton, New Jersey: Princeton University Press, 1996.

Goldberg, Lucianne. *Madame Cleo's Girls.* New York: Pocket Books, 1992.

———, and Sondra Till Robinson. *Friends in High Places.* New York: Richard Marek Publishers, 1979.

———, and Jeannie Sakol. *Purr, Baby, Purr: You Can Be Feminine and Liberated.* New York: Hawthorn Books, 1971.

Hitchens, Christopher. *No One Left to Lie To: The Triangulations of William Jefferson Clinton.* New York: Verso, 1999.

Hubbell, Webb. *Friends in High Places.* New York: William Morrow & Co., 1997.

Isikoff, Michael. *Uncovering Clinton: A Reporter's Story.* New York: Crown Publishers, 1999.

Janeway, Michael. *Republic of Denial: Press, Politics and Public Life.* New Haven, Connecticut: Yale University Press, 1999.

Kovach, Bill, and Tom Rosenstiel. *Warp Speed: America in the Age of Mixed Media.* New York: Century Foundation Press, 1999.

Kurtz, Howard. *Spin Cycle: Inside the Clinton Propaganda Machine.* New York: The Free Press, 1998.

Lyons, Gene. *Fools for Scandal: How the Media Invented Whitewater.* New York: Franklin Square Press, 1996.

MacKinnon, Catharine A. *Sexual Harassment of Working Women: A Case of Sex Discrimination.* New Haven, Connecticut: Yale University Press, 1979.

Maraniss, David. *The Clinton Enigma: A Four-and-a-Half-Minute Speech Reveals This President's Entire Life.* New York: Simon & Schuster, 1998.

———. *First in His Class: A Biography of Bill Clinton.* New York: Simon & Schuster, 1995.

McDougal, Jim, and Curtis Wilkie. *Arkansas Mischief: The Birth of a National Scandal.* New York: Henry Holt & Co., 1998.

Moldea, Dan E. *A Washington Tragedy: How the Death of Vincent Foster Ignited a Political Firestorm.* Washington, D.C.: Regnery Publishing, 1998.

Morgan, Peter W., and Glenn H. Reynolds. *The Appearance of Impropriety: How the Ethics Wars Have Undermined American Government, Business, and Society.* New York: The Free Press, 1997.

Morris, Dick. *Behind the Oval Office: Getting Reelected Against All Odds.* New York: Random House, 1997.

Morton, Andrew. *Monica's Story.* New York: St. Martin's Press, 1999.

Posner, Richard A. *An Affair of State: The Investigation, Impeachment and Trial of President Clinton.* Cambridge, Massachusetts: Harvard University Press, 1999.

Stephanopoulos, George. *All Too Human: A Political Education.* Boston: Little, Brown & Co., 1999.

Stewart, James B. *Blood Sport: The President and His Adversaries.* New York: Simon & Schuster, 1996.

Tyrell, R. Emmett, Jr. *Boy Clinton: The Political Biography.* Washington, D.C.: Regnery Publishing, 1996.

Woodward, Bob. *Shadow: Five Presidents and the Legacy of Watergate.* New York: Simon & Schuster, 1999.

ARTICLES

Beinart, Peter. "Private Matters." *The New Republic,* February 15, 1999, p. 21.

Blumenthal, Sidney. "The Friends of Paula Jones." *The New Yorker,* June 20, 1994, p. 38.

Didion, Joan. "Uncovered Washington." *The New York Review of Books,* June 24, 1999, p. 72.

Dunne, Dominick. "Mr. Dunne Goes to Washington." *Vanity Fair,* May 1999, p. 152.

Dworkin, Ronald. "The Wounded Constitution." *The New York Review of Books,* March 18, 1999, p. 8.

Ellis, David, et al. "The Perils of Paula." *People,* May 23, 1994, p. 88.

Graves, Florence, with Jacqueline E. Sharkey. "Starr and Willey: The Untold Story." *The Nation,* May 17, 1999, p. 11.

Henneberger, Melinda. "The World of Paula Jones." *The New York Times,* March 12, 1998, p. A1.

Kavanaugh, Brett M. "The President and the Independent Counsel." *Georgetown Law Review,* vol. 86, p. 2133 (1998).

Kotler, Steven. "The President's Nemesis" (John W. Whitehead). *GQ,* September 1998, p. 362.

Lardner, George, Jr. "The Presidential Scandal's Producer and Publicist." *The Washington Post,* November 17, 1998, p. A1.

Lewis, Anthony. "The Prosecutorial State: Criminalizing American Politics." *The American Prospect,* January/February 1999, p. 26.

Lizza, Ryan. "Mister Hyde." *The New Republic,* December 28, 1998, p. 14.

Maxa, Rudy. "The Devil in Paula Jones." *Penthouse,* January 1995, p. 107.

———. "The Devil in Paula Jones." *Penthouse,* April 1998, p. 51.

Mayer, Jane. "Dept. of Accomplices." *The New Yorker,* February 2, 1998, p. 25.

———. "Distinguishing Characteristics." *The New Yorker,* July 7, 1997, p. 34.

———. "Portrait of a Whistleblower." *The New Yorker,* March 23, 1998, p. 34.

McClintick, David. "Town Crier for the New Age." *Brill's Content,* November 1998, p. 113.

O'Sullivan, Julie R. "The Interaction Between Impeachment and the Independent Counsel Statute." *Georgetown Law Review,* vol. 86, p. 2193 (1998).

Pollitt, Katha. "After Virtue." *The New Republic,* June 7, 1999, p. 42.

Rich, Frank. "All the Presidents Stink." *The New York Times Magazine,* August 15, 1999, p. 42.

Rosen, Jeffrey. "Jurisprurience." *The New Yorker,* September 28, 1998, p. 34.

———. "Kenneth Starr, Trapped." *The New York Times Magazine,* June 1, 1997, p. 42.

Schippers, David. "Schippers Speaks Out." *Human Events,* May 28, 1999, p. 1.

Semple, Kirk. "Witness for the Prosecution" (Bruce Udolf). *Miami New Times,* August 21–27, 1997.

Shalit, Ruth. "The President's Lawyer." *The New York Times Magazine,* October 2, 1994, p. 42.

Sunstein, Cass R. "Bad Incentives and Bad Institutions." *Georgetown Law Review,* vol. 86, p. 2267 (1998).

———. "Unchecked and Unbalanced: Why the Independent Counsel Act Must Go." *The American Prospect,* May/June 1998, p. 20.

Symposium. "The Independent Counsel Act: From Watergate to Whitewater and Beyond." *Georgetown Law Review,* vol. 86, p. 2011 (1998).

Taylor, Stuart, Jr. "Her Case Against Clinton." *American Lawyer,* November 1996, p. 57.

———. "Jones' Credibility." *Legal Times,* June 23, 1997, p. 20.

Waas, Murray. "False Witness" (David Hale). Five-part series, www.salon1999.com, 1998.

Walzer, Michael. "News Unworthy." *The New Republic,* September 28, 1998, p. 10.

Weiss, Philip. "I Love Luci." *The New York Observer,* June 29–July 6, 1998, p. 21.

York, Byron. "False Witness" (Vernon Jordan). *The American Spectator,* February 1999, p. 24.

INDEX

ABOUT THE AUTHOR

JEFFREY TOOBIN is a staff writer at *The New Yorker*, senior legal analyst at CNN, and the bestselling author of *American Heiress, The Nine, Too Close to Call, The Run of His Life, The Oath,* and *Opening Arguments.* A magna cum laude graduate of Harvard Law School, he lives with his family in New York.